THE LIMITS OF VOICE

Montaigne, Schlegel, Kafka

The Limits of Voice

Montaigne, Schlegel, Kafka

LUIZ COSTA-LIMA

Translated by
Paulo Henriques Britto

STANFORD UNIVERSITY PRESS

Stanford, California

The Limits of Voice was originally published in Portuguese
under the title *Limites da voz* by Editora Rocco Ltda.,
Rio de Janeiro, © 1993 by Luiz Costa-Lima

Assistance for this translation was provided by
the State University of Rio de Janeiro

Stanford University Press
Stanford, California

CIP data appear at the end of the book

Stanford University Press publications are distributed exclusively by
Stanford University Press within the United States, Canada, Mexico,
and Central America; they are distributed exclusively by Cambridge
University Press throughout the rest of the world.

Acknowledgments

It is only in strictly material terms that a book may be said to be written solely by its author. The coauthors are not necessarily mentioned in the text: they are to be found on an underground level, and it is there that they participate, under other names and in other times, in the chemistry of the work.

The idea of this book was first suggested by my friend Wlad Godzich. In a seminar with graduate students at the Universidade Estadual do Rio de Janeiro (UERJ), in 1989, discussing Paul de Man and aestheticization in contemporary thought, Godzich pointed out to me an avenue of research that will not be exhausted in the present work.

More motivation was provided by another friend, Eric Alliez, with whom I collaborated in some courses on the Kantian *Critiques,* also at the UERJ graduate-school program, in 1991. I would be hard pressed to reconstruct the exact way in which a number of ideas—developed particularly in Chapter 2—came into being; but of course I myself must be held accountable for whatever is correct or mistaken in my use of them.

I must also acknowledge the collaboration of a number of other friends and readers, who objected to the wording of specific passages or subjected the manuscript to painstaking revisions. Any attempt to list them all would surely be open to the charge of unfairness through omission; but it would be even more unfair if I failed to single out the names of Heloísa Beatriz Santos Rocha and Thereza Vianna. It is equally important to mention my conversation with Hans Ulrich Gumbrecht in his house in Stanford on October 18, 1992. Most of his comments on the first version of this book have been incorporated into the final text.

The preparation of the third chapter, originally written between August 1991 and July 1992, was partly supported by the Brazilian Conselho Nacional de Pesquisas (CNPq). The book as a whole is deeply indebted to the Alexander von Humboldt Stiftung, which granted me, as a foreign humanities scholar, the Research Fellowship for 1992. This allowed me to rewrite the manuscript in Munich, from October to December 1992.

Last, special thanks to Wolf-Dieter Stempel, for his disinterested support for this representative of a "minor literature."

L.C.-L.

Contents

Translator's Note   ix

Preface   xi

1.   The Consecration of the Individual: Montaigne   1

   Opening Considerations, 1. Montaigne: Subjectivity and the Experience of Heterogeneity, 12. The Problem of the Exemplum, 19. The Corrupting Imagination, 42. Presuppositions for the Treatment of the Portrait, 44. The Requirements of the Portrait, 48. Towards Autobiography: The Essay, 56. Considerations Concerning the Essay, 60. The Book: Presence of the Self and Mark of Criticity, 64. In the Way of a Synthesis, 68.

2.   The Subject and the Law: A Kantian Heritage   71

   The Journey and the Law, 71. An Overview of the Third Critique, 79. The Impact of the Word "Critique" and Fichte, 103. Carl Schmitt: Critic of Romanticism, 107. Schiller and the Aestheticization of Art, 115. Novalis: The Countercurrent of Romanticism, 130. Some Fragments by Novalis: Aestheticism or Criticity? 136. Schlegel as Literary Theorist, 145. A Final Rectification, 170. The End of the Critical Road, 177.

3.   Kafka: Before the Law   183

   Preamble, 183. Kafka and Literature, 188. Kafka and the Question of Representation, 201. Representational Production and Contemporary Literature, 212. Kafka and the Question of Interpretation, 215. "The Judgment," 227. "In the Penal Colony," 234. The Trial, 240. The

Castle: *A Religious Novel? 274.* The Desubstantialization of the Law
and the Status of the Fictional, *294.* Kafka's Context, *303.*

References   325

Index   335

Translator's Note

"Criticity" is a neologism—as is the Portuguese *criticidade* in the original—coined in order to distinguish the act of questioning from both the act of judging ("critique") and the activity by means of which the act of judging is effected ("criticism"). The questioning, non-normative function is certainly already present in Kantian criticism, but the distinction was never captured by a contrasting pair of words, in English or in Portuguese.

In the original version of this book, all quotations from foreign-language texts were rendered in Portuguese by the author. For the present translation, whenever possible I have consulted the original-language edition—particularly in the case of works in English—or an existing English translation. In a number of cases, however, I have had to translate the author's Portuguese text.

Preface

The author of the present work is not a specialist—not, at any rate, if a specialist is taken to be one who is solely concerned with a narrow field of endeavor. What sort of specialist would deal with a French author of the Renaissance, Kant, and Kafka? The academic world recognizes the existence of philosophers, historians of philosophy and of literature, Romanists and Germanists; any author who crosses the boundaries between these fields will not seem serious enough to merit attention. When he disclaims the status of a specialist, the author defines himself negatively in terms of academic discourse; yet his text can be envisaged in no other terms. This inevitably brings to mind the old joke about the man with two professions: as a doctor, he was a good lawyer; as a lawyer, he was a good doctor. A philosopher who should happen to read what is said about Kant on the following pages may well evaluate the author as a good Romanist; a historian of French literature, upon reading the chapter on Montaigne, will perhaps feel that he might do better as a Germanist. But Germanists will surely argue that one whose command of their language is less than perfect can scarcely be called a Germanist!

It would be even less proper to call this book the work of a scholar, unless the word were to be taken in a very loose sense. In addition, the pretension to unity has led to omissions that scholars will surely find unforgivable: How can a study of Montaigne neglect his reading of Pascal and Descartes? How can a discussion of imagination in Kant be limited to the first and third *Critiques*? How can one consider, on the differentiation between individuality and individualism, only what was written about Novalis? Can aestheticization be adequately treated by restricting it to a few authors and then proceeding to make rather generic statements?

The above allusions to omissions are not meant to imply that what has been left out is irrelevant. I acknowledge that at times my approach focuses on a single aspect of a much more complex subject. A prime example of this is the treatment of aestheticization. It is seen as one of two alternatives posited by Kant in his discussion of art, the other being criticity,* the progressive expansion of the former contrasting with the brief existence of the latter. This limited period is represented here by Friedrich Schlegel. But why not take as examples of criticity Flaubert's views as revealed in his letters, Henry James's prefaces, or certain considerations of Valéry on poetry, the subject, and society? There is in fact no reason not to do so. But nothing that could be said about these authors would alter the general fact that criticity is the exception rather than the rule.

Since no systematic historical approach had been adopted, I felt that such examples might be left unexamined without detriment to our central argument: that, of the two alternatives that have been open to art since Kant's third *Critique*, aestheticization has usually prevailed. Further, the reader will perceive that one of the decisive links between the first and second parts of the present work, on the one hand, and the third, on the other, is the statement that the neglected criticity provided the basis for the project of Kafka's fiction. That is: with Kant modern thought found a system that, on the basis of the recognition of the power of the human subject, posed the possibility of establishing and legitimating a world order. Kafka's task is the fictionalization of a world in which this order, based on the premise of the consecration of the individual subject, turns out to be questionable.

The trajectory from the short-lived apogee of criticity in Schlegel to Kafka's fiction points to my espousal of criticity. Here another problem arises: I seem to be defending a position that history shows to have already been defeated. Is the failure of criticity only a historical fact or an inevitable consequence of the human condition? By raising this issue, I intend to do no more than emphasize my own bias. In fact, the very existence of this book depends on the choice of an issue, criticity, that is admittedly problematic. In practical terms, the emphasis on it aims only to underscore the point that the reading of aestheticization proposed here must be seen in the light of my admittedly procritical assumptions.

The Limits of Voice is part of an ongoing project. During the 1980's, in *Control of the Imaginary* and *The Dark Side of Reason*, I attempted to test the hypothesis that, in spite of all appearances, modern reason has never been sympathetic to the imagination. The theory focused on empirical instances, in order to lay down the foundations for a structure to be built later. The time

---

*See Translator's Note, p. ix.

has now come for theorization: What is the meaning of this control? Just what is its close relation to the primacy of the individual and the exacerbation of aestheticization? Is it somehow related to the fact that the prevalence of an effectively critical concern was all too brief? And, finally, what is the connection between this complex of questions and Kafka's work? The discussion of the control of the imaginary is thus now resumed on a fundamentally theoretical plane.

Is this, then, a book of theory? Yes, as long as one bears in mind the affinity between theoretical investigation and the formulation of questions. As a questioning force, theory is quite compatible with passion, without forgoing rigor.

THE LIMITS OF VOICE

Montaigne, Schlegel, Kafka

Since the beginnings of our tradition, the truth claims of literary creation have been challenged. This fact makes literary theory [*die Theorie von Dichtung*] the systematic place for critically evaluating the concept of reality and underscoring its implications.

Hans Blumenberg, "The Concept of Reality
and the Possibility of the Novel"

CHAPTER I

The Consecration of the Individual:
Montaigne

Others conceive man; I describe him.
Montaigne

Opening Considerations

Montaigne is the starting point of a trajectory that, by way of Kant and the early romantics, will take us to Kafka. Four centuries are involved. How many hundreds of pages will be necessary? The answer to this question—perhaps ironical, perhaps anxious—is: as many as you see here.

Just to hear this the reader may experience a sort of vertigo. In Machado de Assis's *Epitaph for a Small Winner*, Brás Cubas rides a hippopotamus on a wild journey to the origin of the centuries. But Brás Cubas was ill, possibly feverish, and as he is about to describe his delirium he tells the reader to feel free to skip the chapter. We could hardly do the same here: were the reader to follow this advice, there would be nothing left.

Although our journey is much shorter than Brás Cubas's, could it be attempted without light-headedness? Its length alone seems discouraging; and this impression is strengthened when we glance at some of the stops along the way: Montaigne, Kant, Schiller, Novalis, Friedrich von Schlegel, Kafka—clearly, each of them would require many more hundreds of pages.

Would it not then be wiser to change our course entirely? This seems quite reasonable, for all of the authors mentioned might be brought together under a single theme: the Law.[1] If we are aware of this fact, why haven't we chosen this path? Fundamentally, we answer, for two reasons: first, because it is not our object to write a history of ideas, even of the small set of ideas that developed in the West over the last four centuries; second, because we do not

---

1. I write "Law" with a capital *L* in order to distinguish between the *principle of regulation* and the statement of a particular norm (or law).

intend to present an introduction to the authors we shall discuss. These two tasks would indeed be redundant or impracticable. Our purpose is different.

The idea is to conduct an investigation that will articulate certain motifs. These are to be the book's structuring themes. The authors to be examined will provide the solid ground on which these motifs will be erected. Although the argument may well take on new hues and will most likely branch off into other byways, lest the reader lose his or her way let us state our themes.

First, there is the circle made up, on the one hand, of the legitimation of the intellectual construct founded on the primacy of subjectivity and, on the other, of the questioning of this very structure. Thus, our first leitmotif is the recognition of the right to speak in the name of the self, the questions that arise from this right, the proffered answers, and, finally, its calling into question in the work of Franz Kafka.

This theme is accompanied by a second, simultaneous with and parallel to the first: the issue of the Law. Let us put it in schematic terms: the self's recognition by itself, that is, outside the nexus with an external and inclusive term that lends it meaning and orientation—the family, or the community, or the nation, or God—automatically raised the question of the objectivity of whatever this self might say; for this recognition implied the granting of an authority that was not self-evident. In empirical terms, the self is no more than a singularity among thousands, hundreds of thousands, millions. How can one be sure that what the self apprehends will be acceptable to the rest of us? What sort of inference can then be made between its apprehension and the order of things, of the world?

Before the consecration of the individual, classical antiquity had conceived a cosmic order that prevailed through the early Middle Ages: a Law that, according to Christianity, was believed to come from a benevolent God, whose magnanimity had built into things the possibility of their being known, used, and transformed for the greater good of his creatures, who then, their conviction strengthened, would sing the glories of the demiurge. Thus, it would be unreasonable to suppose that the individual's claim to primacy could have failed to bring about the downfall of the classical order— or rather, that this claim could have become socialized if such an upheaval had not previously taken place.

Thus, we do not feel it is enough to stress that Montaigne's work consecrates the individual subject's right to express his personalized experience of the world without relying on legitimated models. On the contrary, the individual needed an ordering principle in which to integrate his claim. Now, Montaigne had no such principle; hence the compromise solutions he had to settle for. Nor is his case unique. Pico della Mirandola, Petrarch, the humanists, and Machiavelli were all in much the same situation. For each of them, concentration on the individual subject implied the adoption of a scale of flexibility—vertical for Pico, horizontal for Petrarch, vertical but strictly earthly for the humanists, or commanded by chance, *fortuna*, for Machiavelli (see Greene 1968: 241–65, particularly pp. 249, 258). Whatever the form assumed by the "flexibility of the self," this flexibility had to be conceived in terms of a fundamental order, a Law, that allowed the variant in question. Thus, it is not by accident or due to intellectual inertia that all the authors mentioned, including Montaigne, should attempt to find a compromise with the ancient Law in its Christianized form. Here is the bridge that joins Montaigne's dilemma to Kant's reflections. For it is Kant's thought, and not the Cartesian *cogito*, that will provide a basis for the legitimating Law of the modern subject.

Not only does this second theme run parallel to the first, but the vicissitudes of the latter are projected upon the former. We shall then see that the question of the Law is one thing at the time of Montaigne's consecration of the individual and another when Kant establishes its full cognoscitive legitimation, and that Kafka's calling into question of the problem is associated with issues that were well known to Kant's readers—issues that point to the radicalness with which, in his major novels, he dramatizes the Kantian question of the Law.

The third leitmotif concerns the rise of literature as an autonomous discursive mode. This issue was never explicitly discussed before the *Frühromantiker* (early romantics); it was then that the independence of literature in relation to any other center would be affirmed on the basis of the Kantian postulate of the autonomy of aesthetic experience. But the analysis of Montaigne's *Essays* will show that a rough outline of literature is already to be found there; that, moreover, such an outline is so deeply embedded in Montaigne's practice that, beginning with his work, two conceptions of literature, separated in time, can be contrasted: one deriving from the Renaissance—literature as belles lettres—and the other, modern, founded on the individual subject.

Whereas the first two themes run parallel, each of them being both cause and effect of the other, the third is best described as their consequence. That is, the modern concept of literature—which moves away from the literal meaning of the word, the emphasis on the use of letters, of writing—depends both on the socialization of the experience of the self and on the established role of the Law. This theme would require a specific essay by itself. We shall do no more than observe that the relationship between the third term—the rise of literature—and the issues posed by the theme of the psychologically oriented subject, on the one hand, and those raised by the order that makes knowledge possible, on the other, point in opposite directions. That is, the boundaries of literary space were established when its territory was claimed as that of expression of the self—which also means that the first leitmotif over-determines the third—but it was also defined as that which exempts itself from the search of theoretical justification. Thus, in relation to the self litera-ture has a positive connection that becomes negative when the questioning of the Law that provides its underpinnings occurs. Perhaps it is because the literary work is only negatively related to the issue of knowledge that it has seldom been considered in this light. For instance, Timothy Reiss recently published a detailed study of the shaping of the modern concept of literature without relating it once to the question of the rise of the subject (see Reiss 1992). A single example will provide an illustration of both points.

In 1348, Boccaccio, together with a small group of gentlefolk, fled the plague that was devastating Florence. The book that was to make him fa-mous, the *Decameron* (1349–53), was supposedly written to entertain his anguished companions. It would never occur to any of his listeners or his later readers that the stories, fables, and parables contained in the book were meant to formulate or illustrate any law, even a moral one. Similar works by different authors—for instance, Cervantes' *Exemplary Novels*, or Diderot's *Indiscreet Jewels*, a less obscene and more mischievous collection than Boccaccio's—seem to corroborate our rather trivial observation: such works, precisely because they were literary in intent, had nothing to say as to the determi-nation of the order of the Law, its extension or limits, its operativeness, and so on.

By contrast, the question of the self is conspicuously present in the *Decameron*: the evident resort to themes and topoi inherited from classical tradition was no less important than the contradiction of classical attitudes. Thus, the story of the generous husband who lets his friend borrow his wife presents, if compared to the sort of treatment it would have received in antiquity, an unprecedented complication. An analyst noteworthy for his study of the origins of the novel has observed: "This complication arises above all from the fact that the characters are no longer mere means for the concretization of an idea, but instead *have a consciousness of their own*, which allows them to consider the corresponding situation not as something self-evident, but as *a unique thing requiring consideration*" (Neuschäffer 1969: 45; emphases added).

A break had occurred between the experience of antiquity and that of Boccaccio. The former was integrated in the *order of mimesis*, which had two defining traits. First, the identity of the self was overwhelmingly based on something external to it; classical individuality implied the subsumption of the self into some kind of community. Hence the free circulation of topoi, of rhetorical figures, which passed from one author to another, none of whom claimed any of them as their property, invention, or personal confession. Second, this impersonality of the persona presupposed, in turn, a substantialistic conception of the cosmos: as singular entities, things and beings are part of an order that is inherent to the class of each. It is not this specific stone that is hard; rather, hardness belongs to its class; it is not this stone that crumbles, but rather the property of crumbling belongs to the class of objects in which it is naturally integrated. The order of mimesis was stable and stabilizing; it assumed obedience to models—images of the harmony of a world of substances—and was not to be confused with the servile practice of copying. The production of works led to the multiplication of a sameness that was not as much repeated as it was reiterated by a process of creative change.

When we come to Montaigne, we shall see that the example of Boccaccio was not chosen at random. For the moment, let us simply observe that it is because their characters have a consciousness of their own that the stories in the *Decameron* cannot be fitted into the classical genre of exempla. As Stierle observes, "whereas the exemplum was no more than a narrative transposition of a moral statement," in Boccaccio the anecdote becomes the seed of the novella (Stierle 1973: 365). This highlights the fact that the novella, and particularly the novel later, emphasize the individual anecdote, which cannot be explained by the homogeneity of the model.

The *Decameron*, violating the order of mimesis, is one of the first representatives of the order of *method*. The new order does not replace the old immediately; in between there is an interval during which it is difficult to identify, in abstract terms, what still represents the dying Law and what harbingers the one about to arise.

For our present purposes, we need only characterize the minimal traits of the order that was to distinguish modern times and, within them, modernity: first, the existence of an individualized consciousness, acting in correlation with a self that becomes autonomous from the nexus that previously provided its identity; second, the process of dissolution of the substantialistic concept of the world that underlay the previous order. The order of method thus presupposes a double break, although it is impossible to pinpoint its initial moment or to say whether its two minimal traits took place simultaneously. This implies that if the first trait stands for the irruption of the self and the second for the need to rethink the Law, then their temporal duration is not coextensive; rather, the second requires a centuries-old process of maturation of the need for its formulation.

Since we are simply outlining the themes that will guide our text, we must not dwell on this for too long. Nevertheless, courtesy demands that we attempt to anticipate our readers' doubts, and at least one question cannot be evaded: Are we saying that the notion of the individual did not exist under the order of mimesis? In order to answer the question, we must also establish, again schematically, the distinction between individuality and individual.

Both in Plato and in Aristotle, the search for wisdom assumed a well-established individuality. Individuality and individual are distinct categories inasmuch as the former implies that the constitution of identity is guided by an evaluative standard, both goal and model, whereas the latter is associated with the idea of exploration and expression of a self-inscribed inner core, whose reach is hampered rather than promoted by social relationships. Therefore, in the ancient world it is the a priori value assigned to the nonself as to the conduct expected of each self that is the sufficient component for the characterization of individuality. Without the connection to a community established and fostered by this value, the self was unthinkable. Hence the self's obvious link with the order of mimesis: individuality was a point that presupposed a set. In other words, whereas value is a priori, its locus of geometrical insertion, the set, has the property of generating the points that fill it out. This set is the frame that mediates between every point—or individuality—and the world. No point imitates it but accommodates to it; the work of individuality is achieved under the aegis of similitude. Although the Platonic model is sufficiently distinct from the Aristotelian, since it shapes individuality from the viewpoint of immortality while the Aristotelian model does it from a strictly earthly viewpoint—the polis—both are integrated into the paradigm of classical antiquity for the evaluative precedence they grant to a nonself: in Plato, the fixed horizon of Ideas; in Aristotle, the practice of citizenship.

Clearly, the preceding passage could be no more than a brief explanation, but it runs the risk of proposing an excessively schematic view of two absolutely separate worlds. Against such a view, one should keep in mind the importance of what Foucault called "the care for the self" in the first two centuries of the Christian era, particularly in the treatises of the Stoics. This, to begin with, lends a different quality to the relationship between men and women. "Whereas ancient ethics implied a very close articulation between the power of the self and the power over others," "the care of the self [*le souci de soi*] appears . . . in connection with a 'spiritual service' that allows for the possibility of a game of interchanges with the other and of a system of reciprocal obligations" (Foucault 1984: 105, 69). This, however, should not be taken as an instance of individualism. Foucault himself dissociated "the care of the self" from "the manifestation of a growing individualism," relating it instead to the changes then undergone by the Hellenistic and Roman worlds, which no longer allowed the status of the individual to be qualified by the exercise of a political role; rather, the changes led to a questioning of the political role, the emphasis on personalization in existence and, finally, a stricter sexual morality. Within these limits, the explanation is relevant, lest undue generalizations be drawn from our clearly delimited trajectory.

Beginning our reflection with Montaigne, we take on an issue that is appropriate to modern times and modernity. The problem that arises in this period from the confrontation between the individual subject and the Law and its attendant discursive consequence—the question of literature—could not be automatically displaced to the world of antiquity, not even that of late antiquity.

In order to stress the close connection between the third motif and the two preceding ones, let us remember that in antiquity, in the novel of the Hellenistic period, the merely individual was characterized as "private and isolated": "Therefore, the connection between an individual's fate and his world is *external*. The individual changes and undergoes metamorphosis completely independent of the world; the world itself remains unchanged. Therefore, metamorphosis has a merely personal and unproductive character" (Bakhtin 1981: 119). The very essence of a genre that exploited the private nature of its characters clashed with "the public nature of literary form," and this gave rise to a process that, Bakhtin adds, did not reach completion in antiquity (p. 123).

The renewed contact with ancient sources did not imply the continuous unfolding of a process that, beginning with the epic, incorporated the works of the apogee of classicism and Hellenism, but rather their incorporation into the order of the individual. The presence of this order, of which Chrétien de Troyes and the romance of chivalry are early examples, presupposes not only the decay "of the ancient unity between God and the world" (Köhler 1974: 53) but also the impossibility of its restoration.

The ancient unity mentioned by Köhler was clearly not the order of classical antiquity, much less that of Roman decadence, but that of Christianity. This order, however, had appropriated and preserved, after its fashion, the privilege of a kind of nonself in the determination of the process of identity. Inspired by the Pauline letters, the early thinkers of the Church formulated a concept of the individual in which the idea of the subject remained faithful to Paul's notion of *subditus* (subject). Thus, Paul's saying "What I am, I am by the grace of God" came to imply "that the *fidelis christianus* [faithful Christian] not only had no rights but also had no autonomous standing within the Church itself or within society" (Ullman 1966: 11). This made it necessary to adapt the letter of the Gospel text to the conditions of the day: "Although nature had made all men equal, Gregory declared,

there nevertheless intervened what he called 'an occult dispensation,' according to which some were set over others 'because of the diversity of merits' of
individuals" (p. 14).

Thus, the thought of the church fathers and the medieval society they
helped to build take for granted the permanence of the order of mimesis, even
if in a modified form. In this order, however, the disaggregation was already at
work that would highlight the second meaning of "subject," in which the
sense of *subditus* is replaced by that of autonomous atom. What will come to
be known as literature implies both this conflict and the dominance of the
identification of the subject with the individual.

Let us resort to two of the many paths that could be used to show the
simultaneous presence of the two strands. The first stresses the prestige of the
letter as a literary genre in the Renaissance: "The letter was especially popular
with the humanists, as it allowed them to express their views in a personal and
subjective fashion, although they considered letter-writing a branch of literature, and gave the same polished elegance to their letters as to their other
literary compositions. To these we might add the collections of sentences,
proverbs, and commonplaces" (Kristeller 1965: 28).

Misunderstandings may arise if we fail to note the importance of the
connective "although," which underscores the difference between the domains of the "personal and subjective fashion" and the Renaissance idea of
literature. The dignity of literature called for a rhetorical treatment to which
individual expression had to submit. The personal nature of the content was
not justification enough. In conformity with the prestigious model of Cicero,
the Renaissance letter required ornate language. Novelty of content, the
expression of subjectivity, was not yet considered a sufficient principle, since
the letter was seen as a literary genre only to the extent that it could be
considered a part of belles lettres.[2] Thus, two layers are superimposed, and the
dominant one—the rhetorical conception—represents the permanence of the
public nature of the "literary" genres of antiquity.

The second observation points in the same direction. It may be said—no
longer in connection with a specific genre but as a generic statement—that
the emergence of the self in Renaissance thought took place simultaneously
with the granting of an autonomous status to nature. It was within this
process, which can be observed in the experimental researches that are its
crowning achievement, that Bernardino Telesio discarded the Aristotelian

---

2. That is why it would be best to avoid the term "literature" when dealing with
Renaissance works: "Belles lettres, before being 'literary creation,' was from the outset an
assiduous and intimate intercourse with the poets and orators of antiquity. . . . Belles lettres
is the mark of all cultivated men, and of all Christians to the extent that they belong to a
civilized society" (Fumaroli 1980: 25, 28).

categories in favor of the *juxta propria principia* (proper principles)—that is, proper to nature (see Cassirer 1963: 154). Yet, as Cassirer shows in the passage mentioned, this naturalism was not incompatible with magic, theosophy, even mysticism—that is, Renaissance experimentalism was not adverse to a conception of science that accepted cosmic correspondences and analogies and saw the world as a perfectly ordered and ruled field. The belief in a cosmic order was preserved side by side with the acknowledgment of the individual and kept the exploration of this acknowledgment from disturbing the tranquility of knowledge. The traditional and the new were mutually supportive: "Thus constant reciprocity and conversion are established between man and world. . . . The spirit is equated with the world it conceives" (pp. 200–201).

In Montaigne, this belief in the stability of nature is preserved, but the reciprocal relationship has already been lost. The primacy of the self no longer allows its exploration of infinity to proceed without mishaps. Although, like all his contemporaries, he knows by heart passages from the poets and thinkers of antiquity, Montaigne does not see them as unerring authorities. The primacy of the self leads him into a different path. And as this process takes place, belles lettres gives way to literature.[3] The rise of literature is directly related to the consecration of the individual, to literature's separation from the individuality of antiquity, and to its move away from rhetoric. But it would be naive to suppose that the immediate recognition of the *Essays* implied the acknowledgment that its merit was related to the focus on subjectivity (see note 3).

Pascal's distinction between "author" and "man" is relevant here. Clearly, it already takes for granted the rejection of the rhetorical model, which Pascal attacks for its identification with "all the false beauties which we blame in Cicero" and contrasts with the heart, which he praises: "I hate braggarts and bombasters equally. . . . We only consult the ear because the heart is wanting. Its rule is uprightness. A poet and not an *honnête homme*" (Pascal 1957b: 1096; nos. 33, 22). As Pascal opposes the two terms, the "author" (which, in

3. It should be observed, however, that contemporaries were not aware of this change. Analyzing early receptions of Montaigne, Jules Brody stresses that for both his critics and his supporters what made Montaigne unique was his language: "Montaigne's language is thus defined, immediately after the publication of his book, as a Latinized regionalist idiolect which perceptibly deviates from the urbane, worldly, accessible, polished, and elegant sociolect which was later to be epitomized in the discourse and even in the name of Malherbe" (Brody 1982: 14). Now, not only was singularization through language the established criterion but also, as Brody notes, the deviations themselves were justified by tradition. It was only in the eighteenth century that Montaigne's work was claimed for literature, and the feelings of rivalry it aroused in Rousseau show that he saw Montaigne as someone who had preceded him in the exploration of his own life.

the context, is identified with the poet) remains associated with the use of
rhetoric and separated from the praise of human innerness and naturalness:
"When we see a natural style, we are astonished and surprised, for we expected an author and find a man. Whereas those who have good taste and
who, seeing a book, expect to find a man, are surprised to find an author: Plus
poetice quam humane locutus es [You have spoken more as a poet than as a
man]" (p. 1096, no. 35).

In a later fragment, Pascal shows himself to be posed precisely in between
the rhetorical Renaissance view, which was no longer valid for him, and the
view of literature that was to become canonical. His position is intermediate,
for he praises the natural style or discourse not because it is an expression of
the author-subject, but because of its effect: "When a natural discourse paints
a passion or an effect, one feels in oneself the truth of what one hears, which
was there before although one did not know it, so that one is led to love him
who made us feel it" (p. 1099; no. 44). This more complex process by means
of which the poet was clearly distinguished from his work was soon later
simplified.

Throughout the eighteenth and nineteenth centuries, literature was to
connote a circuit—author, work, reading public—so closely associated with
the self-experience of subjectivity that the link between literature and the
horizon of subjectivity would harden into an incontestable truth. Thus, in
"Éloge à Richardson," Diderot praises the novelist for taking as his model
"the human heart, which ever was and ever will be the same" (Diderot 1965:
40). A few decades later, Novalis established a distinction between works of
art, which can be sold, and poetry "as a character trait, as a manifestation of
my nature," which only a brute would think of as something that could be
bought (Novalis 1978a: 389–90). In a little more than fifty years, the criterion
became apodictic and normative: it was on this basis that Schopenhauer
affirmed that "a *novel* will be the higher and nobler the more *inner* and less
outer life it depicts" (Schopenhauer 1970: 165). It is true that soon thereafter,
in his prose writings, Mallarmé proposed a diametrically opposite poetical
practice; but he was ignored at the time. The exploration of the self's infinity
continued to be the defining trait of literary experience. As late as the beginning of the twentieth century, the writer who was to be considered the great
novelist of the bourgeoisie could write: "Hierarchy [*Rangordnung*] is a good
thing, but I believe the empire of personality is a democracy of kings [*das
Reich der Persönlichkeit ist eiene Demokratie von Königen*]. If one, indeed, is
anything at all, one is, I believe, beyond all comparison. Mastery is a positive
value that allows no comparisons; personality has absolute precedence; it is
rude to offend it with comparisons" (Mann 1960, 10: 415).

What makes Mann's insistence on incomparability particularly notable is the fact that it is antithetical to the criterion of hierarchy. Behind it one senses a liberal political stand, and behind this, in turn, there is the legitimation of literary work.

The consecration of the individual subject, the pressure for a concept of Law that included its primacy, and the legitimation of literature are the three core themes of this book. The third of these issues, in turn, will lead to two major developments. The question of literature will be seen as the point of articulation for the first two themes, and also as implying two decisive effects: (1) the problem of control of the imaginary that accompanies the rise of the literary institution; and (2) the emergence of the question of the fictional, which is dismantled in Kafka.

Let us briefly consider these two points. Concerning (1), even though we stand on the empirical ground presented in *Control of the Imaginary* (1988) and *The Dark Side of Reason* (1992), we must repeat that the establishment of this ground was no more than the stage at which we were testing the hypothesis and verifying its extension. The intent of this book is different: to show the historical and theoretical implications of control, analyzing its link with the correlation between the primacy of the individual subject and the question of a new Law. In brief, we might add: if imagination[4] is seen as the determinant of the approaches that are less amenable to proof, less guided by objective parameters, a kind of spontaneous activity of the self, it would seem to be all the more exalted the greater the legitimation of the discourse of individual subjectivity par excellence: literary discourse. As we shall soon see, this is not even partly true.

As the consecration of the individual increasingly compromised the security previously given by the concept of truth as a correspondence between a state of affairs and a statement, the exaltation of the imaginative capacity came to be questioned in the discussion concerning the status of the "new" truth. This process is best examined in the context of a discussion of Kant's three *Critiques*, particularly the first and the third. It is only after this examination is done (Chapter 2) that we shall be able to make the following two points: that the question of control proper begins with the problematization of the metaphysical concept of the Law; and that aestheticization does not provide an escape from this problem, but rather exacerbates it.

Here we have another opportunity to repeat that the issue of control is not to be confused with the phenomenon of censorship, and indeed, has little

---

4. As in our preceding works, we take imagination to be the actualization—in Saussurean terms, the *parole*—of a faculty or specific capacity to thematize the imaginary, which would be the *langue*.

relation to it. Whereas censorship is punctual, subject to the calculations of political convenience, control is paradigmatic, is inscribed in the very axiomatics underlying modern theory of knowledge. This is not to say that the imaginary and its *parole* (see note 4), imagination, aroused any suspicion in classical thought. But without the disturbing element—the individualized self—the apparatus of classical gnosiology could let it pass with less rigor. As long as they were based on the exploitation of elements codified by rhetoric, imaginative works fit into an established hierarchy of discourses, became acceptable, and, at the same time, were sharply distinguished from "serious" works. This predictable liberality was duplicated, between the end of the Middle Ages and the advent of the Renaissance, by the fact that the competent legislators—the authors of poetics—were unable to bring to heel those works that were related to orality and to popular culture. Thus, the liberality that such authors as Rabelais and Gil Vicente enjoyed was only later subjected to the discipline of taste.

Concerning (2), we shall say even less, since the characterization of the fictional is an urgent task only when the identification of literature with the expression of individual subjectivity becomes threadbare. To say that, on the verbal plane, fictionality finds its vehicle par excellence in literature presupposes the explicit taking up of the question of the Law, something that occurs, not coincidentally, only after Kant's critical philosophy. In due time we shall have to show that the relatively small part of Kant's work that deals with this problem effectively is related to the brief period in which the aesthetic experience was considered from a truly critical angle; and, conversely, that this part of Kant's work contrasts with the predominance of aestheticization (see Chapter 2). Even though this leitmotif is decisive for our argument, it comes into play only two centuries after Montaigne. For this reason, we do no more than mention it in passing here.

Before we close this preamble, a final word must be said about the set of five themes. I repeat that they are no more than structuring motifs. They will not be treated disconnectedly, as pieces of a puzzle that in the end will all be perfectly fitted, but rather as in a musical piece in which developments, repetitions, and improvisations are much more extensive than the generating cells. I have adopted this strategy so that theoretical flights would constantly point to the ground on which they are based.

Montaigne: Subjectivity and the Experience of Heterogeneity

In 1571, when he turned 38, Montaigne resigned from the public offices he was entitled to as a nobleman. A voluntary exile in the estate he had inherited from his father, he began a new phase in his life, centered on the castle library. A Latin inscription in the library stated his decision to retire, while a second one declared his purpose of dedicating to the memory of Étienne de La Boétie *ce studieux appareil dont il fait ses délices* (this studious apparatus which is his delight).

Between them the two inscriptions define the program to be accomplished in the *Essays*. His retirement from political and administrative functions, although at an early age, followed the example of the Roman personalities who, retiring to their estates, dedicated themselves to the task of writing down works that would perpetuate their deeds and their glory. His vow to dedicate his studies to the memory of his dead friend placed an absence at the center of his proposed activity. Although Montaigne decided to devote his full time to conversation with himself, his intent to glorify his deceased friend was also a practice founded on the example of ancient authorities. At first, his idea was to publish the manuscript La Boétie had written as a young man. But in 1574, during the civil war that divided France, the Protestants published an unauthorized edition of La Boétie's *Discours de la servitude volontaire* (On voluntary bondage). Montaigne had not only been cheated of his first objective but also felt the obligation to defend his friend's memory, proving that he was not a rebel, that he did not really sympathize with the cause of those who had published his work, that it was a mere rhetorical exercise, and so on. In addition, the constant self-absorption Montaigne had expected to engage in by renouncing active life failed to materialize. The edition of *Servitude* had only brought home the fact that his plan had been ill conceived. Solitude, he found, "creates me so many chimaeras and fantastic monsters, one upon another, without order or design, that, the better at leisure to contemplate their strangeness and absurdity, I have begun to commit them to writing, hoping in time to make [my mind] ashamed of itself" (Montaigne 1952, I, 8: 15).[5]

The anonymous publication of *Servitude* and the discovery that his goal of dedicating existence to the pleasures of idleness could not be reached led Montaigne to revise his original plan. The pages he had written, instead of celebrating a matchless personality, are suddenly seen to have an empty core. Montaigne proceeds to extract a portrait from them. But a portrait of whom? La Boétie had died far too young to have achieved deeds that could be celebrated. So all that Montaigne could do was to attempt a portrait of their friendship. But a friendship cannot be depicted. The only alternative left, then, was to portray the mourning friend—that is, to produce a self-portrait.

5. The three books of *Essays* are referred to as I, II, and III, followed by the number of the individual essay and the number of the page of the English translation being quoted.

In classical tradition, the exaltation of deeds was a service to the glory one intended to perpetuate; glory replaced the absent figure; the body was gone, but its flesh was replaced by stone, marble, calamus. Montaigne had been defrauded of the opportunity to do this. If he could no longer mediate between the past and the lasting literary monument, all that he had left was a self that now, attempting to honor the memory of the dead friend, could rely on nothing but itself. The portrait he set out to paint was not as much of the absent friend as it was of the effect of his absence on someone who had voluntarily left the scene of glory.

The *Essays* are placed at a neutral point between the ancients and the moderns. The former are given a new inflection; the latter are not yet able to recognize it. The individual now holds the place formerly occupied by individuality. The story of a life need no longer rely on heroic feats: it may content itself with its own "chimaeras and fantastic monsters."

But this description perhaps oversimplifies the initial situation of the *Essays*. We shall soon have to rectify it, drawing attention to the traces of the old honor model still to be found in Montaigne's text. Concerning "Of Constancy" (I, 12) and earlier essays, Thibaudet rightly observes: "These chapters may suggest an original project of Montaigne's, already outlined: a compilation of examples and stories for the benefit of those who engaged in warfare, a book that nobles could read with pleasure" (Thibaudet 1963: 62).

Thus, according to a hunch that Thibaudet himself does not take up, the original project of the *Essays* was that of a work addressed to Montaigne's peers, noble warriors and courtiers. A few passages seem to confirm this hypothesis:

> Were there no lying upon the hard ground, no enduring, armed at all points, the meridional heats, no feeding upon the flesh of horses and asses, no seeing a man's self hacked and hewed to pieces, no suffering a bullet to be pulled out from amongst the shattered bones, no sewing up, cauterising and searching of wounds, by what means were the advantage we covet to have over the vulgar to be acquired? (Montaigne 1952, I, 40: 118–19)

> Teres, the father of Sitalces, was wont to say that when he had no wars, he fancied there was no difference betwixt him and his groom. (I, 40: 121)

> Examples have demonstrated to us, that in military affairs, and all others of the like active nature, the study of sciences more softens and untempers the courages of men, than it in any way fortifies and excites them. (I, 24: 61)

The last of the three passages, with its warlike disdain for the cultivation of letters, highlights the discrepancy between the earlier model and the spirit that later prevails. Such passages and others like them are associated with a conception of *auctor* (author) subordinated to the principle of *auctoritas* (authority)—that is, someone whose voice and relevance are derived from his conformity to tradition. The self, then, has no identity of its own; rather, it is an accident that illustrates and reiterates a paradigm.

It is not by chance that these observations are marginal. Whether the original project they point to is later aborted or, in spite of the obstacles it faces, still manages to survive somehow, the fact remains that in Montaigne the self goes astray and becomes autonomous. It is no longer the material, merely bodily condition for the conception and transmission of a value, but the unmovable point whence the flow of writing proceeds. The break with the ancient model is quite explicit at the end of I, 40: "He who has neither the courage to die nor the heart to live, who will neither resist nor fly, what can we do with him?" (p. 125).

In this chapter Montaigne had attempted to show that the fear of death derives more from the "impatience of imagination," the funerary paraphernalia with which we surround it, than from the mere fact of extinction. The final sentence, however, introduces a new strand: "*Qui n'a la coeur de souffrir ny la mort ny la vie*" (He who has neither the courage to die nor the heart to live): to those who are in this state the ancient lesson is meaningless. Unqualifiable, unclassifiable, this indifference to life and death is the concrete expression of the hand that writes, the eye observing what the hand does, the mind concentrated on the attempt to portray itself. At the zero point where the author stands, the presence of death—blind, brutal, insufferable—is enhanced.

The final sentence of book I, essay 40, summarizes in extreme fashion the gist of the dozens of chapters contained in the three books. The break with the ancient model is concentrated on the use of the exemplum. For the moment, we shall do no more than observe that the search for exemplariness, to be proved by the accumulation of cases, is replaced by the revelation of inner heterogeneity. What is man an example of? Which human behavior could be considered exemplary? "Man (in good earnest) is a marvellous vain, fickle, and unstable subject, and on whom it is very hard to form any certain and uniform judgment" (I, 1: 4). The human condition has such a contradictory nature, so variable as a function of custom, time, religion, and geography, that it seems nearly unbelievable. How, then, could one hope to compose a work that would favor its education? Why add to the store of inevitably useless things one more that we know beforehand to be hopelessly futile? What characterizes Montaigne's moral science is the abandonment of any attempt to codify. The only defining trait of the human condition is diversity.

Such a statement was fraught with danger. In Montaigne's time, France was not only torn by civil war but also suffered the effects of the plague, a population growth inferior to that of other European countries, inflation, and economic stagnation. As long as his words remained within the bounds of his own library, Montaigne could afford to say what he wished without risk. But he was soon exposed to a larger audience, for the first edition of his book had immediate success.[6] Whether by calculation or by option, the author had defended himself with his own text. At least in his lifetime, except for the episode in Rome (see note 6), his book found no obstacles.

Montaigne died in 1592. In 1666, he was to be attacked in the Port-Royal *Logique*; he would again come under criticism in book II of Malebranche's *Recherche de la vérité* (Search after truth); and in 1676 his book was included in the church's *Index*, where it remained until 1783, only a few years before the French Revolution.

We may well assume that Montaigne's text was extremely sinuous and ambiguous because he was aware of the situation in which he lived. Then again, it could be that this characteristic of his work is itself the result of the circumstances under which it was written. His initial idea had been to glorify his deceased friend, but soon he was forced to undertake a composite portrait of an absence *and* a concrete bodily presence; a book originally conceived as a confirmation of the authority of the ancients had ended up doing without them. In their place, as visible surface, presence, and quest, there is nothing but the unprecedented self that writes: "Here, this is not my doctrine, 'tis my study; and it is not the lesson of another, but my own" (II, 6: 180). And: "I do not write my own acts, but myself and my essence" (p. 181).

Whether a defensive measure or a matter of conviction, Montaigne's ambiguity came out clearly in the clash between public and private ethics. Here is a passage that was added to the 1595 edition:

> We owe subjection and obedience to all our kings, whether good or bad, alike, for that has respect unto their office; but as to esteem and affection, these are only due to their virtue. Let us grant to political government to endure them with patience, however unworthy; to conceal their vices; and to assist them with our recommendation in their indifferent actions, whilst their authority stands in need of our support. But, the relation of prince and subject being once at an end, there is no reason we should deny the expression of our real opinions to our

---

6. Circumstances soon forced him to acknowledge this fact. A few months after publication of the *Essays*, after traveling through "heretical" Germany, Montaigne arrived in Rome, in November 1580. In his *Journal de voyage*, his secretary, who jotted down his master's impressions, mentioned the rigor of customs officials. All the books Montaigne was carrying with him were confiscated, including his copy of the *Essays*. It was returned to him only in March 1581. In the meantime it had been examined by church censors. Montaigne was lucky—and perhaps also helped by the protection of the *maestro del Sacro Pallazzo* [master of the Holy Palace]: his book was approved with few restrictions, and it was left to his conscience to "retouch what, as I should see, was in bad taste" (Montaigne 1983 [1580–81], particularly pp. 221–22, 237).

own liberty and common justice, and especially to interdict to good subjects the glory of having reverently and faithfully served a prince, whose imperfections were to them so well known; this were to deprive posterity of a useful example. And such as, out of respect to some private obligation, unjustly espouse and vindicate the memory of a faulty prince, do private right at the expense of public justice. (I, 3: 7)

Here the requirements of public ethics are sharply distinguished from those of private morality. Subjection and obedience pertain to public space; esteem and affection, to the domain of the private. Thus, the subject has the obligation to serve even an unworthy prince; however, once the relation comes to an end, his duty should give way to the voice of justice and the freedom of private feelings. So strict is the separation between the two spaces that we may find the second part of the sentence confusing unless we read it literally: good subjects—that is, those who served faithfully even unworthy authorities—must not be denied the glory they earned, and their instructive example should be handed down to posterity.

It is only in the sphere of the private that the subject is freed from his condition of subjection. But where are the boundaries of this sphere? The very terms of the passage quoted earlier suggest that not even in the privacy of his library is he exempt from the duties of a subject. In this context, Max Horkheimer's observation seems absolutely apt: "In relation to individual existence, inwardness has the same function that churches, museums, places where people seek amusement—that is, spare time—have in social life. In the bourgeois era, the cultural sphere is separated from the economy, on the individual level as well as on the social" (Horkheimer 1988: 244).

Though correct in general terms, this observation deserves closer examination in the particular case in hand. The idea of the subject in Montaigne is not yet identified with the notion of man, as will occur in the Enlightenment. Living in a time when absolutism was still in preparation, Montaigne anticipates the dichotomy that will be theorized by Hobbes. Certainly Hobbes's justification was intellectually and politically more acceptable. If Hobbes "introduces the state as the factor that robs private convictions of their political repercussion" (Koselleck 1976: 23), this is so because "in a civil war it is not easy to say what is good and what is bad, and the desire for peace by itself is not sufficient to disturb the will to power" (p. 23). In short, the dichotomy between the public and the private is of fundamental importance if the sovereign's voice is to make itself heard by the warring parties. But Montaigne's purpose had nothing to do with such august calculations; it was surely because of fear, caution, suspicion of whatever was new, and respect for tradition that he restricted his defense of the prerogatives of the subject.

Now we come to the core of the question: Does not the self's claim to autonomy require that something outside it remain stable? In more direct terms: Does not the autonomy it claims imply stability? But, coming before Descartes and for all practical purposes discarding the substantialistic concept that Christianity had adapted to, Montaigne could not find a fulcrum for his self gone astray. Since he did not claim to be a philosopher, Montaigne was content to acknowledge that nature has its own eternal principles; since he was forced to recognize the power of the church, he compromised with his curiosity, seeing it as a scourge that "prompts us to thrust our noses into everything" (I, 26: 82). And, since he had to find some consistency in his commerce with himself and a part of the world, he admitted, with no tergiversation, that we ought to follow custom.

The Enlightenment authors certainly seem to us unwavering and courageous, whereas Montaigne sounds too slippery. It was in the name of Enlightenment tradition that Horkheimer severely criticized the author of the *Essays*. Our endorsement of this criticism, however, will perhaps obscure our recognition of the fact that the *philosophes* were better equipped to engage in political and philosophical discussions because they could rely on the stabilizing view of the world made possible by the physical-mathematical model and the progress in experimental science. The primacy of the self questions the validity of the ancient Law, which excluded it, and favors the rise of a new Law that should anticipate, recognize, and highlight it. In modern times, this new Law begins to assume a well-defined outline with Descartes and gains its final shape with Kant's first *Critique*. To accuse Montaigne of being indifferent to the world and concerning himself with himself alone is to beg a rather complex question. This qualification does not deny the validity of Horkheimer's observation, but forces us to place it within another frame of reference.

Placed at the neutral point where one Law has broken down and a new one has not yet been established, Montaigne had few tools on which he could rely. *Pace* Horkheimer's contention that "philosophical skepticism . . . is in its very essence conservative" (Horkheimer 1988: 147), Montaigne's conservatism is less the direct effect of his skepticism than of—in addition to strictly personal reasons—the need, imposed by the centering on the individual subject, to postulate some nonself, the firmness of which might contrast with the waverings of the self.

But even if we qualify the applicability of Horkheimer's assertion, we must admit that it points to an issue worth reconsidering. While the consecration of the individual took place at a time when there was no Law to justify its autonomy, it seems that in our time the situation is, in a way, the opposite, for is it not true that we now live under a political order that attempts to legitimate itself in the name of individual autonomy at a time when the Law that justified it is no longer unquestionable? At such a time, the alleged autonomy serves as an excuse to turn one's back on the world as long as one has a roof above one's head. Montaigne himself has something to do with this attitude; but he is not its source. Other points must be examined.

The first of these is the crossroads at which Montaigne found himself. The dying old Law presupposed the involvement of individuality in a complex of meaning and the consequent homogeneity of experience. The new one was anticipated by Montaigne's affirmation of the heterogeneity of each human experience. In the *Essays*, this heterogeneity is all the more categorical in that Montaigne still attempts to find the instruments that will ensure some contrasting means of homogenization, in order to allow examination of experience. When such a means is found, Montaigne is, so to speak, stabilized—that is, when we read Montaigne after Descartes, Rousseau, and Kant have made their impact, we can no longer experience his original horizon. We do, however, gain something from this distancing, and—within a situation that has again become precarious, from an epistemological and an existential point of view—we are led to attempt to understand his dilemmas and the solutions he suggested.

The Problem of the Exemplum

The sententious genres—the fable, the maxim, the exemplum—were the most frequently used media in ancient literature for integrating contingency, chance, and accident into the stability of the model. In the exemplum, "the general appears . . . in the particular. . . . The exemplum refers to a connection between situation and result of situation [*Situation und Ausgang*] which, since it can always be repeated, has general significance" (Stierle 1973: 356–58). The exemplum is the preferred resource for presentation in the *Essays*. But its very ubiquity highlights its evident difference. One need go no further than chapter 1 of book 1 to understand Montaigne's use of it.

The very first sentence is revealing. The classical use of the exemplum had the purpose of expressing contingencies, the heterogeneity of which was contradicted by a general norm, thus underscoring the need to respect the norm. The beginning of the chapter flaunts the traditional practice. Its opening statement may be read as a lesson in prudence for warriors—"The most usual way of appeasing the indignation of such as we have any way offended, when we see them in possession of the power of revenge, and find that we absolutely lie at their mercy, is by submission, to move them to commiseration and pity" (I, 1: 3)—and is immediately followed by an adversative clause that makes the opposite point: "and yet bravery, constancy, and resolution, however quite contrary means, have sometimes served to produce the same effect" (p. 3).

Whereas in antiquity exempla were intended to generate congruence in a melting pot, Montaigne seems to enjoy contradicting their authority. The exempla he then mentions elaborate the initial formulation. He interrupts his first list of cases to repeat: whereas sympathy and pity are to be attributed to weaker natures, "as of women, children, and the common sort of people," "to yield to the sole reverence of the sacred image of Valour" is the mark of those who honor "masculine and obstinate courage" (p. 3). The meaning would seem too univocal, contrary to the heterogeneity of the opening passage, were it not followed by the qualification "Nevertheless, astonishment and admiration may, in less generous minds, beget a like effect" (pp. 3–4).

The passages quoted above stress that weakness is associated with women, children, and common people, strength with those endowed with masculine vigor. So even though Montaigne parodies the authors of antiquity, in his text the old ethos of that nobility of the sword survives nonetheless. It is this ethos that identifies femininity with commonness and opposes to this pair those who are dedicated to *virtù*, that is, those who display virile courage, which is also equated with obstinacy.

It should not be thought that this warlike ethos is denied by the "nevertheless" that follows. The "astonishment and admiration" do not abolish the difference. They do, however, affirm something else: these distinctions are not primary; there is something that underlies them. That is why great warriors are not inflexible.

One might suppose that, in general terms, Montaigne's use of the exemplum faces two resistances: that of narrative and that of its elements. The first is directly contradicted: the cases are no longer shells that come from the same beach. The second, though, is circumvented rather than contradicted: the values that oriented that homogeneity are not exactly denied—for instance, in the above exemplum, the warrior's courage was not negated—but are shown to be unable to lead to the ultimate explanation. This circumvention, when finally revealed, in no way favors normativeness: "Man (in good earnest) is a marvellous vain, fickle, and unstable subject" (p. 4).

Although useful as a synthetic way to present in concrete terms Montaigne's use of the exemplum, this exegesis neither adds anything new to what countless commentators have already shown, nor does it lead to an analytically satisfactory conclusion. According to the earlier discussion, Montaigne is saying that if we would see man as a *sujet*, we must see him as vain, fickle, and unstable. In other words: if, in the old spelling of the word in French, *subject*, the new content, "individual subject," goes beyond the old content, "subject of a sovereign," then the qualities attributed to him make man untrustworthy. If our analysis goes no further than this, our Montaigne is a radical occasionalist, a predecessor of the romantics, who was to be vehemently attacked by Carl Schmitt (see Chapter 2). But Montaigne's image of the human condition cannot be identified with an unpredictable element, thanks to the very statements of his that are usually interpreted as signaling his conservatism: the division between the public and the private, the unwavering respect for church authorities, the submission to custom, the role he assigns to the paterfamilias. This is not to deny Montaigne's conservatism; but if our final judgment of him is to label him a conservative, we miss the opportunity to examine his inner motivation for breaking with the narrative character of the exemplum. And if we fall short of understanding this relationship, we neglect an important element of his expressive and interpretive economy. We must go further into this matter.

In Montaigne's terms, the exaltation of the individual excludes the possibility of his coming under any Law. But to go no further than this would be to see his reflections as indicative of smugness. Montaigne himself, however, defends his position when he states that his work contains no doctrine, that he is simply writing about his own life. We shall see that this line of defense will later be evoked to justify the discourse of literature. But in Montaigne's lifetime literature had not yet been legitimated as a discursive mode, so it could not possibly be used to justify one's writings. Thus, whether as a strategy or out of conviction, adherence to the traditional heritage was the only way to ensure the circulation—even the production—of his work. The time when the *Essays* were written was dangerous not only because of religious conflicts but also, and more importantly, because the principle of order then in force, like the Law it was subordinated to, neither foresaw nor allowed such a vain and fickle subject.[7] In the *Essays* we find less a conscious struggle

7. Natalie Zemon Davis's empirical analysis contains a historically important insight: if the subject's radical inconstancy was doctrinally unthinkable, social practices and beliefs showed, however, that this phenomenon was taken into account: "The line drawn around the self was not firmly closed. One could get inside other people and receive other people within oneself, and not just during sexual intercourse or when a child was in the womb. One could be possessed by someone else's soul; a magician or a sorceress could affect one's thoughts, feelings, and bodily movements, sometimes even without physical contact. . . . The Catholic liturgy had moments, especially during the ritual of exorcism, when the faith and prayers of a group were thought to change one person's inner state" (Davis 1986: 56). Contrary to Romantic attempts to see him as a heroic figure, Montaigne was not entirely isolated in his time. But acknowledgement of this fact only makes his thought all the more unique.

than a tension within the text itself. That is why, before closing our analysis of book I, essay 1, we shall point to the links between it and the themes introduced in the essays that follow. They are selected for their combined treatment of exemplariness, the heroic model of life, and the Christian attitude toward death. When the connection between these themes is observed, it makes sense to associate book I, essay 1, with book I, essay 13.

Of the essays in which Montaigne discusses death, "That the Relish of Good and Evil Depends in a Great Measure upon the Opinion We Have of Them" (I, 40) is not the most notable. In fact, its slighter density is precisely what draws us to it now. After discussing it, we shall be prepared to examine "That to Study Philosophy is to Learn to Die" (I, 19), in which the theme is developed most fully.

What is the point of the "Relish of Good and Evil"? Apparently, no more than the demythification of the fear of death. Death itself lasts no more than an instant; "it is rather the impatience of the imagination of death that makes us impatient of pain" (I, 40: 118). Imagination terrorizes us, and not only as to our thoughts: throughout our lives it influences our beliefs, determines our opinion, and affects the value we attach to things: "not what they bring to us, but what we add to them" (p. 122). Imagination makes us impressionable and makes a weapon out of our frailty. Outside of its sway, however, "things are not so painful or difficult of themselves" (p. 124). It follows, then, that our great enemy is not death. For is it not enough to know that it is inexorable, an inevitable moment, a predictable and unforeseeable circumstance? Our great enemy is the force inside us working in favor of death.

It is unchecked imagination that, through beliefs and opinions, spawns our terror. And the moral that Montaigne draws from this could be taken as a defense of either Christian ethics or the principle of stoicism: "That which makes us suffer pain with so much impatience, is the not being accustomed to repose our chiefest contentment in the soul" (p. 119). But this maxim does not solve the equation proposed. The attempt to demythify the terror of death will only emphasize what was stated in an earlier essay: "fear, desire, hope, still push us on towards the future, depriving us, in the meantime, of the sense and consideration of that which is to amuse us with the thought of what shall be, even when we shall be no more" (I, 3: 6).

Fear of death empties the present and thus poses an obstacle to wisdom, the only wisdom that Montaigne acknowledges in man. Is it not enough to know that death is not in the future where we dimly discern it, but that it patiently lurks, mocking us, at every passing moment? So who has anything to gain from the pomp and circumstance of funerary ceremonies? As he posed this question, Montaigne was well aware of the religious character of these ceremonies and of how intimately they were associated with aristocratic glory. So one would have to rid oneself of such folly in order to experience the present fully, seize the day, and make the best of multiplicity and diversity. In this way, the connection between the loss of exemplariness of the exemplum and the reflection on death heightens the distance between the *Essays* and the established institutions. The Christianized Stoicism or Stoic Christianity that the reflection might seem to lead to is replaced by the eulogy of a lusty virtue, unblessed by official recognition: "Now, of all the benefits that virtue confers upon us, the contempt of death is one of the greatest, as the means that accommodates human life with a soft and easy tranquillity, and gives us a pure and pleasant taste of living, without which all other pleasure would be extinct" (I, 19: 28). This passage reinforces the negation of all idealization—shortly above he had written: "Let the philosophers say what they will, the main thing at which we all aim, even in virtue itself, is pleasure" (p. 28)—in both its religious and its warlike variants.

In this same essay, Montaigne goes even further. The loss of exemplariness of the exemplum not only undermines the foundations of the comfortable union between church and crown but also extracts the consequence: "Where death waits for us is uncertain; let us look for him everywhere. The premeditation of death is the premeditation of liberty; he who has learned to die, has unlearned to serve. There is nothing of evil in life, for him who rightly comprehends that the privation of life is no evil: to know how to die, delivers us from all subjection and constraint" (I, 19: 31). The corrosion of exemplariness, of the aristocratic ethos founded on privilege, the right to glory, the exaltation of honor, and the duty to sacrifice for the sake of one's lord and of the principle of Christian virtue, brings about a violent storm that changes the debris into a paean to freedom.

Such a conclusion, however, is too euphoric. It might be true of the Enlightenment authors who are enthusiastic admirers of Montaigne. But underneath the praise there are dissonant notes; in Montaigne the praise of freedom is restricted to the private sphere: "whatsoever personage a man takes upon himself to perform [*quelque personnage que l'homme entrepaigne*], he ever mixes his own part with it [*il joue toujours le sien parmy*]" (I, 19: 28). The attack on established values is none the less violent—

> In our ordinary actions there is not one of a thousand that concerns ourselves. He that thou seest scrambling up the ruins of that wall, furious and transported, against whom so many harquebuss-shots are levelled; and that other all over scars, pale, and fainting with hunger, and yet resolved to die rather than open the gates to him: dost think that these men are there upon their own account? No; peradventure in the behalf of one they never saw and who never concerns himself for their pains and danger, but lies wallowing the while in sloth and pleasure. (I, 38: 109)

—and just as critical of the principle of privilege: "Equality is the soul of equity" (I, 19: 35).

What, then, would be insufficient in a praise of Montaigne as a champion of freedom? It is not difficult to see the connection between what he attacked and what he proposed: in these passages, Montaigne attacks the alliance between monarchic power and religion in the name of an admittedly individualistic, supposedly protobourgeois ethos. To attack death as a spectacle was to condemn an entire way of life. In contrast, the praise of freedom presupposed individual scrutiny and a conviction to be reached by each one: "The most extreme degree of courageously treating death, and the most natural, is to look upon it not only without astonishment but without care, continuing the wonted course of life even unto it" (II, 21: 329).

But the text of the *Essays* is so sinuous that when analyzing it one should hesitate before starting a chain of inferences. Now that the royal road seems to be sketched out—from the destabilization of exemplariness to the heightening of the value of the self—we had better stop for a while to catch our breath and go over the stations we have passed. As to the point of departure, we ought to stress that once homogeneous exemplariness is broken, the exemplum is used for a purpose that is the opposite of proclaiming a doctrine; the exemplum is now not only what strays away from moral constancy, but only what emphasizes the uniqueness of its creator: "Here, this is not my doctrine, 'tis my study; and it is not the lesson of another, but my own" (II, 6: 180). Hence, the lack of thematic hierarchy: everything fits in his book, from the moment that the value of personal experience is heightened. "There is no subject so frivolous that does not merit a place [*un rang*] in this rhapsody" (I, 13: 22). As though Montaigne had thrown away the board of a game and amused himself moving the pieces around in an absolutely arbitrary way, the exempla, once their exemplariness has been lost, pile up and deny one another, each spinning about in its own orbit.

At first glance, at least, this return to the situation of the exemplum does not seem to have added anything new, for all it did was to confirm the private limit that is a consequence of the attacks on the imposed duties. But perhaps good interpreters of Montaigne will suggest a different path. On the nonexemplariness of the exemplum Hugo Friedrich wrote, "Montaigne is convinced that no individual can be assimilated into the general, as, for instance, the lower to the higher. He searches not for the law, but for the image" (Friedrich 1949: 13). And, drawing the consequences of the inevitable contrast with Descartes's line:

> It is an event of importance that, shortly before the step that will lead the rational
> subjectivity of the modern scientific spirit to technical mastery over the world,

Montaigne should express a subjectivity of a different order: surely no less secular, but not without affinities with a certain feeling of compassion, of unease about individual human salvation, which, the more "subjective" it becomes, the more it limits itself to prudently listening to it and obeying it. (pp. 178–79)

The passage by Friedrich seems not only to confirm that nothing new has been discovered but also that nothing has been said that an intelligent interpreter had not previously shown. But perhaps we have fallen, even with the endorsement of the great interpreters, into a trap. Not that their readings are in any way defective; however, they may have heightened to such an extent the importance of the individual subject that they lack the necessary remove to see beyond (or this side of) the letter of Montaigne's text. Immediately the question is raised, How can such a remove be achieved? The most prudent way seems to be to try to do it where it seems most unlikely.

In a recent book, not notable for its specific treatment of Montaigne, Charles Taylor analyzes the relation between the affirmation of ordinary life and the rejection of ideal values that are external to the plain self and that had been seen as capable of producing the "sense of a qualitative distinction."

A specifically modern variant [of Stoicism] has developed. This is the ideal of the disengaged self, capable of objectifying not only the surrounding world but also its own emotions and inclinations, fears and compulsions, and achieving thereby a kind of distance and self-possession which allows it to act "rationally." . . . Reason is no longer defined in terms of a vision of order in the cosmos, but rather is defined procedurally, in terms of instrumental efficacy or maximization of the value sought, or self-consistency. (Taylor 1989: 21)

This affirmation of ordinary life, effected by each one as a consequence of the destruction of ideal values, adds Taylor, is "one of the most powerful ideas in modern civilization" (p. 14). Note also the uniqueness Taylor seems to see in our age: "The existential predicament in which one fears condemnation is quite different from the one where one fears, above all, meaninglessness. The dominance of the latter perhaps defines our age" (p. 18). This imminent risk of meaninglessness, then, is related to a framework in which "we have the picture of values as projections on a neutral world, something which we normally though unconsciously live within but could perhaps abstain from" (p. 78). That is, if in itself the world is a neutral set of physical properties of matter, and values are mere projections onto it, then the values that bring into being the qualitative differentiation by which a given behavior is privileged, whereas another is stigmatized, and yet another is seen with indifference, are negligible or even harmful properties. The individual subject should then concern itself only with the imperatives of ordinary existence. Thus, the self becomes its own value.

No more is needed for an understanding of Taylor's critical stance towards this dominant trend in modern society. Since Taylor's *Sources of the Self* includes a full chapter dedicated to Montaigne, one might expect to find in it a combination of his general thesis with his particular analysis. This Taylor provides, but not in such a way as to identify the remove we are looking for. Reiterating the obvious opposition between Montaigne and Descartes, Taylor simply underscores the two kinds of individualism that proceed from them:

> Descartes is a founder of modern individualism, because his theory throws the individual thinker back on his own responsibility, requires him to build an order of thought for himself, in the first person singular. But he must do so following universal criteria; he reasons as anyone and everyone. Montaigne is an originator of the search for each person's originality; and this is not just a different quest but in a sense antithetical to the Cartesian. . . . [Montaigne's aspiration] is not to find an intellectual order by which things in general can be surveyed, but rather to find the modes of expression which will allow the particular not to be overlooked. (p. 182)

The differentiation is so inevitable that it fails to explore other aspects. The first of these, however, is so immediate that Taylor would have arrived at it if he had only applied to Montaigne the observation he makes about the procedural character of modern reason—as defined in terms of instrumental effectiveness (see Taylor 1989: 21, quoted above). That is, the primacy of the individual subject brings the issue of the Law to the foreground. This means that the self-centering of the subject will remain an incomplete equation if it is not related to an absent term that subsumes it, unless the individual takes himself to be the Law—a step which is not yet taken by Montaigne. If such a step is taken by a thinker, it will bring into being, or help to bring into being, this new Law. In terms similar to Montaigne's, Rousseau will take this step; more systematically, in the context of modernity, Descartes and Kant are the most conspicuous ones to do so. Montaigne, however, settles for a skepticism that is enough to set him apart from them a priori; one might say he lacked the necessary inclination toward abstract thought to question skepticism itself. Whatever the explanation one may prefer, the fact is that in Montaigne the term that will be formulated only by Kant—the affirmation of the Law in force for all individual subjects—remains absent.

The current reading ignores the issue. To such an extent are we modern—that is, to such an extent do we take for granted the stability brought to the world by the Law as it is scientifically conceived—that we are unaware of the absence caused by the consecration of the individual. Or else, touching that absence just enough to push it away, we justify its concessions to conservatism as an effect of temporal vicissitudes. Passages such as "I have a great aversion from novelty, what face or what pretence soever it may carry along with it" (I, 22: 48) and "The Christian religion has all the marks of the most utility and justice: but none more manifest than the severe injunction it lays indifferently upon all to yield absolute obedience to the civil magistrate, and to maintain and defend the laws" (I, 22: 49) are quoted either with the approval of the interpreter or with the qualification that they were dictated by prudence, or even that they are the peccadilloes of a superior mind. Each of these options, or others that are similar, has the defect of seeing accommodation as a random variable, one that may be replaced by any other stance. In short, what Montaigne does with the subject, the values he adopts and expresses, are seen as irrelevant for a strict understanding of it. Consequently, any discussion concerning the role of absence—which so far we have only outlined—would be otiose. To further illustrate the climate of interpretation we are opposed to, let us mention another recent opinion.

In an extremely short text, Lévi-Strauss emphasizes that the *Essays* are characterized by an ambiguous attitude towards reason: "Every society seems savage or barbarous when its customs are judged by the criterion of reason; however, by the same criterion, no society should be seen as savage or barbarous, since for every custom, in its own context, a well-conducted discourse can find a foundation" (Lévi-Strauss 1991: 281). Thus, Montaigne is shown to profess a relativism that is subversive at bottom, even if "superficially it takes on the color of conservatism" (pp. 288–89). This statement is immediately justified by the comment that "On the practical plane and in the order of speculation, only 'our ancient belief,' as Montaigne says, can counterbalance the effects of the repulsion provoked by the contact with foreign customs and by the philosophical doubt that they might sow and make sprout" (p. 289).

But these passages seem contradictory: If the last-quoted one affirms that radical doubt can be avoided only by the force of "our ancient belief," then this belief plays a role that is at odds with its qualification as a veneer of conservatism (*superficiellement, couleur de conservatisme*). Quite on the contrary, such a conservatism is the necessary consequence of the fact that the irruption of the self, although it destroys the order of the old Law, is not sufficient for the adoption of a new one. We may agree that the acknowledgment of the individual subject in the *Essays* is subversive at bottom, for it undermines a centuries-old order. But it is only then that the most intractable problem begins: What is one to do about the land that has been devastated, particularly since one has nowhere else to go? How should we deal with the dilemma in which we ourselves have involved reason? This is not to say that Montaigne could have adopted no other solution. In fact, his epistemological skepticism presented the following alternatives: (1) It is a passage to a future affirmation. Thus, it is said today that contemporary negative thought makes possible a positive thought that it does not formulate. (2) It strikes some sort of compromise with the destroyed Law. (3) The skeptic subject sees as irrelevant any concern with any "qualitative distinction" (Taylor)—that is, brands as useless all speculative reflection, all mental work that does not result in technical gain; in short, it condemns all theoretical or philosophical effort and conversely recognizes only those opportunities that are conducive to private profit.

The first possibility is applicable to Montaigne only in strictly logical terms. Although it would not be unreasonable to imagine that someone might think of such a transmutation on the basis of the *Essays*, in the work itself no such thing is to be found. And although it seems obvious that Montaigne opts for the second alternative, it is just as obvious that it is only a short step from it to the third, the one that Taylor sees as dominant in contemporary society. Then again, one may wonder whether (2) and (3) are in fact distinct options: (2) might be only a modified version of (3)—what a believer of (3) thinks when forced by circumstances to justify his or her position intellectually.

Be that as it may, the preceding discussion ensures us the right not to take the affirmation of the self as the final stage of a process that began with the destruction of the exemplarity of the exemplum. Instead, this statement is followed by a question: What norms shall I respect? What Law justifies the norms I observe? This question was then shown to imply the existence of an absence, which we were inclined to characterize tentatively as Montaigne's compromise with part of the values of his day. But we must now add that it is not sufficient to fill this absence with a necessary conservatism. This is not to deny what was said earlier: Montaigne's conservatism is no accident, but rather something imposed by his very consecration of the self. All we are doing now is to add that the question of the absence has not yet been exhausted. In order to understand it fully, we must return to the analysis we were conducting before the issue of the absence was posed. Only then will we be able to exploit the significance of this additional observation.

We were saying that once death as a spectacle had been rejected, the present, after the concern with honor and glory had been banished, became an empty space to be occupied. In this field to be cultivated, pleasure is the clear source: "This pleasure, for being more gay, more sinewy, more robust, and more manly, is only the more seriously voluptuous" (I, 19: 28). However, the first proof that this is not enough to fill the gap, to change absence into presence, is the fact that attainment of this desired pleasure is not ensured: "pleasure, to deceive us, marches before and conceals her train" (I, 38: 111). Even such a prudent and carefree pleasure as the one we experience when we read Seneca, Plutarch, and the ancient poets is not safe: "Books are pleasant, but if, by being over-studious, we impair our health and spoil our good-humour, the best pieces we have, let us give it over; I, for my part, am one of those who think, that no fruit derived from them can recompense so great a loss" (I, 38: 111). No pleasure is safe, and it is even less to be trusted that the present will become free and open. The self must then fall back on the pleasure of writing, of continuing this rhapsody until its dying day:

> For these are my own particular opinions and fancies, and I deliver them as only what I myself believe, and not for what is to be believed by others. I have no other end in this writing, but only to discover myself, who, also, shall, peradventure, be another thing tomorrow, if I chance to meet any new instruction to change me. I have no authority to be believed, neither do I desire it, being too conscious of my own inerudition to be able to instruct others. (I, 25: 63)

What pleasure could be greater than that of facing the respected authority of the ancients and assuring them that he quoted them not to speak of them, but to speak of himself? "Neither have I said so much of the others, but to get a better opportunity to explain myself" (I, 25: 63). Pleasure here seems to surpass itself, turning into pride, even hauteur. Clearly, Montaigne's book is for him a source of solitary pleasure. But this chemistry was not able to transmute absence; the effort to portray it had the effect of multiplying it. The friend he had lost, whom he had set out to praise, is not to be recovered by writing; on the contrary, by writing about him and portraying himself in the process, Montaigne can only emphasize the distance. Absence is not conquered by a chemical process, but rather moves to a different plane: what is absent is sharpened into presence, the presence of writing.

This unforeseen result affects the exempla themselves. Undisciplined, heterogeneous, no longer guided by a moral code, they are integrated into a book that will go on being written "so long as there shall be ink and paper in the world" (III, 9: 457). Montaigne's prolificacy is not just an effect of style; by means of it he becomes receptive to the unceasing experience of multiplicity. To him, however, the connotations of multiplicity are not wholly positive: "No French author had the experience of multiplicity in its double sense of liberation and torment as fully as Montaigne" (Stierle 1987: 423–24). Pleasure makes the self spacious. But it is the very condition of its richness that the absence should remain, that it should only move to another plane and shine in the form of writing. This displacement is thus the second strand that interpreters fail to note when they limit themselves to opposing Montaigne's

individualism to Descartes's. Cartesian individualism was consistently opposed to whatever could not be accommodated in mathematical equations.
Absence is not part of its view of the world. The choice made by Montaigne
thus implies two contradictory marks: the first, through the constancy of
skepticism, imposed on him the conservative concession. The second, due to
the permanence of absence, implied the exploration of multiplicity, both
liberating and tormenting. From the intersection of the two, literature will
take shape. But we are not yet in a condition to be able to elaborate this result.
Even before we come closer to the issue of literature, there is yet a third strand
to examine.

The ancient practice of the exemplum corresponded, according to Auerbach's famous thesis, to the division of styles. Serious subjects required
the tragic mode and elevated language, whereas ridiculous or mean subjects, treated in plain language, were the stuff of farce and comedy. Now,
the break with exemplariness, the choice of a subject that was as little
recommendable—according to traditional standards—as the portrait of someone who had not dignified himself enough in the world, would require,
following the old division of styles, the use of *sermo humilis* (humble speech).
As Auerbach himself observed, Montaigne's decision made it impossible for
him to prolong the old practice: "All this is serious and fundamental enough;
it is much too high for *sermo humilis* as understood in antique theory, and yet it
could not be expressed in an elevated rhetorical style, without any concrete
portrayal [*Darstellung*] of the everyday life. . . . His newly acquired freedom
was much more exciting, much more of the historical moment, directly
connected with the feeling of insecurity" (Auerbach 1974: 310). This passage,
with its fine sensibility, should be transcribed with no additional comment.
But we cannot help observing that it is still committed to the idea of the
wholeness of the subject. Montaigne's "creatural realism," to which Auerbach
refers in the passage immediately following the one transcribed above, is more
than just a response to the insecurity of his time: it also includes an ineluctable
absence. Auerbach fails to perceive this fact, and so he not only takes the
modern individual to be a center unto himself but also overlooks the absence
with which he establishes himself—or rather, the absence that establishes him.

The steps immediately following will take us closer to the mark of absence.

The question of man, his dignity, and his capacity for choice and knowledge is the starting point of Renaissance philosophical anthropology. It is
taken up by Montaigne with a significant inflection. Resignation from active
court service contained the initial gesture that gave rise to the *Essays*. The
particular tone in which he poses the question of man no longer admits the

topos of man's dignity, much less the spirit of generalization. Instead, there is a ferocious, uncertain vortex. Against human dignity, which Pico had praised as an inherent trait of a creature that occupied "the interval between fixed eternity and transitory time," Montaigne prefers to echo Seneca: "Oh, what a vile and abject thing . . . is man, if he do not raise himself above humanity" (II, 12: 294). And the comment he adds does no more than cover human weakness with the trappings of Christianity: "He shall rise if God will extraordinarily lend him His hand; he shall rise, by abandoning and renouncing his own proper means, and by suffering himself to be raised and elevated by means purely celestial" (II, 12: 294).

Throughout the *Essays*, preference is given to those authors of antiquity who were not loath to emphasize human misery. The Christianization of their message does little to alter it fundamentally. The introduction of the new theme of the self, though it had been anticipated in the Renaissance, particularly by the genres of the letter and the dialogue,[8] is consecrated in Montaigne by means of a violent torsion: instead of harboring conquering enthusiasm, the heart describes its own tortuous maze, an abyss too dark to be lit by Christian revelation (Greene has observed that Montaigne abolishes the flexibility that Renaissance reflection had given to the experience of the self; see Greene 1968: 259). And example is given by Montaigne's insistent reflections on the monster. The first noteworthy occurrence makes it equivalent to a quite heterogeneous event: the miracle.

> If we give the names of monster and miracle to everything our reason cannot comprehend, how many are continually presented before our eyes? Let us but consider through what clouds, and as it were groping in the dark, our teachers lead us to the knowledge of most of the things about us; assuredly we shall find that it is rather custom than knowledge that takes away their strangeness. (I, 26: 80)

What monsters and miracles have in common is that both give the lie to the established order. Monsters have to do with the order of nature, whereas miracles imply the interference of a supernatural will. By equating them, Montaigne questions the specialists in each area: philosophers and theologians, the men of knowledge and the men of God. All too human, both are guilty of the same arrogance, the product of excessive trust in reason. What proudly passes for science in most cases is not explained by causes, but rather by the action of mere custom. That is, the two kinds of phenomena—the

8. "The Humanist letter, in its original Italian form, was already an 'essay' in Montaigne's sense of the word, touching upon all subjects from the vantage point of a meditating, central self, its only principle of unity in the midst of whimsical diversity" (Fumaroli 1978: 888).

expectable normal, on the one hand, and the monstrous and the miraculous, on the other—are explained most of all not by the use of lofty reason, whether philosophical or theological, but by lowly custom.

True, the author later seems to tone down his violent attack on the pretensions of natural and theological knowledge and deals separately with monsters and miracles. "Those that we call monsters are not so to God, who sees in the immensity of His work the infinite forms that He has comprehended therein" (II, 30: 344); "We need not trouble ourselves to seek out foreign miracles and difficulties; methinks, among the things that we ordinarily see, there are such incomprehensible wonders as surpass all difficulties of miracles" (II, 37: 367).

The figures of the monster and the prodigy had puzzled Renaissance thought: "In Renaissance terms, [they] intensify a sense of decorum by revealing the inexhaustible fecundity of nature" (Greenblatt 1986: 36). But this decorum both provoked wonder at the marvel of the world's machinery and stimulated the desire to experiment, know, and master. One is reminded of the importance of Ambroise Paré's *Des monstres et prodiges* (Monsters and prodigies) (1573) to anatomy. But Montaigne denies that investigative curiosity has any effectiveness. A conformist, he disposes of the problem by saying it does not exist before the eye of God. The experimental plane is thereby annulled, and the question is placed on God's plane. By contrast, the passage from book II, essay 37, denies the value of theological explanations: it is custom, the accustomed eye, that labels "foreign miracles and difficulties" things that, according to a different custom, would be quite ordinary, and that presumes to know what in fact remains strange.

In short, for Montaigne the monster places reason on trial. Like a shrewd lawyer, he uses the arguments that show his viewpoint in the best light. If lay knowledge, at a time when modern scientific endeavor is in its infancy, is seen with suspicion by the church hierarchy, what could be better than to play one against the other? Montaigne's contempt for medicine is not to be affected by the successful experiments conducted by his contemporary Paré. Similar researches are invalidated from the outset by the principle of divine omniscience, against which no opponent would dare raise his voice. But one must take care not to strengthen theologians' hands too much: they are just as presumptuous, ignorant, and dangerous.

For all his shrewdness, however, Montaigne cannot deal with the third clandestine argument raised by the emphasis on custom. Although unforeseen, it was not arbitrary as to its effect on Montaigne's emphasis on human diversity. Clearly, the exploitation of this argument would play against the author's intent, for it would lead to the idea that, by examining the diversity of custom, one might arrive at the conclusion that each custom in itself contained a certain homogeneity, which in turn would allow the development of a science of man—a most ironical outcome for Montaigne's endeavor. But one could always argue that such a result would imply the existence and the manipulation of evidence external to the trial against reason set up in the *Essays*. This would surely be true. But the conclusion fails to capture the fundamental fact: Montaigne had to have a foothold on some constant term. This can be named and diversified on various planes: the divine order, the universal order of nature, the habits and customs of one's time and place. Each of these limits behavior in some way. If Montaigne does not intend to investigate them, if he justifies his lack of interest either by pointing to the futility of reason or by stressing the singularity of his own self, this singularity cannot be believable unless one resorts to some sort of constancy. That is, although they are not explored by reflection, those orders point to a Law.

Nor is it surprising that our skillful lawyer should neglect an unforeseen argument: placed at the point where one Law crumbles and another is only beginning to arise, Montaigne's heteroclite order—that is, an order that was animated by a principle, the individual subject, which pointed to a world view that dispensed with it—was by definition provisional. Montaigne's individual was soon to change into Cogito, into Man, an object that, seeing itself as worthy of philosophical and scientific investigation, would suspend the trial of reason for centuries.

Without the bombast of a preacher or the systematizing zeal of a philosopher, and using rambling as a method—"my style and my wit wander at the same rate" (III, 9: 482)—Montaigne must follow no other path but that of chance, of what he chanced to read and hear and see and particularly experience. Are the *Essays* then an autobiographical work? To a twentieth-century reader, the obvious answer to the question is yes. To show that this is in fact not the case, we shall have to rely on two courses of action. First, let us ask what characterizes autobiography as a genre. After this theoretical elucidation, we can return to Montaigne.

At the beginning of his essay on Augustine's *Confessions*, Eugene Vance writes that the concept of autobiography serves "both as a vehicle of subjective consciousness and as the document of an external, objective history whose alterity is also finally his or her own" (Vance 1989: 1). This seems to be the case in Montaigne. Here is a characteristic passage:

> I am grown older by seven or eight years since I began [this book]; nor has it been since without some new acquisition: I have, in that time, by the liberality of years, been acquainted with the [kidney] stone: their commerce and long

converse do not well pass away without some such inconvenience. I could have been glad that of other infirmities age has to present long-lived men withal, it had chosen some one that would have been more welcome to me, for it could not possibly have laid upon me a disease, for which, even from my infancy, I have had so great a horror; and it is, in truth, of all the accidents of old age, that of which I have ever been most afraid. I have often thought with myself, that I went on too far, and that in so long a voyage I should at last run myself into some disadvantage; I perceived and have often enough declared, that it was time to depart, and that life should be cut off in the sound and living part, according to the surgeon's rule in amputations. . . . And yet I was so far from being ready, that in the eighteen months time or thereabouts, that I have been in this uneasy condition, I have so inured myself to it as to be content to live on in it; and have found wherein to comfort myself, and to hope: so much are men enslaved to their miserable being, that there is no condition so wretched they will not accept, provided that they may live! (II, 37: 365)

We had to let the passage run its course the better to bring out its meaning. Although this particular incident provides material for yet more pages, this is enough to show that the author is less interested in documenting a fact in the story of his life than in illustrating, with resignation and humor, human adaptability. The kidney stone is not reason enough to hurry death on. The reflection on the adaptability to "this uneasy condition" increasingly deviates from a description of the fact it is supposedly documenting. As one who improvises on an initial melodic theme, changing it along the way, Montaigne examines the experience of the ancients concerning the suffering of disease. Each experience follows its course. By bringing them together, he heightens their heterogeneity. And since there is no paradigmatic experience in any case, Montaigne falls back on his leitmotif: "I am in conflict with the worst, the most sudden, the most painful, the most mortal, and the most irremediable of all diseases. . . . I have at least this advantage by my stone, that what I could not hitherto prevail upon myself to resolve upon, as to reconciling and acquainting myself with death, it will perfect" (p. 366)—that is, it will expand and depersonalize it.

The self-portrait Montaigne presents does not exclude diseases and even more intimate details. But these are shown less as documents than as points of departure for a sort of floating, unsystematic, punctual, personalized meditation: "I try myself in the depth of my dolor, and have always found that I was in a capacity to speak, think, and give a rational answer as well as at any other time, but not so firmly, being troubled and interrupted by the pain" (p. 367).

The rhapsodic tone dominates the autobiographical climate, and though the author's eye is constantly fixed on himself he can always address Cicero or the strangeness of what is unknown to reason. Exploiting this strangeness,

Montaigne deftly turns back to personal terms; the illness that began to afflict him after a certain age had been contained in the drop of semen with which his father begat him: "'Tis to be believed that I derive this infirmity from my father, for he died wonderfully tormented with a great stone in his bladder." (p. 367). We may leave aside the long diatribe against physicians that takes up the rest of the chapter.

Thus, what was expected of the chosen example has been achieved: the creation of a solid ground on the basis of which the theorization of auto-biography could begin with Montaigne. Now we are in a position to consider whether what we have here is a conjunction or a disjunction.

Autobiography is frequently associated with the confession, a genre in which, since the Renaissance, Augustine's work has played a decisive role. Undoubtedly, the *Confessions* have since then been read as an emotional testimony to his own life. But this interpretation may not necessarily be correct. For the sake of brevity, let us mention the different positions concerning this point without examining them in depth.

Among those who would answer in the affirmative the question of whether the *Confessions* are an autobiography, we must mention the argument of a competent historian, Peter Brown: "The *Confessions* are a master-piece of strictly intellectual autobiography. Augustine communicates such a sense of intense personal involvement in the ideas he is handling, that we are made to forget that it is an exceptionally difficult book" (Brown 1969: 167). The last sentence is the conclusion of a line of reasoning that is presented in the preceding pages. At first glance, Brown says, it seems easy to classify the book. Augustine was simply following the practice of the Neoplatonists, whose thought he had adopted, of composing prayers to God. And since the Neoplatonic God was *absconditus*, unknown to human reason, philosophical questioning "verged on the concentrated quality of an act of prayer . . . by establishing a direct relationship with God" (pp. 165–66). This identification, however, turned out to be arbitrary, because "such prayers were usually re-garded as part of a preliminary stage in the lifting of the philosopher's mind to God. They had never been used, as Augustine would use them throughout the *Confessions*, to strike up a lively conversation with Him" (p. 167).

Brown's position is implicitly contested by the medievalist Eugene Vance. The belief that the *Confessions* have an autobiographical character is too generalized for Vance to feel the need to name this or that scholar. His argument can be summed up as follows: To Augustine, whereas God is the depositary of truth, human language is no more than the surface layer of memory that must be delved into. It is only memory that gives us access to the divine spark hidden in the creature; it is only by digging into it that the creature can meet its Creator. This encounter presupposes the death of the self and its necessary attendant, mortal and worldly language. The history of the self is then evoked and narrated as the demonstration of an exemplary loss and its transfiguring metamorphosis. Hence, the commemorative character of Augustine's language: "The ontology of the *Confessions* is thus founded not on the model of intersubjective communication between mortals, but on that of possession by a being of a higher order: to speak correctly is to be actually inhabited by the voice of the Other speaking to the 'ear of the heart' " (Vance 1973: 170). The commemorative character of the language implies the mortification of its earthly fleshliness. However, the plunge into memory through the mortal container of the flesh is not completed as directed by confession. That is why "Augustine will become dissatisfied with the narration of his personal life as a source of true wisdom and will consequently invite his soul (as he does in Book X) to reflect upon its own inner, spiritual substance rather than upon the external images of the creation" (Vance 1989: 23).

Vance's argument convinces the reader that his position is better founded than the more common interpretation. Although Peter Brown is a competent and renowned historian, ultimately his argument rests on a neglect of historical time: it is as if the arrow of the *Confessions*, shot in late antiquity, had crossed the shadow of the centuries to hit its target only in modern times: "It is this therapy of self-examination which has perhaps brought Augustine closest to some of the best traditions of our own age" (Brown 1969: 181).

The difficulty with the line of interpretation that refuses to classify the *Confessions* as autobiography, however, is that it treats the autobiographical genre as belonging exclusively to the era of legitimation of the individual. What, then, are we to make of works such as Flavius Josephus's *Vita* if we can no longer include it among the self-encomiastic works of Roman dignitaries? To account for similar cases, must we resort to such improper expressions as "forerunners" or "preparatory forms"? In order to solve this conundrum, it seems we cannot treat the subject—whether ancient individuality or modern individual—as the primary and decisive term. This is what is suggested by John Freccero's formula: "the autobiographical genre . . . implies the death of the self as character and the resurrection of the self as author" (Freccero 1986: 16–17). Instead of the exploration of personal identity in writing, autobiography presupposes the discontinuity caused by conversion—"a conversion is only a conversion when it is expressed in a narrative form that establishes a separation between the self as character and the self as author" (p. 17).

Let us, then, turn to the question of autobiography in Montaigne. The analysis we started before our theoretical digression will now be useful. If

autobiographical narrative emphasizes the unique incidents of a specific existence, it is clear that in the *Essays* the recording of uniqueness becomes a
rhapsodic reflection on life as human experience. Both in autobiography and
in Montaigne the moment of conversion is highlighted. In each case, however, it is connected to a different axiom: in autobiography, the axiom in
question is the uniqueness of the life story being narrated (which is precisely
why it was exceptional in antiquity); in Montaigne, it is the indistinction of
the human condition. But are we now contradicting the emphasis on uniqueness we have previously stressed? This question allows us to underscore the
paradox that accompanies Montaigne's reflection on uniqueness: its need of
contrast. Let us go over the question with caution.

At first glance, we seem to be made up of differences only. Per se, each
human being is an aggregate of dissimilar parts; collectively, we are each of us
different from all others. But something, Montaigne might say, is the same in
all of us: the arrogance and flippancy of our reason. Montaigne places reason
on trial because he denounces as unfounded its pretension to knowledge. It is,
then, in the name of the radical diversity of each human being that reason is
condemned and humbled. Thus, each bearer of this heterogeneity claims the
right to be heard, to describe minute details and personal indiscretions.

All of this places the author in the sphere of the autobiographical. However, we must make a distinction between this general sphere and the autobiographical genre proper. The general sphere is not limited to the autobiographical genre, for it also includes the letter—in which Renaissance
authors, Erasmus in particular, experienced the pleasure of self-expression
free of the constraints of rhetorical formulae and of the Ciceronian model (cf.
Fumaroli 1978)—and the essay. The conversion of Montaigne-as-character
into Montaigne-as-author was achieved less by his retirement to his castle
than by his realization, after the failure of his project of glorifying La Boétie's
memory, that writing is dealing with absences. The conversion leads him into
the autobiographical sphere; the rhapsodic tone consigns him to the rambling
essay.[9]

But by placing the essay in the sphere of the autobiographical we raise a
problem for the argumentative structure of this chapter. We were converging
on a more detailed examination of the question of absence when, before we
had exhausted even the preliminary discussion, a new variable appeared: the
problem of form in the essay. And this occurred even before we finished the
exposition of the present item. Could we not conclude at least this one?
Considering that of the three terms we set out to discuss in this item the third

9. The present reflection is a continuation of "Persona e sujeito ficcional" (see Costa-
Lima 1991: 40–56).

one is yet to be taken up, could we not limit ourselves to reasserting that, in relation to being, Montaigne's position is one of absolute skepticism? This we would do if such an acknowledgment were enough. But all we have said about the close relation between the affirmation of heterogeneity—consistent with epistemological skepticism, to be sure—and the urgent need for a stabilizing ground suggests the opposite. Therefore, rather than adopt reiteration and say, with Thibaudet, that "the *Essays* are the studies, the sketches, for an impossible painting" (Thibaudet 1963: 61), let us accept the impossibility of submitting Montaigne's work to a linear reflection.

If Montaigne's skepticism is apodictic and inescapable, it also establishes, by means of discourse, a proximity that can be illuminating. It is less a matter of seeing it than of knowing how to listen to it:

> Alas, poor man! thou hast enough inconveniences that are inevitable, without increasing them by thine own invention; and art miserable enough by nature, without being so by art. . . . Dost thou think thou art too much at ease, unless half thy ease is uneasy? dost thou find thou hast not performed all the necessary offices that nature has enjoined thee, and that she is idle in thee, if thou does not oblige thyself to other and new offices? Thou dost not stick to infringe her universal and undoubted laws; but stickest to thy own special and fantastic rules, and by how much more particular, uncertain, and contradictory they are, by so much thou employest thy whole endeavour in them: the laws of thy parish occupy and bind thee: those of God and the world concern thee not. (III, 5: 426)[10]

Skepticism is clearly the point of departure for this invective against man—but no more than that. Montaigne's skepticism does not deny the existence of a natural and divine order. This order would make human misery less egregious if only men did not make a point of ignoring it. That is, it is not enough to speak of the failure of reason, for the advent of another force contributes to its weakness. The passage states this clearly enough: unsatisfied with his fate, man "by art" conceives new duties for himself, doubling the misery that he was already doomed to suffer. The failure of reason is parallel to, if not stimulated by, the forge of imagination. Although there are "universal and undoubted laws," the dark side of reason forgets them and, fired by imagination, conceives laws of "[its] own invention," substituting the laws of "[its] parish" for "those of God and the world." The inevitability expressed here is that of the disastrous proximity, discursively established, between reason and the imagination.

In the trial of reason, another defendant appears, an accomplice or instigator: imagination, no less responsible than reason for the state in which

10. Montaigne gave so much importance to this passage that he rewrote it for both the 1588 and the 1595 editions.

man finds himself. It is taken for granted that no trial would have been necessary if man obeyed natural precepts. But where is such a proof of innocence to be found? The diversity of peoples, the recent discovery of a previously unknown continent, failed to reveal the existence of any primitive creature who acted in conformity with the Law of nature. This Law is invoked as an inverted myth. On the plane of reality, man always adds to his natural inconveniences the ugliness created by his imagination. If reason is dark and unreasonable, could it be so because imagination will not let it out of the cave? The conspiracy of the two marks the negative proximity that determines Montaigne's epistemological skepticism. However, as he stages reason's trial, Montaigne still supposes that—theoretically, at least—the world's absurdity might yet be attenuated. (This is the major difference between Montaigne and Kafka. Or rather, this is the difference between the era of the consecration of the individual and that of the questioning of the Law that was set up on the basis of the acknowledgment of the individual.) The attenuation I mentioned was not, in Montaigne, a merely hypothetical possibility; on the contrary, it might actually come to be. This might happen if only human adaptability were not used in order to adjust to the worst of all states, rather than to conceive a less uncomfortable situation. The individualistic ethos may thus be seen as the positive proximity of dark reason. Its manifestations are many. Let us examine a few of them.

Although he does not often praise the Stoics, Montaigne tacitly endorses their position. But he is sharply at odds with them whenever he finds them too much attached to the defense of a value: "truly, a man must confess that there is some phrenzy, some fury, how holy soever, that at that time possesses those souls" (II, 2: 166). Since he was writing in a time of religious wars, when manifestations of holy furor were more numerous than the examples found in books written in antiquity, we may suppose that Montaigne found inspiration in contemporary cases. In this way, even as he professed loyalty to his king, he kept at a distance from the warring parties and branded any fixed position as fanaticism. This would be a sort of constancy founded on the dark side of reason. If reason cannot be enlightening—that is, achieve true knowledge—it may at least prove useful to those who employ it. Pragmatically, the individualistic ethos sticks to down-to-earth positions: I am alive and so I hope to remain; I come from a certain place with certain customs; it is only reasonable that I should follow them. But one should not exaggerate: it is just as unadvisable to follow them under any circumstances as it is to flout them.

Ultimately, then, the condemnation of any fixed position, the defense of flexibility, is based on the decision to remain alive. To stick to a given conduct come what may implies certain qualitative distinctions—better dead than dishonored, misery is preferable to treason, and so on—determined by a scale of values. Now, such a scale is no more than one of the forms assumed by the rules of man's "own invention" that are formulated by the perverse alliance between imagination and reason. Values are unnecessary projections. To obey them is a matter of convenience. To learn to die correctly is to learn how to avoid the ways of hastening death. Reason, placed on trial, was found guilty of a misalliance with imagination; it was this that brought about reason's mad ambition. But even if it cannot be enlightening, reason can at least be sensible. It can refrain from indulging in speculation. Philosophy "forms us [*nous dresse*] for ourselves, not for others; to be, not to seem" (II, 37: 366). Sensible reason affirms a single fact: the individual subject.

Clearly, the individualistic ethos is opposed to a society in which status is fixed. Shortly above the passage just quoted, Montaigne advised philosophy to ignore external appearances: "Let us leave that care to actors and masters of rhetoric, who set so great a value upon our gestures" (p. 366). The followers of rhetoric prize appearances; they are the advisors of the order of show. Sensible reason, however, has to do with being, not seeming. The fact that we have no access to our being is no reason why we should not be mindful of it. Epistemological skepticism exacerbates the proposal of an individualistic ethos. The denial of all values poses the individual as the sole value of a wholesome reason. "I had rather understand myself well in myself, than in Cicero" (III, 13: 520).

Formulated in these terms, however, the affirmation of the individualistic ethos would be redundant. We arrive at it by so many different routes that we would seem to be mimicking Montaigne's own meanderings. The next step is taken by a comparison between two passages concerning the historian's task: "There were never so many historians: it is, indeed, good and of use to read them, for they furnish us everywhere with excellent and laudable instructions from the magazine of their memory, which, doubtless, is of great concern to the help of life; but 'tis not that we seek for now: we examine whether these relators and collectors of things are commendable themselves" (III, 8: 451).

The passage opposes the topos with which the writing of history, *historia magistra vitae* (history, the teacher of life), was classically justified, to the personal examination of the historian. Here are the beginnings of the primacy of the subject's intentionality, and consequently of the role to be assigned to a lay hermeneutics. In any case, our understanding will remain incomplete until we relate the passage quoted above with another, much earlier, text:

There are authors whose only end and design it is, to give an account of things that have happened; mine, if I could arrive unto it, should be to deliver of what may happen. There is a just liberty allowed in the schools, of supposing similitudes, when they have none at hand [*quand ilz n'en ont point*]. I do not, however, make any use of that privilege, and as to that matter, in superstitious religion, surpass all historical authority [*et surpasse de ce costé là en religion superstitieuse toute foy historiale*]. In the examples which I here bring in, of what I have heard, read, done, or said, I have forbidden myself to dare to alter even the most light and indifferent circumstances: my conscience does not falsify one tittle; what ignorance may do, I cannot say. (I, 20: 41)

The affirmation of individualism does not restrict itself simply to disparaging reason's pretensions as absurd, or to accusing it of being the accomplice of imagination, or—even less—to emphasizing the need to make sure of the historian's honesty beforehand. Taking himself as an example, Montaigne adds the requirement of strict respect for the facts. Not that through them one has access to the way of timeless truth—"my conscience does not falsify one tittle; what ignorance may do, I cannot say"—but only to a singular, more modest truth: the truth of what once was. Therefore, the effect of centering on the individual is not simply that of generating a skepticism that incriminates reason and the force exerted on it by the deceptive machinery of imagination, or that of imposing an accommodation with the ancient Law; these are still partial results, which in turn lead to a valuing of testimony and to the authority granted to the trustworthy eye. Against the presumptions of reason and the chimeras of the imagination there is the fact. As an index of what can be known, only the fact is compatible with a world that centers on the individual subject.

Montaigne, the consecrator of the individual, is also the champion of the *fact*, of what seems to be independent of judgment. Devotion to the fact is forced on the individual as the index of a Law, the testimony of a homogenizing principle; it scarcely matters whether or not this Law has already been formulated—it had not, for Montaigne—or that its champion need know only, as it came to be the case since Newton, what "specialists" were able to demonstrate. In either case, the fact was a comforting indication. Thus, we see the encroachment of an element of the new Law. Since Montaigne is not, properly speaking, a thinker, its appearance in *Essays* is more auspicious. Facts are not valued because they are accidents, but because of their usefulness: thanks to them, the heterogeneity of experience seems to find something that is free from subjective arbitrariness.

George Huppert's research on the origins of *modern* historiography in France has shown that this conclusion applies not just to Montaigne: it is revealing of his sociohistorical background. We accept Huppert's hypothesis that the valuing of the factual sprang from the "discipline required by jurists in verification of facts" (Huppert 1973: 27), which discredited the Renaissance model of history and came to be the centerpiece in the characterization of the *culture de robe*—that is, the intellectual training of the administrative cadres in the latter half of the sixteenth century in France. If, in the case of historiography, this is clearly demonstrated by pointing to the *Recherches de la France* (French studies) (1560) of Estienne Pasquier (1529–1625) (cf. Huppert 1973, chapter 3), it is no less true that, in Montaigne, the greater complexity of the *Essays* requires that the relevance of the fact be combined with a much larger problem.

The Corrupting Imagination

To the author of the *Essays*, the force of the imagination is self-evident: "I am one of those who are most sensible of the power of imagination. . . . I take possession of the disease I am concerned at, and take it to myself. I do not at all wonder that fancy should give fevers and sometimes kill such as allow it too much scope, and are too willing to entertain it" (I, 20: 36). Exemplifying with his own impressionability, he observes that the lesson is not addressed only to others. If reason is not qualified for knowledge, the struggle is even more strenuous, for one must also be on the lookout for imagination. Its effects are perhaps even more serious; whereas reason brings about the vanity of mind, imagination is manifested in the body itself: "We start, tremble, turn pale, and blush, as we are variously moved by imagination; and, being a-bed, feel our bodies agitated with its power to that degree, as even sometimes to expiring" (p. 36).

Its seat is the mind, but no part of the body is immune from its effects. And although its power is exerted even over earthly monarchs, it is among common people that it has its most destructive effects. It is because its power is ignored that people speak of miracles and bewitchings. Imagination is the source of superstition: "'Tis very probable, that visions, enchantments, and all extraordinary effects of that nature, derive their credit principally from the power of imagination, working and making its chiefest impression upon vulgar and more easy souls, whose belief is so strangely imposed upon, as to think they see what they do not see" (p. 37).

Imagination is manifested in a rhetoric of the body, the effects of which are more insidious than the effects of professional rhetoricians, for its action is internal and independent of whatever is said. It whispers inside each body, as it were, and dispenses with the attention of the ears. To those who fail to protect themselves against this terrible enemy, anything may happen. Thus it is that the male organ can grow in a maiden, and pregnant girls can give birth to children with the faces of beasts. In this passage, in which he reproduces beliefs current in his day, Montaigne is not postulating the heterogeneity of the exempla. Each belief he mentions points to the same effect. That is why he advises newlyweds to put off the consummation of their marriage until they are less under the influence of agitation and feverish excitement. Otherwise, irremediable shame and inevitable disaster will ensue.

Montaigne is so obsessed with this theme that he returns to it in essays other than "Of the Force of Imagination." He is constantly warning the reader against imagination, for this is the reason why we are ever unsatisfied and thus desirous of what we do not know: "Our appetite is irresolute and fickle; it can neither keep nor enjoy anything with a good grace: and man concluding it to be the fault of the things he is possessed of, fills himself with and feeds upon the idea of things he neither knows nor understands, to which he devotes his hopes and his desires" (I, 53: 149). As to this, Montaigne is undistinguishable from the most rigorous moralist or the most mediocre parish priest. Later—to mention only great names—Bayle was to attack imagination with equal vehemence, although he found Montaigne's epistemological skepticism uncongenial to his own rationalism. The same may be said of Malebranche and Pascal.[11]

If Montaigne insists so much on this point, it is because experience has taught him that, for all his caution, he himself has been infiltrated by the enemy:

> It should seem that to be known, is in some sort to have a man's life and its duration in others' keeping. I, for my part, hold that I am not, but in myself; and of that other life of mine which lies in the knowledge of my friends, to consider it naked and simply in itself, I know very well that I am sensible of no fruit nor enjoyment from it but by the vanity of a fantastic opinion. (II, 16: 304–5)

It seems that sexuality was the only natural impulse against which the West struggled as ferociously as against imagination—we are reminded of Augustine, already an old bishop, accusing himself of yielding to temptations of the flesh. Curiously, Montaigne is extremely candid about eroticism and his own sexuality. One might suppose that the consecration of the individual subject diluted the force of the prohibition against eroticism, part of which was turned against imagination. We believe this took place because imagina-

11. Here is the beginning of Pascal's fragment on imagination: "*Imagination*—This is the dominant part in man, this mistress of error and falsity, and all the more knavish in that it is not so always; for it would be an infallible mark of truth if were of falsity. But, being false more often than not, it gives no mark of its quality whatsoever, endowing the true and the false with one and the same character" (Pascal 1957b, no. 104: 1116).

tion causes a generic commotion—internal and external, bodily and moral—
that compromises the equilibrium of the self, particularly if it is not protected
by an order that previously includes and justifies it. Thus, the commitment to
aspects of the old order would not be enough—let alone the relative stability
given by the customs the self was forced to consider. Without the precautions
against "irresolute and contrary imaginations," the self, particularly when it is
given to such fits, would be disoriented. The fight against imagination does
not derive from Montaigne's traditionalism, but from the valuation of fact, of
objectivity, that increases with the growing primacy of the self. The control
of the imaginary is therefore not unrelated to what will be known as scien-
tism. To do no more than contrast Descartes's individualism with Montaigne's is a concession to the humanistic interpretation; and the price of such
a restriction is to remain blind to what this interpretation could not see.

This insight has the additional advantage of explaining Montaigne's lack
of interest in or aversion to works of fiction (naturally, Montaigne does not
use the term): "Amongst books that are simply pleasant, of the moderns,
Boccaccio's *Decameron*, Rabelais, and the *Basia* of Johannes Secundus (if those
may be ranged under the title) are worth reading for amusement. As to
Amadis, and such kind of stuff, they had not credit to take me, so much as in
my childhood" (II, 10: 195). As an earlier passage makes clear, this lack of
interest seems to have been the effect of a severe education that privileged the
Latin classics and kept him from even knowing the names of the heroes of
romances of chivalry (see I, 25: 79). But this explanation is precarious: in no
other case does Montaigne show such obedience to models. It seems more
likely that the distaste for books that were simply amusing had to do with the
acknowledgment of the fact that they excited his imagination without giving
him any useful result. That is, the romances of Amadis and Lancelot, unlike
detailed descriptions of fact, were not convenient to one who wanted to
explore himself as an autonomous subject, since they did not offer him an
objective scene to be explored and known. The contrasting values Montaigne
attached to fact and imagination, then, are a result of the same search for a
Law that would include both the nonexemplariness of experience and some
frame of reference that might ascribe some meaning to it. This search will also
be present in the praise of custom.

Presuppositions for the Treatment of the Portrait

The core of the present section and the two immediately following is the
antinomy between a passage from book 1 and another from book 2. Although
little noted, it very much deserves our attention.

It is not for outward show that the soul is to play its part, but for ourselves within, where no eyes can pierce but our own; there she defends us from the fear of death, of pain, of shame itself: there she arms us against the loss of our children, friends, and fortunes: and when opportunity presents itself, she leads us on to the hazards of war. (II, 16: 303)

I do not paint its being [i.e., of the object], I paint its passage. . . . 'Tis a counterpart [*contrerolle*] of various and changeable accidents, and of irresolute imaginations, and, as it falls out, sometimes contrary: whether it be that I am then another self, or that I take subjects by other circumstances and considerations: so it is, that I may peradventure contradict myself, but, as Demades said, I never contradict the truth. Could but my soul once take footing, I would not essay but resolve: but it is always learning and making trial. (III, 2: 388)

The first passage formulates what we shall call the "Montaignean ideal self." The role of the soul is not to exhibit us to others; it is inside each of us that the soul plays its role. It is there, unseen by any witness, that it grows resistant to misfortunes. The Montaignean ideal self presupposes a source of constancy. If we fail to communicate with Being, we have no possibility of coming into contact with the metaphysical immutable. If, furthermore, we are assaulted by imagination, we tend to be pushed around by random events and humors. Because of these two conditions, the lesson of the Stoics should be internalized. And the influence of one Stoic in particular is evident here.

In *On the Shortness of Life*, Seneca speaks of the three parts of which life is made up: the present is short, the future is uncertain; only the past is irrevocable. "This, then, is the part of our time that is sacred and cannot be renounced, that remains exempt from all human contingencies, protected from the sway of fortune, immune from the assaults of poverty, of fear, of disease. It can be neither disturbed nor taken away; ownership of it is perpetual and safe from all disaster" (Seneca 1987: x). In order to exert control over oneself, the Stoic points to the part of time that can be possessed to the utmost. The care of the self, Foucault wrote, is not to be confused with the process of the growth of individualism. This is plainly borne out by the passages from Seneca and Montaigne transcribed earlier. To the philosopher, the past is an unchanging territory, which for this reason allows a measure of objectivity. Individuality is placed before it, and the traits of its persona may be judged on the basis of what it did there and what was done to it.

Montaigne, a habitual reader of Seneca, tried to preserve this property, but bringing it into himself; the constancy of the self was to be found not in a transaction with something independent from it, but in its own core. What we are calling the Montaignean ideal self is then the form by means of which the mutable and uncontrollable is changed into affirmation of the constancy that the self provides itself. If this ideal had achieved success, Montaigne would be so close to the philosophers of Roman decadence that we would have to say either that these philosophers were already individualists or that Montaigne cannot yet be considered one.

The other passage, however, counters: the author, like everyone else, inevitably portrays not the being (what is), but the passage (how it is). If, in the description of the ideal self, he speaks of the "part" the soul must play, on the plane of reality he can only deal with its opposite, "a counterpart of various and changeable accidents." If, on the plane of idealized duty, one relied on a role solidified by constancy, on the plane of existence and reality all one can find is the reverse of the role—heterogeneous, multiple, dispersed, dictating the self's chaotic responses to the pressure of events and of imagination itself. The clash between the two planes seems to demonstrate the individual subject's failure to attain its hoped-for constancy. But that is not quite the issue, for constancy, which cannot be reached in itself, is achieved in the form of custom. Let us examine this point so that we can understand the contradiction from which we started.

It is through attention to the force of habit that the individual absorbs and is integrated into the ethnocentric circle. The Greeks labeled "barbarians" those who adopted different customs. "Barbarians are no more a wonder to us, than we are to them" (I, 22: 44). Human adaptability is the mold that shapes custom. However different one may be from the other, within each there is complete homogeneity. "'Tis by the mediation of custom, that every one is content with the place where he is planted by nature; and the Highlanders of Scotland no more pant after Touraine, than the Scythians after Thessaly" (p. 46). Shortly before, in the 1595 edition of the *Essays*, an even more important note observed: "The laws of conscience, which we pretend to be derived from nature, proceed from custom" (p. 46).

Given such passages, we might be misled into seeing Montaigne as the forerunner of anthropology if we failed to take into account what sort of need led the author to place such emphasis on custom. The preceding reflections already suggest the answer: some form of homogeneity had to be found, or else the heightening of the self might lead to anarchy. On the plane of reality, custom is what confers meaning on individual action, hampered by the failure of the Montaignean ideal self; although diffuse and collectivized, it acts as the aggregative factor with which the individual interacts.

This is the context in which we can understand the drift of the *Essays*, which is ultimately ambiguous. On the one hand, the author questions the advisability of any change in customs:

> It is a very great doubt, whether any so manifest benefit can accrue from the alteration of a law received, let it be what it will, as there is danger and inconve-

nience in altering it; forasmuch as government [*une police*] is a structure composed of diverse parts and members joined and united together, with so strict connection, that it is impossible to stir so much as one brick or stone, but the whole body will be sensible of it. (p. 48)

On the other hand, Montaigne speaks approvingly of a Lacedaemonian, mentioned in Plutarch, who had interpreted the law in such a way as to violate its letter in order to benefit his people: "being born to command, he knew how to do it, not only according to the laws, but also to overrule even the laws themselves, when the public necessity so required" (pp. 50–51).

Although the two statements point in opposite directions, the principle they are based on is the same: custom rules over individual action, orienting it and investing it with meaning. But, as we already know, to Montaigne all absolute obedience to a value is harmful and reprehensible. As a kind of value, principles ought to be followed within a certain margin of flexibility. But up to which point is this flexibility legitimate? When does it cease to be advisable? The author never clarifies this point. But a passage from the same essay shows that his conservatism tends to have the upper hand:

These considerations, notwithstanding, will not prevail upon any understanding man to decline the common mode; but, on the contrary, methinks, all singular and particular fashions are rather marks of folly and vain affectation, than of sound reason, and that a wise man ought, within, to withdraw and retire his soul from the crowd, and there keep it at liberty and in power to judge freely of things; but, as to externals, absolutely to follow and conform himself to the fashion of the time. (p. 48)

Montaigne's conservatism is apparent in his defense of the need for the separation between the public and the private, between compromise and personal opinion. The praise of custom does not detract from the defense of individualism—there is always flexibility, as well as private conscience as the court of last resort. Why should appearances matter, as long as even the executioner knows that he has a beautiful soul?

If this consideration adds nothing that is new, it should be noted that the praise of custom leads Montaigne back to reason and to emphasis on another aspect of it. Not that he lets reason out of its pit, or qualifies in any way his condemnation of it. Rather, he acts like a deaf or cynical character who waits for the wind to die down and for custom to crystallize in order to make himself heard with imperative sharpness: "I do believe, that no absurd or ridiculous fancy can enter into human imagination, that does not meet with some example of public practice, and that, consequently, our reason does not ground and back up" (p. 44). Reason interferes a posteriori and justifies what it seems to explain. It is only on this basis that Montaigne can be seen as a relativist. He assumes the primacy of the subject, skepticism, the necessary compromise, and the constancy found in custom.

What is fundamental is to understand the role of custom within a process that begins and ends in reason. A priori, reason is seen as weak and vain, so that the subject endowed with it cannot partake of the homogeneity of Being. In addition, reason is weakened by the pressure of imagination. As a consequence of the action of the two, the self is left defenseless. That is why, as we have seen, Montaigne needed a compromise with the order of the Law denied by his skepticism. The emphasis on custom made his position tenable: "As the central agent mediating between nature and culture, *coutume* [custom] gains an essential significance. It is, as it were, nature under the conditions of culture, and therefore a principle that contains innovation, the only factor that keeps the social world from losing the foundations of its life in common" (Stierle 1987: 438). To say that custom contains innovation is to say that it is the homogenizing agent the self needed in order to impose its primacy. Now Montaigne can reopen the last session of his trial of reason, face the defendant for the last time, and accuse it of cynical pride. But reason is condemned only after Montaigne finds another mold for it. What is proscribed is metaphysical reason, associated with the ancient Law that provisionally still served as an alibi for fledgling scientific experimentation; and imagination turned out to be a defendant as well. However, when Montaigne praises custom and fact, what he is valuing is still reason, though clad in more modest attire. These two point to the affirmation of another objectivity, without which the experience of the modern individual could not be socialized.

The Requirements of the Portrait

The preceding discussion should suffice to allow us to analyze the problem of the portrait. And, with it, after this necessary digression, we can return to the question of absence.

When he first tackled the issue of the portrait, Montaigne had thought of transposing to the domain of the written word a pictorial practice that was quite common in the first half of the sixteenth century. What he did was to appropriate an existing practice rather than to start a new one: "Portraits above all, according to the Dutch tradition, of testimonies or court evidence, and which therefore need not be elaborated, become, particularly when effected in a preparatory medium—pencil—representations in themselves" (Blanchard 1990: 87).[12] Through representation of the self, Blanchard adds

12. It was only when the writing of this book was finished that we had access to Gottfried Benns's magnificent *Bildnis und Individuum: Über die Ursprung der Porträtmalerei in*

(p. 87), the aura that until then had been reserved for monarchs was transferred to the individual.

Even if through a provisional medium, the individual offered himself to the eyes of contemporaries, if not of posterity. But, if they filled in the center, what should painters do with the empty space around it? In order to cover this space, they made use of a procedure technically known as *crotesque*, a term that "referred, in the parlance of the painters of the day, to the ornaments and arabesques [*Rankenwerke*] in which heterogeneous vegetable and fabulous motifs were mixed ad libitum, and the whims of fancy could be indulged in freely, in contrast with the totalizing presentations of serious themes" (Friedrich 1949: 414). Montaigne himself not only clarified the meaning of the term but also made clear how he employed it:

> [The painter] finishes [the picture] with his utmost care and art, and the vacuity about it he fills with grotesques [*crotesques*], which are odd fantastic figures without any grace but what they derive from their variety, and the extravagance of their shapes. And in truth, what are these things I scribble, other than grotesques and monstrous bodies, made of various parts, without any certain figure, or any other than accidental order, coherence, or proportion? (p. 82)

It is not by chance that this observation should appear at the beginning of the chapter "Of Friendship." Here Montaigne not only considers La Boétie but also explains the first void to be filled by his book. Since he can no longer publish *La Servitude volontaire*, how could he show the world the glory his friend would otherwise have earned? Absence had already been introduced in the displacement that was forced on him: since he could not present a portrait of his friend, Montaigne would exalt him for friendship—both the particular friendship that joined them and friendship in general, for its excellence. On both planes, friendship ranked higher than love, since it was free from feverish excitements and apprehensions. The friendship at which they had excelled shone above other possible instances for the perfect fusion it established between them:

> But in the friendship I speak of, [acquaintance and familiarities] mix and work themselves into one piece, with so universal a mixture, that there is no more sign of the seam by which they were first conjoined. If a man should importune me to give a reason why I loved him, I find it could no otherwise be expressed, than by making answer: because it was he, because it was I. (I, 27: 85)

---

der italienischen Renaissance (The portrait and the individual: On the origin of portrait painting in the Italian Renaissance) (Munich: Prestel-Verlag, 1985). Since in what follows we touch on the issue of the arabesque, mention should also be made of another essay that came under our notice only after this book had been written: K. Behnke's "Romantische Arabesken: Lineatur ohne Figur und Grund zwischen." In H. U. Gumbrecht and K. L. Pfeiffer, eds., *Schrift* (Munich: Wilhelm Fink Verlag, 1993).

The very effusiveness of the passage enhanced the absence that was its point of departure. In its central position—in the very middle of book I—La Boétie is the first mark of absence: here is the first impossible portrait in the *Essays*.

On its ruins, Montaigne will attempt to erect another: his self-portrait. His portrait is then defined by a double displacement—it replaces what was originally meant to be there; and what had previously been confined to the margin comes to occupy the center.

And what has become of the arabesques—the *crotesques*? Their ornamental character has now fused with the main motif—someone's portrait—to such an extent that the alleged lack of order and proportion of the ornament has been integrated into the main figure.[13] That is, the arabesque loses its status as ornament; it is intertwined with the subject; the two are fused together. In order to specify the absence that is introduced with this combination, we must resort to a detailed examination.

How did Montaigne intend to acquire recognition? The first relevant passages stress the intention of faithfulness and intellectual autobiography: "I expose myself entire; 'tis a body [*Skeletos*] where, at one view, the veins, muscles, and tendons are apparent, every [one] of them in its proper place. . . . I do not write of my own acts, but myself and my essence" (II, 6: 181). "I universally owe my entire picture to the public" (III, 5: 430). "Permit, reader, this essay its course also, and this further sitting to finish the rest of my picture" (III, 9: 466).

Montaigne is not concerned with feats or external actions; such things interest him only to the extent that they express his interiority. Thus, to speak of intellectual autobiography here is a way to avoid confusing it with autobiography pure and simple. The unceasing, unfinished meditation where

13. The question of the status of the arabesque is here raised for the first time. We will soon come across it again in the discussion of fundamental points of Kant's argument in the third *Critique* and in Schlegel's consideration of the poetic (see Chapter 2). But its fundamental importance lies in the fact that, instead of limiting its relevance to the field of aesthetic experience, its links with apparently unrelated fields is brought out. It was Howard Bloch who showed, in his chapters on the roots of medieval misogyny, that within it the woman connotes not only "body," "the senses," "concupiscence," "letter" (as opposed to "soul," "mind," "reason," and "spirit," which are attributes of man), "ornament," and "metaphor," traits that, taken together, both identify women with the flesh and its aestheticization and theologize this identification: "At the same time the realm of esthetics is theologized, with the result that whatever belongs to the realm either of the feminine or of the esthetic is devalued within an ontological perspective according to which everything conceived to exist beyond the flesh, and thereby gendered masculine, alone has a claim to full Being" (Bloch 1991: 46). The links with the medieval view of the feminine, misogyny, and the simultaneous idealization of women are by no means occasional: in fact, they seem to show that what we have been calling the control of the imaginary is a strand from a much larger skein.

arabesque and body constantly interpenetrate points to the unsystematic exploration of a composite: the portrait reproduces not what was already done, but what can only be done with it. The deviation from the purely autobiographical announces the form of the essay. But let us not go further into it before we exhaust the proposal of faithfulness to the portrayed subject. Another reference to it is in the invocation to the lady to whom he dedicates the essay "Of the Affection of Fathers to Their Children": "*Or, Madame, ayant à m'y pourtraire au vif. . . .*" (Now, madam, having to draw my own picture to the life. . . .) (II, 8: 183).

What this portrait "to the life" presupposes becomes clear when we take into account what Montaigne says about painters:

> For though we are content with painters when they paint heaven, earth, seas, mountains, remote islands, if they gave us but some slight mark of them, and, as of things unknown, are satisfied with a feigned and obscure shadowing forth; yet when they come to draw us by the life, or any other subject which is known and familiar to us, we then require of them a perfect and exact representation of lineaments and colours, and despise them if they fail in it. (II, 12: 259)

These requirements, according to Montaigne, imply that everything that is said about an object be not only verisimilar but also factually true. Without actually writing an autobiography, the author may describe the most trifling events of his own life, the smallest nooks in his garden, all the while being certain that he is not exhibiting himself: "I would that every one should see my natural and ordinary pace, irregular as it is; I suffer myself to jog on at my own rate. Neither are these subjects which a man is not permitted to be ignorant in, or casually and at a venture, to discourse of" (II, 10: 195). "I speak my opinion freely of all things . . . to show the measure of my own sight, and not of the things I make so bold to criticise" (p. 195). "As to the rest, I have enjoined myself to dare to say all that I dare to do . . . the worst of my actions and qualities do not appear to me so evil, as I find it evil and base not to dare to own them" (III, 5: 408).

The fact matters to him because to describe it well is to prove its truth:

> By which we may see, whether the inquisition after truth be not very delicate, when a man cannot believe the report of a battle from the knowledge of him who there commanded, nor from the soldiers who were engaged in it, unless, after the method of a judicial inquiry, the witnesses be confronted and objections considered upon the proof of the least detail of every incident. (II, 10: 199)

Hence Montaigne's aristocratic disdain for "the middle sort" of those whose job it is to write history. Even more important than this prejudice is his disdain for the practice of belles lettres, within which historiography was included: "For the most part, and especially in these later ages, persons are culled out for this work from amongst the common people, upon the sole consideration of well-speaking, as if we were to learn grammar from them" (p. 199).

There is a clear relation between the stringent requirements of faithfulness, the "portrait" of the historian, and what was said earlier about Montaigne's ideal self. Conceived in a process of search for inner homeostasis, the ideal self failed in its confrontation with the mutability of reality and could only find satisfaction—of a relative sort—in the slackening brought about by custom. It was on the same basis that Montaigne required that a portrait be faithful to the appearance of the person portrayed: it reflected a refusal of the court's aura, the pose implied by a role or by the whims of one's own fancy. Just as the historian was expected not to produce well-turned phrases but to prove in detail the truthfulness of what he said, the individual was expected to present a detailed and honest portrait "to the life." It is important to emphasize that the struggle against fantasy was justified both by factual honesty and as a reaction against the ancien régime taste for ornament. Montaigne's lesson would not be forgotten in the coming legitimation of the individual subject.

The association with the historian is not accidental. The writing of history was a part of belles lettres. To expect faithfulness in the verbal portrait and in the writings of the historian implied the same deviation from the code of ostentation. Speaking of writers, and aristocratically excluding himself from their company, Montaigne wrote: "Were I of the trade, I would as much naturalise art as they artify nature" (III, 5: 423). Thus, historiography, essay writing, and the presentation of portraits in painting and in writing all have in common the opposition to codification and the exaltation of the factual as an index of truth.

But the ideal portrait fails no less than the ideal self. As it is actually written, the book does not simply convey what already existed before. The reader is more than a passive witness to the catalyst of truth:

> And though nobody should read me, have I lost my time in entertaining myself so many idle hours, in so pleasing and useful thoughts? In moulding this picture upon myself, I have been so often constrained to temper and compose myself in a right posture, that the copy is truly taken, and has in some sort formed itself; painting myself for others, I represent myself in a better colouring than my own natural complexion. I have no more made my book, than my book has made me. (II, 18: 323)

The self-portrait cannot reproduce its subject because the painter has previously internalized the answer he expects to find in the eye of the other. The other cannot be eliminated; he cannot be excluded simply by the soul's determination to examine nothing but itself. Otherness is already present in the self. That is why Montaigne states elsewhere: "I cannot fix [*asseurer*] my object; 'tis always tottering and reeling by a natural giddiness" (III, 2: 388). If the eye of the other could be seen as an evil presence insinuating itself into a chaste sanctuary, there would remain the possibility of conceiving more effective locks. But if the very self is motion—"I do not paint its being, I paint its passage" (p. 388)—the battle is lost from the outset. Its destiny will remain unnamed as long as the self is placed at the center of the stage.

To say that the portrait is built on an absence literally means that the work is not under the author's control, is not the author's possession. As it permeates the work, the absence frees itself from the subject that supposedly dominated it. Montaigne exhibits his discovery as if it were one of the effects of the melancholia of which he sees himself as a victim. In his case, melancholia was the path chosen by the dangerous imagination. No wonder, then, that after reiterating his obsessive preoccupation with the portrait—"I owe to the public universally my portrait," and defending his habit of calling a spade a spade, "*Et les Roys et les philosophes fientent, et les dames aussi*" (Both kings and philosophers go to stool, and ladies too; III, 13: 526)—Montaigne should justify himself with the argument that he was the way he was because nature had made him so: "'tis not out of judgment that I have chosen this scandalous way of speaking; 'tis nature that has chosen it for me" (III, 5: 430). Nor should it cause any surprise that, until quite recently, the greatest interpreters of Montaigne did not emphasize the fact that the creative subject was defeated by its own creation. One of the very greatest of these wrote: "Thus Montaigne's apparently fanciful method, which obeys no preconceived plan but adapts itself elastically to the changes of his own being, is basically a strictly experimental method, the only method which conforms to such a subject. . . . In the end there is no unity and truth, in the end it is his essential being which emerges from his portraying of the changing" (Auerbach 1974: 292–94).

One may even agree with Richard L. Regosin when he notes, in a short review of a number of works on Montaigne, that Montaigne's reiteration of individual freedom and his contrasting disdain for the outer world were emphasized in these works as a reaction against the threat to the primacy of the self that Nazism represented (Regosin 1992: 135–49). Although the observation is apt, we should keep in mind that the sociocultural motivation for such an interpretation was already centuries old by then: the modern view of literature, and of art, was founded on the previous affirmation of a creative subject that, not distinguishing itself for its deeds, calculations, or discoveries, devoted itself to playing the music of the daemonic human virtualities on the harp of intimacy. By means of literature, man played himself. By means of it, the reader learned what the sciences were unable to formalize. Literary culture made public what otherwise would be ineffable.

If the human foundation was the basis for the understanding of literature and the interpretation of the great authors, making up what we shall call the "humanistic view of literature," the emphasis on absence and the consequent diminution of the author's voice implies a different view. Whereas the humanistic version reaches its apex in Hugo Friedrich's book on Montaigne, the emphasis on absence begins with Michel Butor's *Essais sur les Essais* (Essays on the *Essays*) (1968). Thus, Montaigne now offers us the additional opportunity of seeing an analytic discontinuity in action.

This experiment can be further enriched when we note the resistance to acknowledgment of this break. An exemplary instance of this is the effort—whether conscious or not, we do not know—to explain away the interpretive discontinuity by arguing that the two interpretations are to be seen as complementary rather than incompatible; that, consequently, the same criterion for the identification of literature can and should be maintained. This is what Jean Starobinski argues in his impressive *Montaigne en mouvement* (Montaigne in motion).

Starobinski summarizes the metamorphosis that took place in the composition of the *Essays*:

> The resort to writing transforms the first *readerly* experience into an *authorly* experience. . . . Converted into the receptacle of identity, the book lends a different meaning to identity. It is no longer the equation that establishes an indissoluble fidelity to itself. It is no longer the permanent *essence* of which it had taken possession from inside and that attests the similarity of an image to an "original," itself the author of the image. . . . Identity is conferred on the work, on the production of an image. (Starobinski 1982: 42–43)

The "motion" is then inverted: instead of the author imprinting his personal mark on his creation, it is his creation that ascribes its own identity to Montaigne. The motion points to the failure of the demand for a *substantial* life—that is, one founded on fixed elements: "Inner truth remains inaccessible: it cannot be possessed as a thing, nor can it be fixed as a figure. It refuses all objectification, and retreats as Montaigne believes himself to be moving close to it. He remains in the presence of a confused, unlimited horizon—of an intimate transcendence" (p. 88–89).

All of this is brilliant and well put. What, then, is the question? With his extreme stylistic ability, Starobinski notes the gradual passage from concentration on the subject to emphasis on écriture; it is seen as an effect of a change in the author himself, who, as he wrote, was in effect being written. Subject and object changed places in a smooth transition. Whereas traditionally, literature had been defined as a function of the writer-subject, the emphasis on écriture would also rely on the same center, the self, only now changed from expressive center to "intimate transcendence."

There would be nothing objectionable in this maneuver if it did not conceal the net of contradictions we have been highlighting. In short, there is a contradiction between the stated purpose of presenting a faithful portrait and the autonomous images that are actually produced. In Starobinski *shock* is changed into *fluency*; in this way the motion oversteps the limits that had been set by Montaigne: this motion stops when the self-portrait is finished. Two consequences follow from Starobinski's interpretation: first, the traditional view of literature absorbs the change in the way of envisaging its object and thus gains stability; that is, the incorporation of a different analytical approach to the *Essays* does not affect the modern concept of literature; second, no account is taken of the fact that the failure of the model of faithfulness imposed on portraiture did not make Montaigne convert to a new parameter. That is, although Montaigne came to realize that écriture guided him more than it was guided by him, although he came to recognize that "speaking is half [*est moitié*] his who speaks, and half his who hears" (III, 13: 528), these changes do not affect his original attitude toward imagination, its effects, and its works. Therefore, if one fails to respect the limits Montaigne had set to the motion, one simply distorts the letter of his text. In other words, respect for it is not dictated by a criterion of intentionality—which would be clearly contradictory here—but by the need to keep the analytical instruments adequate to the textual object.

In contrast, although redundant, it would be relevant to examine the role played by the negative identification of imagination in the concept of the ideal portrait. One need only be reminded of Montaigne's horrified reaction: "What, shall mere doubt and inquiry strike our imagination, so as to change us? Such as absolutely and on a sudden give way to these propensions, draw total destruction upon themselves" (III, 13: 526). Montaigne had reasons enough to be wary. Classical tradition had been at best condescending about the use of imagination and had never employed it as the privileged instrument for contemplation with a view to knowledge (*theoria*). In addition, the faculty that tradition prized, reason, had proved to be an accomplice of the accursed imagination. The very emphasis on this changing and meandering being, the individual subject, served by such untrustworthy faculties, implied the need to find something that might provide a support.

The rest of the argument would be otiose here. Let us add only that for these very reasons Montaigne could not possibly approve of the romances of Amadis and Lancelot and such; these could be seen as no more than works of entertainment, relegated to moments of leisure, or even despised. Thus, to ignore this process that runs parallel to the consecration of the individual—the constant (though not always successful) vigilance against imagination, seeing with variable degrees of disdain the strictly fictional work—is to neglect the exact configuration within which, centuries later, the legitimation of literature took place. In this way it becomes easier to explain why the theme of the control of imagination and the imaginary was not integrated into the speculations of humanistic interpreters: from their angle, this control fell on a blind spot. Nor will it seem surprising that only recently has the status of fictionality become systematically high: this correlates with the loss of confidence in the self-sufficient self. Thus, to accept Starobinski's idea that the thematization of écriture harmoniously continues the questioning previously centered on the magnificent power of the creator is to keep those questions in a diffuse and unexplored state. The emphasis on absence as a constituent element of the *Essays* has the purpose of emphasizing this discrepancy. It will then provide the basis for the conclusion of our analysis.

Towards Autobiography: The Essay

According to Montaigne, the essay is to be distinguished from the letter because it is not addressed to a specific person: "For to traffic with the wind, as some others have done, and to forge vain names to direct my letters to, in a serious subject, I could never do but in a dream, being a sworn enemy to all falsification" (I, 40: 114). La Boétie's death had deprived him of his one interlocutor; his disdain for the culture of glory further distanced him from letter writing; the need to write, however, made him search for a form.[14] But what was he to write? and to whom? and what for? What he wanted to express was no doctrine; his addressee was anonymous, if at all existent; his object could only be to bear witness. All of this pointed to autobiography. However, a number of reasons converged in the refusal to write autobiography.

Montaigne says he does not trust himself enough—"I, who am monarch of the matter whereof I treat, and who am accountable to none, do not, nevertheless, always believe myself" (III, 8: 457); he abhors the flowery lan-

14. The relevance of the written character of the essay has already been underscored by Michel Beaujour: "Montaigne considers himself more inspired by epistolary improvisation stimulated by friendship than by the laborious invention of the essay, destined to be mediated by the print shop, and which requires that the writer be shown in his solitude. That is why Montaigne's self-portrait may seem to us a necessary consequence of the breakdown of a privileged oral and handwritten communication and as an attempt to inscribe in the space of the printed book the persona of one who makes us part of his *inspiration* although without actually knowing us" (Beaujour 1983: 24).

guage of letter writers, and to it he opposes his own preference: "I have naturally a humorous and familiar [*privé*] style" (I, 39: 114); above all, he knows he has not achieved great feats that merit perpetuation: "I can give no account of my life by my actions; fortune has placed them too low: I must do it by my fancies" (III, 9: 457). But by differentiating the three motives we in a way deform them, for we seem to suggest they are factors that are added one to the other, whereas they are in fact aspects of the same figure. Their unity is acknowledged in the passage that immediately follows the one we have just quoted:

> And yet I have seen a gentleman who only communicated his life by the work-
> ings of his belly: you might see in his house a show of a row of basins of seven or
> eight days' excrements; that was all his study, all his discourse; all other talk stunk
> in his nostrils. Here, but not so nauseous, are the excrements of an old mind,
> sometimes thick, sometimes thin, and always indigested. (p. 457)

This passage seems to express the modesty of someone who felt unworthy to speak of himself; after mentioning the ironical case of the gentleman whose sole interest was excrement, he speaks of his own style, "humorous and familiar," as equally unworthy. What, after all, does Montaigne believe in if not in himself? But what sort of belief is this if, in order to justify his lack of self-confidence, he says he has to watch out for "*boutades de mon esprit*" (sallies of my own mind) and "*certaines finesses verbales*" (certain verbal quibbles), at which he shakes his ears (III, 8: 457)?

Pascal, who admired Montaigne without following him, answered this question: "It is in this doubt that doubts itself, and in this ignorance that ignores itself, which he calls his master form, that the essence of his opinion is to be found" (Pascal 1957a: 564). The confidence was not in himself, but in his language: the *Essays* "carry sometimes besides what I apply them to, the seed of a more rich and bolder matter" (I, 39: 114). Language is not outside the self, as an object of dignity and mastery, nor is it indistinguishable from the subject's means of expression. The former negation implies that Montaigne could not put aside his aristocratic ethos and see himself as a professional writer; the latter implies that his form could not be the same as Rousseau's, whose *Confessions* are the very epitome of the genre.

In the search for a determination of the form to be used in the *Essays*, all the questions raised in the book come together. Form is the magnet that will make its existence possible. In Montaigne the question concerning this form does not proceed from a previously given answer. It seems plausible, in fact, that he found it only as he wrote his work. This is the conclusion one arrives at after comparing Montaigne's observations on the portrait and those on the essay.

The original model for the portrait had been the work of the painter. We have seen that the ideal portrait was a correlate of the ideal self, understood as the requirement to capture what it ought to be, once the soul were freed of the misfortunes caused by fantasy; we also saw that the failure of one was caused by the same element that had blocked the actualization of the other: the "motion" that unceasingly affects the creature and makes it different from what it was the moment before. Now, the essay has no need for such a planned circuit—or rather, it is born of the ruins of the portrait, ruins that accumulate simultaneously with the effort to achieve the project and are not the result of giving it up. This can be inferred from a factual datum: whereas the decisive passage that denies any plans of autobiographical record—"I can give no account of my life," and so on (p. 457)—was added to the 1588 edition of the *Essays*, in the postmortem edition of 1595 the original formula was reiterated: "I present myself standing and lying, before and behind, my right side and my left, and in all my natural postures [*et en tous mes naturels plis*]" (III, 8: 457).

Although conceived simultaneously and not in succession, the portrait and the essay are opposites. And what Merleau-Ponty said about Montaigne is as apt in relation to the essayist as it is incorrect if applied to the goal of the portraitist. "He does not know this place of rest, this self-possession, that Cartesian understanding is to be. To him the world is not a system of objects facing the idea, to him the self is not the purity of an intellectual conscious-ness" (Merleau-Ponty 1960: 251).

Though distinguished from the record of one's own life, then, the essay as practiced by Montaigne still has an affinity with the autobiographical. As we have observed, within this sphere the autobiographical genre presupposes a moment of rupture, originating in a "conversion" that separates "the self as character" from "the self as author" (Freccero 1986: 17). Given the funda-mental importance of this difference, it will be worthwhile to recall a passage from the paradigmatic work of the autobiographical genre, Rousseau's *Con-fessions*. Although any page would do, we have selected the well-known scene in which Jean-Jacques steals "a little pink and silver ribbon, which was quite old."

When the ribbon was found in his room, the boy defended himself blaming the cook:

> She was sent for, to face a considerable number of people, including the Comte de la Roque himself. When she came she was shown the ribbon. I boldly accused her. She was confused, did not utter a word, and threw me a glance that would have disarmed the devil, but my cruel heart resisted. In the end she firmly denied the theft. But she did not get indignant. She merely turned to me, and

begged me to remember myself and not disgrace an innocent girl who had never done me any harm. But, with infernal impudence, I repeated my accusation, and declared to her face that she had given me the ribbon. The poor girl started to cry, but all she said to me was, "Oh, Rousseau, I thought you were a good fellow. You make me very sad, but I should not like to be in your place." That is all. She continued to defend herself with equal firmness and sincerity, but never allowed herself any reproaches against me. This moderation, contrasted with my decided tone, prejudiced her case. It did not seem natural to suppose such diabolical audacity on one side and such angelic sweetness on the other. They seemed unable to come to a definite decision, but they were prepossessed in my favour. In the confusion of the moment they had not time to get to the bottom of the business; and the Comte de la Roque, in dismissing us both, contented himself with saying that the guilty one's conscience would amply avenge the innocent. His prediction was not wide of the mark. Not a day passes on which it is not fulfilled. (Rousseau 1953: 87)

Among the countless episodes in the *Essays* involving the author's own persona, not one is as detailed as this. The difference has to do with the distinction between the genres adopted by the two authors. Driven by sheer mobility, the essay has no resting point, whereas autobiography remains close to the portrait—it is a branch of the same tree, which raises the intriguing question: How could the latter branch ramify after its failure in Montaigne? Precisely because in Rousseau the individual's own heart is the source of the moral Law, whereas in Montaigne it was seen as errant, finding stability only when enmeshed in custom. That is, in Rousseau the laying bare of one's own heart, which reveals the individual subject, covers up the absence that, since the individual subject's self-sufficiency was not assumed, required that it be explained. If autobiography and essay are both derived from the same emphasis on the self, they are radically distinguished not only by their characteristic approaches—a life confessed versus a life considered in reflection—but, even more importantly, by the way they deal with the absence correlated with the individual.[15]

This question becomes even more interesting when we relate it to the question of literature. Indeed, since literature was to become, with the pre-

15. Our examination must be complemented by an analysis of the fragment. Since its form will be dealt with in Chapter 2, for the moment we need only anticipate that the fragment shares with the essay the characteristics of being unfinished and of being an individuality rather than the expression of something previously existent. The fragment is the minimal form of the essay. The reader himself can verify this assertion. Except for thematic distinctions, what is the difference between one of Pascal's fragments and an essay of Montaigne's beyond the latter's relative expansiveness—or, conversely, the former's concision? One thinks of all the Montaignean expansions that could be made to correspond to Pascal's "Man is neither angel nor beast, and it is man's misfortune that who would act like an angel should act like a beast" (Pascal 1957b, no. 329).

rogatives of the individual subject, beginning with the early German romantics, the discursive form par excellence, a consideration of the different ways
that autobiography and essay treat absence will be decisive for its theoretical reconsideration. We have said that autobiography, assuming that self-
questioning as to the motives of one's own conduct was sufficient, made it
possible to forget the absence. Now, as the question of literature, in modernity, came to concentrate on its articulation with the inner riches of the
subject, it tended to forget its correlate, the shadow of absence. (In the next
chapter, when we examine a temporally distinct aspect of the same Law-
Subject-Literature complex, we shall see that these basic terms are still connected to the alternative between criticity and aestheticization.) In the late
sixteenth century, this alternative did not exist. The essay, however, was
already fully developed. Practiced but not conceptualized, or also practiced as
it was conceptualized and, at the same time, contradicted, the essay as a genre,
in any case, was to have a much less brilliant future. The sequence of the
argument will allow yet another correlation: the essay's less brilliant future
will be associated with its critical bent.

Let us examine the essay as a form, less to contribute to our reading of
Montaigne's work than to strengthen one of the pillars on which our own
work stands.

Considerations Concerning the Essay

In 1910, Georg Lukács published an analysis of the essay that remains of
capital importance to this day. In the following year, a modified version of the
work was published in German. In its very opening, the author questions the
form's ambiguity, which seems to make it unique: its wavering between art
and science, its inability to distinguish itself from both "without blurring the
frontiers of either" (Lukács 1974: 1). This was what distinguished it from
poetry, which had long before become autonomous, in "primitive, as yet
undifferentiated epochs" when "science and art (and religion and ethics and
politics) [were] integrated" (p. 3).

This indefinite status is the core of Lukács's reflection. First of all, he
characterizes the indefinition he must deal with: "Science affects us by its
contents, art by its forms; science offers us facts and the relations between
facts, but art offers us souls and destinies" (p. 3). It might be argued that the
young Lukács was excessively attached to the humanistic conception of art.
Such an objection, however, would be ridiculous, since the only other alternative he had before him was the rhetorical conception of belles lettres. His
conclusion is what matters: "Only when something has dissolved all its con-

tent in form, and thus become pure art, can it no longer become superfluous; but then its previous scientific nature [is] altogether forgotten and emptied of meaning" (p. 3).

This primacy of form points to the first characterization of the essay: it belongs among the works in which "questions are addressed directly to life itself," without resorting to the mediation of literature or art (p. 3). Akin to literature and the arts, since its focus is on the soul's fate, the essay differs from them in the nudity and informality of its body. The difference derives from the existence of two ways of considering the reality of the soul: one emphasizes life, the other living (p. 4). This duality correlates with two means of expression, which are founded on the opposition between image and significance (p. 5). Decades before Sartre formulated the notion of poetry as *mot-chose* (word-thing), Lukács associated the first mode with poetry—"Poetry in itself knows nothing beyond things; for it, each thing is serious and unique and incomparable. That is also why poetry knows no questions: you do not address questions to pure *things*, but only to their relationships" (p. 5). The second mode, presumably, is that of the essay, introduced in the figure of the critic.

This is the basis on which Lukács builds his argument—the differentiation between expression through images and the search for what never reaches their sphere. This brings us close to the decisive passage:

> There are experiences [*Erlebnisse*], then, which cannot be expressed by any gesture and which yet long for expression. . . . The question is posed immediately: what is life, what is man, what is destiny? But posed as a question only: for the answer, here, does not supply a "solution" like one of the answers of science or, at purer heights, those of philosophy. Rather, as in poetry of every kind, it is symbol, destiny and tragedy. (p. 7)

In poetry, form appears as destiny because, dealing with images, it can conceive a figured picture that is destiny and at the same time shapes destiny. The essayist's situation is quite different: his work does not place him in immediate contact with destiny, nor does he give shape to destiny; his task is to speak of objects that have already been made into form: "The critic is one who glimpses destiny [*Schicksalhafte*] in forms: whose most profound experience is the soul-content which forms indirectly and unconsciously conceal within themselves" (p. 8).

In poetry, the question asked of destiny is solved in form. In the essay, instead, the questions burn so brightly that there is no space for them to resolve into form. Lukács gives as an example a comparison between tragedy and Socratic dialogue: "For a tragic life is crowned only by its end, only the end gives it meaning, sense and form to the whole, and it is precisely the end which is always arbitrary and ironic here, in every dialogue and in Socrates' whole life" (p. 14). Hence the errant character of the essay, including the "modern essay." Although it no longer has to serve "books or poets" (p. 15), and therefore has become the genre of problematization par excellence, its own richness will not allow it to assume a form: it remains protean, formless.

Two conclusions ensue: "The essay is a judgment [*Gericht*], but the essential, the value-determining thing about it is not the verdict (as is the case with the system) but the process of judging" (p. 18). And: "[T]he essay is an art form, an autonomous and integral giving-of-form to an autonomous and complete life" (p. 18).

The reader of Lukács's text, or even of the summary presented above, will notice that the second conclusion does not really follow from the preceding argument, but merely restates what had been said in the beginning. But we do not agree with Adorno when he writes that this flaw could have been corrected if the author had observed that "because of its means—concepts—and its claim to truth" the essay has no aesthetic autonomy (Adorno 1958: 12–13). This might well be true, but not sufficient. Although it is acceptable that the problem of science—at least of the so-called hard sciences—is solved outside of the sphere of form, to deny the essay's claim to formal autonomy would be to submit it to the positivistic conception, as Adorno himself observes. That is, the use of concepts and the claim to truth place the essay outside the field of art but do not locate it in that of science; its place is neither here nor there. What, then, is the essay's place?

The difficulty here comes from the identification between art achieved in words—literature—and the idea of expression of the creative subject's, the artist's, soul. The Lukács who wrote *Soul and Form* accepted this identification. His "overstepping" of these limits by adopting the Marxist system only underscores *objectiveness*, the counterpart of the modern emphasis on the individual subject. But not even Adorno subverts that identification,[16] which is not to deny that some aspects of his rectification are of interest.

16. In Chapter 2 the question we have only posed here will be explored at length. As we will see, it is possible to escape the originally romantic conception of literature as the expression of a creative subject through a more rigorous elaboration of the view of literature as fiction—that is, not as a form of compensating illusion, but as a way of seeing truth in perspective or questioning truth without at the same time postulating an alternative truth. However, in Chapter 3 it will be seen that this idea, fundamentally derived from Wolfgang Iser, must be placed in a historical context. Kafka's fictional practice destroys the security that resulted from the view of fiction as a territory where the dominion of other territories is provisionally suspended—the territories of the pragmatic, of beliefs, of knowledge, which are momentarily placed in brackets to allow fruition of an aesthetic and critical experience, it being understood that the old order waits in the wings while the performance is on. As we will see, in Kafka's great novels this suspension disappears before

According to Adorno, the essay's defining trait is its opposition to the system, the finished theory. And what places the essay in a difficult position in our days is its failure to conform to a division of labor in which there is room only for people who deal with hard facts or people who are up in the clouds (*Tatsachenmensch oder Luftmensch*) (p. 12). In rebellion against a regulated world in which a privileged place is awarded to the positive person, with practical sense and strong instincts—the sort of man Thomas Buddenbrook wanted little Hanno to grow up to be—and the "artist" is relegated to the status of ornament, "the essay not only does without indubitable certainty but also denounces it as the ideal of established thought" (pp. 29–30). "In a peaceful way, the essay denounces the ideal of *clara et distincta perceptio* [clear and distinct perception] and doubt-free certainty" (p. 30).

If our intention were to discuss Adorno's problem in particular, we would have to refuse the opposition between essay writing and the order of method, which Adorno reiterates. The essay is not against the method, but against its totalizing pretension. (Even less acceptable, then, is young Lukács's statement that the essay was a "precursor" of the system!) In the case of literature, the dominant idea of method implied that the totalization of literature should be consummated in the subject or—under the influence of Hegel and natural science—in the society that is supposed to determine it. In this way, the control of the motions of imagination, which we have seen at work in Montaigne's work, as well as the discussion of fertilizing absence, particularly in works that can give rise to an aesthetic experience, was kept out of sight—that is, was never elaborated as a concept or questioned in essays. If, on the contrary, these issues are called into question, the method will turn critical, and the praise of the essay will no longer treat it as a melancholy guerrilla fighter who knows from the outset that the system is certain to win in the end.

It is precisely because of its affinity with criticity that the essay is marked more by the forcefulness of its questioning than by the unerringness of its answers. That is why the essay is the form that, though not identified with the literary experience, is closest to it. This closeness becomes more visible when we see literature as the discourse that questions and puts into perspective what a society considers to be true—that is, when we see literature as the verbal actualization of fictional discourse (see Costa-Lima 1989: 68–109, and Chapter 3 of the present work).

---

the avalanche of practices that contradict the empire of "constitutional" norms. This suspension, as it were, was the limit of what could be done within the framework proposed by Kant. Since Kafka, and in the present climate of generalized socioeconomic uncertainty, aggravated rather than diminished by the collapse of "real" socialism, the question is how to develop a *deterritorialized* theory of the fictional that does not simplistically see the world as a make-believe realm.

Since it would be arbitrary to speak of the fictional in the present chapter, which deals with a different historical period, we shall do no more than underscore four points. First, the essay has an "elective affinity" with the fragment: both emphasize what is unfinished or does not seek justification by previously established systems. Second, the essay's very unfinishedness makes it inadequate as a vehicle for the conveying of contents, information, instrumental schemes, so that it tends to focus on its own structure—that is, on form. Third, the essay is not form in the absolute, but belongs in what is previously occupied *by* form, so that what singularizes it is the interval where it remains. The essay is the genre that occupies the interval between the discourse for which form is the principle—poetical or fictional discourse—and those for which questions about meaning are the principle, above all, philosophical discourse. It is less a medium for the circulation of ideas than a medium for questions. As Lukács observed, the essay is not in the service of the literary or artistic work: its vocation is criticism. That is why it is an *excentrical* genre; thus, fourth, treating the essay as a genre makes it easier to draw attention to its varieties. The essay may either be an antisystematic discussion of ideas or, in its constant antisystematicity, keep close to the writing subject's life.[17] In this case, it may assume the form of the self-portrait. Whereas in its first variety the position taken by the author is made explicit by the argumentation—that is, by the way the author behaves in relation to the universe of ideas—in the second variety we face the explicit presence of the writing self before the matter of life. In this context, it is important to remember Michel Beaujour's observation that the Montaignean self-portrait is the mature product of the "confessional variant" of the "encyclopedic *specula*" (mirrors) that the Renaissance had inherited from the Middle Ages and that had been made famous by Erasmus (see Beaujour 1980, particularly pp. 32, 34, and 183).

The Book: Presence of the Self and Mark of Criticity

Since the notion of absence plays a decisive role in my argument, I could hardly finish this chapter without an explicit reference to its introduction in Montaigne studies. This took place in 1968, with Michel Butor's *Essais sur les Essais*.

In a time of civil war, as was Montaigne's time, military valor becomes commonplace and can no longer serve as an indicator of real value. Value,

17. On the difference—but not subordination—between the two modalities of the modern essay, the Baconian and the Montaignean, Jacob Zeitlin's reading remains useful (see Zeitlin 1928: 496–519).

then, was not to be associated with deeds done in worldly life; it was only at the very last moment that it could be recognized, in the way one faced death. Given its location in extremis, this mode of individual singularization implied that recognition of valor was achieved only when the individual in question could no longer be useful to his nation. Thus, Montaigne's defense of La Boétie, his contention that his friend's matchless qualities had not been acknowledged and called for while he was alive, required a different form of proof and demonstration: writing. The Renaissance experience of multiplicity (Stierle) and the praise of individual adventure—previously affirmed as the mark of the Renaissance man—were added to the trance experienced in religious wars, and together they pointed to a task that Montaigne, with his aristocratic disdain for the occupation of scholars, saw as inferior. "The book replaces the joust, the closed field" (Butor 1968: 58).

It is this first determination that leads Montaigne to translate to the realm of words the example of the painters of his time. Before 1574, when the Calvinists frustrated Montaigne by publishing La Boétie's *Discours de la servitude volontaire,* his friend's text "was directly related to the chapter 'Of Friendship' and . . . the chapter that followed did not exist." If this fact is taken into account, Butor adds, "we realize that the two most important 'themes' in the *Essays,* those on which the author concentrates before the first edition, 'Of the Education of Children' and 'Of Cannibals,' these two secondary portraits, are placed symmetrically in relation to the main portrait" (p. 72). But the blow dealt him by the Calvinists forced him to modify his project. The first book would now revolve around a center that was literally absent. But as Butor shrewdly demonstrates, the same scheme was adopted in book II:

> Though the second book turns on the "Apology," as the first had turned on La Boétie's "Discours," it [the "Apology"] is not in the middle position; this is so because the book does not revolve around the essay only, but also around the first book; it is Montaigne's entire literary activity until then that he aims to defend, and the "Apology" itself is part of the defensive shield. (p. 125)

The book is, then, a defense of writing, a defense of the author's own inner voice. But both writing and self-revelation contradict his role as an aristocrat, in the material act itself they imply, in Montaigne's rejection of the standards of cultivated language, in his unprejudiced outlook. Thus both must be disguised by flippancy to ensure that the author will be left alone. The form not only narrates the author but also defends him. Thus, its copiousness derives from a second absence. Even so, the game of composition has not yet involved all its pieces. *Mouvance* (mutability) is still operating, and in book III the function of écriture once again changes: it is no longer conceived as a coat of arms to replace the old insignia of nobility; from a bastion of the self it is transformed into an optical instrument that, like a prism, analyzes itself and the world (p. 193).

It is not necessary to mention Butor's name explicitly to realize that he is the seed from which Marc E. Blanchard's thought grows. One need only quote the passage that best summarizes Blanchard's thesis:

> Starting, traditionally enough, from the reflection of the self writing a portrait of the dead La Boétie, I will begin by searching for what, in the development of the *Essays*, leads Montaigne to see himself as the *parfaict amy* [perfect friend], in this not only borrowing from the poetical fashion of his time but also asking the reader's indulgence for a painting in which the painter, in the attempt to *paint* himself in the likeness of La Boétie, painted someone else. (Blanchard 1990: 23)

The importance of the path opened by Butor is no less clear in Terence Cave's chapter on Montaigne:

> The paper on which the text of the *Essays* appears is, indeed, a place of difference: it allows the rewriting and naturalization of foreign texts; it thereby permits the search for the identity of a *moi* in contradistinction from what is "other"; but at the same time it defers any final access to the goal of the search, since the self is expressly an entirety dissociated from the activity of writing. (Cave 1979: 272)

In spite of this common ascendancy, which is not explicitly claimed by the authors, their respective developments are independent. Thus, Cave will conclude, on the basis of the gap between author and writing, that Montaigne's text is undeterminable: "One may pursue Montaigne's topics as topics, bearing in mind only that they do not function as representation, that they are articulated in fundamentally indeterminate discourse" (p. 297). And with this he repeats a commonplace that is particularly popular among Anglo-American critics today.

The brief allusion to Butor's essay and its influence was made with the intention of stressing its seminal nature. Our major purpose was to underscore the fact that, by contrasting the subject-centered interpretation with the reading that privileges the relation between the writing subject and the absence that is established at the same time, we highlight the series of points that make up the backbone of this book. As one of the consequences of the focus on the individual subject, the legitimation of literary discourse is parallel to the establishment of the control of the imaginary and to critics' inability to capture it. To repeat what has been said before, by failing to differentiate between the portrait and the essay and solving the contradiction by means of the principle of a creative subject, literary interpretation left unexplored the problem that was implicit in this contradiction. In Montaigne, however, it was formulated precisely in the model proposed for the portrait: the expression of the inner voice was not to be affected or disturbed by the motion caused by his own imagination. That is, on the basis of the subject, literature was legitimated by keeping the control of the imaginary it implied outside the reach of analysis. In this way, it was never observed that the choice of the essay and the failure of the portrait showed that Montaigne had bypassed this veto. Thus, in Montaigne the control was simultaneously affirmed and negated—negated and bypassed as individual achievement; affirmed as a precept to follow. In other words, the centering on the individual subject made it possible to break a prohibition in poetical practice—in the *Essays*, that is—and at the same time made it impossible for critics to elucidate it. Hence we arrive at the importance of investigating the question of the absence: as a constitutive—though not an exclusive—element of literary works, it is one of the instruments that allow the establishment of this control and the subsequent problematization of a field that, within a humanistic framework, could not even be envisaged.

Our very brief mention of Rousseau's *Confessions* has an importance here that is not at all proportional to the scarce space devoted to it: if in Montaigne the primacy of the individual placed the issue of the Law in question, it was precisely because the author assumed that the self's actions gained a meaning only as a function of a stabilizing medium. Either he denied a priori that it was possible to find such a medium in himself, or else the failure of the model for the portrait showed the need to find it elsewhere. Hence the emphasis on custom. The same question was posed again by Rousseau, and the answer he gave to it was different: the Law is discovered by listening to the individual's heart. If we recall the relevance of Rousseau's thought for Kant's second *Critique*, we can at least begin to see that the consecration of the individual had the contradictory effect of legitimating literary discourse while leaving in the shadow the dimension of absence and, with it, the control of the imaginary. On these two bases the idea of literature as the expression of the individual was erected. This idea could well leave the question of the imaginary in brackets, as it were, and might even postulate a connection between the creative subject and its imagination, because this expression had previously been stabilized—stabilized from the inside by the Law manifested by the heart (which Kant immediately converted into a moral Law), and from the outside by custom, soon converted into social causality.

In contrast, the questioning of absence, as a constituent of literary works—that is, the questioning of what is not transparent to the writing subject, to its purposes, its intentionality, of what is inscribed in what is

written—allows not only the discussion of control but also a different characterization of the literary: a discourse that neither claims to tell truths nor sees
itself as abstracting the question of truth, but on the contrary literally places it
onstage and discusses it. In literature, the question of the subject simultaneously implies the question of the Law. In order to focus on the relation
between the two, it was necessary to begin with Montaigne, just as it will be
necessary to end with Kafka. In both of them the Law oscillates; it oscillates
and loses its balance between them; in Kant it begins to stabilize, and continues to do so in the reading of Kant adopted by Schiller and in the noncriti-
cal direction taken by the early German romantics; and is affirmed by the
aestheticization that is already triumphant among the latter.

In the Way of a Synthesis

Since our analysis of the *Essays* was forced to follow a rather sinuous path,
it will be worthwhile to stress a few central points.

I have been trying to show that the assertion of the individual subject in
Montaigne is so evident that it has had the effect of leading astray some
interpretations of his work. In order to counter this effect, I found it necessary
to relate Montaigne's affirmation of the subject to (1) his historical situation as
proponent of a thesis—the centrality of the individual—not yet supported by
a congruent Law; and, (2) the simultaneous emergence of the question of
absence, on which the self was to be erected. The self was not built on
nothingness; its expression is connected to the world through absence—that
which does not appear because it fails to penetrate the author's consciousness.

Although the affirmation of absence that is the correlate of the affirmation of the self is nothing new, its consequences are many, and they are worth
going into.

Thus, we tried to show that Montaigne's conservatism was not the reason
behind his defense of individualism, but rather a logical consequence of the
fact that he could not rely on a Law congruent with the centrality of the
individual—see (1), above—and that it is not enough to counterpose Montaigne's and Descartes's individualisms, for what the two require is not autonomous derivations, but rather the determination of a principle of Law. Consequently, if the *Essays* do not propose a systematic theory of knowledge that
legitimates the self, they nevertheless contain elements that will later surface
in such a theory, and the articulation of which has so far gone unnoticed. Two
of these anticipated components are the exaltation of fact and the mistrust of
imagination. Both can be seen in Montaigne's requirements for a self-portrait
and in his suspicion of travel books.

Since we have discussed only the former example, it should be mentioned here that at a time when Europe was awash with descriptions of the New World, Montaigne was stressing the need to substantiate the authenticity of such reports. Narratives about the unknown world should not be fanciful, since their readers could not be expected to submit them to the medieval technique of allegorical interpretation; rather, they ought to be faithful to what had been seen and experienced. Thus, at a time when the self was asserting itself but could not yet rely on a Law that saw it as the core of what could be known, travel became a problematic experience. Little wonder, then, that it should interest the philosopher who was to provide a fuller response to the need to formulate a theory of the Law that, on the basis of the individual subject, could ensure the objectivity of human knowledge.

CHAPTER 2

The Subject and the Law:
A Kantian Heritage

The Journey and the Law

Kant knew the difficulties that his first *Critique* would face. How could it be otherwise when he was challenging the age-old construct of metaphysics? Besides, he was aware of the fact that he lacked "the necessary elegance of statement" (Kant 1965: 37; B xliv) to lessen the difficulties of his endeavor. It was as if his slogan were: no peace to all those who would undertake this journey. The most that his expository method allows is recapitulation of what has been treated; often, however, even here there are obstacles. In Kant there is no place for elegance of form; even so, there is the promise of an Ithaca where a familiar landscape will compensate for the harshness of the journey. Although not as gratifying as Ulysses' Ithaca, Kant's is none the smaller for that. By the time his foothold is secure, toward the end of his "Transcendental Analytic," the philosopher affirms:

> We have now not merely explored the territory of pure understanding . . . but have also measured its extent, and assigned to everything in it its rightful place. This domain is an island, enclosed by nature itself within unalterable limits. It is the land of truth—enchanting name!—surrounded by a wide and stormy ocean, the native home of illusion [*des Scheins*], where many a fog bank and many a swiftly melting iceberg give the deceptive appearance of farther shores, deluding the adventurous seafarer . . . with empty hopes. (Kant 1965: 257; B 294)

Although secondary for the purpose of Kant's exposition, that passage is important for our present purposes. The foundations of critical knowledge as they had been proposed so far, once the Scylla and Charybdis of dogmatism and skepticism were overcome, offered modernity a safe answer to the question, What is it possible to know? In the preface to the second edition of the *Critique* it was stated that "reason has insight [*einsieht*] only into that which it produces" (Kant 1965: 20; B 13). That is, Kant proceeded from the principle—contrary to the assumptions of classical thought—that the real was not to be identified with the rational, could not be superposed on it, was not coextensive with it. Reason does more than simply *re-cognize* what the ear hears, the eye sees, and speech refers to; it cognizes what it itself *poses*, and this activity is precisely what makes its project feasible.

However, from the outset the question arises: How relevant can this comment be if our purpose is not to provide one more presentation of Kant's thought? In order to understand the emphasis given to the passage quoted above and the essential role it plays in the development of our argument, we must relate it to a humble man who lived in the sixteenth century: Menocchio the miller, whom only the readers of Ginsburg's *The Cheese and the Worms* will remember. A modest and poor man, with very little education, Menocchio had the misfortune of being enthralled, as many others had been before him, by John Mandeville's *Travels*. Impressed by the rich diversity of practices, values, and customs described in the book, with the violent clashes between the symbolic systems of different peoples, Menocchio could no longer believe in the orthodox principles of Counter Reformation Catholicism. For centuries, the English traveler's book had aroused curiosity without stirring up any trouble. What, then, had changed?

The first difference is easily detected: the miller lived at a time of religious wars and religious inquisitions. To deny the rigid dogmas of Church authorities then could only be seen as proof of contact with heretical influences. When asked by his inquisitors which was the best law, Menocchio answered: "Sir, I *believe each man thinks his own faith is best, but no one knows which is best*": this was a plea for tolerance, or, as his interpreter writes: "More than tolerance in the strict sense, it was an explicit acknowledgment of the equivalence of all faiths in the name of a simplified religion, without dogmatic or sectarian characterizations" (Ginsburg 1987: 115). The inquisitors failed to realize that the accused man's religious conceptions were rooted in popular belief and saw only their similarities with "the sophisticated religious theorizations of contemporary heretics with a Humanistic background" (p. 116).

The second difference is more problematic. In Menocchio we see the new importance, even in a humble environment, of individual judgment: that is, the recognition of subjectivity. Although the miller was Montaigne's contemporary, the only thing the two have in common is the identical importance they give to subjectivity. A cultured man who owned a valuable library, Montaigne legitimated the self's discriminating power. Menocchio, a very poor and uneducated man, could not resort to the French author's labored evasiveness. He presented his personal judgment in the most straight-forward way; without casting any doubt on the truthfulness of what he had read, Menocchio proclaimed what to the subtle ears of his judges could only sound like a blatant defense of relativism—sheer heresy, since it undermined the foundations of the unity of the Christian world.

As long as it was in force, medieval allegorical interpretation reduced personal judgment to insignificance. The speaking self could always be sub-sumed as an example of a legitimated model; it was not considered as an individual. But with the conflict between rival churches, this was no longer possible. The Law could not be justified impersonally as divinely mandated any more; nor could language be merely the manifestation of what was fully before the intervention of language, nor could words be justified by the community whose values they communicated and proclaimed: now they immediately exposed the speaker. This is not to say that the religious tensions of the sixteenth century were the determining cause of the legitimation of subjectivity, but only to underscore the fact that the clash between sects is evidence of its presence, the importance of which had been increasing for centuries.

The passage from Kant quoted above should be correlated and contrasted with the case of the unfortunate Menocchio. The acknowledgment of sub-jective judgment—precise, punctual, particularized, impossible to assign to any community, irreducible to any allegorical reading—made travel writing dangerous and potentially suspicious. It was dangerous to the writer himself, for how could he be sure he was not mistaken?—and also to the reader—how could he be sure that he was not being deceived? Now, without having ever left his sleepy Königsberg, Kant proclaimed the discovery of an island with "unalterable limits." But this was not a physical island out there in some Edenic region; this island was to be identified with humanity itself. It con-tained humanity's cognitive apparatus, by means of which things were infalli-bly posited and thus made parts of its world. Therefore, the old presumption of knowing things was ludicrous; it was unfounded. This, however, did not mean that the right to know them was arbitrary: the important caveat was that things were to be known *as* parts of humanity's world—that is, as phe-nomena integrated into its experience of nature.

In short, we are proceeding from a simple observation of a fact: from a historical viewpoint, the *Critique of Pure Reason* (henceforth abbreviated as *CPR*) aimed to overcome a moment of confusion and bewilderment caused by the clash between the classical theory of knowledge and the acknowledg-ment of individuality with its subjective dimension. In other words, Kant was trying to demonstrate that knowledge—or rather, a specific kind of knowledge—is no less effective and certain because human reason relies on "instruments" that are not given by things themselves, because only a transcendental apparatus—common to all people—links them with the phenomenality of things, links people and things, allowing the former to arrive at the meanings of the latter.

The above explanation should be taken as no more than an initial step. Its limitation and inadequacy lie not in the simplification it implies, but in the neopositivistic image it presents of *CPR*. In order to counter such an image and take a further step, let us examine the construction of *CPR* itself.

To think of an object is not the same as to know it (Kant 1965: 374; B 416) because the order of reason is not to be identified with the order of reality. Thinking is more inclusive than knowing, because the latter is restricted to the sphere of possible experience. Experience is located between men and things, without identifying itself with actual, material men or things. Thus, to speak of the production of experience presupposes questioning the transcendental apparatus that distinguishes human materiality. This requirement doubly particularizes Kant's position: first, in contrast with the contemplative postulate of classical metaphysics, the act of knowing is no longer seen as a way of retrieving and discovering, but of inventing. Second, this invention, however, is not—in contrast with Vico's more radical position, proposed in *De antiquissima italorum sapientia* (On the ancient wisdom of the Italians) (1710)—a fiction, but rather a "mysterious" fit between human traits and properties of phenomena (Kant 1965: 172; B 164). In other words, the fact that what I see is also derived from myself does not necessarily imply that what I see cannot be trusted. The fact that it is Kant's transcendental apparatus that posits the conditions for human experience does not mean that the experience this produces is no more than a fiction. The medium—that is, the field of experience—is not made up of chimeras and phantoms, but rather of materialities that, in contact with the transcendental apparatus, are made accessible to knowledge.

Critical philosophy begins by limiting and denying: as a human gesture, thinking is not more or less extensive than reality; outside of the field where the two meet—experience—it simply follows a different path. Kant's thought, as the prototypical elaboration of modernity, is defined above all by the subtraction it performs. That is why, for all the proofs the book laboriously presents one after the other, nonetheless a certain feeling of unease settles upon the reader of *CPR*: whereas traditional thought presupposed that the cognoscitively correct statement apprehended and made communicable the substance of what it referred to, in Kant certainty is restricted to the sharply delimited field of the experience of nature. Thus, the Law's presumption is doubly affected: the Law, assuming it controls phenomena by grasping the regularity of their behavior, is related not to the nature of things, but only to their apparition; it pertains only to this apparition-of-things. As conceived by Kant, the Law does away with will and precludes the identification of will with arbitrariness. Before we examine this double bind, which is of fundamental importance to the fortunes of modernity and to an understanding of the problem of art in modernity, let us examine Kant's argument concerning the conditions of possible experience.

The transcendental apparatus implies the joint action of sensibility and understanding—which, nonetheless, have different sources. Sensibility is characterized less by its receptive capacity than by the production of two forms: space and time, the a priori forms of sensibility. To call them "forms" implies that they are not things, that they are not in things, but that they are imposed on things, endowing them with a different character. The space-form is "the subjective condition of sensibility, under which alone outer intuition is possible for us" (Kant 1965: 71; B 42). Similarly, the time-form is no more than a subjective condition of the inner sense. This, however, does not mean that these forms, because they are independent of any experience, are autonomous in relation to experience. Their very characterization as representations that are necessary to all intuitions (*Anschauungen*), whether external or internal, means that they exist only in the medium of experience. They are not phenomena, but exist only in phenomena, of which they are the formal condition. That is why without the experience of time there is no experience of change or, consequently, of movement (Kant 1965: 76; B 48).

But however decisive their importance, the forms of sensibility give no access to the concept of a phenomenon or, even less, to the subject in which they exist. Of the forms of sensibility the representation of something, phenomenal intuition, is derived—in Kant "intuition" always connotes the sensible. Concepts can be inferred from them only after a synthesis of representations, so that the categories of understanding can then operate on it. This synthesis is the work of imagination. Akin to sensibility, imagination is partly receptive—that is, it reproduces what it unifies—and partly productive—since the unification of the multiplicity of representations (like the multiplicity itself) is not implied by the order of things. (Since it is not our present purpose to examine the concept of imagination in Kant, we do no more than note in passing that the two aspects of imagination point to a tension that is a constituent part of it in Kant's system, or even anticipates the instability that came to characterize the system.)

The synthesis brought about by imagination, then, contributes to understanding. Understanding is the ultimate guide to certainty: it never goes beyond the reach of the experience of nature. The self—which is not the operator of the apparatus that invests it with its power, but rather is operated by the apparatus—is excluded from the outset. Kant is clear on this point: "The subject of the categories cannot by thinking the categories acquire a concept of itself as an object of the categories. For in order to think them, its pure self-consciousness, *which is what was to be explained*, must itself be presupposed" (Kant 1965: 377; B 422, emphasis added). "Behind" the categories, then, there is no privileged object that might give rise to a whole array of "new" sciences, which were later to be known as "humanities." On the contrary, behind the categories there is only "the unity of consciousness" (*die Einheit des Bewußtseins*), and the presumptuous proposition "I exist" is only "an empirical proposition," with which the self is reduced to the condition (empirical, necessary only contingently) for the use of the "pure intellectual faculty" (p. 378; B 423).[1] Therefore, instead of the Cartesian foundation, and of what is to characterize Fichte's idealism, what Kant legitimates is not the endeavor of individual self-exploration, but what comes "out" of the individual into the medium of experience.

The emphasis on experience as the rightful place of knowledge is correlate with the meaning assumed by the individual in Kant: what is underscored is not his singularity but his "external," public character, as a member of a "city"—his character as a citizen. It is only to the citizen that the interchange with the other—otherness being the indispensable material for any experience capable of generating knowledge—is ensured. The self is only the unit in which the necessary operations take place. True, Kant also calls it "subject of consciousness," but he immediately adds that from this it does not follow that "I cannot exist otherwise than as subject," but rather that "In thinking my existence, I cannot employ myself, save as subject of the judgment" (p. 371; B 412).

To highlight the understanding's role as sure guide was, then, to privilege the status of the citizen. It was also, clearly, to restrict the legitimation of subjectivity—to restrict it as to the certainties that might comfort it in the trials of existence. What, then, existed outside of the soothing boundaries that authenticated the natural sciences? Did Kant deny any dignity to anything that lay outside the domains of the certain?

What lay beyond this limit was no longer the understanding (*Verstand*) but the exercise of reason. For, like the contrary properties of imagination,

---

1. More descriptively, Kant had written shortly before: "I do not know myself through being conscious of myself as thinking, but only when I am conscious of the intuition of myself as determined with respect to the function of thought" (p. 368; B 407).

although there was no point-to-point correspondence between the two, thinking also included contrariness—in the relations between the understanding and reason. For reason, not being limited to the medium of possible experience, is characterized by the fact that it goes astray. Reason is marked by what, from the viewpoint of the understanding, is excessive: it thinks what cannot be known. The immediate object of its thought is freedom.

What would freedom be in a world entirely ruled by causality if not a vain chimera? Freedom is what cannot be explained by a cause, for a cause starts off a chain of effects and is thus the origin of the homogeneity of phenomena, the condition of certainty. The category "cause" made it possible to justify the physical order of the world and to acknowledge the progressive advance of the sciences dealing with it. But it also raised an obstacle to the "excessive" demands of reason. The only way to break the identification of freedom with chimera consists in taking it as the originator (or cause) of a different set of effects. Now, if the Kantian explanation had abolished the arbitrariness of the physical world, the acknowledgment of the action of freedom necessarily implied its existence on a different plane. This is the moral plane. In Kantian terms, morality does not belong in the order of knowledge. Thus, there can be no such a thing as a science of morals, just as there can be no science of God or of the soul. How, then, can we acknowledge freedom without accepting inevitable arbitrariness? In Kant this is done by converting freedom into moral duty.

Raised to the condition of a cause, freedom is manifested by the effects of duty. Thus internalized, freedom, although it does not become an object of understanding, escapes the empire of arbitrariness. In this it is representative of those areas touched by nontheoretical reason. Whereas the understanding deals with concepts, reason is concerned with Ideas.[2] Through Ideas the human subject formulates what is problematic. This, even if it cannot be known, has its own dignity nonetheless.

The elaboration of the consequences of transforming freedom into a duty would lead to a discussion of the second *Critique*, which would be unnecessary here. We shall then do no more than highlight these consequences as they relate to the Law.

It is only theoretical reason, which relies on the understanding, that is able to legitimate what can be known. In this way the Law is justified, but only within the narrow limits of the possible experience of nature. Its scope

2. As in Chapter 1, we write with a capital initial all those words that, assuming a special meaning, are not to be taken in their usual sense. Thus, we write "the Law," "History," "Idea," and "Logic." Whenever they are used in their usual sense, these words are written without a capital initial.

does not include the sphere of moral Law, since the field of duty has no relation to the field of knowledge other than the fact that both cause or presuppose homogeneity (of behavior and of the object's action, respectively). If there is a real link between theoretical and practical reason, it is a purely negative one: through both of them the individual subject is negated. On the plane of theoretical reason, the self is merely the support of a function; it is no more than the unit of consciousness, permeated and activated by an apparatus that imposes itself independently of any singularities that may characterize this or that individual.

On the plane of practical reason, the individual subject fares no better. True, practical reason presents it with an ideal the achievement of which will depend only on it: the ideal of autonomy. But what is the autonomous Kantian subject if not what is shaped in accordance with the principle of duty? Duty affects the will and asserts itself as it moves the will away from natural appetites. Kant's moral Law has no rewards, nor can it—since it is separated from theoretical reason—ever be demonstrated. Its fairness is given a priori. It imposes itself as an innerly assumed obligation.

> The law is imperious, self-evident, apodictic; the entire experience of human action and judgment would argue against it. It is not a question (a hypothesis); it is not to be discussed or deduced: on the contrary, it is a principle of deduction; of freedom in particular, it is a thesis [*Satz, Gesetz*], it imposes itself, even on itself. . . . Properly speaking, it does not command a subject, it does not address itself or speak to a subject; its voice, sharp and terrible, is mute, but is as it were indifferent, confident that it can never be "unveiled." (Proust 1991: 151)

In comparison with the rigor of the moral Law, the law of science seemed rather mild. Its a priori, universal, and necessary character still implied hypotheses, controversies, and questions. In addition, its determining force, although it did not depend on particular historical or psychological traits of the investigator, required that the individual have critical and inventive abilities. In the moral Law there is nothing of the kind. When commentators of the second *Critique* point to the influence of Pietist rigor on Kant's ethics, they miss an even more inflexible presence: this entire ethics presupposes a God even more terrible than that of the Old Testament. It is as if Jehovah avenged himself on the philosopher's impertinent attempt to treat him as an Idea—inaccessible to knowledge and unfit for science, and to this extent comparable to monsters and chimeras—and directed his choleric voice and his wrathful gaze away from human representation. This wrath indicates that his creature still affects him. Since the divine voice and gaze have vanished, the voice of the moral Law cannot be heard.

Thus, on the one hand, under the empire of theoretical reason, all that remains is a world without mystery, pure mechanism, in which human sensibility is destined to serve the understanding, which in turn serves nature—an utterly disenchanted world, as Weber was to observe. On the other hand, under the empire of practical reason, there is a commanding inner voice that heeds no complaints or protests. Were it not for his respect for everything that pertained to morals, this would be the correct place for Kant himself, in the third *Critique*, to explain the sublime—the sublime of the terrible.

It is, then, not enough to say that Kant's thought deobjectifies knowledge, for it also desubjectifies it. In Kant knowledge depends on the activation of a subjective apparatus, but it is achieved independently of the will, or even to the detriment of it. In the case of theoretical reason, the will does not count. In the case of practical reason, the will, as part of the legacy of nature, counts only to be denied. In both cases, nature is the *tertium comparationis* (third element in comparison) that must be submitted. Rather than enlarge on this point, let us only underscore the rupture in the sphere of the two reasons that the principle of Law points to.

The Kantian world is not only disenchanted—which would still be a positive trait—but also torn apart: what is in force in the sphere of theory is drastically abolished in the sphere of practice, and vice versa. In the former there is pure mechanism: given a phenomenon, there immediately follow the forms of sensibility, the synthesis of imagination, and the categories that situate it in a concept; in the latter there is pure duty. Both spheres, to be sure, are grounded on something related to humanity: the human spirit; its very production and its autonomy, however, presuppose deindividualization. This in no way clashes with the fact that in both spheres the human spirit is the legislator. For our purposes, all that need be stressed is the fact that the legislation proposed is twofold, promoting norms of a radically different nature. (It would not be correct even to say that the scientific Law and the moral Law are contradictory, for this would still presuppose a common ground that does not exist.) Let us go no further than this observation, since it will do for the purposes of the rest of our argument. Its decisive step involves the third *Critique*.

An Overview of the Third Critique

Why did Kant decide to write a third *Critique*? He himself gives two explanations. In the "Introduction" to the *Critique of Judgement* (henceforth referred to as *CJ*), Kant says that the intent of the work is to provide a link between the legislation of understanding and that of reason. Since they are not only distinct but also incomparable, the questioning of judgment as a mediating term between understanding and reason could finally offer the *tertium comparationis* that would put to rights its previous isolated position. Of the faculty of judgment "we may reasonably presume by analogy that it may likewise contain, if not a special authority to prescribe laws [*Gesetzgebung*], still a principle peculiar to itself upon which laws are sought, although one merely subjective *a priori*" (Kant 1982a: 15; B 22). Kant takes to heart the promise implied by the analogy, and adds towards the end of the same section:

> Hence we may, provisionally at least, assume that judgment likewise contains an *a priori* principle of its own, and that, since pleasure or displeasure is necessarily combined with the faculty of desire [*Begehrungsvermögen*] . . . it will effect a transition from the faculty of pure knowledge, i.e., from the realm of concepts of nature, to that of the concept of freedom, just as in its logical employment it makes possible the transition from understanding to reason. (p. 17; B 24–25)

Against the hopes of conciliation and harmony raised by these passages, it should be observed that, in the absence of a legislation of its own, the philosopher expects to find in judgment a *principle* that will articulate the fields of nature and freedom. A principle differs from a body of legislation in that it operates from below, preparing the ground for the erection of a body of legislation. Now, Kant facilitates this preparation by noting the proximity between pleasure and displeasure, the sensations that concern judgment, and the faculty of desire, the object of practical reason; we say he facilitates his task because he writes as if there were an underground circuit between pleasure, displeasure, and feelings of duty and respect. As we advance in the sphere of the judgment proper to the faculty of judging, the reflective judgment, it becomes increasingly difficult to accept the naturalness of the inference. Could it be that it is made possible because the a priori principle of the faculty of judgment is "merely subjective," just as the moral Law exerts its sway only over subjectivity? The answer is no, given the importance of the aesthetic mode in judgments of reflection, which makes aesthetic judgment completely independent of moral judgment.

The difficulty mentioned is then derived from Kant's architectonic intent. Another difficulty immediately appears: the attempt to apprehend what the understanding had expelled from its field—the supersensible. In the "Introduction," Kant observes:

> Albeit, then, between the realm of the natural concept, as the sensible, and the realm of the concept of freedom, as the supersensible, there is a great gulf fixed, so that it is not possible to pass from the former to the latter (by means of the theoretical employment of reason) . . . still the latter is *meant* to influence the former—that is to say, the concept of freedom is meant to actualize in the sensible world the end [*Zweck*] proposed by its laws. (Kant 1982a: 14; B xix)

This passage is an anticipation of the analysis of teleological judgments, which are imposed on natural objects without being constituents of them (i.e., teleological judgments serve to order objects but not to know them). Since the only thing teleological and aesthetic judgments have in common is the fact that both are varieties of the reflective judgment—in other words, the fact that both are of a subjective nature—if the two are confused the supersensible tends to be left unquestioned. So the supersensible—what escapes physical causality—comes to be seen as the source of the sought-for harmony of the system. That is, the architectonic hypothesis rests on a rhetorical maneuver: if *a* (aesthetic judgment) and *b* (teleological judgment) are parts of *c* (reflective judgment), then whatever is said of *b* will also be true of *a*. This, however, is true only if the specificity and autonomy of *a*, yet to be demonstrated by the third *Critique*, are not compromised. The promise of systematicness that seems secure in his thought encourages Kant to stick to his path. We, however, will not immediately examine the difficulties raised; instead, we shall proceed in a different direction, one suggested by passages taken from the same part of the text as the ones we have already quoted.

In an early paragraph of the "Preface," Kant writes that a critique of pure reason would be incomplete without a specific discussion of the faculty of judgment, for otherwise it would fail to explore the ground on which are to be found "*the foundations of the faculty of principles independent of experience*" (Kant 1982a: 5; B 6, emphasis added). Apparently, this passage introduces no idea other than the one we have found questionable. Certainly, the author's intention was to proceed with the development of his argument. This, however, is no reason why we should not establish a differentiation here. As we have seen, the interpretation privileged by Kant is associated with an architectonic design; the legislations corresponding to theoretical and practical reason, being autonomous, autonomously discriminate the fields they encompass. But they are so different and separated that there can be no bridge joining the fields where they hold sway. This, then, is the transitive function that is expected of the faculty of judgment.

If, however, we have underscored such terms in Kant's argumentation as "foundations" (*Grundlage*) and "principles independent of experience" (*von der Erfahrung unabhängiger Prinzipien*), it is because we conceive a second path: it operates not from "above" but from "below"; it is not as much an architecture as an exploration of the underground. More precisely, the reflective judgment points to an archaeological stratum previous to the determinant judgment. This thesis, now defended by O. Chédin, was already anticipated in G. Lebrun's *Kant et la mort de la métaphysique* (Kant and the death of metaphysics). Since we shall take up Chédin's book at length later, for the moment let us seek support in Lebrun.

The task of the "Analytic" in *CPR*, writes Lebrun, was not "to analyze concepts but only to question the a priori concepts given with the understanding." In *CJ*, he adds, the question is on a more elemental level: "Since the philosophy of objectivity *poses itself* concepts in general as already present for judgment, there is a question (and another level of research) that it need not bring up: how is it possible to *form* [*bilden*] concepts in general? And: how can there be a 'power to *think* by concepts'—that is, the understanding?" (Lebrun 1970: 55). Lebrun adds that the object of *CJ* is not just to take up an aspect that had been neglected by its two predecessors. More important, the purpose was to link the possibility of forming concepts in general with the complementation of the reasoning that *CPR* had established for logic.

In *CPR*, the identification between the cognoscible and the object of experience had made classic logic a purely formal discipline,

> an empty and nearly unrepresentable abstraction, unless a relation between its forms and the "world" were taken for granted. . . . To speak of the "conditions of application of logic to nature" is then to speak *also* of the effective (but nevertheless transcendental) conditions without which Aristotelian logic would never have arisen. And, if transcendental philosophy neglects this task of establishing a foundation, one of the following alternatives must be true: *either* it cannot eliminate (except by dogma) the possibility of the right to provide logic with a psychologistic foundation, *or else* it will clash, as if it faced irrationality, with this *de facto* reference that involves, in its origin, formal logic and, *consequently, transcendental logic, to the extent that it accepts the former as given.* Instead, if one is aware of the difficulty, one must admit that it remains to determine, in the (*pre-logical*) root of our knowledge, a transcendental act such that it makes it always possible to pass from any representation whatsoever to an empirical concept. (pp. 275–76)

Within these parameters aesthetic judgment will occupy a major position, although it is not Kant's intention to build an aesthetics—he even complains that the term is misused. To him, aesthetic judgment matters as a privileged instrument to investigate and locate "what *might be* a non-logical judgment" (p. 303), for the very phrase "aesthetic judgment" "can be understood at all unequivocally only if it is taken to mean nonlogical judgment" (p. 303).

The validity of Lebrun's "archaeological" hypothesis is borne out by a comparison between the original "Introduction" to *CJ*, which was eventually expunged from the 1790 edition, and number 23 of the published text. In the "Introduction" Kant stated that "judgment on the sublime in nature should not be excluded from the part of aesthetics concerning the reflective judgment because it, too, expresses a subjective finality, which does not rest on a concept of the object" (Kant 1974b: 66). In contrast, number 23 says: "Hence we see that the concept of the sublime in nature is far less important and rich in consequences than that of its beauty. It gives on the whole no indication of anything final in nature itself, but only in the possible *employment* of our intuitions of it in inducing a feeling in our own selves of a finality quite independent of nature" (Kant 1982a: 92–93; B 78). Clearly, the discordance is a consequence of the emphasis given to the finality attributed to nature. Whereas the beautiful is easily reconciled with a judgment of finality, the experience of the sublime makes no contribution whatever to it, not even as analogy, for all it provokes is "another feeling, to wit that of the inner finality [*dem der innern Zweckmäßigkeit*], in the disposition of the forces of the spirit [*Gemütskräfte*]" (Kant 1974b: 67).

How should this inner finality be understood? Conceivably, by means of a comparison with the role played by imagination in the experiences in which the sublime has no place. In cognoscitive experience proper, the imagination is obviously subordinated to the understanding; it assumes its place between the forms of sensibility, synthesizing the multiplicity of its representations, and the categories. But in the sphere of practical reason no such place is available for it. Here imagination seems idle; it might even be said that it should be kept in chains so that the faculty of appetite can transform freedom into duty. In the sphere of the reflective judgment, in the form of beauty, however, it is true that imagination is not in the subordinate position in which we saw it in *CPR*; here the understanding acts as its partner, with which it can play freely; if imagination also entrusts understanding with its synthesis, such a synthesis cannot coadunate with an exact concept. The synthesis then elaborated by imagination is found to be ineffective from the viewpoint of knowledge, and its free partnership with understanding causes pleasure and does not affect the object. That is to say, in the experience of the beautiful the particular is not subsumed into the universal, the object of experience cannot be seen as one more object under the sway of a general law; the free play between imagination and understanding is the condition for sensing the object of experience in its singularity instead of cataloging it as an instance of a general case.

It should be kept in mind, nevertheless, that even if it is not subordinated, imagination must respect a certain limit: its exercise is free, "subject, however, to the condition that there is to be nothing for understanding to take exception to [*doch unter der Bedingung, daß der Verstand dabei keinen Anstoß leide*]" (Kant 1982a: 88; B 71). In the experience of beauty, imagination is neither servant nor rebel. As we shall see later, in the experience of the sublime, imagination goes rampant, tries to understand it, but finds it "ill-adapted to our power of judgment [*unangemessen unserm Darstellungsvermögen*]" (p. 91; B 77). This is a consequence of the fact that the sublime can only be defined negatively, as "what is beyond all comparison great" (p. 94; B 81). Calling itself into question, imagination can no longer remain in the orbit of the understanding. Now the limit it respected in the "free play" of the beautiful becomes clearer: imagination could then be an equal partner of understanding because in it the "faculty of presentation" was still active.

As it runs rampant, imagination loses the support of understanding and is forced to rely on reason. This, in short, is how Kant explains the specificity of the sublime. Since reason, unlike understanding, is not contented with possible experience, and thus becomes the realm of Ideas—of what man seeks to understand without quite knowing how to explain it—it ends up offering rampant imagination the most fantastic of ideas: the supersensible. Since by definition the sublime is incomparable, it could not possibly acquire a meaning from a comparison with something that is part of nature. Thus, the Kantian argument conjures up the idea that—so it believes—clinches the hypothesis it proposed.

Later we shall see more clearly why Kant's conclusion is not convincing. For the moment, let us simply indicate the different direction in which we shall take his argument: in the sublime, the maximum potency acquired by imagination means that it then reaches its maximum productive capacity—so large, in fact, that, since it cannot be absorbed by understanding, it cannot possibly be known; in order to force some sort of meaning on it, Kant must subordinate it to reason. We say "subordinate to" rather than "articulate with," for the meaning that the experience of the sublime acquires through the introduction of the supersensible implies, to Kant himself, the limit of the autonomy of aesthetic judgment.

The archaeological hypothesis allows us not only to review the relations between *CJ* and the two previous *Critiques* but also to reconsider the problem of imagination in the Kantian system. The second path derives from the observation that the maximum productivity that imagination reaches in the sublime indicates a moment prior to its taming by understanding. The prelogical, to which Lebrun referred, has no connotations of irrationalism; it simply points to what comes before and paves the way for operative rationality. Kant's text contains what in Vico's *Scienza nuova* (The new science) (1744) appeared in a historicized fashion—the poet as the first legislator of the world, before it was possible for the philosopher to emerge. But while Vico's diachronic solution faced the difficulty of having to explain how, after its historically necessary phase was "left behind," imagination could still be pro-

ductive, Kant's text allows more than the examination of temporally successive phases. The attempt to demonstrate this, however, poses a particular
difficulty. In order to make things easier, assuming that the reader is not
conversant with *CJ*, and even though it is not my intention to offer an
introduction to it, I must offer the reader the minimal conditions for following the argument. After this expository parenthesis, we shall return to our
discussion.

THE THIRD *CRITIQUE:* A CLOSER LOOK

The first *Critique* had established a mode of judgment that presupposed,
in experience, an agreement between man's transcendental apparatus and the
phenomenality of things. This agreement is necessarily mysterious to us—
only a different kind of creature could apprehend how the properties of
human thinking are in accord and in consistence with the properties ex-
hibited by phenomena; and it takes for granted that there is a constancy in the
behavior of the "partners" in question—that man's transcendental apparatus
suffers no variations in time or space, and likewise that objects suffer no
changes that cannot be attributed to comprehensible causes.

The presupposition of this agreement and this constancy having been
established, judgment as proposed in *CPR* not only was universal but also
offered a first homogenization of the world. Now *CJ* provides a name for this
judgment: determinant judgment. "If the universal [*das Allgemeine*] (the rule,
principle, or law) is given, then the judgment which subsumes the particular
[*das Besondere*] under it is *determinant*" (Kant 1982a: 18; B xxvi). If Kant, in
writing *CJ*, feels the need to return to this concept and name it, it is because
he understands that the organizing force of determinant judgment does not
come close to homogenizing all experience. "In respect of nature's merely
empirical laws, we must think in nature a possibility of an endless multiplicity
of empirical laws, which yet are contingent so far as our insight goes, that is,
cannot be cognized *a priori*" (pp. 22–23; B xxxiii).

This observation clearly indicates Kant's awareness that the results arrived
at in *CPR*, given their critical and constructive scope, were insufficient.
These results held for possible experience, but were powerless before the
multiplicity of the strictly empirical. Now, unless the phenomenon, however
particularized, could be related to a unifying principle, the medium in which
the experience takes place—the medium the limit of which is the real world
itself—would become chaotic to man. Thus, the faculty of judgment must
supplement the order brought about by the determinant judgment. This
supplementation will be supplied by a second mode of judgment, to be
distinguished from the first in that it could not be conceived of as a party to

the agreement between the properties of the human transcendental and those of phenomena. In other words, the reflective judgment says nothing about the phenomenality of objects, does not affect them or take part in their formulation. "Judgment is compelled, for its own guidance, to adopt it as an *a priori* principle, that what is for human insight contingent in the particular (empirical) laws of nature contains nevertheless unity of law [*eine gesetzliche Einheit*] in the synthesis of its manifold in an intrinsically possible experience—unfathomable, though still thinkable" (p. 232; B xxxiv).

This supplementary principle is that of finality. Its conceptual characterization shows how far we are from the sphere of the purely scientific.

> This transcendental concept of a finality of nature [*Zweckmäßigkeit*] is neither a concept of nature nor of freedom, since it attributes nothing at all to the Object, that is, to nature, but only represents the unique mode in which we must proceed in our reflection upon the objects of nature with a view to getting a thoroughly interconnected whole of experience, and so it is a subjective principle, that is, maxim, of judgment. (p. 23; B xxxiv)

Because it does not affect the object it refers to—since what it does attribute to it, a finality, is not exactly in it—the reflective judgment is defined as what, being given the particular, has to seek the universal to which it corresponds (see p. 24; B xxxvi).

We would not be able to understand the determinant and reflective judgments if we associated the former with what happens automatically and the latter with what requires careful consideration. Rather, the distinguishing criterion is whether the judgment in question is able to penetrate the structure of the phenomenon it analyzes. The determinant judgment characterizes science as it is constituted or capable of being constituted; the supplement of finality indicates that sciences do not satisfy the human need to homogenize their worldly experience.

Therefore, the reflective judgment contains an a priori principle—the principle of finality—which prescribes a law for nature that restricts the margin of chaos that had persisted in spite of the action of understanding. Its presence, in turn, indicates that Kant is no longer satisfied with the distance he had kept from experience, and so, instead of treating it as a possibility, begins to consider it in its concreteness.

This change is accompanied by the acknowledgment of a more complex challenge. Although objects remain stable—copper preserves is ruddy hue and does not liquefy spontaneously—the reliance on the transcendental apparatus is not enough to bring about the desired order. The reflective judgment intervenes to help. But though it prescribes a law for the reflection of nature, as we have seen, it does so not for nature itself, but only for the faculty of judgment (it is heautonomic rather than autonomic—see p. 26; B xxxvii). Thus, the reflective judgment does serve knowledge, but only indirectly. Its proper location is in the subjective sphere. Hence its association with pleasure.

Understanding, in the operation of its categories, "necessarily follows the bent of its own nature without ulterior aim" and does not exert "the slightest effect on the feeling of pleasure" (p. 27; B xl). In contrast, Kant says of the reflective judgment:

> It is true that we no longer notice any decided pleasure in the comprehensibility of nature, or in the unity of its divisions into genera and species. . . . Still it is certain that the pleasure appeared in due course, and only by reason of the most ordinary experience being impossible without it, has it become gradually fused with simple cognition, and no longer arrests particular attention. (pp. 27–28; B xl)

To such an extent is this kind of judgment linked with the feeling of pleasure that even when this feeling is no longer present the mark of its former existence remains. Corroborating its affinity with the idea of the medium, affirmed when the encounter of the transcendental apparatus with the materiality of the phenomenon is so defined, understanding itself is seen as a faculty bounded on the one side by pleasure and on the other by indifference.

Thus, the double connection of the reflective judgment is shown: vertically, it is crossed by the principle of finality, from which its specific functioning—its heautonomy—is derived; horizontally, it expands as the pleasure effect. If we bear in mind this illustration, it becomes easier to understand the reflective judgment's two modalities: teleological judgment and aesthetic judgment.

If any doubt remains as to why teleological judgment is not part of the determinant judgment, one need only reread this passage: "An end [*Zweck*] is the object of a concept so far as this concept is regarded as the cause of the object (the real ground of its possibility). . . . Where, then, not the cognition of an object merely, but the object itself (its form or real existence) as an effect, is thought to be possible only through a concept of it, there we imagine an end" (p. 61; B 33).

Strictly from the viewpoint of understanding, a concept thus conceived—to the extent that its formulation is preceded and presided over by the representation of the end—could only be seen as arbitrary and false. As generated by the understanding, the concept synthesizes only the pure contact between what humanity poses, through its transcendental apparatus, and what the object exposes. The introduction of finality begins the "humanization" of the object of experience. In *La Pensée sauvage* (The savage mind) Lévi-Strauss observes that the difference between magic and science is that the former supposes it operates with an unlimited determinism. Considering that by means of the principle of finality one attempts to account for the very "form or existence" of the object, we could also say that that principle introduces a magical ambition in the "sciences" that adopt it. Finality is not determinant because it has only a regulating character (cf. p. 58; B 343).

At first sight, then, Kant might seem to fall in a rather obvious contradiction when he defined, as he did in the first "Introduction" to *CJ*, teleological judgment as a judgment of knowledge. But Kant adds: "which, however, belongs only to the faculty of reflective judgment and not to the faculty of the determinant judgment," and concludes: "In general, the technique of nature, be it merely formal or real, is no more than a relation between things and our faculty of judgment, solely in which is to be found the idea of a finality of nature and that is attributed to nature only as regards that faculty" (Kant 1974b: 34). Thus, however different the paths they follow, teleological judgment and aesthetic judgment come from a single source, originated by the same principle of finality. Even though teleological judgment has no relevance to our present study we were compelled to describe it before we could arrive at the kind of judgment that concerns us.

Earlier we sketched out a diagram of the reflective judgment, in its vertical and horizontal dimensions. We can now add that the teleological and aesthetic judgments are differentiated by the emphasis each gives to one particular dimension: the former stresses the vertical dimension, the latter the horizontal. This is how Kant describes the aesthetic judgment:

> If the form of an object given in empirical intuition is done in such a way that the apprehension of its manifold in imagination coincides with the presentation of a concept of understanding (the concept being left indeterminate), then understanding and imagination agree with each other to carry out their task, and the object will be perceived as endowed with finality only for the faculty of judgment; consequently, finality itself is considered only as subjective; no determinate concept of the object is required for that, nor is produced in this way, and the judgment itself is not a judgment of knowledge. (p. 34)

The passage quoted deals only with finality (*Zweckmäßigkeit*), describing the conditions for its manifestation: imagination operates the synthesis of the manifold apprehended by intuition, "delivering" it to the understanding. In turn, the understanding "chooses" a concept that coincides with it. But this is an indeterminate concept. Thus, imagination, instead of functioning in subordination to understanding, is adjusted to it. This means that the universal, under the form of a law or rule, has proved unable to subsume the particular object. It is when an obstacle appears in the straight path of the understanding, when the object acts as an impediment, that the cognoscitive apparatus relies on finality. When it postulates that "the object *x* has such and such a form because it is *for* (or *is meant for*) . . . ," reason uses a causal analogy—"if something has such and such a shape, then . . ."—and prescribes a rule that affects only itself, not the object.

So far the text we quoted has only served to make the mechanism of finality more concrete. But it can and should do more. Although the passage does not mention pleasure explicitly, pleasure is present in the cross-reference between understanding and imagination. It arises from the impossibility of reaching meaning immediately, for it lives only as long as automatization does not set in. The advent of a determinate concept puts an end to the commerce with the sensible impression—a commerce that is maintained as long as imagination remains active—and is simultaneous with the finding of a meaning. Once a meaning is found, pleasure is extinguished. In intellectual activity— and all forms of judgment are clearly intellectual activities—pleasure subsists only as long as the concept remains indeterminate. Now, in an oblique way, finality restores, after a fashion, the uniformization of meaning.

This means that the diagram of the reflective judgment contains in potential its own tension. If for a moment we leave aside the two separate kinds, we may describe this tension as follows: verticality (finality) both derives from and controls horizontal expansion (the feeling of pleasure). The tension is neutralized in teleological judgment, since the finality attributed to the object comes with its corresponding end. By this redundance—finality with an end—we mean to emphasize the property, specific to the teleological judgment, of being a judgment "of objective appreciation." And even though the passage quoted above does not define the judgment of aesthetic reflection as "finality without an end," we may say that the idea is clearly present without doing any violence to the letter of the text.

Thus, in aesthetic judgment the finality is preserved, as regards the form of the object, but since this finality does not point to an end its objective and cognoscitive pretensions are undermined. The aesthetic object is invested with a finality without an end because the imagination that elaborates it sees in it nothing but the indeterminate possibility of a meaning or meanings; its finality, as it were, is limited to the intellectual but pleasurable—pleasurable but intellectual—effect caused by its reception. Thus, we can see how the following passage stresses both the effect on feeling and the nonobjective character of aesthetic judgment: "By aesthetic judgment on an object what is immediately meant is that a representation given is certainly related to an object, but that, in the judgment, what is understood is not the determination of the object, but rather that of the subject and its feeling" (Kant 1974b: 36).

Once this difference is made clear, the next one is evident: whereas the teleological judgment responds to an interest, the aesthetic judgment is concerned only with the strict interchange between the object's presence and its effect on the subject: "It is quite plain that in order to say that the object is *beautiful* . . . everything turns on the meaning which I can give to this representation, and not on any factor which makes me dependent on the real existence of the object" (Kant 1982a: 43; B 7).

In the next section we shall examine in a more systematic way the meaning of what we have been discussing. For the moment, let us do no more than underscore the general trend of Kant's argument: the fact that it is unconnected with understanding and outside the sphere of ends makes aesthetic pleasure less an Edenic isle of pleasure, dedicated to the full gratification of the senses, than the depragmatized zone par excellence. Its limits, then, are no less rigorous than the boundaries of morals. The duty that activates morals and the feeling of respect that it generates are in a way depragmatized as well: in Kantian morality there are no rewards (cf. Kant 1971: vii–xxxiv). However depragmatized, its proper territory is nonetheless pragmatic. Risking paradox, we might even say that Kantian morality is depragmatized so that its pragmatization may be moved by a pure motivation: the fulfillment of duty, the impulse generated by respect.

As Kant envisages aesthetic judgment, not even this restriction applies to it. The least sign of the pleasing of the senses or of attachment to the object itself compromises it. Only aesthetic experience satisfies the ambition of absolute depragmatization, of a self-combustion unprovoked by any external stimulus. This circumstance is indispensable to aesthetic judgment; only aesthetic experience ensures its universality. For what Kant writes about the beautiful also applies to the character of the sublime: "Where any one is conscious that his delight in an object is with him independent of interest, it is inevitable that he should look on the object as one containing a ground of delight for all men" (Kant 1982a: 50; B 17). (Kant's often tortured syntax perhaps increases the difficulty of a statement that is in fact quite simple: the awareness that the satisfaction produced by the object was not caused by any specific interest implies that it must contain satisfaction for everyone—a universal satisfaction.)

From a historical rather than a strictly philosophical viewpoint, the need to affirm the universal and verify its effective validity resulted from the acknowledgment of the decisive importance of individual subjectivity. In the case of possible experience—that is, in the scope of *CPR*—this was borne out by the agreement between unchanging transcendental properties and the equally unchanging material structure of objects. Duty played a similar role in the second *Critique*. And yet another analogue had to be achieved for the case of a judgment in which, paradoxically, the mark of individuality was most evident.

Whatever one's stand may be on the subject, one cannot help admiring the genius of the philosopher who was able to go beyond this paradox. To Kant, the beautiful reaches the level of experiences worthy of being the object of reflection because it breaks all bonds with interest; the beautiful attains its unmistakable identity after it divests itself of all links with personalized motivation.[3] Hence he arrives at the surprising property of the judgment of taste to which we shall return later:

> The judgement of taste itself does not *postulate* the agreement of every one (for it is only competent for a logically universal judgement to do this, in that it is able to bring forward reasons); it only *imputes* this agreement to every one, as an instance of the rule in respect of which it looks for confirmation, not from concepts, but from the concurrence of others. (p. 56; B 26)

By taking the judgment of taste (*Geschmackurteil*) as the effect of aesthetic experience, Kant affirms both its universality and the impossibility of its being adequately communicated. That is, aesthetics—the attempt to systematize the study of objects that evoke the judgment of taste—is denied any possibility of being objective. The very reason that invests the aesthetic experience with universality denies it the possibility of objectifying aesthetic value. We may then say that for Kant the aesthetic experience assumes a silent universality— that is, aesthetic experience formally possesses the conditions of universality, but only as long as it remains within the subjectivity of the individual, content to suppose that the same takes place in all other subjectivities. In the next section we shall see other implications of this silent universality and its consequences for theoretical reflection after the reception of *CJ*. For the moment, let us close these preparatory observations by recalling the difference between the experiences of the beautiful and of the sublime.

Kant distinguishes the beautiful from the sublime by means of a number of traits. The object that evokes the feeling of beauty must have a delimited shape, causing satisfaction that is accompanied by the representation of quality, which in turn causes a feeling of elevation; last, it also implies the free play

---

3. The fact that we understand the historical motivation behind Kant's obsession with universality should not keep us from noting that the allegation of aesthetic disinterestedness is one of the prejudices of educated people today: "We in the West tend to dismiss the kinds of powers that were once called divine, all the more when we perceive the deployment of artistry and skill in working the object. But we do so because of our cultural prejudices in favor of what we think of as disinterested aesthetic judgment, and not because the god has departed from the image" (Freedberg 1989: 74).

(interaction as equals) between imagination and understanding. One may speak of the beautiful in the natural world with no difficulty because the above properties are in harmony with the admission of a finality with which the understanding invests the object, taking this finality as given in nature (see pp. 90–91; B 75). The properties of the sublime are opposite. Its experience, which does not properly arouse satisfaction, is accompanied by the representation of quantity, and causes the feeling that the vital forces are blocked; this, in turn, leads not to free play, but rather to the serious activity of the imagination, which connects it to reason. That is why, as we have seen, in the definitive text of *CJ* Kant denies that one can speak of a sublime of nature, for nothing in the object that provokes it gives rise to the Idea of finality (p. 91; B 75).

Before an object that the imagination is unable to synthesize, that for this reason seems formless, but which all the same allows its wholeness to be grasped, the only analogy possible is with infinity. Now, infinity is representable by the understanding, for which quantity assumes a count—that is, a finitude. Thus, only an Idea of reason can give meaning to this analogue. The unease and restlessness caused by the sublime can only be assuaged by an Idea of the supersensible. In plain words: if the relation with the beautiful prepares the transcendental apparatus for an encounter with the concept, the relation with the sublime can only be resolved in the acknowledgment of God.

Kant is thus able to provide his thought with the systematicity that was denied him by the polar opposition between theoretical and practical reasons. Through the experience of the beautiful, the faculty of judgment refers to understanding; through that of the sublime, to reason. The fact that judgment has no legislation of its own but only a principle is most fortunate for the system-builder, for this is the principle of finality that, as it branches off in two, ends up ensuring the sought-for mediation.

Now we can begin to explain why we hesitate to accept this architectonic ending. For the moment, all we shall say is that Kant is able to reach a systematic harmony at the price of ignoring one variable: the infrasensible. In order to understand this more clearly, first let us return to the question of the beautiful and the sublime, from a different angle.

As we know, the beautiful and the sublime, as members of a judgment of finality without an end, make up aesthetic judgment. But the derivations of each are not simply parallel lines that ultimately link up with the autonomous and differentiated faculties of understanding and reason. They are parallel indeed, but of unequal extension. The free play instituted by the beautiful contains a promise of a concept that does no violence to the experience of the beautiful itself. This experience preserves its wholeness whether or not its cognitive "vocation" is considered. This is so because this promise is inferred only as a logical projection. If, from the viewpoint of understanding, the beautiful implies an indeterminate concept, logically it may be admitted that pleasure, sparked off by the beautiful, may find the way out that leads to determination, being then changed into a different thing. Although he does not explore this point, Kant nevertheless brings it up when he touches on an archaeology of the faculty of understanding. We might think, however, that work on this logical projection would be even more fruitful if it were attempted on a synchronic plane, since it would pave the way for the analysis of the creative process in science itself. In any case, it would be inherent to this view that at a certain stage the metamorphosis should take place: as it came upon a determinate concept, the experience of the beautiful would cease to singularize the object that aroused it and begin to treat it as an instance of a general law.

Now, in connection with the relation between the sublime and the supersensible one could not properly speak of a mere logical projection. The sensation of blocking of the vital forces that it arouses—the collapse of any natural finality that might be associated with its absence of form—in Kantian terms implies that reason, relying on imagination, should be forced to resort to the Idea of a Supreme Being. For only such a being seems able to provide a reason for what is experienced as overstepping every measure. That is, the figure of the religious emerges in the midst of the experience and breaks its autonomy. In short, in the beautiful the irruption of the determinate concept is only a logical possibility, whereas the Kantian sublime can only complete its trajectory in God.

Perhaps the interruption of the autonomy of the aesthetic was seen as positive by Kant, who was interested in the aesthetic only as the extreme modality of the reflective judgment, bringing it into the architectonic structure of the global system. But whatever his systematic proposal may have been, the fact is that Kant was responsible for the legitimation of aesthetic experience, a legitimation all the more intriguing because it delimited an area that, imbued with a universal principle, is incompatible with the objectivity of norms, and which thus combines what cannot be combined: it assumes the existence of the territory of a Law—that is, a statement with a universal scope—within which, however, every norm would be arbitrary. Kant would still rely on the figure of the genius in order to explain the overstepping of the norm; but we need not go into the argument here.

Yet the sublime makes Kant uncomfortable, for it threatens his architectonics. Before going into the reasons for this, we must articulate the intention of this discussion with what has been examined before. We have seen that, from the perspective of the present book, the importance of Kant in the

context of this discussion of literature lies in his taking up the limits of the
Law in a world formed under the empire of individual subjectivity. The next
step in the argument could only be taken after a comprehensive overview of
CJ, which is what we have just seen. This is so because the acknowledgment
of the presence of subjectivity raises the question, How can the individual
subject move about in a world ruled by two overlapping legislations? The
architectonic hypothesis was put forth precisely at this point, and its merit lay
in the fact that it allowed for a mediating faculty.[4] But the parts that had been
brought together for this purpose rebelled against the intent that had summoned them. And the autonomy of the aesthetic had the effect not only of
disturbing the hoped-for harmony, but also that of increasing the fragmentation of values.

Our next step, then, is to ask how this autonomy was eventually used
by those who, having meditated on Kant, were concerned with the issue of
art. Let us attempt to answer this question, at first historically, by analyzing
Schiller, Novalis, and Friedrich von Schlegel. The fruitfulness of this analysis
will reflect on the "program" we shall draw from it. This program, to be
announced at the end of the chapter, will be actualized in our examination of
Kafka, which will be the theme of the next chapter. But first let us return
once again to *CJ*. This time, however, our approach will not be descriptive.

AN INVITATION TO A REFLECTION ON THE THIRD *CRITIQUE*

What is the aim of the three *Critiques*? The "Preface" to the second
edition of *CPR* states that the object of critique was to open a safe road for
metaphysics. Kant's intense work from 1781—the year when the first edition
of *CPR* came out—to 1790, when the third *Critique* was published, clearly
indicates that he did not believe his initial efforts were sufficient. If one
considers that at least the general outline of the *Critique of Practical Reason* is
stated on the opening pages of *CPR* and that *CJ* was an attempt to crown the
conclusions of the two previous *Critiques*, we may assume that Kant never
gave up the goal of a new metaphysics. But if the presumption of having
established the author's intention fails to satisfy us, we must ask what indeed is
covered by Kant's three works.

Let us begin with a hypothesis that underscores the philosopher's political beliefs. Kant had not only defended the French Revolution but also, in
contrast with the vast majority of German and British intellectuals of his day,

---

4. In order to make his proposal clear, Kant ended the definitive version of his "Introduction" to *CJ* with a table containing all the faculties, the cognitive faculties (*Erkennt-
nisvermögen*), their a priori operative principles, and their applications (see p. 39; B lviii).

stuck to his position even when Napoleon manifested his expansionist intentions. Thus, we might imagine that, always privileging the citizen over the pure individual, Kant had set out to discriminate the planes of action of each. Cognitive action proper would then correspond to the legislation founded on understanding, which has natural phenomena as its objects. According to this view, Kant did much more than simply draw the gnosiological consequences of the science of nature, which had progressed from Galileo to its ultimate flowering in Newton: he ensured the tranquility of a world that no longer required God in order to be explained.

Thus, the first *Critique* aimed at the socially cognoscitive citizen, whereas the second dealt with the socially active citizen. The second legislation was to be legitimated on the basis of practical reason, and having interhuman relations as its object. But how can concern with the citizen be reconciled with the third *Critique*? In order to escape this difficulty, one might argue that aesthetic judgment, because it is necessarily depragmatized, is not addressed to the individual as such, but rather to the individual to whom a universal judgment is attributed. Although having a private nature, the receiver of aesthetic experience was also an image of the citizen: the citizen-in-private.

As soon as one writes it down, one realizes how poor such a hypothesis would be. Not just because its formulation dispenses with the effort to read the three treatises line by line; such an objection could be neutralized by a textual analysis that arrived at the same conclusion. The problem with the hypothesis is that it is too static: all it does is order in the space of a page the three objects of inquiry, as if Kant's huge effort were the same as that of an encyclopedist who, having outlined his plan, then fulfilled it in the most painstaking manner.

Therefore, we need another hypothesis. We find it in a short essay by Odo Marquard. We need not summarize it; let us simply extract from it what concerns us.

The author considers the dawn of modern times: the separation, which took place in the late Middle Ages, between theology and philosophy made "the world in a way theologically unapprehensible" (Marquard 1962: 235). Reason could then find the conditions for its own emancipation, an idea that was taken up by the tradition of the Enlightenment. Within this tradition, Kant attempted to find in the certainty of the sciences of nature the grounds for the emancipatory leap. But the conclusion of the first *Critique* showed him that he had fallen short of reaching his goal. Marquard synthesizes the thesis he draws from CPR as follows: "First: science is exact only and in the best of cases when it does not presume to provide guidance or salvation [*Führungs und Rettungsanspruch*]. Second: reason justifies its proposal of guidance and salvation only and in the best of cases when it does not equate itself with scientific reason, when it leads to a new form of reason" (p. 241). Thus, the failure of scientific reason is not really its own failure, but rather that of the pretensions with which its examination was carried out.

Realization of this fact leads to the postulation of a second, separate reason. That is why Kant renews his search in the attempt to find a better answer in the sphere of practical action. But again his demand is excessive.

> Moral reason compels man to live "as if" there were a political reality in which men could and did live like men. This "as if" shows that good reality is a postulate [*Forderung*]. The "realm of ends" is not a reality. Thus moral reason manifestly offers only the concept, not the reality, of full being [*des guten Seins*]. Since this fullness is the goal, Kant's philosophy of moral reason gives only the simple concept of end, of goal. (p. 364)

Two roads had been opened, both for the purpose of finding an orienting proposal for the emancipation of man. In both cases, the goal was lost sight of. Kant then turned to the faculty of judgment, moved by the same hope. Could it be that the failure of reason, the impotence it revealed to itself, was the result of the fact that it existed in a world dominated by interests that distorted and weakened it? Should not one then shrewdly conceive of the world of interests as somehow changing into the advocate of the reason that so far had always met with failure? This, Marquard adds, was to suppose that there are interests that give up their own goal, "disinterested interests" (p. 369).

This, then, would be the impulse behind the third *Critique*. But then Kant's interpreter wonders: "Was aesthetic sense the real object of the search? Rather, what was sought was a naturalness endowed with reason [*eine vernünftige Natürlichkeit*], a sensible power of actualization of the goal of reason. What was found was a sensible power, one, however, that was a power not of actualization but only of symbolization of the goal of reason" (p. 369). In Kantian terms, reason proved unable to point the way for the subject. The legitimation that Kant offers to modernity is also the proof of its transitoriness. But this is not quite the path taken by Marquard. Instead, he concentrates on the result of the third and last *Critique*, and then poses the question: "Is aesthetics part of the spearhead or of the funeral procession of the historico-rational endeavor? As the symbol of morality, is the beautiful a spur to achievement or, given its lack of usefulness, a sedative instead?" (p. 370).

The interpretation outlined above has the virtue of drawing a clear parallel between Kant's reflection and the dilemmas that modernity has made familiar, of stressing how the disenchantment (*Entzauberung*) that it brings about comes eventually to take on a double meaning: both demythification and disenchantment proper, both the smashing of idols and the empty-handed return. From our specific viewpoint, it has an additional attraction: the final question it raises may be applied to the interior of *CJ* the better to define the resistance to the architectonic hypothesis. In more precise language: In itself, does Kant's aesthetic reflection have a critical character or is there a compensatory aspect that insinuates itself into it, or even dominates it? We already know that in it the question of the Law becomes less relevant or even secondary, since possession of the a priori principle of finality does not imply possession of a legislation. As we have indicated, this drawback is discarded by the architectonic hypothesis; either by referring to understanding (through the beautiful) or to reason (through the sublime), the judgment of reflection acts as a mediator between theoretical and practical reasons. However, when we observe that this hypothesis can only be maintained if we agree to give up the autonomy of aesthetic judgment, then the absence of the Law assumes a new aspect and a new relevance.

These, then, are the issues from which two immediate questions derive: First, Why is it, after all, that the architectonic hypothesis fails to do justice to the extraordinary richness of *CJ*? Second, What are the consequences of the autonomy of *CJ* from this architectonics, from the viewpoint of an understanding of aesthetic experience? Put more explicitly, the question is whether the aesthetic experience is envisaged in *CJ* from a critical angle or as a palinode to compensate for the impotence of modern reason.

To develop the first question, let us examine a few passages by O. Chédin. The discussion will be brief, since we have touched on it earlier. Thus, it will pave the way for the second.

In brief, Chédin's thesis consists in seeing aesthetic consciousness less as a deficit (the imagination's inability to connect with a determinate concept) than as a specific production: the production of a schematism without a schema and hence without a concept.[5] This somewhat clandestine production does not widen the gap already opened between the diverging theoretical and practical legislations because it dwells in the archaeological underground where the spirit prepares itself for the schema:

> The beautiful object is then the one whose manifold provides imagination with a "schematizing" movement that conciliates it in general with the faculty of concepts, because this movement is exerted in accordance with the condition (schematism) according to which concepts and images associate in order to know objects. The *schematism without a schema* would give rise to a *conceiving without a concept*, which in turn would activate schematism. (Chédin 1982: 113)

5. In order to grasp the boldness of this thesis more fully, let us remember that "schematism is an original act of the imagination: only the imagination schematizes. But it does so only when the understanding presides or has legislating power" (Deleuze 1983: 29).

Such an archaeology, consequently, would not correspond to a primitive creature, to be later surpassed by a more advanced one, but instead would contain—to use Kant's metaphor in a different context—the monogram of the full transcendental design. The monograph is like a name. But which name? We cannot assume a "wild" agreement between imagination and understanding "unless we suppose that the space and time of aesthetic apprehension are presented 'as' concepts—that is, that they *take on the form of the actual power to form concepts*. . . . Therefore this *object* 'realizes' by anticipation the founding principles of the power to know" (pp. 118–19).

Thus, even if we do not apply this insight to the treatment of the sublime, we understand why it is that such a reading of the aesthetic experience does not lead to the supersensible but instead, emphasizing the inner solidarity of the forms of the beautiful and the sublime, underscores the infrasensible, which Kant's reflection, in spite of his own intentions, brings to light. It is not God's acquiescence that assuages the experience of the sublime, but rather a force that prepares man for full conceptual production.

In this way, Kant's text is clearly reinvigorated. The suspicion that reason indulges in a mere compensatory exercise faces a vigorous counterargument. The disinterestedness that characterizes the aesthetic experience in Kant was not, after all, underscored by reason in despair of finding its desideratum, nor does reason shut itself up in a subjectivity that is contented with its own intellectual pleasure: "Disinterestedness, in fact, expresses precisely the opposite of what it seems to mean: indeed, only it can make us perceive existence in itself, the thing itself, with no 'interest' (project) of any concept" (p. 19). But the enthusiasm one may feel on reading this passage should not keep one from noticing that something has been omitted. This is clear in the last part of the quoted text: let us accept that aesthetic consciousness creates the condition for the apprehension of existence in its most elementary form of presence.

But in order to constitute it in fact, something must be added to it: the critical perspicacity of what existence brings. The absence of this perspicacity implies preserving an ecstatic, aestheticizing view of existence. One would escape the identification of the Kantian aesthetic with the compensatory only to absolutize the former: the aesthetic alone would allow the perception of existence in itself, all else merely instrumentalizing it. So what we propose here is not to reread *CJ* in the light of Chédin's new interpretation, but rather to observe, keeping this reading in mind, how Kant's text itself behaves in relation to its interpretation.

We have seen that the architectonic hypothesis fell short of the formulations it contained. It is also clear that the penetration we envisage is made difficult by the fact that Kant, having little familiarity with art, offers only banal examples of the aesthetic experience. But there is nothing we can do about this.

> Flowers are free beauties of nature. Hardly anyone but a botanist knows the true nature of a flower, and even he, while recognizing in the flower the reproductive organ of the plant, pays no attention to this natural end when using his taste to judge of its beauty. Hence no perfection of any kind—no internal finality, as something to which the arrangement of the manifold is related—underlies this judgement. . . . So designs *à la grecque* [in the Greek style], foliage for framework or on wall-papers, &c., have no intrinsic meaning; they represent nothing—no Object under a definite concept—and are free beauties. We may also rank in the same class what in music are called fantasias (without a theme), and, indeed, all music that is not set to words. (Kant 1982a: 72; B 49)

> In ornamental gardens, in the decoration of rooms, in all kinds of furniture that shows good taste, &c., regularity in the shape of constraint [*Zwang*] is to be avoided as far as possible. Thus English taste in gardens, and fantastic taste in furniture, push the freedom of imagination to the verge of what is grotesque— the idea being that in this divorce from all constraint of rules the precise instance is being afforded where taste can exhibit its perfection in projects of imagination to the fullest extent. (p. 88; B 71)

> One who alone (and without any intention of communicating his observations to others) regards the beautiful form of a wild flower, a bird, an insect, or the like, out of admiration and love of them, and being loath to let them escape him in nature . . . takes an immediate, and in fact intellectual, interest in the beauty of nature. This means that he is not alone pleased with nature's product in respect of its form, but is also pleased at its existence, and is so without any charm of sense having a share in the matter, or without his associating with it any end whatsoever. (p. 158; B 166–67)

Let us see Chédin's comment on the first of these passages, noting in passage that our interpretation will be different:

> A beautiful floral design should "confuse" the natural form (of the motif) with the games it provokes. Thus, in itself it becomes a fantasist (artistic)—and natural. The playful shapes that the normal figure inspires slacken their rules while, reciprocally, their preserved regularity "naturalizes" and regularizes their games. Thus, a sort of exchange takes place, an osmosis between the normal regularity of understanding (concept of the model) and the "rule-free" freedom of imagination. (Chédin 1982: 238–39)

This comment is authorized by the fact that Kant himself said that, in such cases, reflection on the object is not elicited by nor leads to any concept; nor is the comment a mere gloss, for it contains a subtle recognition of the obedience and transgression that are simultaneous with the order of the

model. Then what is it that is not being perceived? The fact that this oscilla-
tion still fails to free the aesthetic experience from the function of mere
ornament—an ornament, to the philosopher, of the free play between imagination and understanding, of which these cases would be examples and illustrations; an ornament, also, to the receiver, who is content to understand
the strayings from and returns to the pattern. In other words, the interpreter
does not seem to observe that a remnant is still associated with Kant's praise of
disinterestedness, of the absence of finality.

Is the fault Chédin's or ours? Is it really possible to say more about the
aesthetic experience? The second and third passages from Kant quoted above
suggest that, to him, this is indeed the limit of the sayable: all they do is re-
state what is contained in the first—the beautiful forms of nature reiterate, for
the eye of the nonspecialist, the depragmatized gracefulness they offer; the
excess without usefulness; the complex cornucopia that is indifferent to any
finality. This dysfunctionality leads the observer to understand the singularity
of the aesthetic object. Though long, a passage from *CJ*, number 5, must be
transcribed:

> [The observer] will speak of the beautiful as if beauty were a quality of the object
> and the judgment logical (forming a cognition of the Object by concepts of it);
> although it is only aesthetic, and contains merely a reference of the representa-
> tion of the object to the Subject;—because it still bears this resemblance to the
> logical judgment, that it may be presupposed to be valid for all men. But this
> universality cannot spring from concepts. For from concepts there is no transi-
> tion to the feeling of pleasure or displeasure (save in the case of pure practical
> laws, which, however, carry an interest with them; and such an interest does not
> attach to the pure judgment of taste). The result is that the judgment of taste,
> with its attendant consciousness of detachment from all interest, must involve a
> claim to validity for all men, and must do so apart from universality attached to
> Objects, that is, there must be coupled with it a claim to subjective universality.
> (p. 51; B 18)

The effective actualization of an aesthetic experience is then defined by
the fact that it constitutes a mute universality, one that necessarily cannot be
communicated. It is as if, given this situation, people should content themselves with the presumption of feeling. If it were not for the biographical
arbitrariness this would imply, one might say that in *CJ* Kant incorporates
something of Oriental contemplativeness. It would be less absurd to see here
something close to the mythical. But Kant himself will not allow such an
approach to prove fruitful. Instead, the conclusion he intends to draw is quite
the opposite: "We might even define taste as the faculty of estimating what
makes our feeling in a given representation *universally communicable* [*allgemein
mitteilbar*] without the mediation of a concept" (p. 153, B 161).

The divergence between the philosopher's reading and the interpretation we propose is so blatant that it might cause surprise. However, both have to do with the same phenomenon: to Kant, the universal communicability of the effect of aesthetic experience—that is, taste—is a consequence of the fact that everybody, when disconnected from any private interest, is able to feel it. This means that it is in Kant's text itself that the muteness is affirmed. The Voice, in its transcendental Kantian sense, is, as it were, dumb. This dumbness is its necessary condition, for if I convince someone of the validity of my taste, I transform my taste into a norm and thus move out of the strict field of the aesthetic. Not even here is the citizen replaced by the mere individual, because what is strictly private in the experience is the condition for maintaining its common ground with humanity. The presence of the citizen, however, is supported by the hidden, silent, but universal mark of the Voice. Aesthetic experience alone can unveil it.

The demonstration of the muteness of aesthetic experience underscores the limits of what can be said about it in Kant's terms. But what is the consequence of this conclusion? We have seen that the limit of the Kantian voice kept the aesthetic object from being taken for an ornament or an illustration; or, to use Chédin's comment, without determining concepts, by means of aesthetic experience the object overwhelms us with the pleasure of encountering the very materiality of what is offered us. But if this encounter with the "thing itself" is to elicit pleasure, the sensation of beauty, the thing being experienced must not threaten us, must not shock our understanding; instead, it must decorate it, confirm its rightness. Reduced to this function, the aesthetic object is merely aestheticizing. In this, it may surely play a highly gratifying role; but then it evanesces. Hence, we have the importance of distinguishing between the limit of the Kantian voice and the limit of the object being approached.

Might not a better result be attained if we conceived of the aesthetic object in terms of the pair "syntax-semantics"? The idea is this: outside of aesthetic experience, whether in the most banal pragmatic relation or in the composition of the most abstract treatise, we are all under the empire of the semantic. One can model syntax as much as one wants, rely on the full range of one's language's expressive resources, but the syntax—and, with it, the rhythm made concrete by the modulation of the sentence—will be at the service of the semantic. Written art—for the sake of communicability, let us call it "literature"—implies the provisional suspension of the sway of the semantic. This occurs every time that, given a formulation or even a single word, we suspend the question as to its meaning and instead wonder at the produced pattern itself. The aesthetic experience implies taking syntax as the expectation and interval that precedes semantic (re)occupation.

Expectation and interval: these terms underscore the fact that the detachment from the semantic is only provisional. The full duration of the aesthetic experience is not to be confused with this instant; it lies rather in the very tension between the "syntactic moment" and the imminence of semantic reoccupation. This experience ends only when the full return of the semantic causes the previous attention to the sensible body of the expression to be forgotten. Therefore, it cannot be defined as the absence of interest, for this absence always marks the imminence of aestheticization. Rather, it should be defined by the twofold attention to the syntactic and the semantic, by the tension that accompanies this duality.

The focus on the syntactic relegates the chain of signifieds to the background—not that the two are actually disconnected, as if it were possible, even for a moment, to forget the meanings of the most familiar terms. To relegate meaning to the background means to focus on the actual texture of the construction, the combination of letters—harsh or bland, cold and aggressive or sweet and melodious—in the flesh of words. This does not mean that words and sentences are enjoyed as if they were musical notes. In the "syntactic moment," the aesthetic experience "sees" from a distance the ordinary semantic use to which the same words and turns of phrase are commonly submitted so that, when semantic reoccupation occurs, the distance is assumed and internalized by the semantic; that is, not only intellectually, but also emotionally, the receiver gains a space in which to feel critically what is lost in the merely semanticized—and hence automatized (or automatizable)—world. Ultimately, this experience results less in an object of pleasure—since it also involves the sublime—than in a fictional object. Not that pleasure is absent from it; only, the pleasure is not enough to characterize it.

An empirical correlative of what we have been referring to as expectation and interval can be found in a short text by Elias Canetti, *Voices of Marrakesh*. In addition, the supposition of the encounter between European ears and eyes and an Oriental scene makes it even more operational, due to the contrast then offered to the exotic view of the East, abundantly documented by the "literary" journeys of nineteenth-century writers.

My intention in the last part of this section has not been to "correct" Kant but rather to stress, by contrasting it with Kant's own explanation, the double reading that makes his appreciation of the aesthetic possible, the double reading that now privileges aestheticization, now focuses on criticity. Everything that has been said here about the three *Critiques*, in addition to the purpose of informing the reader who is unfamiliar with them, was meant only to clarify this simple statement. It seemed indispensable to support the statement and show what its effects are because, as we shall see later, the immediate reception of *CJ* was marked by the possibility of this double meaning. But before I demonstrate the connection I have been announcing, I still need to provide more elements for a better understanding of the context we are about to examine.

The Impact of the Word "Critique" and Fichte

As a young man, Walter Benjamin observed:

> In the writings of the early romantics, of all philosophical and aesthetic technical terms "critique" and "critical" [*kritisch*] are probably the most frequent. . . . Through Kant's philosophical work, the concept of critique acquired a near-magical meaning for the new generation; in any case, for them it was not associated preponderantly with the sense of a spiritual attitude, merely judicative rather than productive; to the romantics and to speculative philosophy, the term "critique" meant objectively productive, lucidly creative. (Benjamin 1974a, 1, 1: 51)

This passage emphasizes the impact of Kant on the romantics and their simultaneous distancing from him. (It should be noted that this is true only of the early German romantics: with the sole exception of Coleridge, no foreign romantic—that is, no other Romanticism—kept up the same intense commerce with philosophy.) The three factors we have in mind—Kant's impact, the restrictions to his systematics, and the specifically German phenomenon of poets extremely interested in philosophy—can already be glimpsed in the combination of two passages from fragments 26 and 387 published in the magazine *Athenäum* (henceforth abbreviated *AF*): "Gemanity is the favorite object of characterizers, for the less achieved the nation, the more it is an object of critique rather than of History" (Schlegel 1967c: 169). "Critical philosophy is always seen as something that dropped out of the sky. Even without Kant, it should have appeared in Germany, and indeed it might have, in various different ways. However, it is better as it is [*Doch ist's so besser*]" (p. 237).

The first quotation shows why German political disunity made criticity particularly attractive for German intellectuals. The second, even as it lays emphasis on the contextualization of the phenomenon, seems in a way to lessen Kant's merit. In any case, the final qualification acknowledges that the decisive step was taken by him. From this point two lines derive that will remain parallel—that is, that cannot be conjoined as cause and effect. The only stable relation between them is their temporal and spatial contiguity. The first has as its subject the situation of a nation with no political unity, and hence without an identity as a state; the second is the derivation that criticity will assume among the authors we shall examine here.

Schlegel intuitively perceives that the obsession with criticity is more than the brainchild of a thinker of genius: it was brought about by a political state of affairs. The Germany of his time was an aggregate of about three hundred principalities and sovereign states, governed by ancient feudal privileges or by absolutist power. Because of the absence of a political center, this conglomerate of lilliputian states could not compete with the great powers of the turn of the century—Britain and France. The criticity that aroused enthusiasm among the intelligentsia of the time was as extreme as it was pragmatically ineffective. Unlike other interpreters, I do not define it as a compensatory activity with grotesque results, but I do mean to stress the fact that the critical spirit was activated by the lack of a point of reference on which it could rest. To use Kafka's phrase, Germanity generated a "minor literature." In a metropolitan state such as France, the Enlightenment had been able to help a class break the bonds that kept it from acquiring political power. Nothing of the kind had happened in Germany. Thus, its criticity, even if it is present in all areas, has only a short duration in time. The point is not to set up an opposition between the metropolitan situation and the sort of anticipation of a third-world state of affairs found in late-eighteenth-century Germany and hint at the possible intellectual advantages of this underprivileged situation; I am merely providing a sketch of the context where criticity had its brightest, if brief, moment of glory. We conclude with the first parallel.

The second has to do with the dissatisfaction experienced by the romantics in connection with Kant's thought. In 1796 Schlegel saw a "massacre of reason" in *CPR* (quoted in Ayrault 1961, 3: 139). For Schlegel, the very same man who was able to overcome his cult of the Greeks and of the objectivity they supposedly stood for, could not break free from the old metaphysical unity: "What is reason if not the faculty of ideals?" (p. 139).

As opposed to what was possible in Kantian thought, the old metaphysical unity could somehow be preserved by the influence of Fichte's doctrine. Although Fichte saw himself as a follower of Kant, his version of the *Wissenschaftslehre* (*Science of Knowledge*, henceforth abbreviated *SK*) allowed Novalis and Schlegel to see the individual as a new center. Besides, Fichte's enhancement of the individual justified the emphasis on immediacy. In the only version of *SK* that the early romantics knew, that of 1794, Fichte wrote: "Reason is merely practical and . . . only in the application of its laws to a nonself that limits it does it become theoretical" (Fichte 1988: 126). To which Benjamin added: "Fichte shares with the early romantics the interest in the immediacy [*Unmittelbarkeit*] of higher knowledge" (Benjamin 1974a, 1, 1: 25).

Whereas Kant emphasized the agreement between the properties of the subject's transcendental apparatus and those of objects, thanks to which critical activity was saved from both skepticism and dogmatism, in Fichte every reflective action is concentrated on the activity of the self: "The self determines reality and, through reality, itself. It poses all reality as an absolute *quantum*. Outside of this reality there is no other. This reality is posed in the self. The self, then, is determined, to the extent that reality is determined" (Fichte 1988, 129). It is, then, through the centering on the production of the individual subject that Fichte maintains the primacy of the term "critique." As R. Torres Filho observes:

> *Transcendental* idealism establishes the relations between absolute opposites, the self and the nonself, in what should constitute knowledge in its universality, in terms of a higher *alternance* (reciprocal determination). . . . And with this operation this idealism is also *critical*, for, as long as this higher reciprocal determination is not achieved, as this reciprocal determination maintains, absolutely, an independent activity exterior to it, whether it is conceived as an activity of the self or of the nonself, philosophy will be forced by the principle of reason to postulate an absolute subject or an absolute object, thus falling in the inverse and associated illusions of dogmatic idealism and dogmatic realism, prisoners of the alternative. (Torres Filho 1975: 207)

Given its absolute centeredness on the activity of the individual subject, reality itself, all of it, "is posed in the self" (Fichte 1988: 138). Its very passivity is only a consequence of its own activity:

> Now it may be perfectly understood how the self can determine, by and through its activity, its passivity, and how it can be active and passive at the same time. It is *determinant* inasmuch as, in an absolutely spontaneous way, it poses itself in a determined sphere. . . . It is *determined* inasmuch as it is considered as posed in this determined sphere and abstraction is made of the spontaneity of the posing. (p. 142)

In addition, it is the only originating substance (see p. 142). And, since it is responsible for the unending task of overcoming contradictions through ever higher syntheses, the self is no less than infinite: "To the extent that it is limited by the nonself, the self is finite; but in itself, just as it is posed by its own absolute activity, the self is infinite" (p. 144).

The entire movement described above pleased the romantics. However, the stance adopted towards infinity ended up placing Fichte in opposition to the early German romantics. To Fichte, the unending task—from each contradiction, such as the one by means of which the self poses itself and the nonself and implies activity and passivity, a synthesis derives, which in the case of our example is that of reciprocal determination, which in turn gives rise to a new contradiction and so on, ad infinitum—ends up not resolved but abolished, as its knot is cut through (p. 144). The romantics, instead, came to idolize the self and stamp "its mark on their theory of knowledge" (Benjamin 1974a: 25).

The description presented so far is not only superficial, as it could not but be, but also runs the risk of giving the impression that, after they moved away from Kant, the early romantics ended up moving away from Fichte as well. But the movement between them and the thinkers of their day is not so simple as that. The figure that they actually trace is of a different order. P. Szondi observed this when he wrote that even though "Schlegel's most important philosophical stimuli came from Fichte's theory of science . . . the orientation of his philosophical and aesthetic thought is determined by the Kantian problematic" (Szondi 1978: 32). In order to solve this apparent puzzle, it should be considered that the divergences—particular in a man as hostile to compromises as the young Schlegel—derive from the very viewpoint that had brought them together and which they seemed to share: the affirmation of immediacy on the basis of the centrality of the self. As we have seen, this shared viewpoint seemed to heal—or, more properly, to postpone—the rupture of unity implied by Kant's theory of the limits of theoretical reason. The self was then strategically exalted. The old centeredness on God was merely displaced, and the new divine could expect its worshipers to attribute to it a more visible and less intellectual systematics.

However, as an art critic Schlegel was not inclined to idolize subjectivity. More exactly, it is clear that its adoption would compromise the work to which he was most dedicated. The sarcastic tone he adopts leaves no doubt as to this. Here are fragments 124 and the initial passage of 196 from *AF*:

> Since novels are written and read from a psychological angle, it is very inconsequent and petty to fear the slow and detailed dissection of unnatural pleasures, terrible tortures, scandalous infamies, loathsome forms of physical and moral impotence. (Schlegel 1967c: 207)

> Pure autobiography is written either by sufferers of nervous illnesses, always fascinated with their own selves, the type to which Rousseau belongs, or else by strongly aesthetic or venturesome egoists, like Benvenuto Cellini. (p. 213)

On a philosophical plane, Kant had manifested his complete disagreement with someone who nevertheless presented himself as his disciple: "I see Fichte's *Science of Knowledge* as a wholly untenable system. Indeed, a pure doctrine of science is no more and no less than a mere *logic* which, with its principles, never arrives at the materials of knowledge" (Kant 1922: 370).

Schlegel's divergence, like Fichte's, refuses to center on the pure self. Once again, the young Benjamin observed clear-sightedly: "In the sense of the early romantics, the center of reflection is art, not the self" (Benjamin 1974a: 39). Thus, in order to convert the exercise of critique into an integrating part of creative activity, Schlegel, though he did not adopt Kant's gnosiological proposal, could not help developing the critical method. In this he differs from someone who was much more submissive towards Kant's teachings: "Whereas Schiller relied particularly on some Kantian concepts for his observations [*Vorstellungen*] on the sublime and the playfulness of art, the critical method was applied to aesthetics not by him, but by Friedrich Schlegel" (Szondi 1978: 32).

By now the ground to be covered by the following pages is already clear: they will dwell on the different derivations of criticity in the essays of Schiller and Schlegel. But before we take up this issue, we shall present one more preparatory discussion, concerning the meaning of early romanticism in relation to modernity.

This is made necessary by the very spirit of the present book. Beginning with the discussion of Novalis, there will be an increasingly explicit concern with the character of literary criticism, with the role played in it by criticity; but from the very first chapter the reader is expected to be aware of the fact that this issue will be seen in the context of the question of modernity. In more direct terms, so far this book has been concerned with the legitimation of individual subjectivity as an issue in modernity. The consequence of this legitimation has been the need to reconsider the Law—how to assert its objectivity if it was believed that every judgment was channeled through and colored by individual sensitivity? Hence, we have the central importance of Kant's work, of Kant's attempt to demonstrate the universality of the legislations of theoretical and practical reason. The reconsideration of the Law also has implications for the problem of art. Through the detour of the attraction Fichte has for them, the early romantics, again pioneered by F. Schlegel, shaped literary criticism. Thus, we can understand better why, before we go any further into the problem and investigate dilemmas, limits, and oppositions, we must consider the relation between the early romantics and modernity. The most effective and economical way of doing this seems to be to examine the attacks directed at them by one of their sharpest adversaries.

Carl Schmitt: Critic of Romanticism

Politische Romantik (Political Romanticism) was originally published in 1919, the same year in which Walter Benjamin defended his doctoral dissertation, *Der Begriff der Kunstkritik in der deutschen Romantik* (The concept of art criticism in German Romanticism). In 1925 the second edition came out, with a preface written the year before and an expanded version of the 1920 essay "Politische Theorie und Romantik" (Political theory and Romanticism).

Jurist, professor in Bonn (1922–28), first an advocate of political Catholicism, Schmitt later defended the Weimar Republic, until Hitler became chancellor. Then he joined the National Socialist Party, and became, with Ernst Jünger and Martin Heidegger, one of the three most important German intellectuals to join Nazism. Nonetheless, he must be counted as one of the greatest political thinkers of the century.

For our present purposes, Schmitt's essay interests us only as it expresses the relation between his position in regard to Romanticism and his attempt to delegitimate modernity.

In a straightforward style, in which an almost journalistic agility does not compromise the acuteness of his formulations, Schmitt begins by arguing that the criteria commonly used to define Romanticism are inadequate. Romanticism is not characterized by a preference for certain kinds of scenes or objects. Ruins, lonely mountains, primitive peoples, lyrical poetry, the Middle Ages, chivalry, feudal aristocracy—these are not intrinsically Romantic themes. Nor is a specific psychological state the defining criterion. The escape to far-off places or the cult of the anomalous and uncanny are even less specific to Romanticism. Then Schmitt attacks the opposition, stated by Goethe and popularized by the Schlegel brothers, between Romanticism and classical rationalism. The identification of Romanticism with emotionalism was as false as its identification with Roman Catholicism, which had been attempted after the death of the enthusiasm with which the survivors of early romanticism had greeted the revolutionary spirit—here, again, the key influence was F. Schlegel. "The miraculous structure of Christian order and discipline, dogmatic clarity, and rigorous morality" of the Catholic Church were not to be confused either with eighteenth-century rationalism or—even less—with Romanticism (see Schmitt 1986: 6). The latter identification could be no more than the product of "the curious logic that produces definitions by means of an agreement in negation, and in the fog of such negative similarities contrives ever new connections and admixtures" (p. 6). Romanticism and classicism are not archetypal directions that can be applied to any period; to arrive at a precise determination of Romanticism, one must first demolish confusing and abusive identifications.

There is yet a fourth false criterion: Romanticism is neither politically progressive nor conservative; it is not "a *laudator temporis acti* [eulogist of the times] or a *prophète du passé* [prophet of the past]" (p. 9). The adoption of such approaches only increases the confusion. What, then, is the essence of Romanticism? According to Schmitt, Romanticism is a modality of modern occasionalism, a current of thought whose best known representative is Malebranche. "The problem of the true cause is the initial problem of occasionalism" (p. 85). Instead of causes that imply the existence of preestablished universal laws, occasionalism acknowledges only the existence of occasions that are propitious for a given thing.

To neo-Cartesian occasionalists—besides Malebranche, Schmitt mentions Géraud de Cordemoy and Geulincx—the difficulty raised by the lack of grounds for causality is overcome by the resort to God. God is the true cause, and all events in the world are only occasions. Therefore, it hardly matters that there is no internal legislation in the world to regulate it and justify events in it. Nonetheless, this order is ensured: "God brings about the inexplicable correspondence of mental and corporeal phenomena. Everything taken together—the conscious process, the volitional impulse, and the muscular movement—is a mere occasion for God's activity. In fact, it is not the human being who acts, but God" (p. 86).

Since they rely on God as a point of reference and assurance of worldly order, occasionalist philosophers are, as it were, less occasionalist than the romantics. Wrote Schmitt in his 1924 "Preface": "Romanticism is subjectivized occasionalism because an occasional relationship to the world is essential to it. Instead of God, however, the romantic subject occupies the central position and makes the world and everything that occurs in it into a pure occasion [*Anlaß*]" (p. 18). And what we have said about the reason why the early German romantics found Fichte's thought attractive—an observation that Schmitt does not make—only strengthens his argument the more. Disbelief in causality and the secularization of the experience of the world are, then, the conditions that had the effect of making the individual subject occupy the empty center in Romanticism.

It should also be remembered that in Schmitt's thought the figure of modernity is ever present, on account of its legitimation of subjectivity and the failure of the postulated cognitive unity of the world. The approximation with modernity, however, seems to raise a problem. Mankind and History, Schmitt writes in the important chapter 2, are "modern demiurges" (p. 81). If, we might add, modernity as a whole does not postulate occasionalism, it is because it believes to have found in the social milieu ordering mechanisms that reduce the individual to a cogwheel in a larger order. Should we conclude then that Schmitt's attack on Romanticism does not extend to modernity because modernity is protected from the accusations reserved for the defenders of subjectivism? No. For later in chapter 2 Schmitt says that the supposed action of the modern demiurges is reduced to mere metaphor;

quoting Novalis, he criticizes the so-called action of "a higher, composite human being, the genius" (p. 82). In other words, seen as a whole, modernity is distinguished from Romanticism only inasmuch as it sophisticates or meta-phorizes the individual subject. On this point there is no mistaking Schmitt's position: "Closer examination shows, however, that it is neither of these two demiurges—humanity and history—but rather the romantic subject itself that takes everything as an occasion" (p. 82).

The question, then, is to analyze the social context that favored this state of affairs. Now Schmitt has an opportunity to state his political stand:

> The bearer [*Träger*] of the Romantic movement is the new bourgeoisie. Its epoch begins in the eighteenth century. In 1789, it triumphed with revolution-ary violence over the monarchy, the nobility, and the Church. In June of 1848, it already stood on the other side of the barricades, when it defended itself against the revolutionary proletariat. . . . The new Romantic art develops along with democracy and the new taste of the new bourgeois public. It experiences the traditional aristocratic forms and classical rhetoric as an artificial model and, in its need for the true and the natural, it often proceeds to the complete destruc-tion of every form. (p. 12)

On the one hand, then, all that is left is scorched earth: not only are forms ruined but also the sense of orthodoxy is lost—the sense of hierarchy, the awareness of the world as a huge machinery that infallibly processes the diver-sity of things. On the other hand, there is the centeredness on the individual subject, with its sublimating metaphors and its relegation of the world to the situation of no more than a post of occasion for the exercise of will.

Perhaps because he expected his readers to believe in him solely on the strength of his position as a legal expert, Schmitt does not find it necessary to analyze the vast machinery of the classical conception and the sense it gave to humanity's commerce with the world. Whether or not he was aware of what he was leaving out, his silence is quite effective: whereas he conceals what he defends or proposes, he is painstakingly precise as to what he attacks. Given these premises, his task was to demonstrate the practical consequences of an examination that so far had stuck to the plane of abstraction.

Romantic occasionalism is a subjectivized modality because it conceives the world only as an occasion for the fruition of a personal project. The world is theoretically conceived as a chaotic and anomic agglomerate, in which no order could consider itself legitimate a priori. An understanding of this has immediate implications: "A world that is new arises from ever new oppor-tunities. But it is always a world that is only occasional, a world without substance and functional cohesion, without a fixed direction, without consis-tency and definition, without decision, without a final court of appeal [*ohne letztes Gericht*], continuing into infinity and led only by the magic hand of chance" (p. 19). So what the Enlightenment thinkers saw as a condition for throwing off old shackles and for the advent of the possibility of human emancipation turned into an anarchical razzia. Instead of free agents, men are reduced to the condition of greedy and opportunistic scavengers.

Schmitt's argument now comes to its decisive point. What happens in this situation of opportunism that benefits only the individualized subject? The destruction of all values in the name of the aestheticization of life. Aestheticization, then, implies converting the world into a vast field of operations for the exclusive enjoyment of the self, into an altar for a private priesthood. The aestheticization of the world is then the basic consequence, the last avatar of bourgeois democracy. Schmitt puts it quite bluntly: "Romanticism transposed intellectual productivity into the domain of the aesthetic, into art and art criticism; and then, on the basis of the aesthetic, it comprehended all other domains. . . . An absolutization of art is proclaimed. A universal art is demanded, and everything that is intellectual, religion, the Church, the nation, and the state, flows into the stream that has its source in the new center, the aesthetic" (p. 15).

And, like a sorcerer who turns against his own magic, aestheticization not only reduces all to art but, still unsatisfied, directs its voracity against itself and thus self-destructs. This does not occur by chance: aestheticization does not favor any type of object; it would be a mistake to suppose that it still privileges art; it is part of its own essence to be opposed to any objectification. "Art is absolutized, but at the same time it is rendered problematic. It is taken in an absolute sense, but quite without the obligation to achieve a grand and strict form or manifestation. . . . The new art is an art without works, at least without works in a grand style, an art without publicity [*Publizität*] and without representation" (p. 15).

Whereas in the late eighteenth century Kant optimistically believed that the critique of the unitary view of classical metaphysics was a precondition for man's maturity, in the early twentieth century the self-complacency of subjectivity showed that the world had turned into an object of plunder. A product of the process of secularization, the emancipation of the self had turned into a god more avid than any of the bloodthirsty gods of ancient civilizations. The diagnosis, motivated by the situation of the patient, European civilization, which had already been ravished by the Great War, indirectly sought to avoid the bigger catastrophe. (Ironically enough, Schmitt was to collaborate with the greatest of the catastrophes that were to come.)

In a recent analysis of *Political Romanticism*, K. H. Bohrer observes that Schmitt's analysis dovetails into Hegel's attack on romantic subjectivity,

which accuses it of being vacant and of forgetting objectivity, and into Kierkegaard's criticisms. Schmitt's objections, then, have illustrious predecessors
and cannot be accused of being eccentric or idiosyncratic. It would be even
less reasonable to cast suspicion on their validity on account of the author's
later political preferences. But neither an examination of the convergence nor
an emphasis on this suspicion would be of much help. Instead, it is more
relevant to repeat that "his attack was aimed at romanticism as a paradigm of
modernity" (Bohrer 1989: 288).

Indeed, what is in question is the legitimation of modernity. Romanticism, as a metonymy of modern times, fabricates a world "without a definition, without a decision, without a last court of appeal." It inaugurates a
world unsupported by a substantiality that, expressed by norms, could ensure
its stability; a world, in short, without foundations for the invocation of the
Law. We have seen that this razzia proceeded through an aestheticization that
spared nothing, not even art. And here we may begin to understand why the
author's position could not be interpreted as a preparation for his later ad-
vocacy of Nazism. The decisive argument here is in the passage, already
transcribed, in which Schmitt justifies his attack on Romantic art because of
its nonrepresentational character: "subjectivized occasionalism" was so extreme that Romantic art dispensed not only with the requirement of style but
also with that of representation. But what did the term mean to Schmitt?
"To Schmitt, 'representational' means that great art does not project a self-
sufficient phantom, but instead signifies the reflection [*Widerspiegelung*] of
positive contents. Thus Schmitt's fundamental aesthetic convictions are the
same as Hegel's or Lukács's, and, it should be added, as the approach to
aesthetics and literature that sociology and historiography still adopt to this
very day" (Bohrer 1989: 292).

To the traditional concept of representation,[6] the productive character of
art, to which the early German romantics gave so much emphasis, was repug-
nant. In turn, the concept is affirmed by all those who, irrespective of their
political positions, have a conservative view of art. By denying its productive

6. By using the concept "traditional" I implicitly suggest that my position should not be
confused with one or another variety of contemporary textualism, which starts from the
assumption that the category of representation is inextricably associated with the more
obtuse notion of "referent." I believe, on the contrary, that the referent cannot be identified with a materiality that projects itself and determines the meaning of the sign, but
should instead be seen as a discursive effect—in Foucault's term, "the correlate of the
statement" (see Costa-Lima 1989: 87); likewise, representation is not "the reflection of
positive contents" but rather the effect evoked in the receiver by the interaction between
his value expectations and a particular work. It is on the basis of these notions that I have
found it possible and even desirable to revive an understanding of mimesis (see Costa-Lima
1980).

ability they become its controllers. In contrast, the early German romantics were the first to make possible a theorization of the relation between art and society.

Although I agree with Bohrer's criticism of the concept of representation underlying Schmitt's attack on the romantic conception of art to such a degree that I incorporate it into my own argument, this does not mean I deny that Schmitt's thesis is highly penetrating. Whereas those—historians and sociologists in general—who share his assumption are content to privilege those works of art in which they can find a repetition of what they already know or could know about the society that produced them, Schmitt presents a sharp formulation of the question of aestheticism: "It is only in an individualistically disaggregated society that the aesthetically productive subject could shift the intellectual center into itself, only in a bourgeois world that intellectually isolates the individual in the domain of the intellectual, makes its own point of reference, and imposes upon it the entire burden that otherwise was hierarchically divided among different functions" (Schmitt 1986: 20). Unlike Bohrer, who categorically rejects Schmitt's theses, from my own standpoint I find it important to stress what is fruitful and apt in them. However, I must make two rectifications concerning (1) Schmitt's conception of the role of the individual subject in Romanticism and (2) his rejection of the Romantic legacy.

As to (1), we have already mentioned the purely metaphorical character that the "modern demiurges"—humanity and History—take on for Schmitt. To consider them as metaphors is to treat as enigmatic the relation between the centrality of the individual subject and the primacy of science in modernity. A far larger step is taken by Schmitt's later "fellow traveler," Martin Heidegger: "Clearly, as a consequence of man's liberation, modern times have led to subjectivism and individualism. But it is no less clear that no earlier epoch produced a comparable objectivism, and that in no earlier epoch did the nonindividual impose itself as the collective. The essential thing here is the necessary reciprocity between subjectivism and objectivism" (Heidegger 1972: 81).

In addition, if it does not seem sufficient to end the discussion with the statement of this necessary reciprocity—"the more objective the object, the more subjective—that is, the more imperative—the subject" (p. 81)—we shall later see both aspects as parallel consequences of a term that encompasses both: the self-finality of work in modernity, which distinguishes modern society from all earlier forms:

> In the commodity-producing system of modern times . . . the logic of need has been inverted: as the forces of production, through industrialization and scien-

tism, defeat the coercion and power of "first nature," they coalesce in a second-ary, unconscious, socially produced coercion. The form of reproduction of goods is converted into "second nature," the need for which is placed before individuals in such a blind and demanding way as those of "first nature," al-though their origin was purely social. (Kurz 1991: 16)

Let us examine point (2). Although Schmitt's absolute rejection of Ro-manticism is, to say the least, simplistic, without his analysis of the phenome-non of aestheticization one of the keys to understanding the modern scene would have been lost. We have seen that aestheticization is one of the terms of the ambiguity we found in Kant's appreciation of the aesthetic experience. We are almost ready to examine its consequences. But as we reach the end of this last preparatory section, it should be remembered that aestheticization— the reduction of all values to the aesthetic and the subsumption of the aes-thetic into the receiver's intellectual delight—is not restricted to the romantic age.[7] For instance, the following passage does not refer to Romanticism:

> The classic tradition of *theatrum mundi* [theater of the world] equated society with theater, everyday action with acting. This tradition thus couched social life in aesthetic terms, and treated all men as artists because all men can act. The difficulty with this imagery is that it is ahistorical. The whole history of public culture of the 19th Century was of people who were gradually losing a belief in their own expressive power, who on the contrary elevated the artist as someone who was special because he could do what ordinary people could not do in everyday life. (Sennett 1978: 266)

Although he does not use the term, Sennett is referring to the aestheticization of public life in the nineteenth century.

Thus, things would be easier if we could stigmatize Schmitt's thesis by arguing that totalitarianism is always manifested wherever the prevailing thought denies the productive ability of a certain area of knowledge. Even if this is true, still the conclusion is too generic to be effective. Yet it would be ludicrous to seek support in a decontextualized passage. The reference to Sennett intends to do no more than point to an indication of the presence of a phenomenon the implications of which should be shown by an examination of the reflections on art that followed the reception of *CJ*. In this context, the reflection on Schmitt's book deepens our understanding of the historico-intellectual scene made up of Kant and his reading by Schiller, Novalis, and Friedrich Schlegel.

---

7. For reasons of space, we cannot here fully explore the implications of the following observation: considering that, in the passage just quoted, Kurz uses the Marxist concept of the fetishism of commodities, it might then be associated with the problem of aestheticiza-tion. This approach has yet to be explored.

Schiller and the Aestheticization of Art

In addition to the aesthetic ideals that separated them, there was a strong personal antipathy between Schiller and Schlegel. Nevertheless, in spite of the double moat that lay between them, they shared certain intellectual interests. Both were admirers of Greece, and both founded their reflections on historico-philosophical bases. And these two points of contact motivated the direction they followed in their reflections.

Greece is mythically envisaged by Schiller and Schlegel as the place of wholeness, the time when the gods were close to human disputes and served as mirrors and companions to men. In contrast, they see the modern experience as a time of want. That is why, as Szondi notes, "by Schiller's time *sentimental* poetry could already be considered *progressive*" (Szondi 1978: 95). That is, between the categories created by each of the essayists—sentimental and progressive poetry, respectively—there was a deep-seated correspondence, a consequence of the fact that they could only be applied to a period marked by absence and search: the contemporary period. Their exclusion of the ancient world made clear the philosophy of history practiced by both authors: it assumed a process at a point of which wholeness had been lost, just as the promise of a new unity began to take shape. At the eve of the emergence of Hegelianism, the system of thought in which this promise was to be announced most loftily, the seeds of teleology were already sprouting in the reflections of Schiller and Schlegel. As H. R. Jauss has demonstrated, if their common basis had been established by their enthusiasm over Greece, it acquired a specific inflection with the stands taken by the two authors in a debate that had begun in the Renaissance and had come to a close in the early eighteenth century, in France: the "quarrel of the ancients and the moderns."

In the beginning, Italian humanists considered the ancient writers superior to the moderns, both in the field of letters and in that of philosophical investigation. This evaluation was reversed by Charles Perrault, in a preface that begins with the statement that the just feelings of love and respect for the ancients had become, in time, a "criminal superstition that has sometimes reached the point of idolatry" (Perrault 1964: i–ii). The signs are inverted, and the moderns are seen as the truly excellent.

Let us examine the consequences of this in metropolitan France and provincial Germany. An example of the former is "De l'origine des fables" [On the origin of fables], by Bernard Fontenelle, a minor Enlightenment figure. To him, antiquity no longer meant the ancestors, as it still did, not long before, to Perrault, but rather the first centuries that make up "l'ancienne Histoire d'un Peuple, qui n'est qu'amas de chimères, de rêveries, &

d'absurdités" (the ancient history of a people, which is no more than a heap of chimeras, fancies, and absurdities) (Fontenelle 1742: 270). Fables contain the legacy of these primitive times. They are full of marvelous events because the imagination is not content to "laisser une belle chose imparfaite" (leave a beautiful thing imperfect) (p. 272). In short, they are false and deceitful narratives, either because the authors' reason was feeble or because they were written in bad faith. In metropolitan France, as Fontenelle's words imply, the praise of the moderns anticipated the idea of time as progress.

Fifty years later in Germany, the reception of the debate was quite different. The present was experienced as absence, and the modern poet's effort aimed to overcome it. The idea of progress was there as well, but in an indirect way: the present in itself was not an advance, but a need to overcome.

There is, then, a sharp difference between the two readings of modernity; just as significant, however, is the fact that both start from the awareness that "the works of the ancients and the moderns ought to be evaluated as products of different historical periods, and therefore in accordance with a relative standard of beauty, rather than with an absolute concept of perfection" (Jauss 1970: 71).

The issue of modernity, then, was not a merely German problem, nor did it simply amount to a controversy regarding the excellence of each nation. Rather, it had to do with the way contemporary writers conceived of their own temporality. Within it, however, there began to take shape the idea of progress, of evolution, which was to give it a distinct direction: whereas the German approach, in which the principle of progress is present only in an incipient way, assumed that one's sight was restricted to one's own immediate time, to the concrete appreciation of the works of the present, the other, evolutionary-oriented approach, saw individual works as representatives of a phase, abstracting them, taking them as instances of a supposedly progressive trajectory. This observation is only a rough outline of what was to take place in the early decades of the nineteenth century, under the sway of literary history. But at the time we are concerned with—the period from the 1780's to the beginning of the following century—what interested essayists was the direct, punctual contact with actuality. Let us see how this took place.

In Schiller's case, we are interested solely in two essays written in 1795: *Letters on the Aesthetic Education of Man* (*Briefe über die ästhetische Erziehung des Menschen*, henceforth referred to as *Letters*) and *On Naive and Sentimental Poetry* (*Über naive und sentimentalische Dichtung*, or *NSP*).

The *Letters* are set in contemporary society. The author's intent is not to describe it or express his approval or disapproval; instead, he wants to compare it with the unchanging model of Greece. In particular, in letter 6 he expounds on the disadvantages of life in the present. In antiquity the individual "received his forms from nature, which unites everything," whereas the modern individual "gets them from reason, which separates everything." "The accumulated experience and the more precise thought," together with the appearance of the state, "making it necessary to delimit the estates and business," have the combined effect of moving man away from his natural harmony (Schiller 1989: 19–20). Instead of consonance and harmony, the central metaphor for the modern situation is the machine, in which the individual occupies himself with a minute part and loses sight of the whole. "Even this feeble and fragmentary participation, however, which still joins the isolated parts to the whole, does not depend on forms that are given spontaneously . . . but rather is prescribed with scrupulous severity in a formula that imprisons its freedom of vision. The dead letter replaces the living understanding; the well-trained memory is a safer guide than genius and sensibility" (p. 21).

What was previously animal satisfaction, interaction between the individual and nature, is progressively transformed into "abstract totality," both from the viewpoint of the ruler and from that of the subject's experience. Before this totality that sucks him in without his being aware of it, man reacts by activating his reason; "to this extent he has inevitably become a stranger in the sensible world, losing matter for form" (p. 22). Or else he shuts himself off in the world of business and, hoarding the particular, becomes alienated from the whole. In neither case does the remedy provide a cure. The thinker is left with a cold heart; the professional, with a narrow soul.

The two situations described, represented respectively by the polyp of the Greek city-states and by the centralizing machinery of the modern state, correspond to two modalities of state organization: one natural, the other deriving from necessity. The better to understand the correspondence between the *Letters* and *NSP*, and thus to see how both are part of the same project, it should be observed that Schiller's intention was not to project for the future something like the natural modality. The natural state, "as we may call every body politic originally set up by forces rather than by laws" (p. 9), satisfies only the physical side of man, leaving moral reason idle. Apparently Schiller believed that, under the empire of the natural state, man had no need to develop his reason, but reason became increasingly important as the complexity of society threatened to destroy the primitive idyllic relation with nature. The *Letters* do not discuss this transition, but content themselves with visualizing the second situation: "He is awakened from his sensible torpor, recognizes himself as a man, looks around and finds himself in the state. There he has been thrown by the empire of necessity" (p. 8).

The counterposition between nature and reason associates reason with two other concepts: freedom and morals. Like Kant, Schiller sees them as an indissoluble pair. Man, now awakened, under the yoke of a state created for him by necessity, tries to conceive the state in accordance with a project of freedom and with the plane of morals. With freedom "he recovers his childhood in his maturity, forming the idea of a *natural state* that is not given him in experience, but rather is seen as necessary by his rational determination" (p. 8). The verb "recover" (*nachholen*) here may be mistakenly understood as the actual recapture of an earlier time in the time sought. That this is not Schiller's plan is made clear in the passage in which he formulates the demand of the moral plane. To clarify the passage, we transcribe the sentence that precedes it as well. "Physical man, however, is *real*, whereas moral man is only *problematic*. If, then, reason denies the natural state to replace it with its own, as it must, it confronts the existence of society with its merely possible (even if morally necessary) ideal" (p. 9).

In brief, the contrast between the Greek experience and the modern provides Schiller with a simple set of oppositions: natural state versus state of necessity; nature versus reason; plus an implication: reason → freedom and morals. On the basis of this framework, he projects a third modality: the moral state. It is clearly an ideal, only possible, state and thus the correlate of the progressive poetry postulated by Schlegel. Neither of them will ever be fully actualized. But this is all the more reason for both ideals to be pursued.

Schiller's moral state is a permanent utopia, never to be fully attained, which imposes a task that never despairs of itself, an unending task. Only by identifying with this ideal can the state overcome its modern stage and act "as the representative of humanity pure and objective among its citizens" (p. 13). If this goal is to be conceivable, however, the citizen must not only strive to reach it but also accomplish his own transformation. This is what Schiller says in the passage immediately following the one quoted earlier: "To act as the representative of humanity pure and objective among its citizens, the state must be in relation to them as they are to themselves, and can only respect their subjective humanity to the extent as it is elevated to objectivity" (p. 14). The state can only serve its citizens if their subjectivity is explicitly manifested, rather than preserved or concealed. And this can only occur if their subjectivity necessarily does not contain restrictions or contents contrary to the order of the state. Otherwise this manifestation would generate a climate of criticity, which, as we shall see, Schiller sees as a negative development.

This conclusion we are drawing anticipates an idea of great importance to the present chapter. Let us examine its place in the context of Schiller's general argument.

We know that his objective was not the return to the natural condition of humanity, but rather the construction of a topos—even if it could never be more than a u-topos—in which nature were reconciled with the exercise of freedom. But we do not yet know how Schiller intended to do this.

Schiller's proposal necessarily involved the experience of art—more explicitly, the politicizing of art. This, however, had to be done so as to satisfy the requirement just mentioned: to objectify—to bring down to the plane of the communicable—what was in the spirit of the citizen. Now, considering Schiller's strong attachment to Kant's lesson, we may ask: How could this be possible without damaging the mute universality that, as we have seen, was contained in the Kantian formulation of aesthetic experience? In fact, if we take into account the need for explicit expression, on the one hand, and mute universality, on the other, the clash is inevitable. We have seen that this universality means that each receiver may presume that his or her experience of the beautiful is so free of particularized interests that it can be reenacted in any other receiver, as long as this receiver is also free of pragmatic objectives. The experience is mute because any "justification" of the fact that this particular object seems beautiful would convert the experience into the proposition of a norm, which could only be justified if it were part of legislation or the understanding or practical reason. So how can Schiller defend his argument and at the same time preserve his emphatic faithfulness to Kant?

The difficult conciliation is attempted by the aesthetic education proposed in the *Letters*. This aesthetic education assumes the conciliation of the sensible and formal impulses. The former aims to "make real the necessary that lies in us"; the latter, to "submit the reality *outside* us to the law of necessity" (p. 45). Through them, man's sensible and rational natures oppose each other. But the task of harmonizing them does not seem impossible to Schiller.

To achieve this, he converts the free play of the Kantian experience of the beautiful into an impulse, the play impulse: "The sensible impulse wants change, wants time to have a content; the formal impulse wants to deny time so that there is no change. The impulse in which the two are conjoined . . . , the play impulse [*Spieltrieb*], then, aspires to overcome time in time and combine becoming with the absolute being, identity with change" (p. 57). Only the play impulse constitutes its object for beauty, the "living figure" that is presented as beautiful to man as it harmonizes its disparate impulses. Being a "living figure" means that an object is simultaneously received and respected by our sensation and our understanding. Thus, for instance, as long as we simply *think* about the figure of a man, "he is inert, mere abstraction," and "as long as we only *feel* his life, it is formless, pure impression" (p. 59), so that the conciliation of opposites can be reached solely by means of a work that sets the play impulse in motion. This impulse, then, does not depend on a communication—"this object is beautiful because . . ."—which, in Kantian terms, would destroy the aesthetic experience as such.

Does this mean that the play impulse, which seemed so promising to Schiller, is homologous to what Kant had already formulated? Of course not: Schiller presupposes an aesthetic education, whereas the Kant of the three *Critiques* had no pedagogic pretensions. But to say this is not enough to define the specificity of Schiller's position. Let us attempt to grasp it by considering the predictable relations between the proposed education and the state.

One might have the impression that such a pedagogic process simply assumes that the authorities will diligently pursue a kind of education that will make citizens more appreciative of the beautiful. But this would be to underestimate the author and the reader. The key to a correct understanding of Schiller's position can be found, again, in his comment in letter 4. Let us examine the question further.

The point is to relate the actualization of the play impulse with the indispensable manifestation of the subjective contents of the citizens of the state. The decisive passage is in letter 10. Though an ardent admirer of the Greeks, Schiller does not go as far as to take a Greek model for his proposed state. On the contrary, Greece is included in the following generalization about antiquity: "On whatever point in the past our eyes may fix themselves, they will find that taste and freedom flee from each other [*Geschmack und Freiheit einander fliehen*], and that beauty establishes its empire only at the twilight [*Untergang*] of heroic virtues" (p. 40). Thus, the example of the past should be seen as something to be avoided; the stories of defeated civilizations are cautionary tales that should be considered so that their mistakes may be avoided. For this, it is necessary that the poet himself be educated—that is, that the principles of aesthetic education apply to him as well. Only this way can we avoid repeating what the ancients proudly flaunt: "So many feeble understandings clashed with the social organization solely because the poet's fancy was pleased to erect a world in which everything is otherwise. . . . What a dangerous dialectic is taught to the passions when poets depict them in brilliant hues, struggling against and defeating the laws and duties!" (p. 38).

Clearly, Schiller strongly disapproves of poets past and present when they use their power to question laws. This could only be taken to mean that he sees criticity as intrinsically evil. Thus, it is by discarding the critical spirit that aesthetic education could be seen as favorable to the building of the total state, the aesthetic state. This raises the question: In so doing, does Schiller remain faithful to Kant's thought? At first glance, the question seems preposterous, since it is precisely criticity that is seen as harmful. But it is surely no accident that, with the exception of this admittedly crucial step, the entire essay follows a Kantian line. One need only consider the passage in *CJ* about the free play between imagination and understanding and Schiller's characterization of the play impulse as satisfying both sensation and understanding. So even if Schiller parts company with Kant when he excludes criticity from his aesthetic education, for the rest he closely follows the Kantian model.

But this solution is still not satisfactory: it "salvages" Schiller's "originality" through his unfaithfulness to his model. We can arrive at a better result when we take into account the ambiguity of Kant's aesthetic experience, which has been discussed above: Schiller's exclusion of criticity is only an explicit formulation of one of the possible readings of Kant. The result is not arbitrary, since the source itself allows it. Now we can see that the *Letters* support our earlier observation that Kant's aesthetic experience is ambiguous; that his criticism is internally refuted by the aestheticization that commentators tend to overlook. Even if Schiller's essay were not important for other reasons, it would merit attention for bringing this fact to light. But at the beginning of this discussion we said that the *Letters* should be examined together with the essay Schiller published in the same year. Let us see how this second text supports our interpretation of the first.

At first, it may seem that there is little possibility of learning anything from a comparison of the two. In *NSP*, the Utopian political design is missing entirely; the text concentrates on developing a typology of the artist and his works. Marquard, in a study already mentioned, sees this as a clear indication that the emphasis on aesthetics corresponded to modern reason's acknowledgment of its own impotence. The concentration on the aesthetic as a compensatory activity is then a correlate of the collapse of Enlightenment optimism. Schiller sets out to study "the role of the artist and of art, no longer in relation to the state, but to nature. . . . In this way the Romantic position is fundamentally reached" (Marquard 1962: 373). Through a different path than Schmitt's, Marquard arrives at a similar result: Romantic political thought is irresponsible in relation to the world, either because it is hostile to causal explanations (Schmitt) or because it despairs of understanding and conducting the historical process (Marquard).

Though it is not our contention that there is any agreement, however minimal, between the political projects of the two interpreters—Marquard's essay seems to be inspired by a somewhat leftist Hegelianism—one might say that, on the basis of his argument, the following statement may be formulated: The romantics founded their aestheticism on the feeling, which Schiller manifests explicitly in the two essays under discussion, that the study of History cannot be subjected to a rational plan—that is, to laws.

If adopted, this conclusion would have the advantage of sparing us a fuller examination of *NSP*, for from the outset it would be established that it indeed reinforces the thesis of the *Letters*. If in the *Letters*, inspired by the search for the constitution of a good state, aestheticization was already the proposed instrument to reach the desired end, why bother with the meaning of an analysis that was clearly "formalistic"? But one should beware of the errors induced by supposedly evident conclusions.

The reader may get around some of the difficulties posed by *NSP* if he or she takes into account an elementary fact: the essay appeared as a structured whole only in the 1800 edition of Schiller's works. Originally, its parts were three separate articles, which came out between 1795 and 1796 (see Suzuki 1991, p. 9). Knowledge of this fact makes it easier to understand the contradictions that involve the conceptualization of the pair naive-sentimental.[8] This is not the place to examine them; let us simply take them as indication of a gnosiological work in progress (Szondi's concept; see Szondi 1978: 74) and explore their reach.

In spite of the conceptual oscillations, the distinction between the naive and the sentimental presupposes an awareness of the difference between antiquity and modernity—or rather, of the relation between either and nature. This differential relationship is the first characteristic that should be underscored: the naive and the sentimental imply unmistakable feelings towards nature. Thus, for the ancient Greeks "the entire edifice of their social life was built on sensations, not on a badly finished work of art; even their mythology was the inspiration of a naive feeling, the offspring of a jovial imagination, not of a self-absorbed reason, as is the church faith of modern nations" (Schiller 1978: 24); to modern man, instead, "nature little by little vanished from human existence as *experience* and as *subject* (agent and patient); thus we see it appear in the poetic world as *idea* and *object*" (p. 25).

The distinction Schiller establishes assumes that the Greek experience sprang from a feeling of inclusiveness, whereas that of modern man arises from a feeling of separateness. Hence there are two types of poet: "They either *are* nature or *search* for lost nature" (pp. 25–26). A feeling of inclusiveness here means "that the object which inspires him is *nature*, or at least is considered as such by us" (p. 3), and that nature, in turn, is taken as "the spontaneous existence [*das freiwillige Dasein*], the subsistence of things in themselves, existence [*Existenz*] according to its own unchanging laws" (p. 3).

8. Here is Szondi's summary of the question: "Considered partly as a simple counterpoint of the *naive*, which is attributed to genius only, later also as a possibility for poetry, which is perfectly consistent with the naive, in other passages the *sentimental* is recognized 'under the conditionings of reflection,' as the *naive* itself" (Szondi 1978: 103).

It should be added that, for Schiller, this differential relation to nature did not aim at an aesthetic experience, nor was it oriented by an experimental purpose: "This kind of enjoyment of nature is not aesthetic, but moral; for it is mediated by an Idea, and not immediately begotten by observation" (p. 4). For this very reason, he believes that "nature is in contrast to art and shames it" (p. 3). In itself, the sphere of art is that of artifice, of the merely human, of what is necessarily cut off from its ambience and shown to be separate and imperfect.

The handful of passages just quoted characterize the two members of the pair of concepts that are the central theme of the essay. Wholeness versus want, inclusion versus separateness—these are the contrasting traits. These two concepts, however, imply a third that is no less important: subjectivity. After quoting a passage from Homer—Glaucus and Diomedes interrupt their fight and promise to spare each other in future combats because the latter has told the former about their ties of kinship—the author comments: "A *modern* poet . . . could hardly have waited this far to manifest his joy for such an action. And we should easily forgive him, all the more because our own heart would pause as we read and would willingly *distance itself from the object in order to look into itself*" (p. 29; emphasis added in the second instance).

One clearly perceives the absence and presence of subjectivity in the two epochs; and this is the reason why naive poets see themselves as an integral part of nature whereas modern poets feel pierced by the spear of loneliness. Although Schiller himself does not seem to notice this, the passage captures the essential difference between the ways of experiencing subjectivity. The ancient mode is constituted on the basis of the community and therefore implies the absorption of individuality into a group. Hence the familiarity that characterizes its experience of nature is derived. By contrast, the breaking of this bond is revealed by our modern urge to convert whatever we see into an object of our inner sight. So it is that we observe nature with the curiosity of those who know objects are strange, experiencing them by means of a reorienting introspection.

So far we have been able to follow the argument of the essay avoiding its conceptual duplicity (see note 8 to this chapter). We have adopted this strategy the better to determine the field where the typology belongs. The question now must be raised whether this is the strictly historical field. If indeed this is our first impression, in order to corroborate it we must excise whole passages from the essay. Some of them are clearly of secondary importance; for instance: "We find naive a man without knowledge of the world, but otherwise endowed with good understanding, who tells his secret to another, and by his own sincerity provides the means with which the latter . . . can do him harm" (p. 13). Another example is his identification of naiveté with the child's condition. But even here it will be seen that the sense in which the central term is being taken is by no means historical. Further, the same ahistorical sense is involved in Schiller's consideration of genius:

> Every true genius must be naive, else he is no genius [Naiv muß jedes wahre Genie sein, oder es ist keines]. It is solely his naiveté that makes him a genius. . . . Only to the genius is it given to be ever at home outside of what is known and *expand* nature without *going beyond* it. True, even the greatest geniuses at times go beyond it, but only because they also have their fantastic moments [ihre phantastischen Augenblicke] in which protecting nature abandons them, either because they are carried away by the power of example or because they are led astray by the corrupted taste of their age. (pp. 15–16)

Ever since the *Letters*, Schiller had been stressing the arbitrariness of evaluating the production of the two different eras by the same standard. Should we conclude that now he was contradicting himself and, seeing genius as the privilege of the ancients, affirming the inferiority of contemporary works? Such a conclusion would be absurd; it fails to take into account that "naive" in the passage is not used in a historical sense. Granted, the emphatic statement quoted above coexists with Schiller's later assertion that there are two types of genius, which—most curiously—seems to imply that the naive genius is the lesser:

> I called naive poetry a *favor of nature* in order to recall that reflection has no hand in it whatsoever. It is a stroke of luck: if successful, it needs no perfecting of any kind; however, if it fails, no improvement is possible. The work of the naive genius is wholly contained in sensibility; here lie its strength and its limit. Therefore if the *feeling* has not been immediately poetic—that is, perfectly human—this defect cannot be corrected by any art. (p. 390)

The limit of the naive genius can be grasped in contrast with the opposite kind: "Thus the naive genius is dependent on experience in a way that the sentimental genius is not. . . . The strength of the latter consists . . . in transporting himself by his own power from a limited state to a state of freedom" (p. 77). Both derive from the same starting point, wholeness or want, which had also provided the basis for the initial characterization. We should then understand that this point remains valid and that to either of its types there corresponds one type of genius.

Does this imply that these types are of a historical order? If we consider only the last-quoted passage, the answer is clearly yes. But in order to accept this affirmative answer, we must disregard the two preceding passages, or explain them away as the consequences of the essayist's lack of terminological rigor, since he has no pretensions to being a philosopher. If we wish to avoid such a lame excuse, we must accept the fact that Schiller's concepts are indeed contradictory; his historical intention is evident, but he wavers between this and a psychological definition. To use his own terms, ancients and moderns are said to contrast both in terms of "difference of time" (*Unterschied der Zeit*) and of "difference of manner" (*Unterschied der Manier*) (p. 77 n). The distinction thus involves a typology seen sometimes as historical, sometimes as defining the author's personality.

The traditional biographical interpretation according to which the essay is a sort of allegory of the differences Schiller felt between himself and Goethe, taken as the prototypical naive genius (see Wilkinson and Willoughby's introduction to Schiller 1967, esp. p. xxxix), turns *NSP* into a mere rationalization. But the frank acknowledgment of its flagrant ambiguity allows the interpreter to concede that, for all its flaws, the essay remains a relevant work. However, it is important to point out that *NSP* turns on three, not two, concepts. This becomes clear in a passage that is apparently a mere recapitulation.

> Once man has entered the state of culture and art has laid her hand on him, then *sensible* harmony is suppressed, and he can only manifest himself as a *moral* unit—that is, striving for unity. The harmony between his thought and feeling, which in the previous state existed *in fact*, now exists only *ideally*. . . . If, then, we apply to the two states the concept of poetry, which is none other than *giving humanity its most complete expression possible*, the result is that, in the state of natural simplicity, in which man still acts simultaneously with all his strength as a harmonic unit . . . *what must constitute the poet is the imitation*, as complete as possible, *of the real*—which, on the contrary, in the state of culture, where acting in harmonic concert with all of nature is no more than an Idea, *what must constitute the poet is the elevation of reality to the Ideal*. . . . And these, too, are the two only possible ways in which the poetic genius can usually manifest itself. *They are, as one may see, extremely different one from the other, but there is a higher concept that comprises them both, and it should cause no surprise to learn that this concept coincides with the idea of humanity*. (pp. 31–32; emphases added)

This lengthy passage, in addition to reiterating what has been said before, also presents the common measure that permits a comparison between the naive and the sentimental. This common measure is the "idea of humanity" (on this, see Suzuki 1991, p. 39). But this clarification remains unsatisfactory, for one might construe this idea of humanity as a mere logical constant in which the contrasted concepts overlap and interconnect. Schiller found a more felicitous formulation in a letter he wrote to Wilhelm von Humboldt on December 25, 1795: "Sentimental poetry is surely *conditio sine qua non* of the poetic ideal, but it is also an external obstacle to it" (quoted in Szondi 1978: 99). Since it originated in a time when man was no longer integrated to nature, sentimental poetry is moved by an ideal that, nevertheless, is not actualized; in fact, its actualization is delayed by it. It would then be false to take the "idea of humanity" as a simple logical constancy. Rather, the pair of opposites is in fact a triad, whose third term, the ideal (of a humanity made whole) retrospectively illuminates and gives meaning to the opposed terms.

The conversion of the bipolarity into a triad changes the interpretation of the essay entirely. It affects nothing less than its very significance in the history of the theoretical consideration of literature. Indeed, if we consider only the polarity, we tend to take its terms to refer to a discussion that has long become obsolete; Schiller's work may then be seen as of interest only to historians of literary theory. But now the situation is different. And the decisive argument is given in Szondi's analysis.

Szondi compares the triad with the beginning of Kant's second observation on the table of categories: "In view of the fact that all *a priori* division of concepts must be by dichotomy, it is significant that in each class the number of categories is always the same, namely, three. Further, it may be observed that the third category in each class always arises from the combination of the second category with the first" (Kant 1965: 116; B 110). We transcribe this passage to underscore the acuteness of Szondi's observation: according to him, the passage "virtually contains dialectic in the Hegelian, not Kantian, sense" (Szondi 1978: 100), for Kant himself could not explore it, on account of the matrix on which his thought was based: "The dialectic contained in the triadic principle of his table of categories, as a historical dialectic, could not possibly be utilized in the frame of Kantian gnosiology, which followed the orientation of the ahistorical natural sciences" (p. 101). It was Schiller who had the merit of "applying Kant's thesis to history . . . , thus founding a speculative historical philosophy" (p. 101).

From the vantage point of the present chapter, Szondi's conclusion is most important, since it demonstrates that the formal consideration of the poet and poetry was moved by the same historico–philosophical purpose that is evident in the *Letters*. To realize this, one need only compare the triad of the *Letters* with what Szondi's analytical genius made us see. The same role played by the ideal state in the first triad is in the charge of the Ideal in the second. Each saves the description of modernity from nostalgia for the lost wholeness of antiquity. Each impels its respective author—philosopher and poet—to equally infinite tasks.

However, the perfect match between the two triads will lead to another result, one that is not based on Szondi. From the analysis of the first triad we have drawn a conclusion that can now be reinforced: we have seen that the aesthetic education proposed implied an extreme actualization of aestheticism and the abandonment of critical virtuality; that the emphasis on the former and the ban on the latter made more visible a duplicity in Kant's account of aesthetic experience. Now, if the match between the two triads is to be perfect, this same result must be reached again. But how can this be done without arbitrariness, if in *NSP* there are no allusions to the ideal state and the instrument that was to promote it?

The task is not an impossible one if we focus on the consequences of aestheticization. Its most conspicuous and most often repeated effect is clearly the dissolution of all other values. As far as we know, Carl Schmitt was the first to point this out. More recently, Jürgen Habermas made the same point, though denying that the same reduction occurs in Schiller, because Schiller did no violence to "the independent logics of the value spheres of science, morality, and art" (Habermas 1987: 50). (But this defense is too superficial: the ideal state could recognize the autonomy of other spheres of value, if only because aesthetic education would have already taught students its correct— aesthetic, not critical—use.) By now, however, we are able to perceive that aestheticization has an additional effect: it affects the production of art. Let us return to the end of a passage quoted before: "True, even the greatest geniuses at times go beyond it, but only because they also have their fantastic moments in which protecting nature abandons them" (Schiller 1978: 15–16). The argument that genius actualizes a virtuality of nature had already been formulated in the eighteenth century by Diderot and Kant. Schiller, however, does more than repeat a topos. Geniuses can now be criticized when they overstep their limits, go beyond nature and suffer themselves to be guided by "their fantastic moments."

Two short passages from Kant's "Analytic of the Beautiful" will help us understand the scope of this restriction. Discussing the productive and spontaneous character played by image in the judgment of taste, Kant observes that, nevertheless, it "does not enjoy free play (as it does in poetry)" (Kant 1982a: 86; B 69). Then, discussing the "free play of the powers of representation"— that is, the experience of the beautiful—he makes the parenthetical comment that this takes place "subject, however, to the condition that there is to be nothing for understanding to take exception to" (doch unter der Bedingung, daß der Verstand keinen Anstoß leide) (p. 88; B 71). That is, to Kant there is a limit within which the productive activation of the imagination is permitted; beyond that, as is the case in poetry, its exercise would be an affront (*Anstoß*) to the understanding.

What Kant believed to take place naturally in the experience of the beautiful occurs, according to Schiller, in the very production of the work of art: even the genius has his "fantastic moments"—that is, even he may be led astray, as the rest of the passage goes on to add, by the corrupted taste of his time. Is this not the case of those poets of the past criticized in the *Letters* because their fantasy led them to create worlds in which everything happens in a different way?

The comparison between the passages quoted above brings to light an effect of aestheticization that is only rarely noticed: it implies the exercise of a control on imagination itself, both that of the producer (as Schiller stresses) and that of the receiver (as Kant only hints). In focusing on this second effect, more than merely confirming the absolute consistency of Schiller's two essays, we verify the convergence between aestheticization and the control of the imaginary. We say "of the imaginary" rather than "of imagination" only because the latter, being individual, is like the *parole* in which the imaginary is actualized. Thus, the control of the individualized can be effective only if it extends to its source.

The reader who is familiar with my earlier works on the control of the imaginary will understand the extreme importance of this aspect of aestheticization to our continuing investigation.

For this very reason, we should make another observation at this point: aestheticization is not only intimately connected with control but also modifies its form somewhat. It changes the control of the imaginary as such into something more specific: a ban on the fictional—that is, the product of the imaginary par excellence, made up of words. Reason discovers, as it were, that its enemy is not exactly the power to imagine, but rather its actualization in a product that describes itself as fictional. Just as at the beginning of modern times Renaissance poetics was the basic instrument of control, in modernity literary history and criticism are the basic enforcers of the veto of the fictional. Their effectiveness proved exemplary: though literature was an expected social accomplishment of educated eighteenth-century men, its identification with fictionality remained covert. The prestige of literature, through systematic history and critical pragmatics, was established behind a thick veil: literature as fiction has been the great repressed element in modern thought.

Beginning with the section "An Invitation to a Reflection on the Third *Critique*" (p. 94), I have been introducing concepts an understanding of which will be required for the rest of this book. A short digression is in order here, to clarify my argument.

Our careful reading of the first and third *Critiques* shows the importance of Kant's thought to our work. Retrospectively—that is, taking into account the chapter on Montaigne—this importance is now seen as centering on the explanation of the Law that the consecration of the individual required. In

CPR Kant seems to have satisfied modernity's need for gnosiological justification. But Kant was not satisfied with his own results, and proceeded to develop his second *Critique*. Here Kant's work of exploration is widened and finds a counterweight: the legislations of understanding and reason are not to be reconciled; they are radically opposed, though equally indispensable. The purpose of the third *Critique* was to harmonize them, taking the faculty of judgment, exercised by each human being as the balancing and conciliatory agent between theoretical reason and practical reason. This was the function of aesthetic judgment. Now, this is precisely the point that was to be most privileged in intellectual experience beginning in the late eighteenth century. What is the aesthetic judgment from a Kantian perspective? We have seen that two readings are possible: one critical, the other aestheticizing. The former can be understood, in Kant's own terms, as the form of investigation that eschews both dogmatism and skepticism, seeking the limits of reason and trying to locate them in the object it experiences and considers. Aestheticization, in the light of Schmitt's reflections, is the reduction, in actual practice, of any and all value to the aesthetic dimension.

This recapitulation shows its usefulness as we turn our attention to how each of these lines of thought sees disinterested interest, finality without an end, as defined by Kant. Whereas the critical attitude places itself outside of strictly aesthetic experience, aestheticization instead connects it and extends it to all other modes of experiencing the world. To say of the first that it places itself outside the sphere of the aesthetic is not enough, however. If one prefers to envisage aesthetic experience as a moment of suspension and expectation—that is, as the moment when the absoluteness of semanticity is suspended—we may add that criticity uses this moment and fecundates it but is actualized only outside it. It does so at the moment when the receiver re-semanticizes his or her experience, moves away from the muteness of the aesthetic, and attempts to mediate it to the world of other experiences. He or she moves away from the aesthetic after listening to it, and re-semanticizes it after learning from form unaccompanied by stable meaning.

The development of the entire book is admittedly guided by the critical mode. Since my intention is not only to take a stand on each line of thought examined and to present a detailed reading of Kafka's work, but also to propose a less than optimistic view of the prospect of the cult of image in electronic society, my defense of criticity requires that my use of the concept be clearly distinguished from others'. From the outset it should be clear that my position has nothing to do with the domination of ethical values. Granted, aesthetic experience is not nonethical. But it is no less clear that its ethical ingredient assumes a different position. That is, where the experience of the interval and expectation is extended particularly into the experience of the fictional—I say "particularly" because the experience of the fictional in art covers only the poetical—it means to see, feel, and appreciate at a distance.

Now, this standing at a distance allows the receiver to recognize in a depragmatized way (that is, without being dominated by an immediate interest) the world that, in everyday experience, is close to him or her. This transformation of the proximate into the distant, of the automatized into the surprising, allows the receiver to examine the work also ethically, for this is one of the dimensions of criticity, its "real" world. If, then, criticity is neither to be identified with the domain of the ethical nor is opposed to it, it is because it recognizes the ethical from the vantage point of this distanced position. The ethical, independent of any aesthetic appreciation, judges here and now. Thus, for instance, one says that it is unethical or even immoral to speculate about world peace and ignore the civil wars that once again are popping up around the world. The ethical, which surfaces in the course of a critical process applied to aesthetic experience, arises in another position, in the imagination activated by suspension and expectation.

It should be added that the distinction I am drawing between criticity and aestheticization is not commonly made. On the contrary, the "aesthetic state" is usually exalted on the basis of its Schillerian formulation, which seems to contain the promise of a more human world. This is the argument of a recently published book that, in order to characterize Marx's position, quotes approvingly the following passage: "[Marx] constitutes as 'science' that which in Schlegel, Hölderlin, Novalis was only sensed intuitively: that the actualization of their aesthetic ideal is bound to the course of a temporal process, to the 'fulfillment of time'" (quoted in Chytry 1989: 276). In my view, on the contrary, this confluence of different lines of thought, and particularly the reason for bringing them together, seems, to say the least, paralyzing and naive.

One final observation: criticity and aestheticization are not the only modalities of the aesthetic experience. The experience of the circus, for instance, is contained in neither. It fluctuates between the two, signaling an area of indecision that is eventually assimilated by one of them.

Novalis: The Countercurrent of Romanticism

Friend and collaborator to Schlegel and his most constant interlocutor as well, Novalis was a rare combination—rare even in a milieu of extraordinary intellectual emulation—of poetical and philosophical talent. His countless fragments and encyclopedic notes testify to the extraordinary range of his interests, and though he died prematurely at the age of 29 he was generally recognized by posterity as one of the major voices of early Romanticism. The immediate object of our interest here, however, will be limited; we shall consider Novalis's poetry, and out of hundreds of fragments we shall restrict our attention to only a few. For our object is not exactly Novalis's work, but rather the extremely complex forms of entanglement that the alternative between aestheticization and criticity can give rise to. The emphasis on this fact will act as a preventive against the temptation of oversimplifying dichotomies. With these observations in mind, we shall take as our point of departure the essay "Die Christenheit oder Europa" (Christendom or Europe).

Throughout the present book, we have at times alluded to the slow but constant growth of subjectivity in the few centuries before the period that concerns us, and to the failure of the unitary metaphysical conception of the universe. No attempt was made to present these two phenomena as related in such a way that one would be seen as determining the other. It would have been just as senseless to say that the powerful classical and medieval worldview was gradually undermined by the acknowledgment of individual subjectivity as to hold that the emphasis on the individual subject, its experience, its power of observation, and its initiative, weakened the unifying view. Rather than associated in a causal relation, these phenomena are correlated in the formation of modernity, in the detheologization of thought and secularization of the world. A specific investigation of the issue would take us to a much earlier period, the high Middle Ages. For our present purposes, we need say no more than that the two phenomena are correlates, for the scope of our study begins in a time when the legitimation of individual subjectivity and the failure of an all-encompassing view that explained everything, from the laws of the cosmos to the most trivial aspect of everyday existence, were taken for granted by all except for the upholders of orthodox thinking.

Thus it was that in the late sixteenth century Montaigne asserted the self's right to think without pledging allegiance to ancient systems, bodies of knowledge, genres, or models, and by the end of the eighteenth century Kant had formulated in his first *Critique* a new theory of knowledge founded on the cognoscitive properties of the human subject. At this point difficulties arise for a linear exposition. We must take into account the chasm that separates Kant's transcendental subject from the empirically considered subject. It must be acknowledged as well that the efforts of the two subsequent *Critiques* did not manage to erect an architectonic structure capable of ensuring a new unity. Human reason is a condition not only for the understanding but also for an excess—that is, what merely appears to be known because it has been postulated. Reason is not only constitutive, as in the case of the natural sciences, but also regulative; it not only recognizes the properties of the phenomena that are partly generated by it but also aims to go beyond them and make statements, just as precritical thinkers were wont to do, about the makeup of the world and even of its Creator.

Kant might not have stirred as much controversy among his early readers as he did if he had stated that such excessive use of reason was illegitimate (or, even more cautiously, that his investigations had no impact on traditional doctrine except where they concerned the knowledge of nature). Instead, he tried to legitimate this use of reason. To do this, he tried to determine the limits of the validity of each activity. The final architectonic structure in which all the different spheres of activity are conjugated is a *systemic architecture*—that is, one which aimed to enable its practitioner to understand the chasms that separate each sphere from the others and move about in them. Such a construct was to be mental and not a description of what was already contained in actual reality. In the pure real—that is, before man considers it—properly speaking there are no phenomena, only materialities.

This desubstantialization of the world concerned and even obsessed the early romantics. Two years after Novalis wrote "Christendom or Europe," Heinrich von Kleist described to his fiancée, Wilhelmine von Zenge, his reaction to Kant, whom he had read recently. In a letter dated March 22, 1801, he expressed in language accessible to a lay reader what he had understood and what had alarmed him:

> If everyone saw the world through green glasses, they would be forced to judge that everything they saw *was* green, and could never be sure whether their eyes saw things as they really are or did not add something of their own to what they saw. And so it is with our intellect. We can never be certain that what we call Truth is really Truth [*warhaft Warheit*], whether it does not merely appear so to us. If the latter, then the truth that we acquire here is *not* Truth, after our death, and it is all a vain striving for a possession that may never follow us into the grave.
>
> Ah, Wilhelmine, if the point of this thought does not strike you to your heart, do not smile at one who feels wounded by it to his most sacred inner being. My one, my highest goal has sunk from sight [*ist gesunken*], and I have no other. (Kleist 1982: 95)

We have already mentioned that Schlegel reacted to *CPR* indignantly, claiming it was "a massacre of reason"; but we saw that his repulsion was mixed with fascination. In the case of Novalis, the concern he felt with the loss of unity had a direct political sense—more precisely, politico-religious. The tone of his words could hardly be heard today unless in the voice of one whose duty it was to defend tradition:

With reason, the supreme pontiff of the Church opposed the blatant development of human capacities to the detriment of sacrosanct feeling, and the un-
timely and dangerous discoveries in the domain of knowledge. Thus it was he
forbade daring thinkers to proclaim in public that the earth is an insignificant
planet, for well he knew that men, once they had lost the respect for their own
place, their earthly fatherland, would also lose respect for their celestial fatherland and their own kind, and would prefer limited knowledge to infinite faith,
and would acquire the habit of scorning all greatness, seeing all these things as
effects of a lifeless law. (Novalis 1978e, 2: 733–34)

It was the degeneracy of priests that had caused the Reformation, which
had sealed the church's fate. The Protestants had "separated the inseparable,
divided the indivisible Church, and criminally strayed from the universal
Christian communion, by which and in which only is the true and lasting
rebirth possible" (p. 743). For this reason, the present situation was provisional. In order to overcome it, it was necessary not to scorn or restrict
knowledge, but to develop a higher conception of science:

The more we learn about the objective sciences, in recent times, the more
conspicuous their poverty seems. Nature has come to seem more and more
miserable, and, accustomed to the brilliance of our discoveries, we have become
used to the fact that the light we see is borrowed, and that, with the instruments
and methods we know, we cannot find or build what is essential. Each researcher
should tell himself that no science is anything without the others. This is the
origin of the mystic researches of the sciences. (p. 747)

If the scientific conception of the sciences is the cause of their poverty, it is
the mystic conception that will reconcile them. In so doing, the "mystic"
epistemologist—as the young Novalis probably saw himself—would be working for the new unity. This unity would be consecrated by the restoration of
Christianity: "Only religion can once again arouse Europe and give security
to the nations and institute Christianity, in its ancient and peaceful mission, in
the glory of a new majesty on earth" (p. 749).

This brief summary will do to show that Novalis, in spite of his evident
conservatism, did not envisage a mere return to the state of affairs before the
Reformation and the religious wars. He expected that chaos would reveal its
own fruitfulness and operate—to take a phrase from Fichte, Novalis's favorite philosopher—a higher synthesis. Thus, what might at first seem to be
the most primitive sort of conservatism is in fact something quite different.
The restored Europe of Novalis's dreams, quite different from the actual
Europe that was to emerge after the fall of Napoleon, meant the achievement
of the unity sought by the moderns. Should we then be content to observe
that the actual restoration that took place was a negation of the one imagined

by Novalis in "Christendom or Europe"? This would be too hasty an attempt to rescue the poet. Then again, would not a discussion of this particular point lead us far astray from our argument? Let us try to go deeper into the question and at the same time show its relevance to our theme.

In a passage already transcribed, Novalis referred to the pope's opposition to the development of human capacities to the detriment of the sense of unity that church doctrine stood for. Was the antagonism between the authority supremely responsible for the maintenance of unity before the Reformation and scientific research—which had led the pope to forbid the teaching of the insignificance of our planet—merely occasional, because the new concepts implied a "lower" synthesis, or was it a consequence of the very existence of a unitary metaphysics? The terms in which Novalis formulates his statement force us to discard the first alternative: "*With reason* [*mit Recht*], the supreme pontiff of the Church opposed . . ." From the author's viewpoint, there is nothing fortuitous here. But Novalis would find the second hypothesis just as unacceptable. In short, neither would correspond to his intention, which is clearly set forth in his essay.

What is interesting about the alternatives is that they open a new path, which might be characterized as follows: Could it be that the prenotions implied by the qualification of the modes of the synthesis proposed by his favorite philosopher as "lower" and "higher" made Novalis unable to see the contradiction in his proposal? (The phrases "higher synthesis" and "lower synthesis" do not actually appear in "Christendom," but Novalis was clearly familiar with the concepts.) In more concrete terms: Did the unity that the early romantics sought obsessively negate the autonomy of the different sphere of values a priori? This last question points to a conclusion as strange as it is precious: the margin of freedom that is open to modern humanity, the possibility it gives rise to of conceiving humanity's emancipation, would not be preserved and fecundated by the restoration of a *letztes Gericht* (C. Schmitt), a final and definitive court of appeal, but, on the contrary, by its nonexistence.

The mistake made by Novalis and the early German romantics was—perhaps due to lack of perspective and historical experience—their insistence on a solution conducive to a result that was precisely the opposite of what they intended. That is, the existence of a unitary center, whether religious or secular, that could legitimate what should be valued and subsequently socialized always has the ultimate effect of subordinating differentiated scales of value to a single, unified one. What the desired margin of freedom required was the permanence of controversy, debate, dissension, rules varying according to the different "language game" being played—that is, the irreducible heterogeneity of language games, which unitary reason is unable to shape.

In this way we fulfill our self-imposed requirement of not neglecting to consider the implications of "Christendom or Europe." This treatment has the additional advantage of establishing a link with the central theme of our essay. But to make sure that the link has not gone unnoticed, let us recapitulate the last step taken.

We have been trying to demonstrate the relation between the Kantian issue of the Law—the impossibility of justifying the fullness of its incidence in terms of the understanding—and the emphasis on the aesthetic experience. The privilege we have been conceding to Kantian thought is not arbitrary, since we must verify whether it is indeed Kant that "translates" and attempts to solve the question of the dilaceration that followed the dissolution of classical unity. In his essay, Novalis clearly praises mysticism because it goes beyond the poverty of specific sciences; this praise, we should note now, is close to the way in which aesthetic pleasure was opposed to the mechanism of scientific procedures. Thus, for instance, after announcing the birth of a "mystical experience of the sciences," Novalis added that, if things proceed along this path, "one may easily imagine how propitious to the higher cultivation of intelligence these exchanges between the outer and the inner world must be," and he expects these exchanges to bring about the return of the "ancient heaven" and of "living astronomy" (pp. 747–48). Yet, it is no less evident that the explicit references to the aesthetic are replaced by the emphasis on the political. The articulation between the absent term and the highlighted term is the basis of Novalis's hopes for a religiously oriented restoration of the lost unity.

If we agree that this is a reasonable path to follow, how can we avoid the argument that we are straying from our subject? By simply pointing out that aesthetic reflection involves politics. The exchange of one for the other in Novalis is by no means circumstantial. And here it has the advantage of making us present a more explicit formulation of what perhaps has already been understood. In the preceding section, we saw that the aestheticization required by Schiller's ideal state clearly implied a political program, which could be actualized only in the sphere of art, by means of the interdiction of criticity. No attempt will be made to integrate Novalis's proposed restoration into aestheticization; such a move would be simplistic.

However, the two projects are ultimately linked by a common exclusion. In Schiller, this is made explicit: what is excluded is criticity. In Novalis, it is indirectly implied: in the past—which it is not his intention to restore fully—that is, in the time of the "lower" synthesis, the supreme representative of unity "with reason" forbade the autonomy of science. That is, "with reason" he adopted a normative, dogmatic, anticritical conduct, the opposite of what

Kant recommended. The difference between this and the proposed "higher" synthesis is not that the corresponding supreme authority was more flexible or sensible, but that science itself, mindful of the mystical view, was not to be purely material and partial, but was rather to turn into an instrument of communion and harmony between the inner and the outer, finally leading to the reemergence of the "ancient sky and aspiration [*Sehnsucht*] for it." Thus, it was not to be expected that the new pontiff would remain opposed to scientific investigation because, "with reason," the latter would no longer be dangerous. Therefore, it no longer matters that Novalis neither used art in favor of his intended restoration nor referred to it in the present or in the future. The value he gave to art was already affected by the role—or rather, the elimination of the role—assigned to criticity.

"Christendom or Europe" has played a prominent role among the texts I have selected, since it has brought us to this conclusion. Although in it Novalis does not mention his own art, the text clearly has to do with it as well.

One question remains: Is Kant absent from Novalis's thought? Or, more precisely: Does Novalis escape the ambiguity of Kant's aesthetic experience? Evidence against this possibility is found in the poet's notes for 1797—the "Hemsterhuis- und Kant Studien" (see Novalis 1978b, 2: 212–22). Although they are much less numerous than the observations on Fichte written in 1795–96, they do indicate that Novalis was also interested in the Kantian system. Let us examine some of his fragments in order to see what his position was concerning the pair aestheticization-criticity. Since he maintained a close interchange of ideas with Friedrich von Schlegel, an understanding of his position may help us in our later examination of Schlegel.

Some Fragments by Novalis: Aestheticism or Criticity?

Fichte's presence is almost palpable in many of Novalis's fragments. Our intent is not to point it out, but rather to examine these brief observations for the position towards the theoretical reflection on art that they express. To do this, we must underscore the centrality awarded to reflective consciousness, focused on the inner self, having "humanity" as its content and goal. In itself, this centrality is quite unexceptional, given the youth of the author and his enthusiasm over Fichte. But for our present purposes there is an important consequence: no differentiation is established between the fields of science, philosophy, and poetry.

> Presentation [*Darstellung*] is a manifestation of the inner state, of the inner changes—the apparition of the inner object. The external object, by the self and

in the self, is changed into a concept, and thus intuitive vision [*Anschauung*] is produced. The inner object, by the self and in the self, is changed into a *body that is convenient to it*, and in this way the sign is born. The latter is the object of the body; the former is the object of the spirit. (Novalis 1978b, 2: 195)

Considering that the initial subject, *Darstellung*, implies the act of writing, one might still read the passage as a eulogy of literature (in the strict sense of the word). But this restricted reading is denied by the following passage: "The most wonderful and external phenomenon is *existence itself*. The biggest mystery is man himself. The solution of this unending task, *in facts*, is universal history. The history of philosophy or science in general, of literature as substance, contains the attempts at reaching the ideal solution to this problem" (p. 212).

We live as long as we are driven by ideas. For this reason—Novalis argues in the continuation of the passage quoted above—universal history, in a clearly Fichtean vein, is identified with Being in general (*das Sein en gros*), as is philosophy with thinking in general (*das Denken en gros*). The self is seen for its products. In Fichtean terms, Novalis could have written: the self poses the nonself, with which he would be emphasizing that consideration of its works should not lead to neglect of the source—or, even better, because if the source-self is projected in the world, not everything that is contained in the world is related to the self: "The inner and the outer are opposed. The self is the concept of the inner; consequently, the self is always within" (Novalis 1978a, 2: 198). But does this not mean that the self is imprisoned in itself, or that its intercourse is limited to what, having been conceived by it, has changed into the concept of a work?

As if aware of this danger, Novalis grants the self another extension: the practical self. Both aspects—the creator of externalities and what relates to them—are present in the following fragment:

The self is action and product at the same time. Wanting and representing are reciprocally determining. The self is nothing but will and representation [*Wollen und Vorstellen*]. The practical self is what is differentiated from the outer world. Only the practical self can be perceived; this, then, is also the properly basic self [*das eigentliche Grundich*]. It is only to the extent that it poses itself, and it poses itself only to the extent that it is. To be the full self is an *art* [*Kunst*]. One can be and is what one *wants*. One is more or less a self to the extent that one wants to be. (p. 206)

Certainly, in spite of the extreme centrality of the self in his thought, Novalis acknowledged the independence of the material world. The function of the practical self, if we interpret it correctly, would be to constitute a second kind of nonself: that which, in contrast with the first, is related to the source of meaning. Since this difference does not exist in Fichte, nor is it explicitly presented by his follower, our conclusion must remain tentative.

With the necessary caution, then, we may say that for Novalis the self has two arms reaching out to the world: one is truly creative and is objectified in the works it recognizes as its creations; the other is practical. Both are products of its "will and representation," but the second is distinguished by the fact that it merely regulates its intercourse and does not constitute what interacts with it. In any case, the author's insistence that only the "practical self" can be perceived narrows in a significant way the difference between the two modes of the nonself, to the detriment of the material world that is independent of the self's action. To say that the practical self is also "the properly basic self" implies emphasis on what is common to both relations to the world: the properly creative and the practical. And what could this common trait be if not *poiesis*, the human subject's ability to impose itself? By now it is perfectly clear why no differentiation was made between philosophy, science, and poetry. To do so would be to act like the scientist who ignores the "mystical" conception mentioned in the preceding section—that is, to focus on the part, disconnecting it from the whole and thus failing to perceive its operating center: selfhood (*Ichheit*).

In Novalis, the principle of poiesis surpasses distinctions, both the practical and the properly creative; it implies concentration on the concrete, whether the manipulated (practical) or the properly produced, but without diminishing the simultaneous emphasis on the originating center. If for a moment we disregarded Novalis's religiosity, we might add that poiesis makes God unnecessary. Since this would be unjustified, we may at least say that God in this case becomes a supplementary figure, the support of the court of final appeal, being, however, posed by humanity. One might ask whether it would be correct to say that, against the atomization of the mechanical, against the recognition of the different orders of objects and values that cannot be superimposed or integrated—those that are established by theoretical and practical reasons and by the reflective judgment, postulated both by Kantianism and by empiricism, as well as, outside of any philosophical tendency, by the pragmatism of the state—Novalis proposed integrated attention to both the world of works and its center of creation. But this question must be answered in the negative. Although poiesis is what comes out of—what is not to be confused with, what is freed from—the innerness of the producer, in Novalis the term that is always emphasized is the innerness of the creator. Here is the last note in his "Fichte-Studien": "On humanity. Its pure and full improvement must at first become the art of individuals and then move on to the great popular masses [*die großen Völkermassen*] and from there to the species. To what extent is it an individual?" (p. 209).

The self, the central category in Fichte's theory of knowledge, is now converted into the basis of the utopia of redeemed mankind. The Enlightenment dream of the autonomy of the subject, of its independence of any guardianship, is now translated into the exaltation of the individual. The improvement of the masses and of the species as a whole now depends on the constitution of a special group of individuals. But could the species be envisaged as a plural individual? The question with which the passage ends might be interpreted as expressing doubt about whether the limit of utopia excludes the species or encompasses it in its entirety. Even if this suspicion is dropped, the fact is that the centrality of the individual excludes the image of the citizen that is its correlate in Kantian thought. It is this centrality that originates the immediate projection of a chosen group, an elite that serves as a model and an example for the popular masses.

The passages quoted above are consistent with the restoration Novalis proposed soon after in "Christendom or Europe," even though there is no immediate or necessary connection between the later essay and the emphasis these passages place on the creative principle, poiesis. Thus, we must examine this principle.

Let us proceed from the question, Is the primacy of poiesis as conceived by Novalis equivalent to Schiller's aestheticization? "The sciences in their full form must be poetic. Each sentence must have an autonomous [*selbständig*] character—must be a self-evident [*selbstverständlich*] individual, the hull of an unforeseen incidence [*Hülle eines witzigen Einfalls*]" (Novalis 1978e, 2: 318). The opening deontic proposition does not determine a univocal solution because the qualifier "poetic" may refer either to poiesis, the creative act in general, or to what is actualized in the poem. If the first alternative seems more plausible, the rest of the passage contradicts this impression. The passage says that each scientific statement must be autonomous, have a self-evident individuality, and derive from an unforeseen apprehension. That is, the explanation emphasizes properties of a formal, not conceptual, order. The passage oscillates between the transversality of poiesis and the centrality of poetical art to such an extent that it is impossible to opt in a definite way for one or the other. We must then look for another criterion.

The first fragment we shall consider predicts, with extraordinary foresight, the most drastic consequence of aestheticization: "The ideal of morality has no rival more dangerous than the ideal of supreme force—of a more powerful life—which could also be called the ideal of aesthetic greatness. . . . It is the utmost barbarity. Unfortunately, in our times of degenerate culture, it finds a great number of followers precisely among the weakest" (p. 365).

Whereas Schiller had a beatific vision of what his proposed aesthetic education might result in, Novalis's vision is appalling. Thus, contrary to what the preceding fragment seemed to indicate, Novalis's views here are not to be identified with those of the author of the *Letters*. A passage that follows shortly afterward underscores this divergence: "Morality and philosophy are arts [*Künste*]. The former is the art of choosing well, among motives of conduct, a moral idea, an a priori idea, and thus invest all conducts with a great and profound meaning . . . the latter is the art of doing the same to thoughts, of choosing them: the art of producing our set of representations in accordance with an absolute, artistic idea" (p. 366).

Undoubtedly, the two are called arts as forms of irradiation of poiesis. If the two characterizations are trivial, for our present purposes they present the advantage of showing that they have no point of contact with aestheticization: morality and philosophy presuppose artificial rules and procedures, whereas Schiller's aestheticization implied the internalization of preexisting norms.

Here are two more examples to undergird our contention:

> We know something only as far as we *express* it—that is, as we can do it. The better and more variously we can *produce, accomplish* something, so much the better we *know* it.

> Our states are hardly more than *legal* institutions, *defensive* devices. The educational institutions, the artistic academies and societies are not educational or artistic, or are only a little. Men must supplement them with specific coalitions. (p. 378)

If, by itself, the first example simply reaffirms the power of poiesis, the second emphasizes the extreme contrast between it and the state. To Novalis, Schiller's trust in the state, even the ideal state, was clearly, to say the least, excessive. It is true that the drastic opposition between individual poiesis and the state's defensive power opens a troublesome gap—hence, as the rest of the fragment notes, people have the need for particular alliances to supplement institutions that have no such defensive power. In any case, this gap would not exist if there were some direct link between the producer and the merely defensive—that is, respectively, the individual and the state.

One might argue that these are mere notes not intended for publication, that the author had no intention of composing a treatise on a constitution that would be at least less imperfect. Although these qualifications are obvious, it is no less obvious that the identification of the individual with poiesis indicates more than the praise of man's productive ability: there is also an expression of the satisfaction with the merely individual. And it is on the basis of this contentment that, in his own way, Novalis revives aestheticization:

> The self must be constructed. The philosopher prepares, provides artificial [*künstlich*] elements and thus proceeds to construct. There is no *natural history* of the self—the self is not a natural product, not a nature, not a historical being [*kein*

historisches Wesen], but an artistic being, an art, a work of art. Man's natural history is the *other half*. The doctrine of the self and the history of mankind—or nature and art—fuse together and complete *each other* in a higher science—*the doctrine of moral education.* (Novalis 1978d, 2: 485)

What is exalted in this fragment is the artistic construction of the self. Even though this construction is to be surpassed by a "higher science," its character remains that of a *moralischen Bildungslehre* (doctrine of moral education). It then comes as no surprise that a passage from the same series, "Das allgemeine Brouillon" (The general draft), should express the dream of a life filled with beautiful works: "It will be a beautiful time, the time in which only *beautiful compositions* will be read, only works of literary art. All other books are means and will be forgotten as soon as they are no longer useful means" (p. 510).

But what are we saying? Is Novalis's position, after all, similar or opposite to Schiller's? In fact, both answers are correct, but partial. The aestheticization proposed in Novalis's fragments is of a different kind. Whereas for Schiller aestheticization was public and served as an instrument for conceiving a state that would be consonant with the interests of citizens, for Novalis it offered a future appearing only as a daydream of a "beautiful time." The present unbridgeable gap between state action and the individual's private ability makes it impossible for Novalis to agree with Schiller and forces him to choose his own path. The aestheticization proposed in his fragments is of an exclusively private kind.

However, there is yet another contradiction: the self-contentment with the individual's singular voice clashes with a sharp criticism of the individual who takes himself as his single object: "Through excessive self-reflection, man becomes saturated with himself and loses the proper sense of his own self" (Novalis 1978c, 2: 347). But perhaps we see a contradiction here only because we have not yet quite grasped Novalis's distinction between the exaltation of individuality and the rejection of individualism. Another passage underscores the importance of making such a distinction:

Every satisfaction is a solution of itself. Need is born of discord, external influence, vulnerability [*Verletzung*]; which must recover its balance by itself. The solution by itself of impulse [*des Triebes*], this self-combustion of illusion, of the illusory problem, is precisely what is voluptuous in the satisfaction of the impulse. What is life if not this? Despair, fear of death, are exactly illusions of this kind. . . . Each story *contains a life*—a problem that solves itself. Thus each life is a story. (p. 352)

For all the obscurities of a text meant to be read only by the author himself, it is clear that the satisfaction (*Befriediging*) praised here is not to be identified with that of individualistic banality. Even more arbitrary would be to identify it with moralistic rigor. To say, as the fragment says, that it depends on a solution found by the subject for itself, on the vulnerability or injury (*Verletzung*) that impels it to its need does not mean finding a sedative—the individualistic solution—or the inner ability to repress the injury. What it does mean, as the text states clearly, is the self-combustion of illusion—*diese Selbstverbrennung der Illusion*—itself a source of voluptuousness. It thus means a product of the subject. Its satisfaction, with the mitigation of despair and fear of death, occurs after poiesis has operated on the self. (Hence the insistence on compound words with *selbst-*, or "self-".)

Now we can clear up the difficulty mentioned before, and affirm that the private mode of aestheticization found in Novalis does not contradict his rejection of individualistic self-contentment because it is founded on the praise of individuality, which produces not objects but existence itself. This self-producing individuality ultimately points to a vague mysticism, to a mystery the doors to which may be opened, but which leads to no doctrine that assures salvation; it neither conforms to nor proposes any church, for such an institution would necessarily be based on the defensiveness Novalis attributes to the state.

However fascinating we may find this solution—which Novalis suggests rather than formulates—we must repeat that it is articulated with what we have been calling the private mode of aestheticization. This point is brought home by a note almost immediately following the one transcribed above: "Life should not be a novel given to us, but one we make ourselves" (p. 352). Poiesis and poetics continually alternate. Although poetic achievement is not the only aim of poiesis, it would be impossible to find in Novalis a poiesis without poetic properties.

The lack of such a distinction seems to have serious consequences. How could the value of a philosophical or scientific work be evaluated? Whether private or public, aestheticization reduces all scales to one. Thus, if public aestheticization implied the control of artistic production, as if for its privilege it had to pay the price of being set up as an example, private aestheticization exempts only the artistic from the mechanisms of control. Art, instead of being controlled, becomes the controller. Now, how could this controlling agency be critical? How could it preserve for itself only what it would deny to other values? One may conceive of a solution: in the pilgrim's progress of individuality, it might turn out that the indispensable self-combustion of illusions made the return to criticity indispensable. But if this were indeed the case, the link with aestheticization would have to be broken, for either aestheticization or criticity would have to be asserted. Criticity is the dissonant note in the final chord of the tune.

Let us, however, leave aside such speculations and return to the texts themselves, seeing from a different angle the aestheticization at which Novalis arrived. We saw that it started out from the emphasis on the individual's productive force. Poiesis was then seen as the ineradicable mark of this being, fated to death and the ephemeral. But we are rushing to a conclusion. Let us first examine what Novalis did not consider an authentic production.

Here is a relevant passage: "One may pay for genuine art-poetry [*echte Kunstpoesie*]. Poetry as need, as a trait of character, as a manifestation of my nature—in short, *sentimental poetry*—could only be paid for by a brute" (Novalis 1978c, 2: 389–90). The opposition established here assumes the inferiority of alienable products, among which even genuine art-poetry is included. "Sentimental poetry" here is identified with the expression of the idiosyncratically personal. The opposition between "genuine art-poetry" and poetry that manifests the creator's need is rooted in the existence, in the late eighteenth century, of a book market that allowed and even required writers to take into account the demand and the public's level of understanding. Thus, a differentiation was made between uncompromising treatises and essays written in accessible language. Even philosophers like Kant and Fichte had this division in mind, using less technical language and relying on simpler reasoning when they wrote for the general public. Although the backwardness of the German bourgeoisie was well known, there was a large market for German books (see Fontius 1983: 184–87).

Although neither Novalis nor Schlegel enjoyed a comfortable financial situation, and though Friedrich, like his brother August Wilhelm, was always doing journalistic work to support himself, the two friends, the poet and the critic, both held the public in contempt. In the same year when Novalis is thought to have written the passage quoted above, Schlegel published in his "Athenäum Fragmente" fragment 275: "German authors are always criticized for writing for a very small circle, and often for each other. This is all to the good. In this way German literature will only gain in spirit and character. And in the meantime a public will perhaps arise" (Schlegel 1967c, 2: 212). For this attitude, they could either be accused of being the proponents of an aristocracy of the spirit or praised for not submitting to the emerging law of the market. But the passage from Novalis quoted earlier points to a more adequate interpretation: the commercialization of the product, he believes, affects its spiritual value. It indicates that the product is not a manifestation of "my nature." Whatever is marketable issues from its creator combined with an alien, material, worldly element. That is: the praise of poiesis does not encompass the entire field of poiesis, but only what is supremely spiritual, identified with pure inner need to create. The fact that an object—such as a poem—is marketable stigmatizes and diminishes it.

We arrive at the same conclusion after reading a passage from "Das allgemeine Brouillon": "Philosophical history. It is a philosophically strange and *unanswerable* question whether the human race is advancing; why not ask also: does the human race change? This question is the higher one: only from change can one infer improvement or decline" (Novalis 1978d, 2: 619). Against this early version of the notion of social progress, Novalis propounds the idea that the species must change beforehand. No contemporary reader would have made the absurd mistake of taking him to refer to material change: the ethical and intellectual connotations are quite obvious, so that once again poiesis is identified with the spiritual. Consequently, all human products—whether objects or institutions—that are associated with materiality are seen as intellectually inferior or contemptible. This connotation had already been visible in Novalis's view of the state—"our states"—as a merely defensive device. Thus, the "spiritualist" prejudice is also present in Novalis's quite reasonable implicit criticism of "man's aesthetic education." The state necessarily builds its house opposite to that of the individual, for while the individual aspires to the condition of a bird or a dancer, the state cannot help being a machine solidly planted on the ground, heavy and pedestrian.

The aesthetic privatization proposed by Novalis largely depends on the early German romantic's prejudiced view of the material world. The ideals of purity and sublimity projected an image of the poet and of the intellectual that did not disconnect them from the world as much as it made them naturally inclined to defend proposals of restoration—by definition, restorations imply regaining a lost aura.

These considerations do not mean that our examination of Novalis has corroborated Carl Schmitt's views. It would be preposterous to see the poet as an occasionalist who found in the world no more than an opportunity for self-fruition. But one cannot help agreeing in part with the author of *Political Romanticism*: an examination of the conditions that the world presents to the autonomous self leads to a precise mode of aestheticization, which is the correlate of a biased view of spirituality that despises the material.[9] This second aspect is enough to make the aestheticization deduced from Novalis's notes less viable than the public variety. The latter, instead of despising materiality, accepts it as part of the Law to be internalized. Though bearing in mind that both reject critical virtuality, we must conclude that Schiller's proposal had better chances of flourishing.

9. This prejudice is extraordinarily durable: it remains alive to this day, and provides the basis for many of Adorno's attacks on the barbarization of American culture in the mid-1940's, when he was in exile. The reader of *Minima Moralia* should carefully distinguish Adorno's acute observations from what is no more than rehashed German Romanticism.

One final point must be made: what relation could be established between what we have said in the present section and what was said before about "Christendom or Europe"?

It would be unwarranted to set up a direct link between the emphasis on "spiritualized" productivity and the political conservatism of the essay. At the most we could say that this emphasis favored the conservative solution. But it would be more reasonable to say that the essay does not actually contain the consequence of these speculations, which are only preparatory in nature, but rather presents its brutal side. It is as if Novalis, grown weary of an unending lucubration, like his beloved Fichte and the question of infinity, with contradictions that kept turning up, had suddenly put an end to this process and established a compromise between possible reality and the eternal adjournment of the desired communion. This is the paradoxical aspect of programmed spirituality: hatred of materiality, at certain times, turns into its very basis. "Christendom or Europe" illustrates the hard ground that is sometimes the angel's choice.

Was Novalis anticipating what his friend Friedrich would soon attempt in a practical and irreversible way? In other words, was early Romanticism, at some stage of the lives of its members, fated to stigmatize criticity, exalt aestheticization, and turn its revolutionary fervor into narrow conservative integration?

Schlegel as Literary Theorist

Friedrich von Schlegel was not a playwright, a poet, or a novelist who, out of ennui or financial need, turned to writing about the work of others; in fact, the opposite would be closer to the truth. He was the first man of letters to devote himself entirely to criticism.

We have seen how prestigious the word "critique" had become among the early romantics, due to the influence of Kant. But the examples of Novalis, Ludwig Tieck, and his own brother, August Wilhelm, only bring out the more the singularity of Friedrich von Schlegel. Novalis, his closest and most constant collaborator, had, in spite of his youth, an encyclopedic fund of knowledge, but above all he was a poet, the author of *Vermischte Gedichte* (Mixed poems), of the *Hymnen an die Nacht* (Hymns to the night), and a novelist, the author of *Heinrich von Ofterdingen*. Tieck was to become famous as the translator of Cervantes, and was also known for his essays; but it is in his novels that his best work is to be found. The same cannot be said of August Wilhelm, who in his long life wrote no more than histories of various literatures. But the similarity with his brother's case is only apparent.

Friedrich von Schlegel alone was able to imbue critical appreciation with extraordinary theoretical force. This fact is of the utmost importance; what Benjamin said of the romantics is true particularly of Schlegel: "It was only with the romantics that the term 'art critic' [*Kunstkritiker*] definitively replaced the older term 'art judge' [*Kunstrichter*]" (Benjamin 1974a, I, I: 52). Since he remained an isolated example—in the first half of the nineteenth century only Coleridge came close to him, and in our own century only Valéry's critical talent is comparable to his—the importance of his distinction is often neglected. By contrast, the term "art judge" would be more adequate in connection with Boileau or—to mention a name closer to Schlegel in time—Lessing.

Like any judge, the "art judge" relies on a body of applicable legislation. It sometimes happens—as was the case in the Renaissance—that the "art judge" is also the legislator; he lays down the law and then judges in accordance with it. But the critic is different: the term in its strict sense applies to one who produces theory instead of merely applying previously existing rules. This means that theoretical work becomes an urgent necessity whenever the values behind the legislation in force have lost their effectiveness. One might think that, in the case of France, Boileau's precepts lost their force when court society no longer imposed its taste on a production mostly addressed to a class—the bourgeoisie—most of the members of which did not frequent the court. With the Enlightenment, particularly through the work of Diderot, a new body of legislation arose that took into account the individual, exalting his feelings, his family relations, and a mode of conduct that owed nothing to the aristocracy.[10]

However, the Enlightenment pattern in art, represented in Germany by Lessing, did not reach the time of the early German romantics. In Germany as in France, the Enlightenment thought of art not as an autonomous sphere, but as the proper field for the socialization of values erected on the cult of reason. According to a neo-Habermasian author, the Enlightenment failed in the field of art because "the Enlightenment project of coupling art and life through graphic presentation of contextually (also politically and economically) important constellations of norms and values totally neglects or contradicts the dissociation of different, independent spheres within society" (Schulte-Sasse 1988: 111). For this reason, the author adds, whereas Kant believed that the aesthetic experience could be harmonized with the laws of theoretical reason and the norms of practical reason—that is, that it served to relieve for a moment the "instrumental reason" without questioning it—to

10. For an appreciation of Diderot as art critic, see Costa-Lima 1992, chapter 5.

the early romantics "such acts of emancipation were the basic condition necessary for the *possibility* of subjectivity" (p. 146).

Although Schulte-Sasse is right as far as the Enlightenment is concerned, he misses the point when he discusses the romantics. In his view, the Enlightenment's failure to make art the field of mediation of values gave rise to the "institutionalization of art as a compensatory medium" (p. 111). In the terms we have been framing the issue, this would mean that there is no alternative between aestheticizing fruition and criticity; the failure of the Enlightenment necessarily implies the former. Consequently, it would be arbitrary to highlight the intervention of a theoretical period, to which Friedrich von Schlegel's contribution was outstanding. With the romantics, then, a "progressive" conception was simply replaced by an "esoteric" and compensatory one. And, in addition, Benjamin's distinction between the critic and the judge would be otiose.

But such a view makes sense only within a unitary and totalizing conception of society, according to which art either mediates and amplifies the circulation of values—which are not seen as belonging to art, but to society— or else it is no more than an officially sanctioned sedative.

Instead of assuming such a haughty posture, in which the interpreter invests his theory with absolute power over the historico-social world and attributes this intelligence to himself, neither Schlegel nor Novalis resorts to a body of legislation ready to be applied. The contradictions between either of them and the others, and their internal contradictions as well, derive precisely from this fact. Both theorize because the situation they face does not allow them to content themselves with the inherited values. It is because they are living in a situation of crisis that they are driven to the exercise of criticism. To argue a priori that they had the answer or that their answers turn out to be identical would be to attribute to their work a univocality that does not really exist, that could only be affirmed by one who has never taken the trouble to attempt to understand them.

The fact that the men we are discussing were involved in the same situation of crisis does not mean it was this that made them opt for a critical path. As we have seen, this was not Schiller's or Novalis's case, though there was no convergence between their paths either. For the moment, we do not know whether their example may be applied to Schlegel. All we have attempted to do so far is to open the way for an appropriate discussion and to highlight the intellectual poverty or (what amounts to the same thing) the deplorable intellectual arrogance of those who take it for granted that their positions are equivalent.

As I reject this possibility, I am inevitably reminded of an early passage in

Benjamin's essay: "The objective foundation of the concept of art criticism given by Friedrich Schlegel involves only the objective structure of art, as an idea, and of its products, as works" (Benjamin 1974a, 1, 1: 13). Schlegel provides the objective foundation for the concept of art criticism because instead of being content to accept previously existent norms, as he did early in his career, he takes on the task of grasping the "objective structure" as it is manifested in the works. This objective foundation can only be glimpsed to the extent that the critical exercise is moved by a theoretical question: What is art? What constitutes this particular work? We can then add that what singularizes modern criticism and distinguishes it from earlier forms of appreciation is the fact that it presupposes not a norm, but rather the question: Given a work of art, are there norms to be formulated? What is the legitimacy of norms conceived in order to judge art?

We do not mean, however, that every age necessarily contains a discontinuity of some kind, which implies that past values are no longer in force. Such a principle here would be dysfunctional and futile, for if Enlightenment values are no longer valid for the early German romantics and the men of the Enlightenment were clearly living in the modern age too, we implicitly acknowledge the fact that within modernity itself there is a discontinuity between the Enlightenment and Romanticism. What we are emphasizing here is something much more specific: that the uniqueness of modern criticism cannot be accounted for without an examination of the impact of Kant. It is Kant who teaches us to eschew totalizing and reductionistic generalizations.[11]

The primary questions that, on the basis of Kant's work, were raised by Schlegel's reflections presupposed the exercise of criticity. Put more precisely, art criticism becomes objectified as it asserts itself as a theoretical enterprise. However, this sort of criticism was to die out a short time later. All the more reason, then, for us to examine its brief existence. Before doing this, two facts should be emphasized: first, that Schlegel's attempt to understand was com-

11. The critique of totalizing systems is introduced here in a somewhat abrupt manner. In order to provide its proper contextualization, it would be necessary to examine Hegel's thought, which would break the unity of the book and perhaps even make it unpublishable. But there is a way of narrowing this gap. At a time when he was not yet under the spell of the Hegelian tradition, but was already fighting off the seduction of the early German romantics, Lukács wrote, in his essay on Kierkegaard: "A man who wants to be 'honest' . . . must force life to yield up its single meaning [dem Leben die Eindeutigkeit abzwingen], must grasp that ever-changing Proteus [diesen ewig gestaltwechsenden Proteus] so firmly that, once he has revealed the magic words [wenn er ihm einmal den Spruch offenbar hat], he can no longer move" (Lukács 1974: 29). Reacting to the subjective absolutism of the early German romantics, Lukács postulates an absolutism just as categorical. In other words, the urge towards totalization, the extreme effort to favor it, predominates, even if in inverted form, in the context we are examining.

promised by a theoretical frame of reference that postulated a unitary and totalizing conception of society. Considering that the romantics did so much to promote a new unitary view with which to resist Kant's thought, we may find it ironical that the contempt in which they came to be held was based on a unitary conception (in fact, there is nothing extraordinary in this: the theoretical debate we are referring to simply reiterated Hegel's restrictions against the romantics). Second, that Schlegel's enterprise is favored by the link established by Benjamin between the foundation of art criticism and concrete concern with the concrete properties of works. As Benjamin observes, "When he writes about art, [Schlegel] is thinking particularly of poetry" (Benjamin 1974a, 1, 1: 13). This makes his object even more concrete and particularized.

Thus, Schlegel attempts to understand works in their own right, rather than—as is common among thinkers—to present them as examples or illustrations of something that precedes them (more often than not, the system developed by the thinker in question). "The romantics, unlike the Enlightenment thinkers, did not see form as a rule of beauty in art, or its observance as a necessary premise of the work's pleasing or edifying effect. . . . The idea of art as a medium [*eines Mediums*] thus opens for the first time the possibility of a free, nondogmatic formalism—or, as they would call it, a liberal formalism" (Benjamin 1974a, 1, 1: 76–77).

The emphasis on form both inspired the search for objective understanding and disallowed the Romantic identification of art as a compensatory activity. For if this function were previously ensured, why should the critical endeavor be necessary? We may go even further: the compensatory interpretation and the Enlightenment conception of art are not contradictory and are in fact equivalent in that both subject art to a mechanism of control. Both the Enlightenment attitude and aestheticization control art a priori, the former because it forces art to propound supposedly universal and superior moral values, the latter because it requires that the producers and the receivers of art internalize the values of society beforehand. Whereas Enlightenment authors failed to question the autonomy of art, to Schiller it implied the simultaneous homogeneity of citizens: they were not to have any reservations (secrets, reticences, restrictions) as to the principles of order. If in these two cases art is controlled, Novalis's private aestheticization makes it the controlling agent: its formal traits are by themselves invaluable indicators of quality.

These three proposals about art, then, though they cannot be said to be exactly the same, connect art to power, submitting the former to the latter or identifying one with the other. The inoperativeness of the metaphysically justified Law—that is, of a Law assumed to translate the substance of the cosmos—ultimately results in a number of laws that conflict with one another and thus give rise to the yearning for another unitary justification. If power always lurks behind justifications of control, the power that would be unitary is the one that expresses the will to control most explicitly. And when it not only would be unitary but is so in fact—and is consequently centralist and absolute as well—control (and not only of art, of course!) is the instrument with which it operates.

This is one more reason for a detailed examination of the critical path. An understanding of criticity is interesting not only in historical and academic terms but also in that it helps us to understand the contemporary situation. Let us then see how Friedrich von Schlegel considers the issue.

THE CRITIC OF POETRY

Schlegel began to publish quite early. He was only twenty when his first essay of any importance came out: "Über das Studium des griechischen Poesie" (On the study of Greek poetry; published in 1797, but submitted to the publisher in late 1795).

A philologist by training, who shared Winckelmann's enthusiasm for the art of antiquity, Schlegel opened his critique of modern poetry with the words: "It is evident that modern poetry has not yet received the goal it seeks, or else that it seeks no concrete goal, that its history has no connection founded on laws [*gesetzmäßig*] and the whole, no unity" (Schlegel 1971b, 121). Thus, the category he applies to it—the interesting—has no more than "provisional aesthetic value" (p. 119), whereas "there are pure laws for beauty and for art, which are in force and admit no exception" (p. 115). In this way, "the lack of characteristic traits seems to be the only trait of modern poetry, bewilderment the common mark of its works, and skepticism the result of its theory" (p. 125).

The vehemence of Schlegel's critical attack suggests that poetry is not its only target. In fact, as a passage from a review of Friedrich Jacobi's philosophical novel *Woldemar* makes clear, Schlegel is inveighing against the entire modern age: "The original sin of modern culture is the total separation and dismembering of human forces, which can survive healthily only in free association" (Schlegel 1971a: 260). The Greek poets were praised for their attainment of "objectivity," whereas the moderns were concerned only with the "individual" and the "interesting." Modernity was identified with the primacy of the individual, and since this necessarily meant a transgression of the "pure laws" that should govern everything, its products were held to be inferior. Schlegel's position was thus the opposite of what Schiller defended in 1795, in the first article that was later to become a part of *Naive and Sentimental Poetry*.

This article—which Schlegel probably read after he had sent in the manuscript of "Das Studium" to the publisher (see Eichner 1955: 260–64)—caused a revolution in Schlegel's thinking. On June 11, 1796, he wrote to his brother: "In the introduction to 'Studium,' I showered praises on the sentimental poet Schiller and, towards the end of the same article, particularly on his poetry" (p. 262). Apparently the introduction he mentions was added to the essay, the publication of which had been delayed. Rather than see it as an opportunistic move in order to make the Schlegels more acceptable to the magazine that Schiller was then editing, *Die Hore*, it seems more sensible to agree with H. Eichner that the playwright's consideration had served to rectify the young critic's position.

The fact is that Schlegel retracted his earlier views both in the "Kritische Fragmente" (Critical Fragments) of 1797 and in a review of Gotthold Ephraim Lessing published in December of the same year. In the review the author of *Hamburgische Dramaturgie* (Hamburg theatrical criticism) is praised for his revolutionary spirit—"In theology as well as on the stage and in criticism, he not only distinguished himself but also produced a total and lasting revolution" (Schlegel 1980a, 1: 106)—and also for his individuality, whose richness surpassed his manifold talent: "*He himself had more worth than all his talents*" (p. 119, emphasis in the original). The individual is valued as he is manifested in his works: as a "perfect expert in his art," "the ideal and the concept of the individual seem to be almost fused together here" (p. 109). Thus, "Über Lessing" indicates, together with the two series of fragments we shall analyze, a different view of the critic's approach to the chasm between the ancient and the modern.

Independently of the question of how Schlegel behaved in relation to Schiller, who had had a decisive influence on him, there is a problem that must be pointed out from the outset: it is clear that Schlegel gave up the primacy of the criterion of objectivity that he had proposed in the "Studium" under the influence of an opposite view of poetical work. Now, this criterion, from Renaissance poetics to Winckelmann, had been founded on a systematic aesthetics—that is, a legislation that offered positive norms for the judgment of works "without exception." Does Schlegel's abandonment of this criterion—considering that he was a reader of Kant—mean that he gave up the pretension of attaining an objective, systematic aesthetics? This is where the importance of examining Schlegel's work as literary theorist becomes most visible. For Schlegel abandoned the legislation he had originally adopted without embracing another; instead, he set about passionately searching for a different criterion. Our task now is simply to formulate the problem; later we shall come to terms with it as we examine Schlegel's decisive texts.

THE FRAGMENTS

The first question that interests us is: What does Schlegel's preference for the fragment mean? To avoid a psychological explanation, let us rephrase it: Is there a way to specify the fragment as a form?

Admittedly influenced by Sébastien Roch Nicolas Chamfort's *Maximes* and by fragment 206 of the "Athenäum Fragmente"—"Like a small work of art, a fragment must be totally separated from the world surrounding it and complete [*vollendet*] in itself, like a hedgehog" (Schlegel 1967c: 197)—R. Ayrault offers the following comment: "If 'fragment' is replaced by 'maxim' or 'sentence,' the formula still holds, no other change being necessary, not even the ironical image at the end" (Ayrault 1961: 124). But this equivalence is equivocal. True, the maxim and the epigram have in common with the Schlegelian fragment the sharp wit (*Witz*), which was, as such, the basic stylistic feature of conceptism and of metaphysical poetry. But the Schlegelian fragment is not a prolongation of the baroque. It is distinguished by the presence of individuality, of the individual subject that animates it. In addition, whereas baroque acuteness was addressed to the subtle ear, the fragment is conceived for the written page. It is a testimony of individuality and, at the same time, the constituent of an autonomous individuality: "The fragment functions at the same time as a remainder of individuality *and* as individuality" (Lacoue-Labarthe and Nancy 1978: 63).

As a testimony of the author, of his singularity, the fragment is always an unfinished product. In that, it is indeed close to the Montaignean essay: "The fragment is a statement that does not aim at exhaustiveness and corresponds to the idea—no doubt a properly modern one—that what is unfinished may or even should be published (or also to the idea that what is published is never actually finished)" (p. 62). Why call it unfinished if not because it aims to do more than express the subjectivity that generated it? This is not a property of all the forms that are immediately related to a subjective source. The acuteness distinguishes the fragment-as-form from the confessions, the characteristic genre of expressivism. We have seen earlier, with Benjamin, that what distanced the early German romantics from Fichte was their obsession with the work of art. It is its individuality—the constant effort to understand it, to absorb it to such an extent that its theory would thereby be constituted—that distinguishes Schlegel's fragments from pansubjectivism.

Two subjectivities coexist in the modern fragment—one is expressed, the other produced. We have inherited from Romantic hermeneutics, through intentionality, the bad habit of seeing form as the property of an author, of subordinating it to the manifestation of something that already existed before it: the idiosyncrasies of a self. The Schlegelian fragment cannot be reduced in this way. Little would be gained by the addition of intentionality.

If two individualities are contained in the fragment, if the first appears in unfinished form, why should the same be true of the second—the individuality produced? The answer seems clear: Romantic poetry, as Schlegel will say quite explicitly, is an ongoing task; he might have called it inexorable and infinite as well. Unfinished, the fragment points to the Book that is ever being written, that for this reason is always being taken up again and always being dropped. That is why we say that the fragment is the minimal seminal form of the essay. By this we mean both that the fragment-essay is a modern form, rooted in the experience of a self, and that it is of the nature of a search that is never concluded—that is, its nature is incompleteness. On the basis of these considerations, let us examine the two series of fragments, with particular emphasis on those that are more salient.

In the series of "Critical Fragments," the first one worthy of emphasis is number 14: "In poetry too, every whole could well be a part, and every part could be a whole" (Schlegel 1967b: 148). Here the approximation between fragment and poem is all too obvious. The fragment takes on a critical appearance not because it stands above the poem, in the sense that a judge may be said to place him or herself above the litigants, but because both share the same nature. This clearly poses a difficulty: is Schlegel really saying that criticism, as an autonomous genre, should have the same literary character as the poem? It should not be thought that this is a question raised only to be explained away immediately. Fragment 117 is quite explicit: "Poetry can only be criticized by poetry. An evaluation of poetry that is not in itself a work of art, either in its substance as a presentation of the necessary impression in its becoming, or in its beautiful form and liberal tone in the spirit of ancient Roman satire, has no right of citizenship in the realm of art" (p. 162).[12] On the other hand, the ironical fragment 57 argues: "If certain mystical lovers of art, for whom every criticism is a dissection and every dissection a destruction of pleasure, were consistent in their thinking, then the best evaluation of a work of merit would be an 'Oh!' Many critics do no better than that, only with more words" (p. 154).

It would be impossible to resolve this ambiguity. It derives from the fact

12. This corresponds to Novalis's fragment: "He who cannot compose a poem can only judge it negatively. True criticism requires the ability of producing what it criticizes. By itself, taste can only then judge negatively" (Novalis 1978c: 323).

that the idea of literary space here is not stable, firm, with established boundaries. With the demise of the "art judge," the position of criticism shifted, from outside to inside the bounds of literature. Literature, much more than philosophy—let alone the sciences—had the individual subject as its basic raw material, although it was not yet identified with the expression of the author's subjectivity, as would be the case later, in the "normalized" Romanticism of the early nineteenth century. In such a context, the logic of fragment 117 would seem self-evident. But the circuit formed by authorial subjectivity and work does not exhaust the issue. By itself, it does not account for what the early romantics most privileged: poiesis, or actual production. Thus, the work is defined not as a transposition of the writer's idiosyncrasies to the realm of words, but as the production of a text—that is, of something that cannot be immediately justified by a determined end, that says from the outset no more than what its purpose is *not*. The "mystical lovers" of art—the irony is all the stronger for the fact that "mystical" had strongly positive connotations in the author's circle—do not know that a text requires much more than their enthusiasm.

Thus, confusing criticism with an exclamatory utterance, these "mystical lovers" once again expel criticism from literature and feel they have solved the problem that the early German romantics themselves could not solve: What is the status of literary space? Contrary to Kant, Schlegel is not content to acknowledge the judgment on the beautiful as a universal property. Such a property could be the receiver's "disinterested" fruition. To Schlegel, the problem is the particular work of art. The issue only appears to become simpler. From the beginning the problem is vexing, because—as we have seen—the abandonment of an objective aesthetics gave rise to the question: How can judgment on a work of art evoke more than a mute communication? That is, criticism, as Schlegel conceives it, involves a theorization of its own activity that can only advance in function of its actual practice.

The fact that Schlegel ironizes over those who are exasperated with the exercise of criticism shows that not only in theory but also in practice he distances himself from Kant's explanation of the aesthetic experience, and that he uses the term "criticism" in a sense that oversteps the limits of this experience. Thus, the contradiction between fragments 57 and 117 is not resolved; rather, the former points to the insufficiency of the latter, whereas the latter, for all its insufficiency, emphasizes the fact that criticism is not entirely outside or above the literary object. In itself, this contradiction is decisive: it suggests that if criticism was to be emancipated from the ambiguity we have seen in Kant's explanation of aesthetic experience, it would have to break its strict identification as a literary genre or as an explanatory appendix to literary works, while avoiding delimiting a separate space of its own. To choose between the two fragments and affirm, against fragment 117, that criticism will not advance as long as it is included in literature, or else take sides against fragment 57 and accuse it of opposing criticism to "the pleasure of the text," would be to choose a sterile path. What is fascinating about Schlegel's approach is precisely its paradoxical nature.

The paradox is clearly stated in fragment 117 of the "Critical Fragments": a judgment of art must itself be a work of art. This statement is immediately extended to apply to two alternatives. The first possibility is rooted "in matter" (*im Stoff*). It is said to be constituted by the "presentation of the necessary impression in its becoming," which may give the impression that it is born of an impression (*Eindruck*) that cannot be reduced to the biographical explanation of the work under criticism. (In this case, the critic would have to justify his interest for such a work because the author comes from the same town as he, or because he had experiences similar to those described in the work, and so on.) Instead of such an accidental impression, what we have is an impression formulated in such a way that becoming is condensed in it—that is, is incorporated into the letter of the critical text that becomes readable through it. Now, how could the becoming—the time interposed between the object text and the critical object—be incorporated unless such an impression were impelled by a "fictional drive"? Thus, we believe Schlegel, in the passage in question, proceeds along the same lines as the tendency in present-day criticism formulated by Hartman: "Everyone has known the feeling that in Henry James or Sartre, let alone Borges, criticism is not independent of the fictional drive. The most insidious question is whether any critic has value who is only a critic: who does not put us in the presence of 'critical fictions' or make us aware of them in the writings of others" (Hartman 1980: 201).

The interpretation of the second possibility, however, presents no difficulties. In this case, the work of criticism is a work of art due to its "beautiful form" and its consonance with the liberal tone of ancient Roman satire. While "beautiful form" (*schöne Form*) subordinates the work of criticism to the strict condition of a literary genre, its affinity with satire emphasizes its character of questioning against the grain. On the basis of this interpretation, we can return to what was said about the first possibility and include both in a single assertion: criticism is neither inside nor outside literary space. It is part of poiesis but is not to be identified with the poetical. The poet may or may not be a critic: Kafka is, while Rilke is not; or, to take examples from Brazilian literature, João Cabral de Melo Neto is, while Carlos Drummond de Andrade is not. The presence of the critical dimension does not imply greater merit, nor does its absence signalize a fault. But what is a critic without poiesis (fictional drive) if not an art judge in disguise? The place of criticism is a certain interval. As Schlegel himself puts it, criticism materializes the dilemma between adopting a system and not following any. "It is just as pernicious to the spirit to have one system as it is to have none. Therefore one must simply decide to combine them" (Schlegel 1967c: 173). The combination alluded to at the end of fragment 57 points both to its need and to its lack of resolution, its openness to unceasing questioning.

The material we have seen so far does not indicate whether Schlegel went any further in concretely establishing the territory of poetry or of criticism. All we can do is ask: How could criticism escape arbitrariness if the author had early given up the possibility of judging according to pre-established rules?

The first fragment we analyzed in the present section was number 14. Let us now examine number 15: "The foolish master in Diderot's *Jacques le fataliste* perhaps does more honor to the author's art than his mad servant. The master's foolishness borders on genius, which was much more difficult to create than a madman who is a full-blown genius" (Schlegel 1967b: 148). Schlegel is then saying that the master in Diderot's novel is a better fictional character than his servant because the madness of the latter was easier to create than a foolishness bordering on genius. Clearly, the hierarchy between master and servant points to the emphasis on pure textual productivity. Schlegel applies to Diderot the considerations Diderot himself had presented in his *Paradoxe sur le comédien* (The paradox of acting). Just as the actor's quality depends on the distance he keeps from the character he plays, the quality of the characters in a novel depends on the distance between the characteristic displayed—foolishness or madness in the case in point—and the density achieved by textual means. Thus, the master is said to do more honor to Diderot's art because his foolishness can only be compared to that of a foolish genius. What in reality would be a paradox in literature is a virtue.

To go beyond mere paraphrase, we should say that here we are close to a category that is not actualized in Schlegel: the category of fiction. For a text whose greatest virtue is to make verisimilar what outside of it would seem incredible is precisely a fictional text. Thus, our initial concern with the determination of the fragment as a form led to an issue we have not yet examined: the author's implicit—never fully worked out—view of the fictional.

Let us leave the discussion of this question for a more appropriate opportunity and, to conclude this section, return once again to fragment 206 (Schlegel 1967c: 197). It lends support to the statement that criticism is not an autonomous activity unless it simultaneously asserts the autonomy of its object. Discrete and self-enclosed, the work of art and the fragment do not claim to exclude or exempt themselves from what surrounds them. Otherwise, it would be impossible to understand how practically every possible topic—the French Revolution, contemporary philosophy, the relation between writer and public, the question of marriage, and so on—is treated in both forms. The autonomy in question does not place poetry and criticism inside a cordon sanitaire that isolates them from the world.

The fragment, as the minimal form of the essay, suggests what is the territory open to criticism: criticism is a mode of the essay. As such, it is a quintessentially modern genre. So the second sentence in fragment 24 applies to the form: "Many works of the ancients have turned into fragments. Many works of the moderns are born as such" (p. 169). What is usually presented as criticism of antiquity will not be anachronistic only if one is careful to note that it corresponded to a different conception of literature, one founded on rhetorical criteria rather than on the experience of individual subjectivity (see Wellek 1982: 13–16).

THE CONSTITUTION OF TEXTUALITY

Earlier, we referred to wit as a springboard to the characterization of the fragment form. The question now is to see it as a part of the dynamics of the work.

In one of the first "Critical Fragments"—number 9—wit is defined in terms of the spirit of sociability: "*Witz* [wit] is the spirit of unconditional sociability or fragmentary genius" (Schlegel 1967b: 148). The statement seems to contradict what we said earlier about the difference between the fragment and baroque poetics. Thus, we must juxtapose it to fragment 394 in the second series: "It is a grave mistake to attempt to restrict wit to its use in society. For its devastating force, its infinite concentration, and its classical form, in its best manifestations wit often brings about an embarrassing pause in conversation. Wit, like laws, can be well thought-out only in writing" (Schlegel 1967c: 239).

There is a clear logical inconsistency between the two passages. If, however, we insist on the logical aspect and neglect the historical angle, we shall fail to see their richness. Even if the author was unaware of the fact, these two formulations spell out the dramatic change suffered by wit in a period of two centuries. Although by "spirit of sociability" Schlegel probably had in mind his experience of Berlin salons, where as a young man he circulated among men of letters and intellectual women, from the historical viewpoint these parties were no more than the remainders of an obsolete means of socialization (which, admittedly, was to survive for quite a while longer, as Proust was to show in his novel).

Baldesar Castiglione's *Il libro del cortegiano* (The book of the courtier) (1528) and Baltasar Gracián's *El discreto* (1646), translated as *The Compleat Gentleman*, are the great documents of courtly socialization. Both are intended to teach how to become the perfect courtier. The authors discuss in minute detail the adequate forms of conduct, the necessary learning, and particularly the proper forms of expression. Gracián writes in the beginning of his treatise: "Thus your character should be unique, but not anomalous; seasoned, not paradoxical." In order to adapt to what is required of him, the courtier must automatize the proper way of speaking. It must be witty, since "the truths that matter most to us are always only half said" (Gracián 1986: 21). However, these truths must be subordinated to decorum, as is emphasized in a passage from a dialogue between the author and "Doctor F. Francisco Andrés": "Author: Learning is never harmful. Doctor: But it may bring sorrow, and just as prudence prevents what others will say, discernment observes what others have said" (p. 22). The courtier's carefully chosen word, the recommended circumlocution, are purely oral in nature. And the refinement he seeks is not consistent with the exploration of personal potentialities: just as wit serves decorum, genius is admired as *ingenium*.

Courtly society no longer existed by Schlegel's time. Between Castiglione and Gracián's day and his own—between the court of Italian princes and of the Spanish king, on the one hand, and the private Berlin salons, on the other—there was the case of La Rochefoucauld. He had had the upbringing of a nobleman and had served in Louis XIV's court. His disapproval of absolutism and his participation in the Frond culminated in his estrangement from the court. La Rochefoucauld retired to his estate and, to while away his empty days, wrote his *Réflexions ou sentences et maximes morales* (Reflections or moral sentences and maxims) (1664).[13] The exercise of wit lived on, now in the printed page. But outside the court decorum had lost its practical function. For the nobleman expelled from the circle of power, orality was replaced by writing, and the intention of teaching refinement gave way to the ruminations of a disenchanted courtier. The very change in the organization of power had led to the displacement of wit to the written medium.[14]

When we consider the decline of the courtier, we realize the fruitfulness

---

13. For an in-depth analysis of this issue, see Costa-Lima 1992: 47–64.

14. This is not the place for a more detailed examination, which would conclude that in La Rochefoucauld (cf. n. 13, above) and in Schlegel the first elements for the analysis of the fictional appear.

of the fragments quoted last. Wit is now recruited for a different mission. Genius is encouraged not to acquire polish, but rather to discover its own voice. Wit then becomes one of the foundations upon which the text is built. But does it have limits? So it would seem, to tell from fragment 17: "Nothing is more contemptible than sad wit" (Schlegel 1967b: 148). What is Schlegel referring to? To find out, we must contextualize the fragment in the series.

Since Schlegel's admiration for Shakespeare knows no bounds, clearly he does not mean that as a critic he despises or is indifferent to tragedy or drama. Schlegel's target, in fact, is the lachrymose and the melodramatic, because they require no more than a flabby reception. Thus, sad wit would be a contradiction in terms. For wit signals a dense, unpredictable, lightning-quick reason. In place of the banal association between the "Romantic soul" and daydreaming or melancholic meditation, the early German romantic's praise of fancy—still understood as a synonym of imagination—did not imply the cult of irrationality. Here is fragment 104: "What is usually meant by reason is only one of its kinds: the diluted, watery one. There is also a thick, incandescent reason, which makes wit what it is and endows genuine style with elasticity and electricity" (p. 159). This dense reason is elsewhere re-ferred to as a chemical activity. This analogy makes it clear that Schlegel did not mean simply to value certain textual properties to the detriment of others; the following observation on Novalis would be just as apt, or even more so, in relation to Schlegel: "The application of chemical elements to aesthetic discourse . . . invests the latter with the quality of a revolutionary fact" (Moser 1989: 235).

Thus, to understand the role played by wit in Schlegel's thought we must understand the relation between this concept and various elements. On the one hand, it is a channel for the exploration of individual potentiality; but the latter is always considered as raw material to be transformed. The resulting product then becomes part of a different space, no more subordinated to the principle of "physical" reality than to the others—the political, the moral, the philosophical—it will have to rule over. In the fragments, this space is meta-phorically described as dense, electrical, unpredictable, instantaneous, chem-ical; the last adjective suggests that the transformation is to be not only aesthetical but political as well. On the other hand, being suffused with an undiluted reason, this space must extend its sway beyond the boundaries of the merely intellectual. That is the meaning behind fragment 350, attributed to Friedrich Schleiermacher, which states that "only the magic wand of affection [*Gemüt*] can make everything emerge" (Schlegel 1967c: 227). The emphasis laid on affection by the early German romantics, however, is not to be identified with the exclusiveness established by "normalized" Romanticism. Like Schiller's sentimental poet, they value affection and sensibility not in opposition to reason, but as means to thicken it. So the reason alluded to in the fragments is both "sentimental" and acute, both affectionate and piercing. Once this fact is understood, the emphasis on irony becomes more comprehensible.

Whereas wit was associated with the fragment, irony points to another genre: the novel. True, in the first series we find a fragment, number 42, the opening of which—"Philosophy is the true fatherland of irony" (Schlegel 1967b: 152)—points to a different theme: the unity to be attained between poetry and philosophy. But let us leave this fact aside for the moment and associate the passage with fragment 26: "Novels are the Socratic dialogues of our time. In this liberal form, knowledge of life escaped the schoolroom" (Schlegel 1967b: 149). The fragment does not actually speak of irony; rather, it exudes it. Whereas the Socratic dialogue was seen since the Renaissance as the epitome of schoolroom wisdom, its modern incarnation has the peculiarity of avoiding it. In addition, in order to ensure its liberal form, knowledge of life flees from the legitimated form of knowledge. The ironical critique of the official suggests another break looming in the horizon of time.

Even if we do not pause to examine Schlegel's considerations on the novel as the "Romantic book" par excellence, it is important to see how he justifies his statement. In a work published after the fragments, he introduces the term that mediates between irony and the novel: whereas "ancient poetry wholly relies on mythology to the point of avoiding any material that is properly historical," he argues, "Romantic poetry rests entirely upon a historical basis"; "Boccaccio is almost all true history" (Schlegel 1980b, 2: 177–78). History, not mythology, is the underlying layer common to the ironical procedure and the genre of the novel.

If we combine these passages, we arrive at the link between the ironical procedure and the poetics of the novel, and we add its mediating term, History. But we have not yet explained why History makes its entrance at this point. Let us turn to the ending of fragment 42:

> Only poetry . . . can still rise to the heights of philosophy without relying, as does rhetoric, on ironical passages. There are poems ancient and modern that exude from all their parts the divine breath of irony. In them there is a truly transcendental buffoonery. Inside them, the mood that suffuses all and infinitely towers above all that is conditioned, even above art, virtue, or genius; outside, in their execution, the mimic mode of the common Italian buffoon. (Schlegel 1967b: 152)

Irony is of capital importance to the novel because, its matter being historical, it deals only with human subjects. Without the use of a distancing technique, the presence of the merely human might compromise the meaning of the scene, suggesting that the intended goal was the human types represented by the characters and not the text in which they are presented. Even as it ensures the contact with the human, irony keeps the human from usurping the place of the text. To put it concisely: "Irony is the means of self-representation in art" (Strohschneider-Kohrs 1977: 70).

Being autonomous, literary space is not an altar to humanity. Being historical, the novel is not an instrument of divinization of the creature. In this all-too-brief moment when criticity flourished, the novel is not seen as a more or less disguised allegory of common men or of heroes. The individual—the human element—is the means for the creation of another materiality that chemically consumes and transforms it. What is required of the text is that it contain, in a limited space, a multiplicity of planes. That is why fragment 48 of the first series subordinates irony to paradox—"Irony is the form of the paradox. A paradox is everything that is great and good at the same time" (Schlegel 1967b: 153)—and number 108 praises Socratic irony. Its justification, at the end of the fragment—"It contains and excites the sense of the ineluctable struggle between the unconditioned and the conditioned, between the impossibility of and the need for full communication" (p. 160)— points to the very opposite of a poetics of complacency. To hammer this point home, let us turn once again to fragment 251 of the next series: "There are so many people today so tender and kind that they cannot stand a tragedy, and so noble and dignified that they will not hear a comedy. What testimony to the delicate morality of our century. Only the French Revolution gives it a bad name" (Schlegel 1967c: 207).

Irony has yet a supplementary use: it is able to subvert the very texts that would seem to forbid it. What genre could be more antithetical to the ironic procedure than the confessions? Nevertheless, even there irony instills its acid; so that Schlegel could write of Rousseau's *Confessions* that as a novel it is unsurpassable (*ein höchst vortrefflicher Roman*), far superior to *La Nouvelle Héloïse* [The new Heloise] (Schlegel 1980b, 2: 182). But the transformation of Rousseau's lachrymose seriousness into novelistic humor is so instantaneous as to seem magical. Indeed, in order to see the critical nature of this metamorphosis, one must realize that it relies on a formal transformation of the confessional object: the naive method (*auf dem Wege des Naiven*) used in its composition must be perceived as *arabesque*.

An examination of Schlegel's use of the term "arabesque" will bring into sharper focus the opposition between his version of criticity and the practice of aestheticization. To him, the arabesque is on the same plane as the *hieroglyph*, and both are connected to the praise of *chaos* in the work of art. A few brief examples will do. Fragment 173 of the *Athenäum* series states: "In the true poet's style, nothing is ornament; everything in it is a necessary hieroglyph" (Schlegel 1967c: 193). The formulation should be juxtaposed to a passage from "Brief über den Roman" (Letter on the novel) (an integral part of the "Gespräch"). After mentioning examples that would best contribute to a theory of the novel, he adds that they would be "veritable arabesques" (Schlegel 1980b, 2: 181); previously he had described them as "witty, bizarre paintings" (*witzigen Spielgemälde*) (p. 173). This description of the arabesque becomes clearer when we learn that it was formulated in connection with *Tristram Shandy*. But even this is not enough to make it satisfactory.

The difficulty is probably lessened, however, when we realize that Schlegel is trying to apprehend the experience of the sublime. This is what we are led to think when we read two passages. The first is Schlegel's description, in fragment 424, of the French Revolution, "the greatest and most incredible phenomenon in political history," as "a nearly universal earthquake, an immeasurable flood in the political world, or the archetype of revolutions," and as "the most terrible grotesque of our age" and "an amazing chaos" (Schlegel 1967c: 247–48). The second is a fragment he left unpublished: "The most important thing in the novel is chaotic form—arabesque, fairy tale" (quoted in Brown 1979: 92). Arabesque and chaos fascinate Schlegel and are incorporated into the values of the work because they contain so much complexity that—to quote the closing lines of João Cabral de Melo Neto's poem "Uma faca só lâmina" (A knife all blade)—"in trying to grasp it / every image explodes."

In chaos and in the arabesque, wonderment and astonishment are combined. In this, they are functions of the necessary hieroglyph, opposed to ornament, as fragment 173 observes. An ornament is what gives pleasure and is undemanding. It is tamed beauty. Nothing could be more antithetical to it than the functions of the hieroglyph, from its wildest outer limit, chaos, to the artistic elaborations of the arabesque and the bizarre. Just as ornament is the motto of aestheticization, the arabesque is the sign of criticity. The former is driven by the agreeable, which sweetens and legitimates the existing world; the latter is driven by the sensation that the world requires of men more than complacency and "understanding."

If our conclusions are valid, they have the immediate effect of allowing us to emphasize the distance between Schlegel's positions and Kant's view of the aesthetic experience. Consider, for instance, the passage where Kant discusses the experience in which the object is not subordinated to an objective finality. When this happens, "nothing is left but the subjective finality of the representations in the mind of the Subject intuiting. This gives [*angibt*] a certain finality of the representative state of the Subject, in which the Subject feels itself quite at home in its effort to grasp a given form in the imagination" (Kant 1982a: 70; B 47). Is not the ornament the best expression of this "well-being of the subject" in the sphere of the imagination?

Against this, one might argue that Kant's object was not exactly a judgment on the work of art: the example he gives in this context is a clearing in a forest, so that he seems to be reflecting on the experience of nature. Nevertheless, it might be counterargued that, whatever Kant's purpose in his examination of what he calls reflective judgment, he was to find in aesthetic judgment the purest form of reflection. Thus, starting from the aesthetic experience of the work of art, one may retrace the trajectory of Kant's text and find that, independently of the author's purpose, he privileges the ornamental in art—for the ornamental does not respond to any objective finality and satisfies and relaxes the contemplator fastest. Last, it should be understood that my intention is not to find flaws in Kant's edifice, but rather to affirm the difference between the function of art in Kant's time and what it must be today.

The equivalences we mentioned earlier have also another implication: the functions of the necessary hieroglyph are emphasized as a consequence of the autonomy of the principle of reality in relation to the poetical which is ensured by Schlegel's theory. Here is the definitive formulation of this idea: "The allusion to chaos and Eros symbolizes the abandonment of the function of imitation and reflection; it symbolizes the correlation between 'free and creative activity of imagination' and the denial of all links and restrictions, by means of an established world of laws, which restricts or orients the poem" (Preisendanz 1967: 64).

THE SPACE OF THE POETIC

The fragments mentioned shortly before emphasized the technical procedures responsible for the metamorphosis operated in the poem. Since Schlegel refused an objective, systematic, and consequently normative aesthetics, it would be absurd to expect him to believe that these procedures ensured quality. These instruments are only the condition that make the poetic effect possible; the latter is then the counterpart and the complement of the former. Thus, fragment 20—"A classical work should never become entirely understandable. But people who are cultivated and who cultivate themselves should always want to learn more from it" (Schlegel 1967b: 149)—naturally points only to the work's "arabesque" effect. An idea that was to become commonplace in our own time—that the historical situation itself favors, hampers, or blocks the reader's motivation—did not occur to Schlegel.

To him, on the contrary, a classic is what generates an infinite effect, ensuring the work its (supposed) form of eternity. It is also important to consider, in fragment 20, the constituent role of the receiver in the formation of the work, ancient or modern.

It is important to emphasize the effect of the poetic work, lest Schlegel's theorization be seen as the forerunner of what in the twentieth century was to be known as immanentist criticism, the most popularized form of which was New Criticism.

Attuned to the formative characteristics of literary works, the effect has the reader as its subject. The reader, thus, is considered in consequence not of a generic centering on the individual self, but of his displacement in favor of the object of experience. The fragments deal with the receiver by emphasizing poiesis objectified in a product. For the moment, let us consider only fragment 28: "Having the sense (of a particular art, science, man, and so on) is a division of the mind, a self-restriction and, thus, the result of self-creation and self-negation" (Schlegel 1967b: 149).

The constant concern with education that characterizes Schlegel's time here opens a new front. Consider, first, that this newness is indirectly related to reflection on art, for the receiver was brought to the fore by the examination of the poem's effect. Thus, instead of an aesthetic education, the consequences of which we have already seen, there is a critical education. However, its fruits transcend the boundaries of art and formulate a parameter for individual maturation. For this is what is newest about the proposal: rather than exalt the infinite expansion of the individual, it stresses the need for self-limitation (*Selbstbeschränkung*). Like the poem, the substance of the individual may be compared to a gas that must be compressed in a narrow container so that it will not be diluted and lose its force. What is self-denied in this way becomes a condition for what is self-created. The imposition of limits conditions the possibility of concentration.

This helps us to understand why there is feedback between criticity and poiesis. Here Schlegel exhibits his extraordinary capacity to formulate a theory of poetic experience that, serving as a model for the receiver's critical education, does not reduce the other activities to the aesthetic principle. And since this capacity is founded on the use of wit, we must add that it is no less surprising that the incisive, witty word should establish not a direct but an oblique circuit—the examination of the poem is not extended in a program that would necessarily be aestheticizing, but rather unfolds into an unspecific mirror, one that is adequate to all and any sort of intellectual formation.

The same obliquity may be seen when Schlegel returns to a consideration of the strict field of the experience of art. Fragment 172, attributed to

August Wilhelm, states: "It may be said that a characteristic trait of poetic genius is knowing much more than it knows it knows" (Schlegel 1967c: 192). The consequence of this is that no relevance is given to grasping so-called authorial intent. It should be noted, in passing, that there is complete disagreement among the members of the Jena group. It is a well-known fact that Schleiermacher not only was Schlegel's friend and a contributor to the fragments Schlegel published but also was interested in a hermeneutics that was not restricted to biblical texts. Now, one of the principles of this founder of Romantic hermeneutics was to establish, for the interpreter, the goal of recovering what the author really meant to say, even if unaware of it. Through this "divinatory" method, the interpreter would have access to the author's poiesis.

In its incisive formulation, fragment 172 forbids all psychologism. Further, if we associate it with number 299, which seems unquestionably to have been written by Friedrich, we get a result with implications beyond the sphere of the literary: "As to sheer unconsciousness of genius, it seems to me philosophers are quite the match for poets" (Schlegel 1967c: 215). The statement is clearly heretical. To see the philosopher as the poet's equal in being possessed by a "daemon" that speaks for him is to question the secular legitimation of philosophy. What is most important, however, is that the autonomy of the text in relation to the intention behind it goes beyond the sphere of poetry. So exceptional is the statement that one laments that it is no more than a fragment.

We have saved for the last part of this section the discussion of three of the most important fragments. They are those numbered 116, 238, and 74 (all from the second series). We shall translate only the parts that interest us here.

> Romantic poetry is a progressive universal poetry. Its destiny [*Bestimmung*] is not only to reunite all the separate genres of poetry and place poetry in contact with philosophy and rhetoric. It wants to—and also must—combine and fuse poetry and prose, genius and criticism, art poetry and natural poetry; make poetry alive and communicative, life and society poetic; poeticize the wit; fill and saturate the forms of art with the genuine stuff of culture and animate them with the vibrations of humor. . . . Only [Romantic poetry] can, like the epic, change itself into the mirror of the whole world around it, in the image of its time. . . . Other poetic genres are finished and may be fully dissected. The genre of Romantic poetry is still in formation; its proper essence is being eternally in a state of becoming, never completing itself. No theory can exhaust it, and only a divinatory criticism can dare characterize its ideal. Only it is infinite, and only it is free and recognizes as its first law that the poet's whim [*Willkür*] tolerates no law. The genre of Romantic poetry is the only one that is more than a genre and,

so to speak, is poetic art itself: for in a certain sense all poetry is or should be Romantic. (Schlegel 1967c: 182)

There is a poetry that is fully the relation between the ideal and the real, and that, by analogy with philosophical terminology, should be called transcendental poetry. It begins as satire, with the absolute differentiation between the ideal and the real, in the middle, drifts as elegy and ends as idyll, with the absolute identity between ideal and real. But, just as one would attribute less value to a transcendental philosophy that were not critical, so this poetry should add to the transcendental materials and exercises that are frequent in modern poets a poetic theory of the faculty of poetizing. (Schlegel 1967c: 204)

In a faulty use of language, *verisimilar* means *almost true* or *somewhat true* or *what may yet come to be true*. All of this, however, according to its composition [*Bildung*], cannot apply to the word. What seems to be true need not necessarily be true, to any degree; but it positively must seem to be so. The verisimilar is the object of sagacity, of the faculty of singling out, among the possible sequences of free actions, the one that will turn out to be real; it is something entirely subjective. What some logicians have thus labeled and attempted to describe is possibility. (Schlegel 1967c: 175)

The first fragment deals with the tension between the inexhaustibility of Romantic poetry and the desire for unification with which it is infused. Its first qualities—being progressive and universal—point to what makes it different from the older mode, corresponding to a world entire unto itself, as well as the need to be integrated in a future time that cannot be visualized. (It is hardly necessary to point out the manifest influence of Schiller's idea.) Though opposed, the old and the modern modes reveal the correspondence between them through a comparison of the role played by the epic in the past and that which is expected of the modern mode, of which the novel is the genre par excellence. Further, the inability of any theory to exhaust it again underscores the incomplete, tentative character of Romantic criticism. To Schlegel, then, criticism operates along the axis whose opposite poles are the fragment and the essay. Criticism remains essayistic as long as it does not become associated with a systematic aesthetics. This, in turn, forces it to remain on the plane of theorization.

The commentary on fragment 116 was brief because the fragment only combines aspects that had already been analyzed separately, because an exhaustive treatment of it would be dysfunctional here,[15] and also because the desire for union that it stresses will be taken up only later. And, although this

---

15. Thus, for instance, the statement that the poet's whim (more precisely, the ability of being an arbitrator, *arbitrariness*) will tolerate no law can be understood both as a reiteration of the autonomy of aesthetic judgment and as a consequence of an implicit social hierarchy, at the top of which stands the artist. It seems that both readings are valid in the

is not the proper moment to do it, the reading of this fragment already paves the way for the discussion, since it introduces the issue of unity.

In this context, we should remember Benjamin's observation that the phrase "transcendental poetry" is a "mystifying allusion" (Benjamin 1974a, 1, 1: 95). Indeed, to define, within a seemingly Kantian context, the transcendental as that which unites and deals with the relation between the real and the ideal, as the end of fragment 22 does again (Schlegel 1967c: 169), would be flagrantly to violate Kant's distinction between the transcendental—an examination of the conditions in which reason, from the viewpoint of the intended knowledge of the object, can be effective—and the transcendent, which includes the excessive pretensions of reason.

It might be argued that our concern with detail risks missing what is relevant in the fragment. This is the point of an eminent interpreter. In poetical reflection, writes Strohschneider-Kohrs about this passage, "the integral parts, in a transcendental achievement [*Vollzug*], are changed into a synthesis: the synthesis that joins subject and objectivity, but in such a way that the components of artistic creation, the created and the creator, are recognizable in coexistence" (Strohschneider-Kohrs 1977: 48). But the problem with this reading is that it neglects the connection between art criticism and a view of History that is always present in Schlegel.

The synthesis effected by transcendental poetry presupposes not only poetic achievement, as Strohschneider-Kohrs underscores, but also a historical approach, in which the idyll announces the conciliation of opposites at the end. The interpreter's observation implies that the second layer does not interfere with the first, so that there is nothing problematic about Schlegel's thought. It would be more precise to stress the underground presence of a force opposed to criticity in the "idyllic" aspiration of transcendental poetry. So far, this opposing force reveals no more than its unifying ambition. However, it has a more precise name. It is a religious intention. It is, in fact, a religion, which, as Lacoue-Labarthe and Nancy write, "is art itself, but art henceforth thought of as *Darstellung* [representation] (absolute, with no remnants) of truth" (Lacoue-Labarthe and Nancy 1978: 203).

To test the validity of this qualification, we must proceed with our examination. For the moment, all we can do is warn the reader that under the edifice of Schlegel's theorization, something points in the opposite direction. The movements of this contrary layer are hardly noticeable. Sooner or later, however, an earthquake will topple the entire structure. But if it would be

context of this phase of the author's. To these the religious dimension should also be added. But all of this would be relevant only in an analysis that centered on Schlegel himself.

rash to ignore the existence of this "archaeological fault," one must also take into account fragment 74.

It is much less famous than the two others, and it raises a point that, surprisingly, has largely been neglected. To understand it fully, let us look also at fragments 100 and 101: "Poetic appearance [*Schein*] is a game of representations, and the game is an appearance of actions" (Schlegel 1967c: 180). "What happens in poetry either never happens or always happens. Otherwise it is not real poetry. It is not necessary to believe that this is actually [*wirklich*] happening now" (p. 180). What is said about the verisimilar, what is denied of it and, later, what is asserted of it, always assumes the relation between truth and appearance (*Schein*). Ultimately, then, appreciation of the verisimilar implies appreciation of the work of mimesis.

Since classical antiquity, the treatment of mimesis has led to a dichotomy. The oft-quoted passage of Aristotle's *Poetics*—"though the objects themselves may be painful to see, we delight to view the most realistic representations of them in art, the forms for example of the lowest animals and of dead bodies" (Aristotle 1952: 682; 1448b 10–11)—is one of the alternatives. It is expressed in the statement that the image is not received in the same way as its source; the unpleasantness of the perception of the source is not necessarily caused by its image.

Now, what is perceived—as long as we are certain that it is not an illusion, that we are not the victims of our own imagination—is traditionally taken to be true, or at least the basis of truth. The image's specific power of action thus raises a difficulty for the theory of truth on substantialist bases—truth as that which states what *is* without the decisive interference of the agent or the form the thing is given—of which Aristotle is one of the major exponents. How could a substantialist theory of truth, which sees truth as *re*-cognizance, be reconciled with and do justice to the tendency to emphasize the autonomy of the image and its deviation from what is perceived? How to accept the tendency if not by somehow bringing it back to the community, like the shepherd who brings the stray sheep back to the fold? Because of the difficulty of such a task, the other alternative has more simply consisted in repressing the autonomy of the image and treating it on the level of *percepta*. As classical thought came to prevail over "pre-Socratic" tendencies, the substantialist tradition of truth came to dictate the legitimated interpretation of mimesis, mimesis and *imitatio* and, consequently, conformity to a model, that is, to something perceived or perceivable—no matter how far the model or how idealized the perceived—that is real, empirical, given.

This digression has served to show the direct link between the classical reading and its rejection by Schlegel. Fragment 74 denounces the arbitrariness of interpreting the verisimilar in terms of the scale of truth. Its refusal to accept the usual reading of the term implies that the true and the verisimilar correspond to two differentiated scales. Now, to the extent that the verisimilar is manifested in an image or that it is the product actualized by an image, it belongs in the area of mimesis. From this it follows that it is only in an improper sense, the effect of a usage already adopted to the substantialist paradigm and no longer integrated to the order of mimesis (see the opening of Chapter 1), that mimesis can be understood as imitation. Consequently, the statements that the verisimilar does not belong in the scale of truth and is entirely contained in *Schein*—appearance, that which shines, the shine of appearance—are entirely consistent with the beliefs of Schlegel, who from the beginning had broken with an aesthetics that claimed to know a priori what is the objectivity of value in art and where it is.

If these two statements were predictable from a strictly logical point of view, there is nothing predictable about the most incisive point of the fragment: though what seems to be true need not be true at all, it "positively must seem to be so" (aber es muß doch positiv scheinen). Appearance can neither be directly submitted to the scale of truth nor can it be restricted to the property of having an illusionary shine. The whole problem has to do with how the need to positively seem what is not does not affect the autonomy of the scale of the verisimilar. Earlier, we said that this autonomous scale was logically predictable since Schlegel abandoned the positions he had defended in "Das Studium." We must now add that the explicit presentation of this view, however, clashed with what we have described as his desire to achieve unity once more—that is, to have or give access to a position that left behind the fragmentation of values of the modern world. The plain sentence "Was wahr scheint, braucht darum auch nicht im kleinsten Grad wahr zu sein" (What seems to be true need not necessarily be true, to any degree) contains the entire dilemma that characterizes early Schlegel—in fact, his decisive dilemma. The aestheticizing path, in the two variants we have described, had been able to disguise or even suppress the issue of the relation between the artistic verisimilar and truth. By so doing, it brought about the control (on art, or, instead, based on art).

Schlegel had the extraordinary merit of formulating the decisive question. This discovery, however, took place in the context of a line of thinking that aspired to recapture a comprehensive unity. This is the reason of the conflict: to contribute to the hoped-for union, or to help the liberation of a scale proper to verisimilitude? The two proposals cannot be reconciled. Unity may be attained to the detriment of art or in its favor. In the latter case, the scale of verisimilitude would triumph over that of truth and ridicule every proposal that did not see truth as a specific case of the properties of verisimilitude. This, then, is the limit of Schlegel's position.

Nonetheless, to return to a deduction previously arrived at in connection with a different fragment, it is only fair to note that the sentence that sums up Schlegel's dilemma contains, though unnoticed, the key to the following step. For a product that cannot be identified with a true statement but must positively seem like one can only be a fictional product. The fictional is a *Schein* that is not content with its own shine, that is, the effect—emotion, effusion, transport, or mere satisfaction—it causes; it must appear to be true so that its receivers may consider what they take to be true, question it, have something solid—the text and its effects—to stand for the concretization of their questioning of the truth.

Thus, it is not enough to speak of the specific scale of verisimilitude; it is also necessary to relate it to its neighbor, the scale of truth. This is what Schlegel does, even if unconsciously. By combining the verisimilar and the true—i.e., through the interconnection of their scales—the verisimilar in art appears as a functionally *different* element: it makes the work of art autonomous from the requirement of truth in order to place truth in perspective—that is, to submit it to examination by the community of receivers. Thus understood, the fictional is, in sum, the figure that arises with the adoption of criticity.

Last, it should be added that to say that the figure of the fictional was imminent in Schlegel's reflection but was never made explicit means that its full formulation was blocked by a contrary force. We are now in a condition to put together the conclusions of the two arguments: the condensed figure of criticity does not emerge because it is resisted by the desire to recapture unity, to legitimate an obligatory Law—that is, one that would apply regardless of the particularities of nations and their spatial location.[16] This is a fact that must be taken into account in our analysis: in the work of the great proponent of criticity—Schlegel, whose life makes one think of a Rimbaud *avant la lettre*—the ideal of criticity was corroded from inside by the opposite current.

A Final Rectification

The last fragments to consider concern criticism and the individual, and are presented for a double purpose: to reinforce the observations made previously and to prepare for the final treatment.

16. The reader who is acquainted with Wolfgang Iser's work will recognize the importance of the idea of the fictional as a questioner of historically acknowledged truths in Iser's thought. It follows then that I am saying that Iser's thought transcends Schlegel's limit.

The prominence of the issue of criticism was, generally speaking, a result of the feeling of dissatisfaction, the sense of crisis, and also the urge to respond in a revolutionary way to Germany's peripheral position in the second half of the eighteenth century. Hence, we have the extreme variety of topics covered by the fragments, and the central place they reserve for the French Revolution. Further, in the sphere of literature in particular, the variety derives from the situation of the moderns in relation to the ancients. Schlegel writes in fragment 93 of the first series: "In the ancients, one sees all poetry in full flower; in the moderns, one foresees the spirit to come" (Schlegel 1967b: 158). The dissociation between the two times had been well formulated by Schiller. Schlegel does not intensify this dissociation; rather, he steers it in a new direction: that of criticity.

So far we have been content to characterize Schlegel as the "other" of aestheticism. This, however, we know now, was only possible at a certain stage of our argument. Now we are in a position to state that this simple opposition is fictitious. Though to a slighter degree, aestheticization was also present in Schlegel. The weakening of his critical thrust could already have been detected when we observed that its manifestation was accompanied by an underground force in the opposite direction. Now is the time to focus on this opposing force. In his "Speech on Mythology" (Rede über die Mythologie), a part of the "Gespräch," mythology is said to be the element that gave cohesion and unity to the ancients, and the absence of which provided the driving force for the moderns: "I maintain that our poetry lacks that central point [*Mittelpunkt*] which mythology was for the ancients, and that the essential reason why modern poetic art ranks below the ancient can be summed up in these words: we do not have a mythology" (Schlegel 1980b, 2: 159).

Shortly later, he added: it was the contact of ancient poetic expression with mythology that transformed chaos into "a harmonic world" (p. 161). By identifying "supreme beauty" with "the supreme order . . . of chaos" (p. 161), he implicitly attributed to modern beauty the qualities of being progressive and infinite. (What the author called "supreme beauty" corresponds to the concept of the sublime.) So far, there is nothing new here. However, also in the early chapters of the "Speech," he adds: "We are on the verge of reaching [a new mythology]; or rather, there is an urgent need that we seriously collaborate in its production" (p. 161). This was not an unreasonable demand, for the very existence of German Idealism was "a very significant sign and a remarkable confirmation" of the fact that the new mythology was to be generated "from the innermost depth of the spirit" (p. 160). It should be remembered that this text was written in 1800—that is, before Schlegel's political and intellectual about-face, at a time when he was still fired by a revolutionary urge. This clearly indicates that his criticity was accompanied by an opposing tendency, associated with the determination to contribute to the creation of a new mythology that would harmonize the creative chaos. From this viewpoint, criticity was seen as a provisional instrument, to be used for the purpose of promoting the advent of a time when it would no longer be needed.

Certainly Schlegel did not mean to detract from the merit of Romantic, contemporary works because they were driven by a chaos devoid of a center. Criticity seems to him legitimate in the meantime, for the works of his time. But this implies that the thought of an entire existence devoted to criticity would be unbearable. Unfortunately, this intolerance was manifested not only in Schlegel's own lifetime but also in the entire period that began with the fall of Napoleon and the conservative restoration.

It was, then, during this very brief period—beginning in 1797, with the appearance of the first series of fragments, and ending in 1800—that Schlegel produced the most extraordinary part of his work. As literary criticism proper—that is, practical actualization of a theoretical elaboration—this work was driven by the need to provide a different alternative for the unsatisfactory state of affairs mentioned in the beginning of fragment 167: "Almost all judgments on art are either too generic or too particular" (Schlegel 1967c: 191). One year earlier, in an article in honor of Lessing, he had provided the definitive formulation for the conception of criticism as he practiced it: "Criticism is thought of as a mediator between History and philosophy, which are connected by it. In criticism, History and philosophy ought to come together so that a new, third field might arise. Without philosophical spirit, criticism cannot prosper—on this all agree; but neither can it flourish without historical knowledge" (Schlegel 1971c: 399).

In order to understand this passage, it is important to keep in mind that the view of History it implied assumed a vehement denial of the factualistic tendency already present in Herder:

> Since hypotheses are often spoken ill of, someone ought to attempt to write a History without hypotheses once. A thing cannot be said to be if it is not said what it is. If one thinks of facts, one relates them to concepts and cannot possibly be indifferent to them. If this much is known, then among the possible concepts one determines and chooses those that are necessary if facts of all kinds are to be related. If one does not wish to acknowledge the fact, the choice is left to · instinct, chance, or whim, and the investigator is flattered to have a pure, solid, a posteriori empirics, when in fact he has a highly partial, dogmatic, transcendent a priori view. (Schlegel 1967c: 201–2)

Lest I be accused of overinterpretation, here is a straightforward criticism of Herder, at the end of Schlegel's review of the *Humanitätsbriefe* (Letters to humankind): "The method of considering each flower of art without appreciation [*Würdigung*], but taking into account only the place, time, and manner, could ultimately lead to no other conclusion than that everything should be as it is and has ever been" (Schlegel 1967a: 54). Contrary to what is affirmed by the triumphant factualistic conception of history, Schlegel realizes that there are, properly speaking, no facts, but only interpretations of facts; and that, properly speaking, there are no interpretations of facts, but only the practical working out of concepts, the predominance of which is all the greater when the factualistic historian is not aware of their existence.

In short: inside this small but rich body of work, the very forces that will lead to paralysis are already contained.

Before ending our discussion of Schlegel in his capacity as a critic, we must come to a conclusion concerning what was his final word on the status of aesthetics—whether he gave up objective aesthetics; whether he diverged from Fichte when he privileged examination of the poetic object; whether he affirmed that the poetry of his time was fated to be progressive and thus necessarily experimental, so that no theory could ever exhaust it or establish a set of norms on which judgment could be based. In short, the question is: According to Schlegel, what criteria should be adopted by a critic who refused to settle for subjective values?

On the basis of what we have seen, we may say that Schlegel did not formulate a theoretical answer to this question. His conclusion is rather a negation:

> To the historical conscience of modernity, beauty is given only as an ideal to be attained. Since art had become emancipated from the old aesthetic's "ideal of beauty," defined in terms of content, the question, in short, was whether aesthetic criticism should be justified, should take into account an ideal of beauty that had never been legitimated, without grounding art on a psychological— and therefore historically relativistic—disposition. (Weber 1973: 177)

It is only fair to add that, for all his claims to the contrary and his greater admiration for Fichte's *Doctrine of Science*, Schlegel always kept within the limits of Kant's third *Critique*. This is confirmed by a passage from one of his many unpublished writings: "The modern *supremely beautiful* of artistic form is never reached; it is a regulative Idea" (Schlegel 1958: 199). The phrase clearly relies on the Kantian concept. To Kant, a regulative principle is one that can be inferred from an Idea (such as God, freedom, or the soul) which, being indispensable to reason, is, from the viewpoint of the understanding, no more than a problematic, inaccessible concept (Kant 1982b, 57; B 341). "Judgments passed in this manner"—led by concepts that "exceed the capacity of understanding [*überschwengliche Begriffe*]"—"cannot be constitutive" but only regulative (p. 58; B 342).

The passage from *Nachlaß* (Posthumous writings) reinforces this idea: the values that guide judgments on art are based on a regulative principle, and thus can neither be automatic nor declare the structure of the object they concern. Hence, judgments inevitably risk arbitrariness; hence, there is urgent need for a criticity to watch over their every step. (Or, as a correlate, throughout the history of criticism, with the appearance of each norm—ethnic, national, sociological, etc.—criticity is forgotten for a time.) Now, as we have seen, this criticity was always accompanied by an opposite current. We are not saying that Schlegel's theory of criticism was simply hampered by his belief in the need for a new, harmonizing mythology; we do say that it was cut short, neutralized, and ultimately abolished by it. Let us see how this took place.

Schlegel's anticritical tendencies also originated from his thoughts concerning the individual. Two fragments are relevant here: number 116 of the first series and number 414 of the second series: "Germans are said to be the foremost nation in the world when it comes to excellence of artistic sense and scientific spirit. True; only, there are very few Germans" (Schlegel 1967b: 161).

> If there is an invisible Church, it is the Church of the great paradox that cannot be separated from morality and should not be confused with the merely philosophical. Men who are eccentric enough to be and to become gravely virtuous everywhere understand one another, find one another easily, and make up a silent opposition against the ruling immorality, which dons the trappings of morality. A certain mysticism of expression, which, together with Romantic fantasy and grammatical sense, can be a very good and attractive thing, and is frequently used by them as a symbol of their beautiful mysteries. (Schlegel 1967c: 243–44)

The Christian phrase "invisible Church" makes its one appearance in these series of writings hitherto characterized by irreverence. But it plays a major role, for it is what makes it possible to gather the new elect mentioned in fragment 116. In order to understand the connection we are making, it will be necessary to see beyond the irony that is so impressive in a first reading of fragment 116. The vaunted exceptionality of Germans is true, says the fragment, as long as it is observed that they are few. But few because Germany is small? This is the key to the irony of the text, and the way to go beyond it. Germans are few not because Germany is small, but because only a few have the qualities mentioned. Thus, the fragment expresses not patriotic pride, but elitism.

Fragment 414 of the second series extends the domains of these chosen few beyond the borders of the German world. Further, such phrases as "a certain mysticism of expression," "a Romantic fantasy," and "grammatical sense" clearly underscore the Romantic cosmopolitanism of this aristocracy of the spirit. A true aristocracy, it holds the material world in contempt. Thus, in obvious consonance with what we have seen in Novalis, fragment 410 of the second series states: "Everyday existence and economy are the necessary supplement of natures about which there is nothing universal" (Schlegel 1967c: 243). The concept of "invisible Church" undergoes a significant shift: it is made up not of Christians, but of men of spirit—that is, Romantics.

Hence, fragments that might seem irrelevant take on a surprising importance. The poetic object, which had been illuminated by critical examination, now serves as a means to legitimate a certain elite. Outside of the aristocracy of blood, the intellectual justifies his right to superiority. When we realize this, we see that—with regard to an understanding of Schlegel's work, though not of his theory of criticism—his idea of fusing poetry, science, and philosophy cannot be disregarded. His search was motivated not only by an abstract metaphysical worldview, by a new, tranquilizing Law, but by the legitimation of a new aristocracy, an aristocracy that would represent the cream of a deified humanity. In this context, another "irrelevant" fragment, number 262, acquires significance: "Every honest man is ever coming to be God. Becoming God, being a man, cultivating oneself [*sich bilden*] are equivalent expressions [*die einerlei bedeuten*]" (p. 210).

Finally, fragment 406 proves that the link between art, the artist, and religiosity is not an effect of overinterpretation: "If every infinite individual is God, then there are as many gods as there are ideals. The relation between the true artist and the true man and his ideal is also a complete religion. He for whom this divine inner service is a lifetime goal and occupation is a priest—that which each one can and should become" (p. 242).

These last-quoted fragments all date from the same period as the previous ones. Thus, it could not be said that they point to some change undergone by the author. We are forced to conclude that, in Schlegel, criticity is accompanied by a sense of the aristocracy of artists, understood as the indispensable condition for becoming a member of an "alternative" church.

This conclusion is, in turn, reinforced by a curious letter sent by Schlegel to Novalis on December 2, 1798. Explaining more clearly the announcement of his intention of "writing a new Bible," contained in a letter also addressed to Novalis on October 20 of the same year, Schlegel now adds: "My Bible project is not literary but biblical, absolutely religious. I am thinking of founding a new religion; or rather, helping to announce it: then it will come and conquer without my aid" (Schlegel 1975, 4: 507).

We have seen that to Novalis private aestheticization implied a mystical encounter independent of any church. To Schlegel, the situation is more complex: simultaneously, we find a theory that, through its criticity, is a genuine theory of literature, and the postulation of a religion of art. These tendencies are antagonistic, because the first is inspired by a progressive, experimental drive that does not aim at a predetermined point of arrival, whereas the second affirms precisely the reaching of a goal, a new *re-ligio*—a new re-linking—that was to absorb what till then had been dispersed and fragmentary, and would make criticism superfluous, even suspect. But it should also be added that the second tendency is motivated by the fact that the first was unable to satisfy the desire for harmony and unity felt by Schlegel. Paradoxically, then, Schlegel's criticity was accompanied by a private aestheticization even more radical than his friend's: it actually led to a new church. That is why we say that Schlegel's criticity was accomplished in the brief period during which his fantastic idea of founding a new religion did not give way to the more pragmatic act of converting to a church already in existence.

In short, criticity among the early German romantics was as short-lived as it was because no center, no existing institution or intellectual system, satisfied them. Heading in all directions, criticity, particularly in Schlegel's case, concentrated particularly on understanding the art of poetry. Thus, Schlegel was to arrive at the frontier of a concept decisive to the specificity of the poetic: its fictional character, which, being placed at the crossroads of the scales of truth and of verisimilitude, conferred on it a peculiar position in relation to truth. For the fictional, since it cannot be taken to propose some truth, is located at a place from which truth can be seen in perspective. This is what we meant when we said that the fictional is the very condensation of criticity.

Against its formulation, however, there was the other tendency in Schlegel's thought: the search for a unity of meaning for the world, one that would be unequivocal, creating a communion for those who adhered to it. If this tendency could no longer be motivated by criticity, it had art as an object of cult. The religion of art, the supreme incarnation of aestheticism, was then the earthquake that demolished the critical edifice. In its place, that religion helped build, outside the idealization of bohemianism, the recognition of the writer, the man of letters, and the artist as embodiments of the ideal of culture, as models of the man of refined spirit and sensibility. This image was to last in "civilized" Europe until it was destroyed by the consequences of the Great War. However, after the anarchical and creative turmoil of the 1920's and 1930's, aestheticization found new allies for its triumphal march. Since it is outside the scope of the present work, let us simply highlight, at the end of the chapter, some of the trends that led to that march.

The End of the Critical Road

For the sake of convenience, I offer here some relevant biographical information.[17]

Novalis died in March 1801. Although the adventure that had culminated in the publication of the *Athenäum* magazine had already ended, the death of his friend, together with the fact that his brother had moved to Berlin, convinced Schlegel that there was nothing left for him to do in Jena. In April he followed August Wilhelm to Berlin. But he was unable to make a living there either. Then he decided to move to Paris, where he was to found an international magazine. He left Berlin in 1802, traveling through Dresden, Leipzig, and Weimar. In late July, he settled in Paris with Dorothea Veit (the daughter of the Jewish philosopher Moses Mendelssohn), with whom he had been living in Jena and who had followed him in his travels. They married in Paris, in 1804. But the ambitious project that had brought him abroad failed, and the magazine he had begun to publish, *Europa*, did not earn him enough to survive on. The couple began to make their way back.

In Cologne, where they settled first, Schlegel tried to get himself appointed to a university post. Again, he failed. In 1808, still in Cologne, Friedrich and Dorothea converted to Roman Catholicism. In the summer of the same year, Schlegel went to Vienna, where he expected to get support from influential friends and finally achieve the success that had proved elusive in France. In November, his material difficulties having been overcome, he told his wife to come join him. Late in March 1809, he was notifying his brother that he had finally managed to get hold of a position in the Austrian administration. From then on, he was politically active as a journalist, defending Austria's war against Napoleon, doing a stint in the diplomatic service under Metternich, and also lecturing. Until his death in 1829 Schlegel was to be an exemplary (and obscure) defender of the ruling order. Although his intellectual production continued incessantly, his brilliance was gone. More precisely, he had become reconciled with the common early-nineteenth-century view of literature.

To see this, one need only glance at the lectures he gave in Vienna from February 27 to April 20, 1812. Published in 1815, with a dedication to Metternich, they were titled *Geschichte der alten und neuen Literatur* (subsequently translated as *Lectures on the History of Literature*).

17. Taken from Peter 1978 (especially pp. 50–66).

From the very first, Schlegel's lectures stress the relation between literary works and the national spirit. The poetic work is no longer a particular requiring a subtle understanding of its parts, but a bloc expressing and illustrating the nation that gave birth to it: "For the later development and full intellectual existence of a nation, the most important factor, from the historical and comparative point of view, consists in the fact that the people have a reserve of national traditions. The most admirable mission of poetry is to preserve and exalt these traditions, particularly when they are lost in the distance from their origin" (Schlegel 1961, 7: 15). "First-rank poets and philosophers are always rare; where they do arise, however, they are rightfully taken as proof and criteria of the spiritual force and the education of the nation to which they belonged" (p. 17).

Tellingly, poetical works were no longer seen as productions, achievements, but rather as documents, testimonies, objects of reverence. Poets had become the guardians of the treasures accumulated by their people. And with the nationalization of literature, theoretical terms became mere ornaments. One can hardly believe that such passages came from the pen of the same author who had written "Über Goethes 'Meister'" (On Goethe's "Meister") (1798) and the "Gesprächt." The name "Friedrich Schlegel" designates only one individual, but two quite different writers.

The expository scheme of the lectures is the one most adequate to the expectations of his exclusive audience. After a few introductory pages, filled with the sort of elevated sentiments we have seen, the different national literatures are presented. All in all, there are twelve lectures, beginning with Homer and the ancient Greeks, covering the Latin, Hebrew, Persian, and Hindu literatures—when he came to Paris, Schlegel was already interested in the East—the Middle Ages, and finally the modern literatures; here Spain, for its ancient national unity and its conservatism, is held up as an example and a model; also examined are the literatures of Italy, France, and England, and the last two lectures discuss German literary art. Though Schlegel, we may suppose, had firsthand knowledge of these works, his synthesis never ventures beyond illustrative comments. This is much to be expected. The critical thread had been consciously left dangling, and a different measure had been picked up. The most interesting aspect of an analysis of Schlegel's work— something we shall not attempt—would be a study of the changes suffered by the author's original analytical categories. Thus, for instance, the praise of imagination is now combined with the emphasis on preservation of the past: his praise of Cervantes is founded on the fact that the Spain of his time still contained traces of chivalric life. And he praises the poets of Cervantes' period for their attempt to "escape narrow reality and achieve an opening, some access to a realm in which fantasy could move in freedom" (pp. 274–75).

Nevertheless, it should be noted that this emphasis on a fantasized past, although now guided by a political and pragmatic motivation that did not exist before, was the fruit of a root planted in the earlier phase. As we have seen, Novalis and Schlegel valued spirituality and on this basis justified their contempt for pedestrian reality—everyday existence, money concerns, tasks for men who had no access to what was universal.

The contempt for material life found its ideal habitat in a court that was then the quintessence of European conservatism. Drawing from its values, Schlegel tried to ennoble himself by adopting objective norms for judgment. These norms were based on Christianity and on the morals of his day. Both implied a repudiation of mythology, not even Homer being spared, for this mythology, "in the historical times we know, deserves censure, not only because it clashes with particularized moral concepts but also because its vision was material, objectionable, and impious" (p. 49). Schlegel's old fascination with mythology, which had inspired the idea of recapturing a unitary conception, was now eschewed in the name of Christianity, for Christian poetry "dispenses with a mythology of its own due to its *natural basis* [*dagegen der natürlichen Grundlage*]" (p. 284, emphasis added). Clearly, the search for a substantialist basis for the Law that characterizes Schlegel's trajectory is best exemplified by the argument with which he justifies the refusal of mythology: Christianity can do without it because it has a "natural basis."

Christianity and the moral standards of good society, then, are the bases on which objective norms rest. Besides, their proper turf is the field of historical investigation. It is not the idea itself that is new, but the concepts to which the facts are now subordinated: the poetic work is a document of the treasures accumulated by the nation to which its author belongs; thus, there is no need to delve into its specificity; Christian values provide the *natural* measure for *objective* judgments. Is not the "present relevance" of this phase of Schlegel's thought quite evident? Is it not even more obvious than the role of criticity for which we had so much praise?

In spite of the dramatic change in his positions, quite clearly Schlegel strove to salvage some of his earlier positions. "Romanticism" remains his key term, only now in a Christianized sense. Schlegel's Christianity seems to have found its first form of expression in the allegory of his worldview. Romanticism was distinguished from it for taking as its matter individual life, and having as its goal the purification of individual life. If in the earlier version Dante had been considered *il miglior fabbro* (the best craftsman), in the later phase Calderón de la Barca was the model (see pp. 285–86). In utter seriousness, Schlegel transmogrifies his concepts; the effect sometimes approaches parody. For instance, in a discussion of the language of the Scriptures he alludes to the hieroglyph. He compares the Hindu maxim (*Spruch*) with its

Hebrew counterpart, notes the similarities, and emphasizes the difference: the metrical irregularity of the Hebrew maxim influences its mental construction, equally irregular and with a higher-flying imagery, "so that in the richer passages each sentence almost forms a hieroglyph in words [*eine Hieroglyphe in Worten bildet*]" (p. 109). With a sort of dissociation of sensibility, Schlegel fails to see that this comment would only be valid—indeed, it would be brilliant—if he were not forced by his objective criterion to subordinate the biblical passage to its function of confirming a preestablished doctrine. What could possibly be the role of a complex—hieroglyphic, as Schlegel might put it—formulation that complicates what has been established as doctrine, if not that of ornament or illustration?

It might not be fair to say of such passages that they read like parodies of early Schlegel. But we are justified to say that ornament and illustration are now the functions he assigns to the poetic. If ornament is associated with aestheticization and illustration with the idea of the historical event as an explanation of national substance, we may well speak of the aestheticization of History, which is quite visible here. Thus, the intellectual decline in Schlegel's career is indicative of much more than the disastrous personal consequences of his choice: it points to the profound change undergone by theoretical approaches to literature in only twenty years.

The first modern literary theory was developed in a very brief period of four years—from 1797 to 1800. After this fleeting flowering, criticism, having begun to explore the prospects opened by Kant's three treatises, took a quite different turn. The dissolution of criticity is seen both in the reappearance of objective and predetermined criteria for evaluative judgments and in the role now played by literary history. Schlegel was the first to make "history a determining category in speculation on the beautiful" (Witte 1990: 71). After his political and religious conversion, and particularly in the lectures, "the social function of literary history is . . . perceived as contributing to the formation of national identity, as it opens the way to a new understanding of its own origin, interpreted according to the political interests of the historian" (p. 76).[18]

If we compare this with the passage from "Von Wesen der Kritik" (The essence of criticism) quoted above on the role of History and philosophy in the constitution of literary criticism, it becomes clear that literary history has taken the place of criticism. Thus, Schlegel became one of the forerunners of literary historiography, the most important instrument for the legitimation of the teaching of literature since the period of Restoration in Europe. He would certainly not subscribe to the view of a later historiographer, Ger-

18. Witte believes this change had taken place before, at the time of the "Fragments."

vinus, who stated in 1842: "Aesthetic judgment on objects does not concern me: I am not a poet, nor am I a lover of belles lettres" (quoted in Witte 1990: 77). But the divergence would be a surface phenomenon only, for both approaches are based on a category that is formulated at the end of the lectures: "True knowledge . . . consists in having a vision and an intuition of the whole, and, then, in discerning or distinguishing what is right" (Schlegel 1961: 412). Totality is the category that allows literary history to replace criticism. But, this much being said, more remains to do before we can end this chapter.

So far, my analysis has led to the conclusion that the constitutional ambiguity of Kant's explanation of the aesthetic experience paved the way for two developments: the aestheticizing and the critical. Then I showed that the critical road, which gave rise to the first theory of literature, came to an end quickly. Its replacement by literary history allows me to underscore the close links between the then dominant idea of History and aestheticization.

In a recent essay, David Lloyd demonstrated how Schiller's reflections became paradigmatic for a master of English historiography in the second half of the nineteenth century, Matthew Arnold, and for the parallel observations of Samuel Ferguson. Let us quote only his conclusion: "Writing in the 1830s and 1860s respectively, Ferguson and Arnold have at their disposal a discursive configuration in which philology, ethnology, and historiography are intimately linked with aesthetic criteria in a manner upon which it never seems necessary for them to reflect critically" (Lloyd 1985–86: 161). Although the aim of both authors would have been unthinkable to Schiller—the justification of British hegemony—they are in agreement with him to the extent that to them the aesthetic "provides the criteria by which the formal development is seen as the measure of political maturity" (p. 147). Duly pragmatized, Schiller's utopia is converted into the equation culture = state, and is adapted to imperial legitimation.

However, the demise of criticity and the predominance of aestheticization are also useful outside the sphere of literary history. Before the publication of Lloyd's essay, Hayden White had already stressed that the establishment of History as a discipline and its academic legitimation were accompanied by the substitution of the beautiful for the sublime:

> For both the Left and the Right, this same aesthetics of the beautiful presides over the process in which historical studies are constituted as an autonomous scholarly discipline. It takes little reflection to perceive that aestheticism is endemic to what is regarded as a proper attitude towards objects of historical study in a certain tradition, deriving from Leopold von Ranke and his epigones,

which represents the nearest thing to an orthodoxy the profession possesses. For this tradition, whatever "confusion" is displayed by the historical record is only a surface phenomenon. . . . If this confusion is not reducible to the kind of order that a science of laws might impose on it, it can still be dispelled by historians endowed with the proper kind of understanding. And when this understanding is subjected to analysis, it is always revealed to be of an essentially aesthetic nature. (White 1982: 70–71)

White's observation is of crucial importance, not only because it spells out the connection between the aestheticism of the model of historiography that has prevailed since then, but also because it associates the privilege conceded to the beautiful with the comforting feeling that the human world is also ruled by laws or something almost as stable as laws.

In short, the overwhelming prominence of aestheticization is a response to the modern dilemma posed by the absence of a universal law-giving center, having in its place no more than the fetishism of commodities, according to a hypothesis that can be derived from R. Kurz. So our investigation has more than purely academic interest; its relevance is political, even urgently so. What led us to study Schlegel was the desire to understand why the theorization of literature was so short lived, to discover its internal and external weaknesses, in order to attempt another use of criticity. The next chapter is the consequence of this search.

~✦

CHAPTER 3

Kafka: Before the Law

I am the end or the beginning.
—Franz Kafka, February 25, 1918

Preamble

Franz Kafka could not possibly have predicted his present fame. When he died, in 1924, one month before he turned 41, he had published, aside from contributions to literary magazines, seven short books (*Meditation* [*Betrachtung*], in 1913, containing 18 stories; "The Stoker" [*Der Heizer*], also in 1913; *The Metamorphosis* [*Die Verwandlung*], in 1915, reprinted in 1918; "The Judgment" [*Das Urteil*], in 1916, reprinted around 1920; "In the Penal Colony" [*In der Strafkolonie*], in 1919; *A Country Doctor: Little Stories* [*Ein Landarzt: Kleine Erzählungen*], 14 stories, in 1919; *A Hunger Artist: Four Stories* [*Ein Hunger Künstler: Vier Geschichten*], 1924). The longest of these books, *Meditation*, had fewer than 100 pages.[1] If we consider the slightness of his output, then the limited critical reception of Kafka's works, amounting in compilation to no more than 150 pages (see Born 1979), though for the most part polite and formal, contains some surprising exceptions. Contrary to what was commonly stated at the time his fame began, Kafka was by no means neglected in his lifetime or immediately after his death. Let us examine the comments of his more perceptive early readers.

In 1916, Oskar Walzel published in the *Berliner Tageblatt* a review of "The Stoker," a fragment later incorporated into *Der Verschollene* ("The Man Who Disappeared," later known as *Amerika*), and *The Metamorphosis*. Walzel displays tremendous critical acumen when he compares "The Stoker" to Kleist's

---

1. For a complete list of Kafka's works published in his lifetime, including technical writings for the Workers' Insurance Office (Arbeiter-Unfall-Versicherungsanstalter), see Dietz 1965: 85–113. For a chronology of the writing of his works, see Pasley and Wagenbach 1965: 55–83.

stories. "This short narrative," he writes in the beginning of his brief essay, "is reminiscent of Kleist" (Born 1979: 33). But he does not leave it at that: comparing Kleist's and Kafka's approach to the uncanny with that of the German romantics (Arnim, Chamisso, Hoffmann), he contrasts the romantics' practice of leading the reader slowly into the fantastic atmosphere with the surprising, mesmerizing swiftness of Kleist and Kafka. "With his very first sentence, Kafka hurls his reader into the uncanny" (p. 36). The difference of treatment implies a rejection not only of the commitment to verisimilitude and of the author's role as his reader's guide but also—and this is the point emphasized by Walzel—of the possibility of presenting characters from a double perspective, externally and internally, as a creature seen from the outside and as someone endowed with an unconscious. To achieve this, in addition to presenting the uncanny abruptly, Kafka, instead of multiplying its strangeness, treats it as a common fact, placing on it such a "stamp of reality" that, the critic observes somewhat ironically, "it may arouse the envy of a naturalist" (p. 37). "It is as if the entire narrative presented no more than the representation of a logical key [*einer logischen Schlußkette*]" (pp. 36–37) and the "naturalistic" developments were only its consequence.

Walzel assumes a reserved and ironical stance toward his own reading. He could not know that, in his felicitous comparison with Kleist, he had put his finger on the tension on which Kafka based his narrative—the tension between dream element and realistic development, as others would soon observe. Nor could he be aware of the implications of the relation he set up between the swiftness of Kafka's leap into the uncanny and the logico-mathematical resource the author employs—the "logical key" he mentioned. But we can already detect in this double effect—the critical finding and the ironical reaction—the point of friction that Kafka aroused even this early. Curiously, this same double effect was to reappear independently in another early critic of Kafka.

In the *Weltbühne*, on June 3, 1920, and March 9, 1926, respectively, Kurt Tucholsky (under the pen name "Peter Panter") reviewed "In the Penal Colony." In the first review he also compares Kafka with Kleist and notes the damage wrought by dream logic on traditional causality: "This little book . . . is a masterpiece. Ever since *Michael Kolhaas*, no German novella has covered up with such conscious force the apparent inner participation [*Anteilnahme*]— which, however, is so disseminated—of its author. . . . And then the image shifts, and, in a causal nexus that becomes comprehensible only in the terms of a dream, the officer frees the condemned man" (Born 1979: 94–96). Like Walzel, Tucholsky is simultaneously attracted and repelled by a text of whose novelty he is profoundly aware.

Even more surprising is Tucholsky's bewilderment when confronted with the first of Kafka's major posthumous works. Three short observations of his are priceless. "It becomes clear that Joseph K. has fallen into a gigantic machine, the ever-active, industrious, well-oiled machine of the court" (Born 1983: 107). Then he notes that K.'s relations with this machine take place through "a cruel mixture of the sharpest reality and what is most unearthly [*Unirdischem*]" (p. 108). What could such a mixture mean? *The Trial* is not "a satire of justice, no more than "The Penal Colony" is a satire of the military or *The Metamorphosis* is a satire of the bourgeoisie; these images are autonomous, not allusive" (p. 109).

These reactions are patently contradictory. Tucholsky's enthusiasm finds a serious obstacle: in "The Penal Colony" the author's internal sympathy is checked by a conscious force, but it permeates the entire work. For this reason, the novella could not be taken to be a satire of the military, as the reviewer, we may presume, would have liked—after all, he was forced to flee the country when the Nazis came into power and died in exile in 1935. His interest in Kafka is disturbed by the question: How can these works be interpreted?

It is this very embarrassment of Kafka's earliest intelligent critics that makes their texts relevant. It shows clearly that they not only were able to identify the uniqueness of Kafka's fiction but also realized that it could not be approached by common interpretive models.

A final confirmation of the critical friction Kafka aroused is given by an essayist who adopted, however, a quite different approach. In "Über Kafka" (On Kafka) Walter Muschg qualified the author as "a master of the short form, of the fantastic arabesque" (Born 1983: 101) and resorted to a historical conditioning that was to become a standard fixture of Kafka criticism: "The guilt of existence [*Dasein*], first experienced by writers [*Dichtern*] and other supersensitive organs of creation, has in our time become the fundamental mood of an entire generation" (p. 104). Then Muschg attempted to analyze Kafka, underscoring what others had pointed out before: the importance of the dream element. "The episodes in this work, the settings in which they take place, the figures that loom in them, the torment of fear and bliss they experience are of the kind one knows only from dreams: inescapable and unforgettable. Kafka is one of the most important examples of the abundant and profound effects that psychoanalysis exerts on our time" (p. 106). Thus, Muschg resolves the tension in which Walzel and Tucholsky were caught up by the resort to a theoretical model—psychoanalysis—that seemed to him to make sense out of that strange object; and this solution proved so persuasive that psychoanalytic readings of Kafka eventually became a veritable plague.

Also in 1929, in Berlin, *Die literarische Welt* published a transcription of a

radio lecture given by its editor in chief, Willi Haas, upon the fifth anniversary of Kafka's death.

Since he described Kafka's work as a "mystical narrative," one might think
that Haas was simply repeating the religious interpretation put forward by
Max Brod. But such is not the case. The mysticism that Haas refers to was
related to a profoundly negative religious experience. To Haas, Kafka's world
contains two powers, one over man, characterized by grace, and another under man, marked by the lack of mercy and by condemnation. The distinction
between these two powers, however, is only spatial—the first being presented
in *The Castle* and the second in *The Trial*; in fact, they work in close unison.
The higher power is as cruel, capricious, and cunning with its victims as the
lower. "Both worlds are a shadowy, dusty, narrow, stifling labyrinth, with
desks, offices, waiting rooms, an immense hierarchy with lower clerks and
higher, inaccessibly high officials and assistants, scriveners, lawyers, collabora-
tors, and messengers, who seem to act out a parody of a ridiculous, senseless
staff" (Haas 1929a: 3). Kafka is said to have a religious sensibility, which makes
him "the only legitimate descendant of Kierkegaard and Pascal," but a quite
heretical one, for his basic religious motif is that "before God, *man is always
wrong, even if, before man, God is also wrong*" (p. 4; emphasis in original).

Haas justified this equivalence with an allusion to Isaac's sacrifice. God's
conduct toward his servant Abraham would be incomprehensible if the deity
did not show himself, by his own conduct, to be a degraded God ("der
Gott . . . *schon gewissermaßen, ein erniedrigster Gott*," p. 4). Kafka, then, is a
"Judeo-Faustian poet" whose sources—which Haas does not imagine to be
conscious—are "primitive, Oriental myths, almost incomprehensible even to
present-day Jews" (Haas 1929b: 6).

An allusion to this remote mythical background is also present in Benjamin's essay on Kafka. Haas, like Benjamin later, is not contented with this
abysmal displacement, through which he rediscovers "extremely ancient Semitic ceremonies and institutions" (p. 7), but must find his way back to
contemporary reality: "This dreaminess, with its accompanying mysterious
mechanical precision, operating with perfection but far from any causal
mechanism—this mechanical dream world, in which everything is functionally connected to everything, but in complete disagreement with the Law
of human understanding, is the characteristic trait of Kafka's world and art"
(Haas 1929c: 7). It would not be too much to say that this reading of Kafka,
one of the earliest, is also one of the most remarkable, and it is all the more
surprising that it should be only rarely mentioned in specialized studies.[2]

2. For a critical appreciation of Kafka's reception and a critical bibliography of studies of
his work, see Beicken 1974, esp. pp. 21–33.

If such was the situation in the late 1920's, now one may say, as a Kafka specialist has written, that "more critical literature is published on Kafka each year than on any other writer except Shakespeare" (Corngold 1988: 24 n).

There are various reasons for this critical avalanche—from the strictly commercial, through the publish-or-perish imperative of the academic world, to the intellectually legitimate one of trying to find a path through these wild woods. The result of this has been the development of an industrial conglomerate, a veritable Kafka industry that would certainly have surprised and pleased old Hermann Kafka. With a melancholy and sharp irony, Adorno observed that the author had become an "information bureau of the human condition" (Adorno 1969: 245).

The close links between his work and his biography, the ready availability of his diaries and letters, the countless translations of his narratives, the un-equivocal (though enigmatic) relation between his work and the dilemmas of the contemporary world, all stimulate a curiosity that is often sterile and sometimes downright negative and disastrous—some purely positivistic, such as the neverending philological discussion, started by Hermann Uyttersprot, about what should be the true sequence of the chapters of *The Trial*, others trying to find in Kafka's texts illustrations of some thesis or theory. Through *A Hunger Artist*, Kafka himself ironically depicted his own fate, although he was lucky enough to die before the public grew bored with his exhibition.

This state of affairs is mentioned here in order to state the purpose of my study: it is not my intention to open a new branch office of the powerful industry that awards the post of managers to interpreters. Even to dare such a thing, one must first explore the network already built and, having examined the ever-growing critical literature, find one's own niche in it. However, we shall deal with no more than a small part of this literature.

The relatively limited access to the bibliography on Kafka might perhaps prove a fatal flaw if my purpose were to deal with the entire corpus of his works. But I shall be concerned only with a well-delimited part of it: those of his writings that allow us to think about the questioning of the modern status of fiction. In this way I shall try to link Kafka to the central argument of the present work—the issue of the Law under the sway of individual subjectiv-ity—and the covert theme that underlies it: the question of the control of the imaginary in modern times.

Although it is fitting that writers should state their intentions, it is no less advisable that they should avoid treating their object as the mere illustration of a hypothesis. The interpretation of a work runs the risk of turning into an "industrial" practice when the raw material must be laminated in order to fit the specifications required for the product. Thus, we have had a Freudian

Kafka, a Heideggerian Kafka, a religious Kafka, a revolutionary Kafka, and so on. I do not mean that such appropriations are arbitrary, but that they overlook the tension that is characteristic of Kafka's text and ignore its fictional specificity. Criticism is often accused of tending to be reductionistic, but this does not make it any easier to avoid falling into this trap. What seemed to me the most plausible way of escaping reductionism was to adopt a curved, quite ungeometrical path, created by the very intractability of the object.

Kafka and Literature

Kafka's view of literature had little to do with the heroic age of avant-gardism in which he lived. Since Dada, the basic trend in avant-garde movements was to break the boundaries that marked the territories of the arts and of literature. Relegated to moments of leisure and the space of the museum, art had moved away from everyday reality; at best, it described the formation of a personality, but more often than not it turned into a sumptuary activity, a way of reinforcing status. Whether in the salons of the ancient aristocracy frequented by Swann or among the ornaments of the suspicious wealth amassed by Gatsby, artistic objects were symbols of luxury and carefree living.

Whatever the political positions they might come to defend, the avant-gardists were concerned with restoring freedom in the domains of visual images, sounds, and words, breaking down the dams and barriers that differentiated and limited works of art, making art once again a living presence in the streets and in everyday existence. The random word order of Dadaist poems, the free associations of the Surrealists, the introduction in paintings and sculptures of "low" materials—newspaper clippings pasted onto painted surfaces, a urinal enthroned as a piece of sculpture—these were all consistent with the search for freedom. If slightly more than one hundred years earlier Kant had been able to think of aesthetic judgment on the basis of a reflection on morality, to the young avant-gardists any relation between art and morality had become unthinkable. Such a link was felt to be an effect of the pharisaism that attempted to reconcile the irreconcilable: the whistles of factories and the harmony of musical chords, the dismal urban wastelands and the peacefulness of a "luncheon on the grass."

From the standpoint of the avant-garde, Kafka's attitude is timorous, provincial, backward-looking. Not that his work was opposed, alien, or indifferent to experimentalism. His debt to expressionism is quite evident. But we are not yet discussing his work, only his attitude toward literature.

It may be said that Kafka placed literature on a plane previous to and more elementary than that which avant-gardists aspired to. Avant-gardists took their personalities as a vehicle for an aggressive production. In Kafka, instead, literature does not shirk from the attempt to fix the earlier image: "My talent for portraying my dreamlike [*traumhaft*] inner life has thrust all other matters into the background; my life has dwindled dreadfully, nor will it cease to dwindle. Nothing else will ever satisfy me" (Aug. 6, 1914; Kafka 1972: 302).

Although this statement must later be qualified—its absolutization would only have the effect of justifying the reductionism to which Kafka has been subjected—it captures more than a fleeting mood. To take one's own individuality as the essential material of one's writings was to think of oneself as a kind of ground, however floating and unstable and dreamlike. Nothing is changed even if we add that this stable ground might be as disturbed as Antonin Artaud's, for we are considering the question in expressive, not psychological, terms. In Kafka, the need for literature is rooted solely within the boundaries of his own self. One might even speak of an extreme, "neurotic" egoism: nothing can be seen but is incorporated into his internal inscribing. But this is not yet sufficient; the quality that is specific to this internalization consists in the metamorphosis it will perform; through it, the obsessively inward-looking eye will change into an object, the idiolect of the self will turn into a language for the other. For the moment, we do no more than announce the transmutation and underscore the intense commerce between obsessive introspection and the no less obsessive search for the right word.

To Kafka, literature is an absolute. As he wrote to Felice in a letter dated November 30, 1912: "To write badly, yet feel compelled to write, or abandon oneself to total despair!" (Kafka 1978: 185). And the anxious fixation is mentioned again in a letter dated December 11–12 of the same year: "But now, this evening, I had the chance to write, which my whole nature has been irrefutably demanding—if not directly, then with an inward-spreading despair; but I write barely enough to let me survive another day" (p. 211).

The amorous relationship between Kafka and Felice may be compared to a two-way traffic system. From Kafka to Felice, there is a flow of refuse, the physical process of discharge; in the opposite direction, Kafka receives from Felice food, the chemical process of strengthening. The examples we have given are both of the first kind. Examples of the other flow will have to await the analysis of the texts that depend on this relationship.

To Kafka, the act of writing is a response to an urgency of redemption and liberation: "I have written nothing today, and the moment I put the book down I am promptly assailed by the insecurity that follows my not writing like an evil spirit" (Kafka 1978: 275). And, if the page is not written, the passing of time does not lessen the insistent demand. If the discharge is not directed to Felice, it is diverted to the diary: "Since I am nothing but literature and can and want to be nothing else, my job will never take possession of me, it may, however, shatter me completely" (Aug. 21, 1913; Kafka 1972: 230). Literature might be compared, rather than to a Medusa-like deity, to a voracious whirlpool that gushes out everything, but wants to suck in one thing only—the soul of the one it devours. Before the magnetic eye of the terrible deity there can only be either surrender or perdition. Thus, Kafka renounces everything in favor of the blank page:

> When it became clear in my organism that writing was the most productive direction for my being to take, everything rushed in that direction and left empty all those abilities which were directed towards the joy of sex, eating, drinking, philosophical reflection, and above all music. I atrophied in all these directions. This was necessary because the totality of my strengths was so slight that only collectively could they even half-way serve the purpose of my writing. (Jan. 3. 1912; Kafka 1972: 163).

That is why work is an inexorable burden to him, whether in the office or in the factory that his father makes him a partner in. He writes of the former: "I need only throw my work in my office out of this complex in order to begin my real life" (p. 168); and of the latter: "Through this empty effort spent on the factory I would . . . rob myself of the use of the few afternoon hours that belong to me, which would of necessity lead to the complete destruction of my existence, which, even apart from this, becomes more and more hedged in" (Dec. 28, 1911; Kafka 1972: 156). The office and the factory are burdens no less than family life or the desire to start his own family. On March 9, 1914, just before he became officially engaged, only to break the engagement immediately after, he wrote in his diary: "I couldn't marry then, everything in me revolted against it, much as I always loved F. It was chiefly concern over my literary work that prevented me, for I thought marriage would jeopardize it" (Kafka 1972: 262).

In his mind, Kafka anticipated what was yet to take many twists and turns before it actually happened in his real life. The "decision" he announced then was, however, part of a continuing process that could already be detected in his July 21, 1913, balance sheet of the pros and cons of marriage:

> The connexion with F. will give my existence more strength to resist. . . .
>
> I hate everything that does not relate to literature, conversations bore me (even if they relate to literature), to visit people bores me, the sorrows and joys of my relatives bore me to my soul. Conversations take the importance, the seriousness, the truth of everything I think. . . .
>
> The fear of the connexion, of passing into the other. Then I'll never be alone again. (Kafka 1972: 225)

Torn apart, Kafka feels close to madness. Is madness what is confused with damnation, once the literary absolute is lost, or is it what feeds the very need for the absolute? The two statements occur to him, and he wavers between them. Thus, he will write to Felice on July 13, 1913: "*Simply to race through the nights with my pen, that's what I want. And to perish by it, or lose my reason, that's what I want too, since it is the inevitable and long-anticipated consequence*" (Kafka 1978: 411). In the same vein he was to write, many years later:

> Writing sustains me, but is it not more accurate to say that it sustains this kind of life? By this I don't mean, of course, that my life is better when I don't write. Rather it is much worse then and wholly unbearable and has to end in madness. But that, granted, only follows from the postulate that I am a writer, which is actually true even when I am not writing, and a nonwriting writer is a monster inviting madness. (Kafka 1977: 333)

But perhaps the attractiveness of madness is even stronger, more intimate to Kafka than he acknowledges when he sees it as opposed to the obsession with literature. Between the two, rather than opposition, there may well be an overlap. Kafka admits as much in a humorous passage in a letter to Milena: "A 'Tribuna' reader told me recently he thought I must have made extensive studies in a lunatic asylum. 'Only in my own,' I said, whereupon he continued trying to pay me compliments on my 'own lunatic asylum' " (Kafka 1954a: 149). Although humor, even in the most anguished situations, is frequent in Kafka, it is in a tone more somber than mocking that he returns to the connection between madness and obsession with literature in a letter to Robert Klopstock, the friend of his last days:

> In the interval, after being lashed through periods of insanity, I began to write, and this writing is the most important thing in the world to me (in a way that is horrible to everyone around me, so unspeakably horrible that I don't talk about it)—the way his delusion is important to the madman (should he lose it, he would become "mad") or the way her pregnancy is important to a woman. (Kafka 1977: 323)

The double connection that literary effort maintains with madness— both an outlet for it and a way of avoiding its complete domination— reappears on the plane of religious imagery. Thus, in a letter to Felice dated August 14, 1913, Kafka tells her the story of a monk whose voice was the devil's own voice, and adds: "The relationship between me and literature is similar, very similar to that, except that my literature is not as sweet as that monk's voice" (Kafka 1978: 428).

Most of the time, however, his passion for writing is referred to as his only means to save himself—and saving himself was precisely his "mission":

"That, indeed, is why I am here, that is quite clear to me" (June 21, 1913; Kafka 1972: 222). But the word "mission" (or "calling") is not exactly appropriate. Common as it is in religious discourse, here it might be taken to mean that Kafka's obsession with literature is part of a process of conversion, even if a sui generis one. Though not denying the religious element in Kafka, we should make clear that this would only be partly true. What, after all, does literature redeem for Kafka? Let us recall the incisive tone of the letter he intended to send to Felice's father: "My job is unbearable to me because it conflicts with my only desire and my only calling [*Beruf*], which is literature" (Aug. 21, 1913; Kafka 1972: 230). This sentence is a cry for help addressed to Herr Bauer, whom Kafka was implicitly asking to put an end to the engagement he himself was unable to break.

What did Kafka see on the other side? What sort of salvation could literature offer him, that was worth sacrificing the most fundamental social duties? Let us examine a passage marked by a euphoric tone that is rare in Kafka. In this famous diary entry, written on September 23, 1912, the day following the composition of "The Judgment," Kafka says: "The conviction verified that with my novel-writing I am in the shameful lowlands [*in schändlichen Niederungen*] of writing. Only *in this way* can writing be done, only with such coherence, with such a complete opening out of the body and the soul" (Kafka 1972: 213). Even when he writes in conditions that seem ideal to him, the results only place him on the lowest rung of literature. The tone of the entire passage, which is not at all depressing, does not allow a self-deprecating reading of the image; rather, it is revealing of Kafka's intuition concerning the kind of soil on which his writing operates. And the association with Freud he finds natural—"thoughts about Freud, of course [*Gedanken an Freud näturlich*]" (p. 213)—only stresses Kafka's connectedness with his inner world. The "calling" (*Beruf*) Kafka feels is not materialized in any sublime or luminous product, the highest forms of literary expression. His mission has to do, not with the God of his people, Jehovah, but at best with the God of the Gnostics. Haas seems to be right when he says that it puts Kafka in contact with primitive Semitic myths, in which God is an awful figure, whose angels claim earthly women as their property (see Haas 1929b: 6).

This "optimistic" hypothesis is not an attempt to make a Gnostic out of Kafka; all we are doing is highlighting what the writer and Gnostics have in common. As far as we know, Eric Heller was the first to make a comparison between Kafka's work—*The Castle*, in particular—and Gnostic thought (see Heller 1975: 223).[3] But Heller fails to notice a difference: "In Gnosticism,

3. "The castle of Kafka's novel is, as it were, the heavily fortified garrison of a company of Gnostic demons, successfully holding an advanced position against the manoeuvres of an impatient soul" (Heller 1975: 223).

there is an alien, wholly transcendent God, and the adept, after considerable difficulties, can find the way back to presence and fullness. Gnosticism therefore is a religion of salvation, though the most negative of all such saving visions. Kafkan spirituality offers no hope of salvation, and so is not Gnostic" (Bloom 1989: 167). This difference again reinforces the correctness of Haas's insight.

This rectification helps to understand the parallel drawn by Kafka between literature and the devil, the connection he sees between writing and confusion and disaggregation. But not even this emphasis on the religiously negative provides the interpreter with a satisfactory clue to Kafka's obsession with literature. It may even have the unintended effect of endowing Kafka's work with a potentially univocal meaning. This possibility, however, is negated by his private writings. Let us return to them.

Here is a passage from a letter to Felice dated June 16, 1913:

> All I possess are certain powers which, at a depth almost inaccessible under normal conditions, shape themselves into literature, powers to which, however, in my present professional as well as physical state, I dare not commit myself, because for every inner exhortation of these powers there are as many, if not more, inner warnings. Could I but commit myself to them they would undoubtedly, of this I am convinced, lift me out of my inner misery in an instant. (Kafka 1978: 388)

By now it should be obvious that indecision is the constant trait in Kafka's search for an existential definition. It should be added, however, that his father's figure is an indispensable element in the economics of his indecision. Thus, the December 14, 1911, diary entry relates one of the many arguments with his father in which the old man rebukes him for not taking seriously his work at the factory. Instead of complaining or lamenting his father's lack of understanding and excessive pragmatism, Kafka says he is surprised to realize that, later on, he felt he "could put up with my present situation very contentedly, and that I only had to be careful not to have all my time free for literature. . . . I disputed my ability to devote all my time to literature" (Kafka 1972: 138).

Two days later—December 16, 1911—these reflections continue, no longer connected to the actual event, and turn into an objective and critical appreciation:

> If a disorganized education having only that minimum coherence indispensable for the merest uncertain existence is suddenly challenged to a task limited in time, therefore necessarily arduous, to self-development, to articulate speech, then the response can only be bitterness in which are mingled arrogance over achievements which could be attained only by calling upon all one's untrained

powers, a last glance at the knowledge that escapes in surprise . . . and, finally,
hate and admiration for the environment. (Kafka 1972: 139)

This dense, convoluted sentence weaves a labyrinth that favors the constancy
of indecision. Kafka is probably referring to his own intellectual work and the
displeasure he felt for his own writings. The text searches for a cause and is
caught up in a web of effects. The consequence of it all is increasing paralysis.

His very permanence in Prague has the same effect. The city had always
displeased him; early in his professional life he had even imagined that his
company might groom him for a post in Latin America or, at least, in Berlin;
but it was only in his last days, when Germany was ravaged by postwar inflation—and thus in the most unfavorable circumstances possible—that Kafka
actually moved to Berlin. The idea of leaving his father's house and starting a
family of his own had always seemed to him a way of concentrating his
dispersed powers, but in his letters to Felice he does all he can to convince her
that he is the most inadequate of fiancés. And because Felice was not easy to
convince and in his mind it was his father who fed his indecision, Kafka tried
to enlist the interference of Felice's father. The fact that he sent the letter to
Felice rather than directly to her father only reinforces his need to remain
undecided, as though, in spite of his anguish and despair, he wished to prolong this state as much as possible. However, a passage from the letter he
meant to send to Herr Carl Bauer gives us a clearer view of the situation:
"And is your daughter, whose healthy nature has destined her for a happy
married life [*zu einem wirklichen Eheglück*], to live with this kind of man? Is she
to tolerate a monastic existence with a person who, though he loves her as he
can never love anyone else, spends most of his time in his room or wandering
about by himself—simply because of his irrevocable vocation?" (Aug. 28,
1913; Kafka 1978: 439).

The allusion to his inability to offer his fiancée a truly happy married life
is revealed as a euphemism when set side by side with other documents. Two
of these will be enough. One year after meeting Felice for the first time,
under the impact of his impression, Kafka wrote in his diary, on August 14,
1913: "Coitus as punishment for the happiness of being together. Live as
ascetically as possible, more ascetically than a bachelor, that is the only possible way for me to endure marriage. But she?" (Kafka 1972: 228). There is no
need to interpret the covert reference contained in the letter to Herr Bauer.
Kafka puts the matter plainly enough, with no reserve or ambiguity, in a letter
to Felice dated April 1, 1913:

My one fear—surely nothing worse can either be said or listened to—is that I
shall never be able to possess you [*daß ich Dich niemals werde besitzen können*].

At best I would be confined, like an unthinkingly faithful dog, to kissing your casually proffered hand, which would not be a sign of love, but of the despair of the animal condemned to silence and eternal separation. (Kafka 1978: 349)

Although he could not—or felt he could not—function sexually in marriage, the idea of a stable union was never far from his mind. Proof of this are his 1919 engagement to Julie Wohryzek and his relationships with Milena Jesenská and with Dora Dymant, not to mention his somewhat obscure involvement with Grete Bloch, Felice's friend and perhaps her rival as well. We may assume that Kafka's sexual inhibition was brought on only by the woman of his choice.

This problem is discussed even more clearly in two passages of a letter to Max Brod, written in mid-July 1916:

> Basically I never had that kind of intimacy with a woman [war ich noch niemals mit einer Frau vertraut], except for two cases—the time in Zuckmantel (but there she was a woman and I was a boy) and the time in Riva (but there she was half a child and I was altogether confused and sick in every possible way). . . . I have never feared anything so much as being alone with F. before the wedding. (Kafka 1977: 117–18)

In someone who expressed himself with such clarity and who, in addition, was an admirer of Freud, the nature of the symptom could not possibly be misinterpreted; it is precisely because he knows he is not sexually impotent that Kafka is tortured by indecision. Another relevant passage is in a diary entry dated August 14, 1913. It immediately precedes the reflection on coitus as punishment, and concerns the contradiction aroused in him by Felice: "Conclusion for my case from 'The Judgment.' I am indirectly in her debt for the story. But Georg goes to pieces because of his fiancée" (Kafka 1972: 228). This brief entry sums up the dilemma caused by Felice. "The Judgment" had been written a few days after Kafka was introduced to Felice; he knew he had felt attracted to her (see entry dated Feb. 11, 1913, Kafka 1972: 214–15). Yet, in the story Georg is condemned because of the existence of his fiancée. Felice is both seductive and threatening, both a stimulus to creation and the imminence of disaster. The unpretentious girl from Berlin, who never really understood the role she had played in the mind of this strange man, was only the catalyst in a chemical reaction that was already in the making.

Although many pages of diaries and letters by Kafka are now available, the passage that best shows how he saw the formation of his individuality is perhaps an autobiographical fragment published not as part of his diaries, but in a collection of various texts, *Hochzeitsvorbereitungen auf dem Lande und andere Prosa dem Nachlaß* (Wedding preparations in the country and posthumous prose).[4] Since the fragment would be too long to quote in its entirety, let us transcribe the most significant passages:

> Every man is peculiarly, and by virtue of his peculiarity, called to play his part in the world, but he must have a taste for his own peculiarity. So far as my experience went, both in school and at home the aim was to erase all trace of peculiarity. In this way they made the work of education easier, but also made life easier for the child, although, it is true, he first had to go through the pain caused him by discipline. A boy, for instance, who is in the middle of reading an exciting story in the evening will never be made to realize, merely by an argument bearing solely upon himself, that he must stop reading and go to bed. . . . That was my peculiarity. It was suppressed by means of turning off the gas and leaving me without a light. . . . All I felt was the injustice done to me, I went to bed sadly, and here were the beginnings of that hatred which has in a certain respect determined my life in relation to my family and hence my life as a whole. Although being forbidden to read is only an example, it is a characteristic one, for this prohibition went deep. My peculiarity was not accorded any recognition. . . . If even this openly displayed peculiarity met with condemnation, how much worse then must those peculiarities be which I kept concealed for the reason that I myself recognized something a little wrong in them. . . . The peculiarities I displayed increased more and more the nearer I came to the life to which I had access. Yet this brought me no liberation, it did not cause the quantity of what was concealed to diminish, and on more refined inspection it appeared that it would never be possible to confess everything. (Kafka 1954b: 201–4).

It little matters whether the actual incident had the impact Kafka attributes to it; the important thing is that he chooses to interpret it in this way. According to the fragment, then, Kafka's socialization began with a prohibition, a precise one: he was not allowed to go on reading after a specified hour. This prohibition was retrospectively converted into the origin of the hatred he came to feel for his environment. What might have been an irrelevant incident is changed into resistance against the repressing voice. It grows and is eventually transformed into Kafka's singularity as an adult.

This does not explain in a deterministic way the indecision that would become a part of his personality. Certainly various other consequences would have been possible. Between the explanation and the final result there is always a gap, and the links are either nonexistent or missing. The singularity of each individual trajectory is precisely what cannot be explained. What is

4. The passage in question was published for the first time under the title "Skizze einer Selbtsbiographie" (see Kafka 1953: 165). The editor of the French translation included it in the diaries, dating it "July–August 1916" (see Kafka 1984, 3: 419 ff.). But in the volume of the *Kritissche Ausgabe* (Critical works) the original presentation is maintained (see Kafka 1992, 2: 7–13).

relevant in the case in question is that a clear gap is opened between the prohibition against reading and the institution imposing the prohibition. Since this division never hardened into pure opposition, the terms involved—reading and family—will forever and insolubly haunt Kafka. That is why the father, contrary to the traditional psychoanalytical reading, is not a character in the Oedipal drama, but an embodiment of social power: "The judges, commissaries, bureaucrats, etc., are not father-substitutes; rather, it is the father that sums up all of these forces, to which he submits himself and invites his son to submit also" (Deleuze and Guattari 1977: 19).

It is also because the discontinuity between the preferred act—reading—and the prohibiting institution—the family—is not transformed into pure opposition that Kafka's work follows a direction that is the opposite of Rousseau's. To the Rousseau of the *Confessions*, words had the strength to reveal, against all hypocrisy, every commitment to convention and authority, "the heart laid bare." In Kafka, words do not purify; they refer to waste matter heavier than they:

> Even if I had not kept any secret to myself, but had flung everything so far away from me that I would have stood there in complete purity, in the next instant I would again have been choked with the old muddle and confusion [*Durcheinander*], for in my opinion the secret would not have been completely recognized and assessed, and in consequence would have been restored to me by the generality and imposed upon me anew. (Kafka 1954b: 204–5)

What, then, could be the value of words that attempt to cleanse the soul of its innermost secrets? Kafka is dealing with a topos of central importance in the Christian tradition. Since Augustine, at least, the common belief had been fixed: the soul that confesses moves closer to the divine source, and in this way achieves absolution. Rousseau and Schiller, with the *Confessions* and the *Letters on the Aesthetic Education of Man*, replaced God with public opinion and the state. In both cases, however, the divulging of secrets remained, together with the conviction that human intercourse could be transparent. In Kafka, although he was unaware of the change he brought about, no such liberation is possible any longer. To return to the long meditation we have quoted from before:

> If, for instance, one confesses to a friend that he is miserly, for that moment and in relation to his friend, that is to say, in relation to a person whose judgment is authoritative, he has seemingly freed himself from his miserliness. For this moment it is, besides, of no account how his friend takes the confession, that is, whether he denies that there is such miserliness in him or gives advice about how to get rid of miserliness, or even defends miserliness. It might not even be decisive if the friend were to break off the friendship as a result of this confession.

> What is decisive, however, is that one has confided one's secret to the generality, perhaps not as a penitent sinner, but at least as an honest one, and in this way hopes to have reconquered one's good and—this is the most important element of all—free childhood. But one has only made the conquest of a brief folly and much subsequent bitterness. (p. 205)

What had been prohibited now flourishes as a secret; the guilt that accompanies it and the very "material" character of what is hidden from the sight of others cannot be redeemed by its conversion into expressed words. All it brings about is a short-lived madness. Changed into writing, the reading that had been prohibited in childhood is metamorphosed into non-redeeming literature. Its absolute urgency betrays its proximity to madness—a proximity that, as we already know, is ambivalent: literature is both a defense against madness and a road to madness.

We have said that Kafka's introspection does not explain the ambiguity attached to the terms "prohibited thing" and "prohibiting institution." Kafka himself is aware that there is no necessary link between his early experiences and his fate: "I cannot grant that the first beginnings of my unhappiness were inwardly necessitated; they may have indeed had a necessity, but not an inward one—they swarmed down on me like flies and could have been as easily driven off" (Jan. 24, 1922; Kafka 1972: 405). Kafka is also aware that his fate is best explained not by a causal explanation, but by his own imitative ability: "My development was a simple one. While I was still contented I wanted to be discontented, and with all the means that my time and tradition gave me, plunged into discontent—and then wanted to turn back again. Thus I have always been discontented, even with my contentment. Strange how make-believe, if engaged in systematically enough, can change into reality" (Jan. 24, 1922; Kafka 1972: 405).

It is hardly accidental that the acknowledgment of this ability of a mimesis voluntarily invoked onto himself should have focused on language. We have observed that in this Kafka differs from Rousseau. Whereas Rousseau saw language as an instrument of revelation and transparency, Kafka realizes that between the thing to be revealed and the moment of revelation there is an indeterminate distance. It is here that he resorts to *staging by means of language*, through which he invokes or even produces causes that supplement those from his actual childhood. This mise-en-scène is achieved in language; it does not simply occur with the aid of language, but rather is produced in it and not just "recaptured" or represented. Language is the occasion for an event and not a simple means of access to an "essence."

It is thus an obvious fact that Kafka is extremely conscious of the potential contained in the pair mimesis-language. The reflections on the relation between individuality and writing, which—as we saw in the previous chapter—were thoroughly explored by the early German romantics, now take an important step forward: there is no direct relation between the two; writing begins even before the act of writing. In the present case, this observation cannot be disregarded; otherwise the emphasis we have been laying on indecision would eventually have a negative impact on the reading of the work.

For the moment, let us simply note that it is because he observes intently the staging put on by language that Kafka is not a monothematic writer, and that his vision of the absurdity of the Law—that is, of a world in which men move instead of limiting themselves to a monotonous pathos—tends to lead to a comic view of situations. The comic does not come easily to him, particularly when one realizes that he himself is aware of the impasses he faces and feels discontented with his situation: "Why then do I add to the unhappiness that this shore causes me by longing to cross over to the other?" (Jan. 14, 1922; Kafka 1972: 412). However, awareness of the power of language counterbalances paralyzing ambiguity. Were it not for this awareness, Kafka's work would be at the mercy of the wish to be the expression of the misfortunes of a certain existence, and analysts would have a "stable object" to explore. Thus emphasized, the focus on indecision does not run the risk of falsifying the analysis we have before us. And now that we know the elements that are to be highlighted—indecision and the mimesis-language pair—we may return to the former with a surer step.

Indecision is an ever present note in the intense correspondence with Felice. And it does not follow the typical pattern, coming after what would have softened its impact—passionate declarations of love. Instead, the passion is protected by the distance that separates Prague from Berlin. Thus, passion could flare up without affecting the hard core of indecision. The coexistence of passion and indecision is exasperating at times. Among dozens of incidents, let us single out one from a letter dated November 11, 1912:

> I don't want to know that you are fond of me. If I did, how could I, fool that I am, go on sitting in my office, or here at home, instead of leaping onto a train with my eyes shut and opening them only when I am with you? Oh, there is a sad, sad reason for not doing so. To make it short: my health is only just good enough for myself alone, not good enough for marriage, let alone fatherhood. (Kafka 1978: 139)

Kafka both acts in a seductive manner and courts rejection. Health complaints are as common in the diaries as expressions of dissatisfaction with his own body. In the letters to Felice, however, these complaints play a definite role, although an unconscious one. Years before meeting Felice, Kafka had confided to his diary that the strength he gained through writing in it was drained by his daily suffering (Nov. 1, 1911; Kafka 1972: 101). But Felice is a more resistant source. As convinced of his own frailness as he is of his "calling," Kafka sees in Felice the possibility of a continuous source of vital force.[5] This is indicated in the beginning of a letter dated December 7, 1912: "I have still got you, dearest, a second justification for living, but then it is shameful to draw one's justification for living entirely from the existence of one's beloved" (Kafka 1978: 201). And if the ending of "The Judgment" seems weak to him, he knows exactly to whom he can resort in order to make it better.

In "Kafka's Other Trial," Elias Canetti has insuperably demonstrated that Kafka acted like a parasite sucking energy from the woman he loved (Canetti 1978: 7–94). It will not be necessary to repeat his arguments here, or to stress how much Kafka's literary legacy has depended on "sucking." We need only mention that Kafka drew strength from her in two phases: at the beginning of their relationship, when he wrote "The Judgment," "The Stoker" and five more chapters of *The Man Who Disappeared*, and *The Metamorphosis*; and when the engagement was broken. "Disillusionment brought, after the first period, an end to his writing. After the second period the effect of estrangement was the reverse: it led him back to writing" (p. 86). But the two motivations are not contradictory, for their opposite signs—the search for intimacy in the first, the yearning for freedom in the second—have one element in common: indecision. It is indecision that explains why, on an unconscious level, Kafka tried to conjoin things he believed to be irreconcilable: a wife, a family of his own, and literature.

Kafka's obsessive pursuit of literary creation aroused astonishment in one of his best interpreters: "How can one commit one's entire existence to the frenzy of ordering a certain number of words?" (Blanchot 1949: 21). To Kafka, literature was the only shield against the indifference, aggression, and cruelty his sensibility, lucid to the point of morbidity, found in the world—which calls to mind a passage from a letter to Milena: "I understand your Czech very well, I can also hear the laughter, but I'm burrowing into your letters even between word and laughter, then I hear only the word, and besides, my nature is: Fear" (Kafka 1954a: 71). But such an interpretation is

---

5. Observes Canetti: "The important thing about Felice was that she did exist, that she was not invented, and that, the way she was, she could not have been invented by Kafka. She was so different, so active, so compact. . . . The love that she turned upon him flowed through his heart like blood, so he declared in one letter, and he had no other blood. He asked her whether she had not noticed that, in his letters, he did not really love her, for, if he did, he would have to think only of her and write about her. As it was, he worshipped her, and he expected help and blessings from her for the most absurd things" (Canetti 1978: 28).

too easy; indecision in Kafka contaminated his relation to literature and the world. These two are not directly opposed, as his belief in salvation through literature might lead one to suppose; the stamp of the worldly is evident in his figures, the more so because indecision is not the only psychological mark upon them, for it is manifested side by side with an acute awareness of words.

These conclusions will serve as a basis for later analyses.

Kafka and the Question of Representation

The term "representation" is used so often and in so many different ways that it is difficult to propose a definition for it. However, at least in common usage, it may be characterized as the innerly conceived image corresponding to the perception of an object. The proportionality between what is perceived and the inner image evoked is of fundamental importance to the definition. In fact, its importance remains even when the object is placed in the position of subject—that is, if, instead of envisaging an object as something we perceive, we take it as the subject of a production. Whatever this agent does is then seen as proportional to it. In other words, what is produced *represents* its producer.

In the particular case of fictional works, this conception of representation is reinforced, if not determined, by a view of expression rooted in Romanticism: the value of the work is directly proportional to the degree it expresses its creator. In fiction, authenticity—that is, opposition to the mere imitation of models—implies the multiplication of representations of a way of seeing, conceiving, and articulating reality.

I am summarizing these common views to analyze how they fare in Kafka's work, and subsequently, to ask what is the significance of this work in our times. I shall go on examining Kafka's private writings for now.

In Kafka's letters and diaries, the most frequent complaints and negative allusions have to do with his own body. One of the earliest diary entries reads: "I write this very decidedly out of despair over my body and over a future with this body" (Kafka 1972: 10). The observation is repeated, in a provisionally optimistic tone, on August 5, 1911: "I have stopped being ashamed of my body in the swimming pools in Prague, Königssaal, and Czernoschitz" (p. 50). But even if this statement is to be believed, shame was not the decisive element. On November 21 of the same year he wrote an extensive description of how he saw himself. Here is the beginning of the passage: "It is certain that a major obstacle to my progress is my physical condition. Nothing can be accomplished with such a body. I shall have to get used to its perpetual balking" (p. 124). This mood was intensified on November 24: "Then at the junction with the Bergstein I once more thought about the distant future. How would I live through it with this body picked up in a lumber room? The Talmud too says: A man without a woman is no person" (p. 126).

These quotations are enough. Rather than find additional and redundant examples, it would be more interesting to pose the question: What is it about Kafka's body that repels him so strongly? The answer lies in the constant references to the idea of strength, always seen in a positive light. Thus, in one of the rare expressions of self-approbation, as he reflected on a lecture he had given early in 1912, Kafka writes: "In all this are revealed powers to which I would gladly entrust myself if they would remain" (Feb. 25, 1912; Kafka 1972: 182). This passage, read in isolation, might mislead one into thinking Kafka meant that the powers in question derived from himself, from the joyous awareness of his own "proud, unearthly consciousness," from his self-possession before the audience, his "strong voice" and "effortless memory" (p. 181). But the context rectifies this impression. The enthusiasm has to do only with his work for the Jewish Town Hall—or rather, for the actor Jizchak Löwy, for whose benefit Kafka had organized the evening in which he was to speak himself.

The powers he felt in him came from the community he had assembled by his personal effort. His own presence side by side with his friend fills him with enthusiasm and expansiveness. The episode is all the more notable because at the moment we are not discussing Kafka's relations with the Jewish community. What is important to note here is that his awareness of the powers in him is countered by the conditional clause relative to their permanence: "powers to which I would gladly entrust myself *if they* would remain" (emphasis added). Saddled with a weak, ungainly body, a most inadequate tool to ensure his own future, Kafka tries to find powers that might animate him, dispel uncertainty, confusion, and apathy.

As is well known, he was to draw such strength for some time from a kinswoman of Max Brod's. Having met Felice in August 1912, on September 23, only three days after sending her his first letter, Kafka is telling her about the excitement of writing "The Judgment" in one sitting: "How everything can be said, how for everything, for the strangest fancies, there waits a great fire in which they perish and rise up again" (Kafka 1972: 213). Felice's name is not mentioned; but then Kafka never writes what is obvious. It was she, the uncomplicated girl with whom he had exchanged a few formal words, that inspired him with the strength that impelled him. So close were the links between this strength and this fire that, in the entry in which he explicitly associated Felice with the story, Kafka referred to its composition as "eine regelrechte Geburt mit Schmutz und Schleim"—"a real birth, covered with filth and slime" (Feb. 11, 1913; Kafka 1972: 214).

In the summary of arguments for and against marriage he wrote not long after, the effect "borrowed strength" is literally replaced by its cause, "strength drawn from Felice": "The connexion with F. will give my existence more strength to resist" (Kafka 1972: 225). The contact with the girl from Berlin once again sparked the sensation he had experienced, encouraged by Löwy, in contact with the Jewish community. Both, however, were short lived. His relations with the Jewish community were blocked by the reservations he felt simultaneously with his enthusiasm. As to Felice, although from the outset he had misgivings, the process was to be somewhat slower. The strength she inspired in him was protected by the physical distance between them. Kafka himself acknowledged that he was terrified of the possibility of having her near him, which would leave him unprotected.

Thus, the dilemma is clear: he needed this strength and was quite conscious of his need, but he also felt that the source of this need made his independence impossible. This will be the pattern of Kafka's relations with power, as they are expressed in his works: though extremely sensitive to it, he nonetheless shuns it all of the time. Like strength, power is what is denied his body a priori; like strength, power is what his work needs—the power to make his work move, to provide a setting for it. In order to treat the issue of power in Kafka, we shall need to go into his fiction; we are bringing it up at this point only in order to point to its homology with the question of strength.

As we have seen, to Kafka there was complete incompatibility between family and marriage on the one hand, and literature on the other. The terms of this opposition become more complex when we add to them the weakness of Kafka's body and his reliance on an external source of strength. This articulation points more clearly to the fate of his sexuality—active only in relationships where love is not present, or at least not manifestly revealed as such. When love was clearly manifested, as in the case of Felice, bodily contact was to be avoided. Thus, the breaking off of the engagement was very much to be expected.

Canetti stresses Kafka's exceptional inability to avoid making the same mistakes again and again. Perhaps Canetti would also agree that even more exceptional was his ability to point to the source of his mistakes. For Kafka does more than simply complain of his weakness. He seems to believe, contradictorily, that his survival is the result of a last remaining force: "No push is really needed, only a withdrawal of the last force placed at my disposal, and I fall into a despair that rips me to pieces" (Dec. 11, 1913; Kafka 1972: 246).

The sentence, however, seems to deny what it states: if all that is needed is the withdrawal of the last force at his disposal for him to be flung into utter despair, such a force—necessarily external—would have to evoke an inner force in him to contradict it. Without such a tension, the sentence is meaningless. But the passage expresses the situation from an angle that conceals the source of resistance. This becomes more visible if we write: no push is necessary, because if there is no external pressure there will be no resistance either.

This brief exegesis shows how partial our examination had been so far. There is no incongruence in the acknowledgment of an inner energy, as long as one notes that this energy depends on another one coming from outside. It must be added that this inner force does not act solely as a defense against despair. Its action is not necessarily positive. In fact, most of its effects are negative: a body that refuses the contamination of the external force contaminates itself. Kafka's letters show that this is the case. Writing to Max Brod in April 1921, he comments on his own illness: "Tuberculosis no more has its origins in the lungs than, for example, the World War had its cause in the ultimatum. There is only a single disease, no more, and medicine blindly chases down this one disease as though hunting a beast in endless forests" (Kafka 1977: 275).

Although he was not particularly enthusiastic about psychoanalytical interpretation, Kafka was a careful and intelligent reader of Freud and in this passage relies on him to illuminate his own case. In an earlier letter, to Minze Eisner, written in February 1920, he discusses his hesitation over whether he should spend his vacation in the north or in the south in a passage that is only apparently lighthearted: "My head, I think, prefers the north, my lungs the south. But since the lungs usually sacrifice themselves when it becomes too hard on the head, so the head in reciprocation has gradually conceived a longing for the south" (p. 225).

The two passages quoted above are in fact derived from a decisive text, contained in a letter to Brod written in mid-September 1917:

> In any case my attitude toward the tuberculosis today resembles that of a child clinging to the pleats of its mother's skirts. If the disease came from my mother, the image fits even better, and my mother in her infinite solicitude, which far exceeds her understanding of the matter, has done me this service also. I am constantly seeking an explanation for this disease, for I did not seek it. *Sometimes it seems to me that my brain and lungs came to an agreement without my knowledge.* "Things can't go on this way," said the brain, and after five years the lungs said they were ready to help. (p. 138, emphasis added)

To the extent that Kafka's complaints directed at his own body *expressed* his opinion, they had to do with the fact that his body was not consistent with his physical and aesthetic values. But the passage quoted above clearly has another meaning.

With an ironical detachment that deflates all pathos, Kafka stages for his friend's benefit a short play in which the central characters are the brain and the lungs. They are not seen as *his* organs, for in this case they would act as instruments of self-expression for him; rather, they act as formulators of an unexpected equation. In the best tradition of the early German romantics, wit turns back on itself. To reduce the cause of his suffering to a physical malady would be, as in the case of the war only recently ended, to mistake the effect for the cause. This, he writes Brod in 1921, is the sort of reasoning of those who hunt an animal in forests where it is not to be found. The tuberculosis is only the effect of a decision made by the real protagonists; illness is the physical effect of a symbolic cause.

This cause could only be found in the mind. What if not his mind could Kafka be accusing when he criticized himself for the insensibility he detected in himself in relation to the Austrian defeats in the Great War (see Dec. 13, 1914, entry, Kafka 1972: 314)? Detaching itself, leaving what should be its subject in a state of torpor and confusion, his mind left him dependent on the stimulation of external forces. Its sabotage went even further: it made its subject believe that there was nothing but passivity inside him. But does it make sense to speak of a subject here when what should be the subject of *cogito* behaves as if it did no more than obey orders? By deviating from the expressive tendencies of "normal" Romanticism, Kafka revived the sharp irony of the early romantics. But he used it to destroy something they left intact: the individual subject as central point.

The transformation of subject into object, of the unifying element into a setting for disputes it cannot control, is repeated in the letter to Minze Eisner when Kafka refers to the mind's acceptance of the lungs' wishes. Both in the serious and dramatic context of the letter to Brod and in the lighthearted one of the letter to young Minze, the body is the receptive medium. Its strength, as we have seen, can be brought out only by an external stimulus. However, the brain itself may be the external source in question.

Kafka's belief in the symbolic origin of his disease allows us to understand his stand on the issue we brought up in the beginning of the present section: the problem of representation.

We have seen that the modern (let us now characterize it as such) use of representation had been closely related to the privileged treatment given to the idea of the self, of subjectively oriented individuality. In theoretical or philosophical terms, Kafka was not interested in the problem. Nevertheless, it is worth investigating whether his introspection led him to a view of the issue that contradicted the approach favored by modernity. Disease is seen not as resulting from an external physical aggression, but from an internal symbolic cause. This, however, implies that, contrary to the physicalist view of the organism, the different parts of the human body interpret the orders issued by the brain independently from the will or the consciousness of the self.

From the viewpoint of literary production, the consequence is immediate: instead of expressing the centrality of the self, infinite selfhood, the work is a system of production in which what is voiceless speaks, using the body as its stage. Thus, the concept of representation is limited to a precise historical period, its apex being located in the centuries during which individuality reigned supreme; otherwise the concept must be redefined. Before turning to Kafka's work, let us reflect on the effects of this change.

Against the tradition on which the prestige of representation is based, Kafka's works, even his private writings, stress the impossibility of postulating the presence of a unity that could be expressed. The critique of this pretension is clear in the diary entry dated December 10, 1913:

> It is never possible to take note of and evaluate all the circumstances that influence the mood of the moment, are even at work within it, and finally are at work in the evaluation, hence it is false to say that I felt resolute yesterday, that I am in despair today. Such differentiations only prove that one desires to influence oneself, and, as far removed from oneself as possible, hidden behind prejudices and fantasies, temporarily to create an artificial life, as sometimes someone in the corner of a tavern, sufficiently concealed behind a small glass of whiskey, entirely alone with himself, entertains himself with nothing but false, unprovable imaginings and dreams. (Kafka 1972: 245)

Why are "unitary" judgments—yesterday I felt that way, now I feel this way—false? Why does Kafka say such affirmations of unity lead to an artificial life, comparable to drug-induced fantasies, if not because they postulate the unity of the self?

It is well known that reduction to unity, subordination of differences to a constant, is the necessary prerequisite to the operation of concepts. "Without minimal homogeneity, no understanding is possible" (Lebrun 1970: 270). Kafka's opposition to this rule is not based on any contrary theoretical postulate; it is his sensibility, long dedicated to self-examination, that leads him to the realization that, under the empire of the self, "minimal homogeneity" balloons to an inordinate size. And here, in addition to reminding ourselves once again of Kafka's dramatic sketch involving the brain and the lungs, we must read with attention a passage from the December 12, 1913, entry:

I looked closely at myself in the mirror a while ago—though only by artificial light and with the light coming from behind me, so that actually only the down at the edges of my ears was illuminated—and my face, even after fairly close examination, appeared to me better than I know it to be. A clear, well-shaped, almost beautifully outlined face. The black of the hair, the brows and the eye sockets stand livingly forth from the rest of the passive mass. The glance is by no means haggard, there is no trace of that, but neither is it childish, rather unbelievably energetic, but *perhaps only because it was observing me, since I was just then observing myself and wanted to frighten myself.* (p. 247, emphasis added)

This detailed description might be taken as a display of naive narcissism, were it not for its closing section (which I have emphasized). The positive trait he finds in his own look—"*unglaublicherweise energisch,*" he calls it—immediately receives an antiexpressionistic qualification: perhaps it seems so simply because his look is observing him and, resenting the fact that it is being observed, decides to frighten the one who is observing it! The focus on the self, concentrating on material description, cannot be exact or pure because the one being observed, instead of remaining passive, reacts by interfering with the "observer." And this interference consists not only in confusing his understanding but also, in a much more active sense, in staging a scene that makes it difficult to draw a definite conclusion. Who intended to frighten him? The syntax of the sentence is clear enough: it unambiguously describes a "dialogue" between *er* (it)—that is, *der Blick* (the glance) and *ich* (I), the subject (if indeed we can go on using the term) of the action.

The passage we have just examined deserves special attention because, since it was not meant to be published, we may assume it is free of literary artifice. (The validity of this assumption remains even if we agree that, as someone has observed, it is very difficult to draw a sharp line between Kafka's private writings and his manifestly fictional work.) So important is this point that we may as well test it again:

The best things I have written have their basis in this capacity of mine to meet death with contentment. All these fine and very convincing passages always deal with the fact that someone is dying, that it is hard for him to do, that it seems unjust to him, or at least harsh, and the reader is moved by this, or at least he should be. But for me, who believe that I shall be able to lie contentedly on my deathbed, such scenes are secretly a game; indeed, in the death enacted I rejoice in my own death, hence calculatingly exploit the attention that the reader concentrates on death, have a much clearer understanding of it than he, of whom I suppose that he will loudly lament on his deathbed, and for these reasons my lament is as perfect as can be, nor does it suddenly break off, as is likely to be the case with a real lament, but dies beautifully and purely away. It is the same thing as my perpetual lamenting to my mother over pains that were not nearly so great as my laments would lead one to believe. With my mother, of

course, I did not need to make so great a display of art as with the reader.
(Dec. 13, 1914; Kafka 1972: 321)

The entire passage, with its mixture of coolness and involvement, self-
irony and sincerity, detachment and commitment, clearly presupposes the
power of mimesis. Nothing could be more absurd than to imagine Kafka
carried away by the intensity of his feelings. Mimesis is evoked in his relationship with the reader and with his mother. In the former case we have the
writer; in the latter, the actor. The effectiveness of mimesis, at least according
to Kafka, depends on the discrepancy between his own attitude toward death
and the receiver's different expectation. This discrepancy generates the effect
of intensity: since Kafka imagines himself contented in his deathbed, he can
write about his characters' complaints with a poise born of detachment that
has a more forceful impact on the reader. Also, the reader cannot see the
scaffolding behind the text, which increases the effect all the more. For all
that, the reader is not entirely mistaken; only, the expressiveness derives not
from the sincerity of the confession, but from the skillfulness of the staging.

It would be false to call this falsity: the stage director is shrewd; what he
relies on is not an artifice—a stylistic flourish designed to meet the reader's
demand—but the shrewdness of detachment, reminiscent of the opening of
Fernando Pessoa's famous poem "Autopsicografia":

> O poeta é um fingidor.
> Finge tão completamente
> Que chega a fingir que é dor
> A dor que deveras sente.   (Pessoa, 1965)

> The poet is a pretender.
> So completely does he feign
> That he passes off as real
> His all-too-actual pain.

Thus, Kafka channeled into literary practice a game strategy rooted in childhood, in his relationship with his mother. In both cases—the shrewdness
aimed at the reader and the strategy calculated to attract his mother's attention—there is mastery of detachment, a specialized mastery in the former case
and a form common to many who are not writers in the latter: the habit of
seeing oneself or one's products as things that must be examined and pursued,
with dissatisfaction but also with curiosity, the very opposite of confession.

The difference between detachment and confession does not imply a
distinction between artificial, potentially fraudulent conduct and natural,
ethical behavior. The distinction is merely one of degree: confession necessarily implies a specific kind of dramatization, or at least the naiveté of pre-

suming that, when one confesses, one hands over to the other a pure self, shorn of any artifice. Confession and detachment are only diversified strategies of the same mimesis of action.

What is the origin of Kafka's preference for a certain strategy of mimesis? A text written on October 19, 1917, explains: "There is no such thing as observation of the inner world, as there is of the outer world. At least descriptive psychology is probably, taken as a whole, a form of anthropomorphism, a nibbling [ein Annagen] at our own limits. The inner world can only be experienced, not described.—Psychology is the description of the reflection of the terrestrial world in the heavenly plane" (Kafka 1991: 14–15). This will sound shocking only to those who believe that the world of Kafka's writings and his own inner landscape are one and the same. The passage just quoted not only denies the truth of this equation in Kafka's specific case but also affirms that there is no access to this inner universe. One cannot express what one experiences descriptively because there is no direct expression of how one lives. There will always be the mediation of the manner in which the one who lives can express to him or herself and to others how he or she lives. This manner is the mark of inevitable mimesis. And, because it is inevitable, to ignore its existence, to refuse to deal with it, to believe instead in a would-be substance known as the self, inevitably has the effect of making one a bad actor: the sort of actor who, because he evokes his own testimony constantly, is convinced he must be believed.

"All human errors are impatience, the premature breaking off of what is methodical, an apparent fencing in of the apparent thing" (p. 15). Unconsciously, Kafka protects himself from impatience by resorting to indecision. But there is nothing unconscious about the way he avoids being a bad actor. Two decisive consequences ensue: (1) the nonrepresentational character of his fiction, if representation is understood in its usual sense of expression of the authorial self; (2) his expectation of finding salvation in literature. In consideration of (1), in addition to the passages already quoted, let us examine one more:

> "Know thyself" [*Erkenne dich selbst*] does not mean "Observe thyself." "Observe thyself" is what the Serpent says. It means: "Make yourself master of your actions." But you are so already, you are the master of your actions. So that saying means: "Misjudge yourself! [*Verkenne dich*] Destroy yourself!" which is something evil—and only if one bends down very far indeed does one also hear the good in it, which is: "In order to make of yourself what you are [*um dich zu dem zu machem, der du bist*]." (Kafka 1991: 20–21)

Written at a time of spiritual and religious search, this extraordinary passage is born of the refusal to accept the cliché. It implies that one should

not confuse the classical advice with the commonplace (it is no longer necessary to add: and modern) observation of oneself. This prohibition does not
derive from any aesthetic principle. If such were the case, it would be enough
to add: for in this way you will arrive at nothing. At the same time, however,
the serpent's interference would not make sense. The foundation of the
prohibition is ethical. It lends the classical injunction a paradoxical meaning:
to know oneself is to ignore oneself, to destroy oneself, which in turn leads to
the conclusion, in which the ethical and the aesthetic are fused together. In
other words, the aesthetic way is in the method—to avoid banality—on
which the ethical way is built. If the method is to become operational—that
is, not reduced to a mere cliché—it is necessary to adopt a manner. In the
terms of the passage in question, this manner could only be that which avoids
excessive proximity to oneself—detachment. In this way one avoids both
being a bad actor and doing what the serpent says.

It would be irrelevant to introduce an ethical argument here but for the
fact that it allows us to emphasize the close association between the ethical
and the aesthetic in Kafka. This brings into sharper focus the nonrepresentational aspect of his fiction: it is so not as an escape or out of prudishness; it is
intentionally nonrepresentational for ethical reasons—because it refuses to
collaborate with the devil, or, in more straightforward terms, because it refuses to endorse individualistic narcissism.

This has the additional advantage of stressing the inadequacy of those
analyses of Kafka's religiousness that are based on such facts as the degree of
his familiarity with the Talmud, his effective links—clearly weak—with the
religious core of Judaism. About this, all we can say is that Kafka's interest in
Jewish life is more cultural than religious. But the decisive point is rather the
link between the ethical and the aesthetic in Kafka—more precisely, the fact
that the principle of operation of the former presupposes activation of the
method proper to the latter. But before we proceed, let us conclude our
discussion of representation.

All we have said would be enough if it were possible to speak of representation only as the expression of an authorial self that showed itself through representation and therefore found in it a way of socializing itself. But this would
be incorrect. To shorten this discussion, let us turn to a passage by Kafka.

The text in question is a draft of a letter to his friend Franz Werfel,
written in December 1922, in which he evaluates Werfel's play *Schweiger*. His
tone could not have been more critical. Even without having read the play,
we can plainly see the reason for the harshness of Kafka's judgment.[6] Kafka is

6. For information concerning the play, see the translator's, C. David's, comments in
Kafka 1984, 3: 1615 n.

indignant because the play is approached as if it were not clearly localized in place and time, and because what happens to the central character appears to be merely trivial. With a rude frankness not to be found anywhere else in his correspondence, Kafka accuses the author of "a betrayal of the generation, a glossing over, a trivializing, and therefore a cheapening, of their sufferings" (Kafka 1977: 366). What is so offensive to their generation about the random nature of the character in the play can only be the fact that its triviality makes it inadequate as a representation of its time. But if this is indeed what Kafka means, how can it be reconciled with what we have said about the nonrepresentational character of Kafka's work? Do we mean that Kafka was so blatantly contradictory as to reject as a reader what he did as an author?

There is no contradiction here, for a quite simple reason. Kafka attacks Werfel's work because the time and place common to both of them, as writers who belong to the same Jewish community in the same Czech nation, could not be identified. Clearly Kafka was not calling for "local color," picturesque detail, or other surface traits, but for the "objective correlative" of a situation that Werfel surely knew as intimately as he did himself. This is not a gratuitous conjecture. According to Gustav Janouch, when he criticized *The Metamorphosis* for being "an awful dream, an awful representation [*Vorstellung*]," Kafka answered: "The dream unveils the reality under which representation remains [Der Traum enthüllt die Wirklichkeit, hinter der die Vorstellung zurückbleit]" (Janouch 1951: 27).

Kafka rejected the cult of the self and the confidence in its centrality, not under the influence of any philosophical doctrine, but because he was aware of the false unity this belief presupposed, although he was always attentive to his own dreams, which he frequently mentioned in his letters. Thus, the emphasis on the antirepresentational character of Kafka's work will be misleading unless one is aware of what it leads to. For in Kafka another representational scene is elaborated: one that intends to speak of its own time not as though the self stood outside of it, like an onlooker, but by bending over it so as to incorporate the character of its time to its own form.

It would be an oversimplification of the issue to which the present section is dedicated to conclude that Kafka uses all his resources merely in order to avoid self-expression and achieve representation of his place and time. This would be tantamount to conceiving him as an epigone of realistic or terror fiction. One does not represent one's time by recreating through language what is already contained in one's time before the writing itself. The time does not make the work. It is the work that, through its manner of production, makes the time.

Now we see that seemingly irrelevant details make sense. Thus, for instance, in a letter to his publisher, Kurt Wolff, dated October 25, 1915, Kafka insists that the insect protagonist of *The Metamorphosis* should not be depicted in an illustration. "The insect itself cannot be depicted. It cannot even be shown from a distance" (Kafka 1977: 115). Gregor Samsa does not take on the shape of what he already is. His transformation does not begin at the moment he realizes he cannot get up from his bed, nor does it end after he terrorizes his family. The horror he embodies is a horror in progress; it is elastic rather than shapeless. If it is not compatible with a drawing, it is because it does not exemplify a homogeneity and thus cannot follow a law. Its nonrepresentational character has to do with the fact that it is the objective correlative of its time. It is as such that it represents the horror of a historicized form of life. But it represents it by producing it. Representation in Kafka, being nonexpressive, does not illustrate, describe, or exemplify. Like the work he is part of, Samsa-as-insect is an event—that is, what cannot be explained according to what is previously known; though not explainable, however, he explains what is already present.

I am not playing with words here. What I am describing is characteristic of all true production. "Is an event something like a *Witz* [wit] of history?" (Proust 1991: 123). Being antirepresentational, representation in Kafka is the production of a wit, a flash of lightning revealing what was previously unseen and that only now makes sense; what could not be seen, not because of a sort of collective nearsightedness, but because, though it was already there, it could not be integrated into any homogenizing pattern that could make it meaningful. Wit and event are, therefore, on the planes of form and of history respectively, correlative phenomena. No wonder, then, that the first perceptive readers of Kafka should have felt stunned. Their unease could not be explained in purely literary terms.

Does fiction, then, contain the salvation potential that Kafka searched for? In order to see that we cannot conclude that it does, let us examine the second consequence of Kafka's antiexpressivism.

Representational Production and Contemporary Literature

Is what we have been calling representational production, on the basis of the conclusions stated earlier, a consequence of Kafka's view of literature? In order to understand his view, let us examine three important passages. The earliest is dated December 27, 1911. To express his discontentment with the works he had produced until then, Kafka wrote a short text, of which we transcribe the beginning and the ending:

In front of two holes in the ground a man is waiting for something to appear that can rise up only out of the hole on his right. But while this hole remains covered by a dimly visible lid, one thing after another rises up out of the hole on his left, keeps trying to attract his attention, and in the end succeeds in doing this without any difficulty because of its swelling size, which, much as the man may try to prevent it, finally covers up even the right hole. But the man—he does not want to leave his place, and indeed refuses to at any price—has nothing but these appearances, and although—fleeting as they are, their strength is used up by their merely appearing—they cannot satisfy him . . .

How weak this picture is. An incoherent assumption is thrust like a board between the actual [*tatsächlich*] feeling and the metaphor of the description [*vergleichende Beschreibung*]. (Kafka 1972: 155)

The second and third texts are dated December 8, 1917, and December 6, 1921, respectively:

For everything outside the phenomenal world, language can only be used allusively [*andeutungsweise*], but never even approximately in a comparative way [*vergleichweise*], since, corresponding as it does to the phenomenal world, it is concerned only with property and its relations [*vom Besitz und seinen Beziehungen*]. (Kafka 1991: 30)

Metaphors are one among many things which make me despair of writing. Writing's [*des Schreibens*] lack of independence in the world, its dependence on the maid who tends the fire, on the cat warming itself by the stove; it is even dependent on the poor old human being warming himself by the stove. All these are independent activities ruled by their own laws; only writing is helpless [*hilflos*], cannot live in itself, is a joke [*Spaß*] and despair. (Kafka 1972: 398)

The topic common to these three reflections, written over a period of ten years, is the inadequacy of metaphor. The first passage is quite straightforward about it: metaphor is an unjustifiable operation. The second is more difficult to decipher, although its point of departure is clear and consistent with the other two: the opposition between the allusive and analogical modes of language. But only this much is clear. If we identify allusiveness with nonsymbolic language (see Corngold 1988: 54) and see metaphor as the instrument of analogy par excellence, the vexing question is: How can the allusive mode be possible in literature? According to the second passage, however, this is a must, for language, as regards the sensible world (*entsprechend der sinnlichen Welt*), "is concerned only with property and its relations." Surely it is inconceivable that Kafka should attempt to produce literature without dealing with what is not sensible. But what does he mean by what is beyond the sensible? To C. David, the author of the commentary to the French translation of Kafka's works, the solution seems quite simple: "The sensible world as a flaw in the purity of the spiritual world" (see Kafka 1984, 3: 1417).

This explanation fails to answer the question: What spiritual world did Kafka intend to write about, in relation to which the analogical was an obstacle?

One possible answer is to be found in Corngold's suggestion that "human inwardness" stands outside the parameters of the "phenomenal world" (Corngold 1988: 37). Thus, it is in relation to this stance that analogy, or metaphor, is arbitrary and falsifying. Unfortunately, however, such a solution will not do. We can understand Kafka's dissatisfaction with the use of a worldly language to express innerness. We have already seen how Kafka rejects descriptive psychology as mere anthropomorphism and a trick with mirrors. But just how could one create a nonmetaphorical language? Curiously enough, the dilemmas that had been the concern of the Vienna Circle now resurface, quite independently, in Prague. It is surely no coincidence that, in the third passage, Kafka should say that metaphors make him despair of literature. It may be said that the issue ends in an impasse, for both the writer and his interpreter: literature is entertainment (pleasure, a joke, *Spaß*) and despair; it is what cannot justify itself ([es] *wohnt nicht in sich selbst*), among other reasons because, unlike simpler phenomena such as the cat or the old man warming himself by the stove, it does not obey its own laws (*eigengesetzlich*).

But to say this is to neglect the practical solution that is formulated by Kafka's work itself. To say that, with regard to the sensible world, language "is concerned only with property and its relations" implies emphasis on allusiveness and its deictic power, its ability to indicate. What, then, is property if not what points out, since the entire legitimacy of property is a metaphorical leap—an arbitrary leap, in Kafka's terms? What are relations of property if not deictic elements or derived indications? Thus, to emphasize the deictic nature of allusiveness means to highlight relations of contiguity—that is, to make the principle of metonymy predominate over that of metaphor. It means to submit to this angle all the subject matter of fiction. The metaphorical "transport" or "leap" is subjugated when it is treated as a succession of small shifts. In this way the writer can deal with the nonsensible without infringing upon his self-imposed ban on metaphor.

Later we shall return to the impasse of metaphor. For the moment, we do no more than stress that, to Kafka, literature ultimately proved unable to provide the redemption and salvation he had expected. Such an expectation was the effect of a transference from the sphere of religion. In Kantian terms— and here the parallel between Kant's and Kafka's reflections is striking—it would amount to treating a subject that is by definition transcendent, that is, derived from the excessive pretension of reason, as if it were transcendental! Given the same prohibition that Kafka imposed—a consequence of the fact that language concerns only property and its relations—Kant had attempted to legitimate the distinct spheres of practical reason and the reflective judgment. In a nonspeculative way—Kafka himself said he was uninterested in philosophical speculation—the parallelism between the writer and the philosopher is maintained: Kafka's work is a practical response to the impasse that had not been solved theoretically.

It is then precisely because of the failure of his highest aspiration—to produce writings he could find satisfactory—that he became a contemporary master. Thus, it is not accidental that the following reflection by Maurice Blanchot should be based on Kafka's work: "If language, and literary language in particular, were not constantly pushing forward, from the outset, towards its own death, language would not be possible, for it is this movement towards its impossibility that is its condition and its foundation. . . . Language is real because it can project itself on a nonlanguage that it is and does not actualize" (Blanchot 1949: 28).

It is because Kafka's work follows this path consistently that it is one of the cornerstones of twentieth-century literature. For it affects nothing less than the very way we conceive the literary work. We have seen how it attacked one of the foundations of the conception that had been in force since the late eighteenth century, frustrating the usual expectation that the work should be the representation of a rich, unitary subjectivity. Let us now see how it affects another foundation, the correlate of the one we have just examined.

Kafka and the Question of Interpretation

Modernity secularized the creative subject. This does not mean that a single, unitary position was then adopted in relation to the secularized subject. Montaigne's epistemological skepticism could not be identified with the certainties of Descartes's *cogito*, which in turn was denied by Vico's ideal eternal history and by Kant's subject of transcendental apperception. Though not in the privileged position it was to occupy in Descartes's system, in Montaigne the self was central in a different way. In any case, for him it is not humanly possible to attain certain and unequivocal knowledge; Montaigne's individual ruminations about the self's errancy, capriciousness, and idiosyncrasies, unprecedented in antiquity, made his work unique. Whereas in Vico ideal, eternal history assumed an inexorable succession of phases of which even decline and recurrence were predictable, the process, although imperious and impersonal, emphasized the human subject nonetheless. Vico's principle—one can only know what one makes—separated the plane of the deity from that of the creature, making the needs of the human subject the core of his investigation. Similarly, in Kant, although the empirical subject—each self—is not the source of certainties that Descartes saw in it, and although knowledge depends not on its active intervention but on the apparatus with which mankind is endowed, still the individual subject remains central in the reflective judgment.

For all the divergences between the systems of thought of the seventeenth and eighteenth centuries, the centrality of the subjectively oriented individual was a constant. Hence derived the importance of the principle of representation, analyzed in the previous section. Its centrality, we may now add, was bound up with the way modernity interpreted the fictional text. Again, divergences existed. The traditional historiographical model, which reduced works to the homogeneity of the periods they belonged to and the extraindividual constants that corresponded to these periods, was opposed to the no less traditional approach that saw life as the determining factor of the work's character. And the latter tendency was not to be identified with the immanent, textualist, antihistorical, and antibiographical approaches that would dominate twentieth-century literary criticism. All of these different approaches presupposed either that individual works were integrated into a unity or that they were themselves this unity, so that the set of canonical masterpieces formed a sort of constellation. No wonder, then, that the romantics should speak of the *organic unity* of the work of art and that, in our own century, the integration of the various strata of the work should be seen, by the Polish philosopher Roman Ingarden, as a criterion of value.

Even when these interpretations did not fall back on the banality of equating life and work, they all assumed the centrality of the subject. Just as the subject was whole and living, the work was harmonic and integrated, hence the principle that interpretation consisted in providing the real meaning of the text. Just as each individual—particularly the creative one—was unique, each text was unique as well, and the searched-for uniqueness was also applied to the interpretation. This led to the maxim that each text contains one interpretation, which, being the true one, allowed no other.

It is understandable, then, that rejecting the critical babel of the contemporary scene, E. D. Hirsch, Jr., should propose a return to authorial intentionality: "The question I always want to ask critics who dismiss authorial intention as their norm is . . . : 'When you write a piece of criticism, do you want me to disregard *your* intention and original meaning?'" (Hirsch 1976: 91). The answer to the question is so predictable that a disciple of his adds, in the same vein:

> It is not logically possible for an author both to express the belief that "You do not surmount nature by denying its prime claim of sexuality" and *not* to express

this belief. If a literary work is a speech act, it cannot have logically incompatible meanings. (Juhl 1980: 221)

> If the meaning of a work is logically tied to the author's intention, or what a work expresses is linked to the author's beliefs . . . then there is good reason to believe that any interpretation of a given text can in principle be shown to be correct or incorrect. (p. 236)

If, therefore, interpretations vary in time, this is so because "the relation of [a text's] meaning to changing historical circumstances, is potentially unlimited" (p. 230).

However, even those who find absolute intentionalism too narrow will adopt—only less emphatically, perhaps—the corollary of "correct" interpretation. An interpretation is more correct to the extent that it succeeds in capturing the integration of the various traits of the work in a layer (evidently hidden to common readers) discovered by means of painstaking analysis. The unity of the source—the subject as creator—corresponds to the semantic stability that is constitutive of the work, whether the work in question is a "classic" or merely a nonchaotic text. The modern concept of the subject is projected onto the work, explaining it—from the expressivism of "normal" Romanticism to the attempt to restore it through Hirsch's intentionalism—and justifying it against the chaos of theories[7] which does no more than hasten the death of literature and strengthen a certain conception of language and literature.

The various layers of language provide the support for a semantic axis. That is, language aims at communication; everything else—phonology, phonetics, morphosyntax—is either a preparation for this goal or an ornament. Although the literary work is distinguished by a strangeness and power of organization that are not sought by usual communication and, as opposed to the scientific work, by the fact that nothing may be added to it after it is understood (see Juhl 1980: 222 and 224, respectively), these effects do not affect the thoroughly semanticized structure common to all language, however it may be used.

The idea of "strangeness" has the additional advantage of allowing us to escape from the narrow circle of intentionalists and showing that their conception of literature agrees with other tendencies that at first do not seem to be involved in the discussion. Indeed, the statement "Literary works captivate

7. This is not the place to demonstrate that the expressive-intentionalist position today is more than simply conservative. Let us only add that it is not content to be one position among dozens of others, but presents itself as a defender of Western values. For a highly instructive example of this argument, see Kernan 1990, one of the most complete defenses of the critical establishment.

readers by their strangeness" would be acceptable, with modifications that are irrelevant here, both by the proponents of a stylistic approach and by Slavic formalists. This strangeness is then seen as the mark of the literary, without affecting the semantic stability preserved by works.

It is not necessary to go into a long demonstration in order to see that both strangeness and semantic stability are implicit in the explanation of aesthetic experience that has become traditional. All we need observe is that if strangeness attracts one to its cause—deviation from the authorized norm— semantic stability acts as a counterweight, ensuring the receiver that the effect of deviation from the norm will not open a "black hole" in language. It is, in short, the agreement between the effect of strangeness and the semantic stability that is the source of aesthetic pleasure.[8] In other words, intentionalism is part of a paradigm to which such different theoretical currents as stylistics and formalism belong. Their common ground is the traditional explanation of the aesthetic experience, on which the notion of semantic stability is based, and which in turn is connected to the principle of the true interpretation.

A quotation from Adorno's study on Kafka will make it unnecessary to analyze the mass of premises on which these interpretive practices are based: "Through the power with which Kafka commands interpretation, he collapses aesthetic distance. He demands a desperate effort of the allegedly 'disinterested' observer of an earlier time, overwhelms him, suggesting that far more than his intellectual equilibrium depends on whether he truly understands; life and death are at stake" (Adorno 1969: 246).

According to the parameters that were seen as traditional at the time Kafka wrote, fiction was no more than an arabesque that could not compromise the solidity of the pillars. So tenuous was its pattern that one could contemplate it with no fear of losing one's serene composure. The observer could enjoy it in such a disinterested way as to imagine that what he or she was seeing was only the subject in full command of its reflexivity, its infinite self-fruition. Surely Kafka was not the first to undermine the stronghold of the self, nor was he the first to attack the principle of representation of a self-made unitary subject. To see this in Kafka brings to mind a whole line of ancestors. Immediately before him there was Kleist; then came Flaubert, Mallarmé, Baudelaire. In each of them, the supposed semantic stability of the work of art was dealt a mortal blow. Fiction could no longer be seen as a graceful arabesque on a solid building—that is, an arabesque that submitted to

---

8. There is a clear if superficial similarity between this explanation of aesthetic pleasure and Kant's description of the beautiful. It is no less evident or less symptomatic, however, that it is incompatible with Kant's description of the sublime. This explains Kant's difficulties in dealing with the sublime and ultimately subordinating it to the idea of the supersensible (see Chapter 2).

the values of the society of which it was a part—but rather something that imposed its own themes. Properly speaking, one could no longer see the arabesque as equivalent to an ornament.

But before we return to Kafka's work, let us see how the principle of interpretation and the status of fiction go together in it. Kafka's private writings provide abundant material for such an investigation—precisely the sort of material that might be exploited by the kind of interpretation we reject, whether in its biographical variants, such and such a life explains such and such a work, or in its more "noble" variant, given a work, only one meaning may be attributed to it. Let us examine some passages that show how inadequate these approaches are.

Take the issue of guilt, for instance. Kafka often manifests guilt over his decision to devote himself exclusively to literature. These passages would easily fit an expressive reading: they may be seen as expressing the remainder, the mark, the weight left by an antagonist whom the subject is unable to overcome. It might also be added that the German word *Schuld* means both "guilt" and "debt," so that for Kafka guilt is also a debt. In the case of guilt, his antagonist is morality; in the case of debt, his father. But what could such a reading do with the following observation, made in 1920? "Original sin, the old injustice committed by man, consists in the recrimination brought by man, and which he will not give up, that he was the victim of an injustice, that original sin was committed against him" (Kafka 1989, 5: 219). The injustice that, according to the Bible, was committed by man is subverted here: man is no longer the agent, but the object, of original sin. A negative God seems to make an unexpected appearance: he makes his creatures the victims of an evil and an expulsion for which they are later to be considered responsible.

But the passage does not say whether man is right or wrong when he accuses his creator. If the passage adopted the Gnostic viewpoint, the inversion would not interfere with semantic stability: original sin is the sin committed against man. If such a Gnosticism had indeed taken root, the explanation of guilt would be reversed. In the Christian interpretation, the personal life secretes the motives that are the ground on which guilt sprouts. In the case of Kafka, his "neurotic" guilt is associated with his exclusive concern with unprofitable literary work. The Gnostic inversion would give rise to a different reading: guilt, once depersonalized, is the byproduct of the recrimination man indulges in for being the victim of injustice. Correspondingly, Kafka's recrimination is directed against his family, particularly his father. But the passage fails to endorse the inversion; it simply poses it and leaves undefined whether or not the creature is right to complain. That is, instead of a saturated semantic space, in which the positions of subject, action, time, mode, and object are clearly filled, we have an unstable and unlimited world. How could such a "document" be used in the context of traditional interpretation?

Here is a second example. In a letter to Kurt Wolff, dated October 11, 1916, Kafka explains the tone of "The Penal Colony" as the result of a mark present not only in himself but also in his time: "The painfulness is not peculiar to it alone but . . . our times in general and my own time as well have also been painful and continue to be, and my own more consistently than the times. . . . The way I feel now, all I can do is wait for quieter times; in saying which I am representing myself, at least superficially, as truly a man of our times" (Kafka 1977: 127). Unlike one who confesses or uses every occasion to speak of oneself, Kafka sees himself as a testing ground for the possible extension of what he refers to. He may know the torture of guilt better than anyone, but guilt is not his private property: it is common to all his contemporaries. If his story is "painful," the story of a dilaceration that his publisher found disturbing, the reason is both in himself and in the times.

Taken together, the two passages point to three extensions: the world, the times, and the individual subject. Apparently the stability of interpretation remains unchanged. This is indeed the case if the three variables act as follows: the world brings about the feeling of guilt; the times manifest it; the individual introjects it; and each variable behaves in a univocally constant way. Now, as we saw earlier, Kafka's awareness of mimesis made him reject the supposed univocity of the self—that is, the principle of its unity. Let us consider the consequences of this by examining a couple of examples.

On October 22, 1911, Kafka reflects on the group of Jewish actors who are performing with Jizchak Löwy: "The sympathy we have for these actors who are so good, who earn nothing and who do not get nearly enough gratitude and fame is really only sympathy for the sad fate of many noble strivings, above all of our own. Therefore, too, it is so immoderately strong, because on the surface it is attached to strangers and in reality belongs to us" (Kafka 1972: 86).

The following day, he comments on his own reflections:

> The actors by their presence always convince me to my horror that most of what I've written about them until now is false. It is false because I write about them with steadfast love . . . but varying ability, and this varying ability does not hit off the real actors loudly and correctly but loses itself dully in this love that will never be satisfied with the ability and therefore thinks it is protecting the actors by preventing this ability from exercising itself. (p. 86)

If we combine the two passages, we find that sympathy (*Mitleid*) and love made his appreciation false because the feeling not only came unaccompanied by energy (literally *Kraft*, translated above as "ability") but also inhibited it.

The emotionally positive sentiment toward the actors was not enough to give Kafka the strength he always found wanting in himself. In contrast with the constant strength he drew from Felice at the time he was writing *The Trial*, the love accompanied by varying energy (*wechselnder Kraft*) produced a tender tone that, satisfied with its own emotion, failed to touch the object in its concreteness. Why should this be felt as unsatisfactory if not because Kafka could not be content to indulge in good feelings and their expression? The limitation of the expressive soul is the fact that it cannot touch what touches it.

It is because he is aware of this limitation and does not want it for himself that Kafka made a point of exercising his "objective" view of himself, of presenting himself as an external object. Let us consider from this angle a passage that is otherwise of little significance. The writer describes an encounter: "We hadn't spoken so intimately for a long time, or perhaps never at all—I felt my face, which had never before been so closely observed by him, reveal parts to him in spurious frankness that he hardly understood but that nevertheless surprised him. I was unrecognizable to myself. I know him quite well" (Oct. 24, 1911; p. 88). Before the other, Kafka's face reveals what Kafka himself as a subject does not know. The impossibility of self-knowledge betrays the failure of the center that was supposed to express itself. The position of otherness is the only adequate alternative if one is to know oneself.

Valuing detachment over self-affection, observation over introspection, Kafka is not guided by an artistic intention, but by the concern with truth. It is in the name of the requirement of truth that he refuses to share the presumed identity of the self and hence the need to express it. In this context, the entry of December 8, 1911, is particularly important: "I have now, and have had since this afternoon, a great yearning to write all my anxiety entirely out of me, write it into the depths of the paper just as it comes out of the depths of me, or write it down in such a way that I could draw what I had written into me completely" (p. 134). No otherness is invoked in connection with this desideratum: there is no object, such as a mirror, with the aid of which he might examine himself, or someone else on the basis of whose reactions he might come into contact with what he ignores about his own face. To him, it is writing that has the task of functioning as an interposed external medium, capable of extirpating anxiety. Writing does not express: it contrasts.

We may then say: in Kafka, words move in a direction opposite to introjection, which is rejected because it would enmesh him in subjective presumptions—in the subject's preconceptions about itself and external things. This displeased him, for he wanted his writing to be a production of truth, hence his striving toward objectification. In the terms of a passage quoted earlier, the allusive mode would be compromised if it allowed facile metaphors. The allusiveness he strives for depends on the emphasis on literalness. It thus implies a language opposed to the curvilinear and the manneristic. Rather, it requires a dry, dense, cold, austere language. The exclusiveness of literature for Kafka cannot be understood unless one considers its consistency with the search for the objectification of truth. Uninterested in abstract speculation, Kafka always has to deal with sensible situations. The fictionality with which they must be treated must operate in a way that is uncontaminated by subjective presumptions. Not that Kafka believes in the sufficiency of an objective materiality, or that he avoids personal observations. His goal is to approach personal material in such a way that his treatment may move from inner to outer space—that is, transform the ghosts of innerness into objects that were revealing of himself and of his times.

To the extent that this entire examination has set out from the premise that Kafka's work has a disturbing effect on the assumptions on which modern interpretation is based, it is time to ask what conclusions we have reached. Two points should be emphasized.

On the one hand, dissatisfied with and even irritated by the psychological tradition in literature, Kafka strives to discover ways of objectification. He is not trying to protect himself from public curiosity but rather to find a medium interposed between subjectivity and the outer world that makes it possible to objectify the former. Thus, it would be just as absurd to describe his work as impersonal as to call it confessional; in addition, if we exclude the pathetic element, Kafka's attitude shows affinities with that of expressionist painters.

On the other hand, the requirement of truth Kafka imposes on his stories, emphasized by statements in his diaries and letters, points in the opposite direction. That is, if the first point implies that Kafka violated the principle of interpretation based on the deep expression of a self, and thus destabilized the exegesis that saw itself as capturing the subject's view of itself and its world, the second point instead implies that in principle there was no incompatibility between the will to objectify truth and the assumption of the semantic stability of the text.

This means that the issue of interpretive stability presents two quite different courses. The first results from the set of assumptions we examined in the beginning of the present section: there is one correct interpretation, and it ultimately amounts to the discovery of the authorial intention (it is irrelevant here that this discovery should show intentionality in a more clear and precise way than the author himself would be able to see it). The second course is much more radical: here the stability of interpretation becomes a chimera, and the search for it is no more than a gross mistake, for the text that it attempts to examine has no semantic stability whatsoever—that is, there is no way to say conclusively what it is that the text says. Although the first text we examined (Kafka 1989, 5: 219) favored such a path, the other two make it impossible to say that it is adequate to Kafka. His will to objectification as a way of showing the truth is not consistent with the sort of instability that would make textual interpretation undecidable.

Should we then conclude that Kafka's work remains undecided on the issue of semantic stability? No. Though not yet on a definitive basis, let us say that the semantic instability that characterizes Kafka's texts, even on the level of plot—in *The Trial* Joseph K. is arrested, and yet remains free; in *The Castle*, the voice K. speaks to on the phone confirms that a land surveyor had been sent for, but nevertheless K.'s right to remain in the village is not acknowledged—is the very form assumed by the characters' search for truth. Here we have an "objective correlative" for a temporal situation in which truth is manifested only through a questioning of what the truth refers to—that is, through the question as to what would be revealed by the truth. To arrive at a conclusive examination, we emphasized Kafka's need for interposing mediums which, avoiding subjective distortion and emotional limitation, might bridge the gap between the almost dreamlike nature of his material and the objectification of the text he sets out to write. One of these mediums is the omnipresent *tribunal*.

THE OBSESSION WITH THE TRIBUNAL

Kafka was only 27 when he wrote, on December 20, 1910: "I have continually an invocation in my ear: 'Were you to come, invisible judgment!'" (Kafka 1972: 31). Three years later, in a letter to Felice (September 16, 1913), this idea is amplified by the relation between the permanence of condemnation and the impossibility of deflecting it (see Kafka 1978: 445–46). The same thought recurs in a letter to Brod written in late December 1917, with a small but significant addition: the evidence with which he intended to defend himself was flawed. "What is the sense of saving such 'even' artistically misbegotten works? Because one hopes that these fragments will somehow combine to form my whole, some court of appeals [*Berufungsinstanz*] upon whose breast I shall be able to throw myself when I am in need?" (Kafka 1977: 184).

But it was to Felice that he confided, on September 30 or October 1, 1917, the most revealing explanation:

> When I examine my ultimate aim it shows that I do not actually strive to be good, to answer to a supreme tribunal. Very much the opposite. I strive to know the entire human and animal community, to recognize their fundamental pref-

erences, desires, and moral ideals, to reduce them to simple rules, and as quickly
as possible to adopt these rules so as to be pleasing to everyone, indeed (here
comes the inconsistency) to become so pleasing that in the end I might openly
act out my inherent baseness before the eyes of the world without forfeiting its
love—the only sinner not to be roasted. In short, my only concern is the human
tribunal, and I would like to deceive even this, and what's more without actual
deception. (Kafka 1978: 654)

Given our purpose in transcribing it here—to verify Kafka's obsession with
the tribunal in order to have more elements with which to consider the
question of the stability of interpretation—we ought to give the passage close
attention.

He begins by denying that his efforts are in any way related to the
expectations of a supreme tribunal (*einem höchsten Gericht*), and says that what
matters to him is the human tribunal, which he would like to win over
without fraud, gaining the love of all without sacrificing his inclinations. The
transformation of the divine tribunal into an earthly one, with the admission
that, through prior understanding and adoption of human preferences, he
would then try to deceive it, may seem mysterious. But it is this very mystery
that is important for the stability of interpretation.

It should be noted that the secularization of the tribunal is not always
present in later texts. Thus, in a letter written in mid-January 1918 on Brod's
conflicts with his wife and his friend's possible responses to her complaints,
Kafka observes: "But in so doing you transfer the matter to so high a court
that it will never deliver a verdict, but let the trial begin again from the
beginning" (Kafka 1977: 186). The ambiguity (or indecision) about the nature of the tribunal that obsesses him becomes all the more important because
the trial is inexhaustible. The extension of the tribunal is infinite in both the
horizontal and the vertical directions; that is, it appears on the human and the
divine planes. This surely does not mean that the presence of one implies that
of the other; in this case there would have been no ambiguity. In Kafka's
obsessive dealings with the tribunal, it is never clear whether it is to be taken
as religious or as purely earthly; and for this reason the interpretation remains
undecidable. More precisely, it is impossible to decide whether Kafka's text is
open to a religious interpretation, which could not possibly treat its object
only within historical and temporal parameters, or whether its sole referent is
Kafka's time and the inexhaustible tribunal is an institution afflicting his
contemporaries.

However, it is of decisive importance that we should not confuse this
undecidability with the issue of expression, which we examined earlier. That
is: to Kafka, the tribunal does not wait for him only; it is not a merely personal

issue, a way of dramatizing his own personal dilemmas. What is undecidable is the nature of the tribunal. This conclusion, in turn, immediately requires another preliminary study.

THE QUESTION OF THE LAW

Kafka's frequent references to the Law always assume that its limits are undetermined. It is at this point that the question of the Law in Kafka is closely related to the presence of the tribunal. And the ironical "liberalism" of his diary entry of January 5, 1914—"All things possible do happen, only what happens is possible" (Kafka 1972: 251)—is in fact rooted in the inscrutability of the Law. Many of Kafka's texts are rooted in this same soil. The following passage is reminiscent of a variant of the parable of the doorkeeper in *The Trial*:

> Seen with the terrestrially sullied eye, we are in the situation of travelers in a train that has met with an accident in a tunnel, and this at a place where the light of the beginning can no longer be seen, and the light of the end is so very small a glimmer that the gaze must continually search for it and is always losing it again, and, furthermore, both the beginning and the end are not even certainties. Round about us, however, in the confusion of our senses, or in the supersensitiveness of our senses, we have nothing but monstrosities and a kaleidoscopic play of things that is either delightful or exhausting according to the mood and injury of each individual. (Kafka 1991: 15)

This fragment was written on the same day—October 20, 1917—as another, which only superficially seems more enigmatic: "The decisive moment in human evolution is perpetual. That is why the revolutionary spiritual movements that declare all former things worthless are in the right, for nothing has yet happened" (p. 16). To man, it is always possible to revoke the entire past at any moment, for mankind always stands in the situation of the travelers in a train that has stopped in the middle of the tunnel, from where they can see a light neither at the beginning nor at the end. It should be observed, however, that the passage does not deny the existence of light at either end, but only stresses the impossibility of using it as orientation. In other words, the indeterminate nature of the Law, the nonassertion of its nonexistence, brings about a situation in which one can neither deny the presence of a religious unease in Kafka's work nor see it as the center of his concerns. Both possibilities would allow a comfortingly stable interpretation, and would in addition rule out the alternative: the proponents of a religious-existential reading would reject (as indeed they do) the social-historical reading as superficial and contingent, and vice versa.

Now, it is precisely in this situation that Kafka is the end or the beginning. Both in modernity and before it, philosophical reflection had attempted to dispel the insubstantiality of shadows and establish the solid rock on which its concepts could be founded. It was on them that the homogeneity of experience, and consequently the stability of its interpretation, were based. When, in modern times, this effort is based on the notion of a subjectively oriented individuality, the situation is not radically new, only more difficult, for one has to build on an empirical unit—the self—that is impalpable and invisible.

Although he claims to have no speculative talent, Kafka undermines the certainties that modernity had accumulated. He does not discuss whether somewhere there is a Law, the solid, homogenizing core the "contemplation" of which would lead to the correct interpretation of phenomena; he only acknowledges, half in terror, half in acceptance, that it is not accessible to the traveler. His objectifying practice will not let him place himself in the position of a victim. His terrible reflection (September 21, 1917) on his relationship with Felice makes him realize that "she is an innocent person condemned to extreme torture" and that he is "the torturer" (Kafka 1972: 385). For even in his most private writings Kafka does not offer himself to the reader as an object for identification—a device that, as Adorno observed, had traditionally been employed to ensure the effectiveness of aesthetic experience. Once again, then, we must note that in Kafka the ethical and the aesthetic are inseparable: the indetermination of a Law the existence of which is nevertheless assumed can transform the best-meaning person into a torturer. In fiction, this makes it impossible for the reader to identify with the sufferings of the protagonist.

The solidarity between the ethical and the aesthetic also implies an almost complete blurring of boundaries. Thus, if Kafka usually saw himself as physically weak, to him weakness had a scope of action well beyond the boundaries of the private: "With this [universal human weakness]—in this respect it is gigantic strength—I have vigorously absorbed the negative element of the age in which I live, an age that is, of course, very close to me, which I have no right ever to fight against, but as it were a right to represent" (Kafka 1991: 52).

Inner weakness is neither contained within individual boundaries nor does it reflect on a necessarily sweetened view of his own time; instead, it produces an unexpected aspect of Kafka himself. Caught up in inevitable darkness, how do men think of the tunnel they are in? Rather than blame them for entertaining themselves, Kafka prefers a fable that "explains" the origin of customs: "Leopards break into the temple and drink to the dregs what is in the sacrificial pitchers; this is repeated over and over again; finally it can be calculated in advance, and it becomes a part of the ceremony" (p. 22). If, then, we are satisfied with the regularity of the coming of the leopards, and consequently of the established ceremony, the issue of the Law may be left aside, and the stability of interpretation may be preserved. But if we think of it as a degrading capitulation, we shall be forced to admit that often the question of interpretation is undecidable.

What is the meaning of such a statement? Literally, it means that we can no longer count on having a criterion that tells us what is *the* true interpretation. The positive certainty such an interpretation contained becomes a merely negative certainty: all analysis can do is identify the incomplete or false interpretations. But this is not the most relevant consequence. To say that interpretation is undecidable means that one can no longer postulate that the language of fiction is founded on and finds resolution in a stable semantic ground. Hence, it is clear that although Kafka's name is not mentioned, his experience is presupposed in the following statement by a major literary theorist of our times: "If semanticization and the resulting acts of meaning attribution derive from the tension experienced by the receiver of the fictional text due to the fact that the nature of the imaginary is that of an event, then the meaning of the text is only the pragmatization of the imaginary and not something inscribed in the text itself or belonging to it as its ultimate reason" (Iser 1983: 147).

Semantic instability is then postulated as a characteristic trait of the fictional. If we historicize the statement—which is not Iser's proposal—what could it mean but that we can no longer count on the stabilizing experience of the individual, center and navel of the world? But it means more than that; it will require that we historicize, at the proper moment, the fictional narrative that brings about instability. This will be the central subject of a later discussion.

We have now concluded the first part of our task, in which we exploit the proximity between Kafka's private texts and his fiction in order to test the analytical tools we will later apply to the fictional part of his work. Let us begin by examining two stories, "The Judgment" (1913) and "In the Penal Colony" (1919).

"The Judgment"

From the window of his room, Georg Bendemann gazes at the river that runs through the city, the bridge that joins its two halves, and the hills on the farther bank. He is holding a letter he has just written. The letter is to a friend who, years ago, dissatisfied with his prospects at home, emigrated to Russia.

The business he started was successful at first, but then went downhill. On his increasingly rare visits to his native city, his friend complains of his situation, and on his yellowish face his beard fails to conceal the fact that his health seems to be getting progressively worse. Not having made acquaintances in the city where he now lives, he leads an isolated existence and has no prospects of marrying.

The first two paragraphs in the story describe the addressee of Bendemann's letter. In indirect speech, the questions Georg asks himself are stated: "What could one write to such a man, who had obviously run off the rails, a man one could be sorry for but could not help" (Kafka 1971: 77). What could the emigrant do but come home and rely on the help of those of his friends who had remained? But even this might not be a good idea after all, since his friend has told him that he no longer understands trade in his native country. Such has been the stuff of the correspondence that Georg manages to keep up with him, if letters containing no more than this sort of triviality can be said to make up a correspondence.

His friend has not visited his native country for three years. Meanwhile, Georg's life has changed. His mother has died; he has moved in with his father, and—most important—gradually assumed control of the family business. Either because his father did not let him take over earlier or because his mother's death weakened the old man, the business is now flourishing more than ever: the staff has doubled and sales are five times as great as before. But Georg has not mentioned any of this in his letters to his friend. Prosperous and active, he is the very opposite of the failed emigré. His reticence about his own success has been dictated—or so he feels—by a sense of delicacy. For the same reason, he has not mentioned his engagement; instead, in several letters he talked about the engagement of someone who was unimportant. He justifies the fact that he has not told his friend about his own engagement by telling himself that he must leave undisturbed his friend's idea of the home town he had left behind. Obviously, Georg has not told him about his imminent wedding. But now his fiancée is forcing him to change his course.

The undisturbed flow of indirect speech is suddenly interrupted by his fiancée's warning: "Since your friends are like that, Georg, you shouldn't ever have got engaged at all." The oddness of this remark, however, does not seem to cause Georg any surprise, for his enigmatic reply is: "Well, we're both to blame for that; but I wouldn't have it any other way now" (p. 80). Georg does not seem to find anything strange in this dialogue, as he recalls it now. If it did give him any misgivings, they seem to have been quieted by the promise to write to his friend. The strangeness of this interchange remains unexplained, like a corpse floating on the water that is unnoticed by those who see it quite plainly. Just as strange is the comment with which Georg seems to end the conversation: "That's the kind of man I am and he'll just have to take me as I am. . . . I can't cut myself to another pattern that might make a more suitable friend for him" (p. 80). This is the end of the long parenthetical passage that begins immediately after the opening sentence; from now on the narrative follows a linear path. Georg writes the letter he has promised to write and decides to discuss it with his father.

Though the two live in the same house, for months Georg has not entered his father's room. He justifies this with the thought that he constantly sees his father at work, they have lunch together, and at night, when he does not go out with his friends or visit his fiancée, they sit in the same room, each with his newspaper. Georg still seems to be in a mood of dreamy absent-mindedness; he emerges from it only when he steps into his father's room, where it is quite dark, in sharp contrast with the sunny morning.

The second scene of the story begins with his father's greeting—"Ah, Georg"—and Georg's unspoken comment: "My father is still a giant of a man." If the reader is as absent-minded as the protagonist, he may not notice the change. The father's immediate reactions seem to indicate only that he is senile. When Georg tells him about the letter he is going to send, the old man seems puzzled: "To St. Petersburg?" Still in his vacant mood, Georg thinks how different his father is in business hours. But he does not know how strong his father still is.

This will become obvious only when his father, still pretending that he does not believe in the existence of his son's friend, begins to change the tone of the conversation. Since the death of Georg's mother, he says, unpleasant things have happened. The course of nature—his failing memory, his sagging strength—has combined with the blow of his wife's death, which, he claims, affected him more than it did his son. Georg feels embarrassed to hear his father ask him not to deceive him. But still the old man pretends to be senile. This pretense has the effect of making his son say that he has not been taking good care of his father and promise that a radical change will take place. He considers moving him to the front room, where there is more ventilation; he will make sure that his father eats properly, take him to the doctor, and follow all his recommendations.

As the father goes on playing the part of the senile old man, Georg tries to make him recall how his friend was their guest once; how his father, who did not like him at first, later got on with him well, and even repeated a story of the Russian Revolution he had heard from his friend. Georg notices that his father's underwear is not very clean and reproaches himself for it; concerned with his father's weakness, he carries him to bed. Everything seems to be well after all; his unexceptional relationship with his father seems to be normal again. Once in bed, his father covers himself and, with his questions, encourages Georg to tuck him in. Then Georg says: "Don't worry, you're well covered up." This statement has the effect of eliciting a furious reaction from the old man, prompted by the ambiguity of the verb *zudecken*, which means both "cover up" and "bury." "You wanted to cover me up, I know, my sprig, but I'm far from being covered up yet. And even if this is the last strength I have, it's enough for you, too much for you" (p. 84).

One might think that his father's senility has degenerated into madness. The old man now not only says that he was perfectly aware of the existence of Georg's friend but also accuses his son of being false to his friend for many years. He adds that he thinks of this friend as a son after his own heart—"Er wäre ein Sohn nach meinem Herzen" (p. 85)—and that for this very reason he has secretly been writing to him regularly. He accuses Georg of having, on account of his fiancée, "the nasty creature" (*die widerliche Gans*), disgraced his mother's memory, betrayed his friend, and stuck his father into bed so that he could no longer move. All Georg can do is exclaim: "You comedian!"

By now even the reader who failed to notice the change in the mood of the story the moment Georg entered his father's room will have perceived the transformation that has taken place. In contrast with Georg's surprise, the old man seems to be quite self-possessed; he accepts and even approves of the epithet his son flings at him. By feigning weakness but secretly hoarding the strength his dead wife had given him, he kept up the connection with Georg's friend, and now has in his pocket the names of his son's customers. This is his accusation. He reacts to his son's disloyalty by showing off his strength. Georg does not react any longer. The father accuses him of having been "an inno-cent child . . . but still more truly . . . a devilish human being" (p. 87), whom he now sentences to death by drowning.

Like a sleepwalker, Georg rushes out of the tribunal, crosses the roadway, jumps over the railing, and drops into the water. The sentence has been executed.

Kafka had good reason to thank Felice for having given him the strength, even if involuntarily, to write "The Judgment." This was the first of his stories to display his singularity. We shall use it only to provide illustrations for points already brought up.

The above summary, intended as no more than ancillary to the analysis, cannot possibly give the reader a clear idea of the story, the peculiarity of which derives from its dreamlike character, which in its second part progres-sively changes into a nightmare. Dream and nightmare, however, do not receive the usual literary representation but instead are presented in direct transposition, as it were. That is, Kafka refrains from adopting any procedure that might "prettify" the subject matter and shows it in all its coarseness. It is not, however, the coarseness of waking everyday reality, but that of the shadows of the dreamworld. This combination of realism and dreamlike material is the direction his work will take henceforth. That is why the plot contains very little or no explanation at all. From a conventional literary outlook, the change is too abrupt, too unpolished. And that is also why metaphor is presented the way it is. Unlike what goes on in realistic plots, the seed of the plot is not a fact but a metaphor: the judgment, the son's sentencing by the father. As Greenberg has pointed out, the title in German, *Das Urteil*, has both the concrete, literal sense of "sentence, verdict, judgment" and the abstract one of "critical evaluation, opinion" on someone or some situation. Just as in dreams metaphors are literalized, so also in Kafka's stories the abstract sense is joined to the literal, primary one (Greenberg 1968: 48).

The shift in discursive territory by which the recognizably literary is replaced by the oneiric, which, however, is intended not as a document or symptom of the dreamer but as an autonomous object, requires a change in the very act of reading: "Read from inside, the metaphor is felt as literally true" (p. 51). The misgivings Kafka was to express in relation to metaphor and that had the effect of making him despair of literature forced him to adopt, in his first characteristic narrative, an experimental solution. Kafka's interest in dreams, unlike that of the Surrealists, does not lead him to transcribe them automatically; what concerns him is the literalization of metaphor. For this he sacrifices the dramatization of plot, the slow development of character, the sort of composition traditionally identified as literary. A reserved man who frequented a small circle of friends in his native Prague, having at his disposal only a borrowed language, apparently reduced to its basic syntactic and lexical pattern, Kafka becomes, with this story, an experimental writer. His experimentalism, focusing on the use of metaphor, makes no less stringent demands on the reader, who must see in the father-son conflict much more than a mere transposition of Kafka's own personal experience: the confrontation between the younger generation and the older one that refuses to retire.

Greenberg must also be credited with having observed that "The Judgment" was written in the same year (1912) as Freud's *Totem and Taboo* (see Greenberg 1968: 56). Bendemann senior may thus be seen as none other than the *Urvater*, the primeval father, the tribal chief threatened by his son, whom the course of nature—"*der Ablauf der Natur*"—was grooming to replace him in all vital functions. By reducing the conflict to its most primitive form, Kafka could include himself without confessing. Doubtless his personal experience was behind his choice. It is no less clear, however, that that experience would not have been enough for the actual composition of the story. What might have been confession is replaced by allegory. The change in the way metaphor is treated corresponds to the reader's need for a reorientation. This, however, will end up compromised if it does not lead to its own interpretive practice. In order to understand this, we must consider all the main characters.

In the first part of the story, Georg Bendemann is characterized as absent-minded, dreamy, and selfish. The reasons given to explain why he wrote the sort of letters he did to his friend abroad suggest, at the very least, that Georg thought of him as an albatross around his neck, a burden beyond help. As described by the narrator, Georg does not seem to be responsible for what is said about him. Accustomed to the practice of indirect speech, the reader accepts that it is Georg who reflects: "What could one write to such a man." But who is responsible for this sentence? Once we become aware of Kafka's experimentation, we realize that, behind the uncommitted surface of indirect speech, free indirect speech interferes. Whereas the former implies that the narrator is responsible only for transcribing words actually attributable to the character, in free indirect speech the voices of the narrator and of the character are combined. That is, there is no longer a clear distinction between one and the other, and the receiver cannot count on any clues as to how he or she should interpret what is being said. It is the stability of interpretation itself that is questioned. Kafka's experimentalism is then more than merely a matter of expressive technique. The literary use of dream material subverts the entire circuit actualized by the narrative.

This observation is reinforced by Georg's treatment of his father. He does not reproach himself for not having gone into his room for months, for never having realized how dark it is, for not taking proper care of his father, for having taken for granted, with his fiancée, that the old man would remain alone in the old house. And all the promises Georg then makes fail to affect his own characterization. His power had seemed secure only because old Bendemann had pretended to be frail, unprotected, helpless. And when he tells himself that his father is still a giant of a man, Georg involuntarily realizes that his own power is only a delusion. It is at this point that the reader is forced to revise his or her interpretation.

The reader who is already familiar with Flaubert—a writer whom Kafka particularly admired—will be aware of the traps that indirect discourse is apt to lead one into. But this is not to say that Kafka's peculiarity boils down to the use of free indirect speech. On the contrary, it is only in the second part of the story that Georg's attitude forces a change in the position of the receiver. Indeed, Georg's passivity when he is sentenced to death and the promptness with which he executes the sentence cannot be explained in terms of coherence. The same unavailability of coherence applies to the father's conduct, with all the more reason. As another interpreter has put it: "The name Georg does not signify at the beginning what it signifies at the end; the name of the father does not designate at all times during their interview the same law. For intelligibility's sake the initial posit as to their value must in both cases be changed, but that is the end of consistency" (Corngold 1988: 33).

This does not mean that the inconsistency of the characters is the main axis of the narrative, but that hermeneutic stability, supported by the characters' consistency, is compromised and lost. The son's passivity can be understood only in terms of an allegorical enactment of the primal conflict with the primeval father. This, however, is not enough to attribute unity to the story, for it adds nothing retrospectively to the earlier characterization of Georg. The two scenes that make up the story, the second of which takes place in the father's room, in fact belong to two different registers. The best explanation for this fact has been given by Greenberg. Georg Bendemann's struggle consisted in freeing himself of the symbol embodied in the figure of the father. His image of strength and power, imposed on the son since childhood, no longer corresponded to the truth. The old boss could not only be removed from power at the office but also—in two senses of the word *zugedeckt*—covered and buried. The image preserved since childhood begins to be corroded by the shadows in the father's room: this darkness seems to indicate that the old man is no longer in a position of authority. Georg's absent-mindedness seems to be the proper attitude for one who is now the master of his own life. But this impression is merely the product of his father's defensive pretense. Georg's ultimate submission, his inability to defend himself, are indicative of the contrariness of the course of life: the new force is not sufficient to replace the old. The biological process is subverted, and the image of the primeval father prevails (see Greenberg 1968, esp. pp. 47–68).

Greenberg's interpretation is valid for Georg, but less so for his father. To what an extent is he really a comedian? The two protagonists, father and son, agree that the latter's dotage was part of the comedy he put up. But his mad behavior that culminates in the final sentence—can it be explained as play-acting as well? Whatever the answer, old Bendemann's theatricals cannot be explained in Freudian terms. The "implicit multivalence" of the characters simply impugns a unified, totally consistent interpretation—as if Kafka, when treating his dream material, had incorporated into his narrative the undecipherable "navel" that Freud says, in *The Interpretation of Dreams*, every dream contains. This is the key element.

As we have been stressing, in "The Judgment" three points are the most likely causes of the story's peculiar character: first, the abolition of the separation between two modes of exposition—indirect speech and free indirect

speech; second, the enactment of the mythical conflict between the generation weakened by old age and the new one that is impatient to replace it; and
third, the absence of consistency in character, which would indicate the
interpretive stability that should be ensured by the reading. It is now apparent
that the first two points can be properly understood only if we subordinate
them to the third. It is on this that the treatment of the dream material
depends. Its most radical and ambitious aspect does not consist in presenting
material that contradicts the facts of everyday reality and that could then be
used to emphasize the uniqueness of individuality, but rather, on the contrary,
in connecting the oneiric with the real. It is in this sense that one may speak of
Kafkan realism, though it cannot be grasped in the terms of what may already
be called classical realism—that of Balzac or Fielding, of Stendhal, and to a
certain extent that of Flaubert as well.

Since our analysis is not meant to be exhaustive, for the moment we need
not consider the character of Georg's friend.

"In the Penal Colony"

No in-depth analysis is necessary to bring out the connection between
"The Judgment," "In the Penal Colony," and *The Trial*: in all three narratives,
someone is sentenced to death.

But a superficial reading will not be enough to show the different position occupied by the death sentence in each. In "The Judgment," the sentence is related to a conflict of which it is the denouement, whereas in the
other stories the sentence either has been previously pronounced ("In the
Penal Colony") or is being delayed (*The Trial*), it being impossible to know
what role might have been played by legal action. In short, the specificity of
each narrative has to do with the *position* occupied by the sentence in each,
who is involved in its circle, and the space the poles of which are the Law and
the defendant.

"The Judgment" is characterized by the final pronouncement of the sentence, which even before it becomes visible hovers over the story like the
sword of Damocles. In "The Penal Colony" and *The Trial*, the position of the
sentence is different: in the latter, the action involving the accused man and
the invisible tribunal takes place before an audience that either pretends not to
see or else considers the whole business a routine misfortune; in the former,
on the contrary, the condemned man and his judge are undisguisedly observed by the foreign explorer, the *Forschungsreisender*. Due to its position at
the end, the sentence in "The Judgment" is the focal point for all the accidents in the plot, all of which it motivates and explains a posteriori. In the two

other narratives, taken a priori—whether explicitly ("In the Penal Colony") or implicitly (*The Trial*)—the sentence makes it possible to treat the machinery of justice as the central theme. No more is needed to bring out the higher complexity of the two later works. In "The Judgment," the experimentalism of the narrative ended by connecting the dream material to brutal reality but stood too close to the terms involved to allow a critical treatment of them. "In the Penal Colony" and *The Trial* benefit from a more detached point of view.

Before we discuss these two works, it should be noticed that the story and the novel are connected by the time in which they were written and the events that led to the composition of both. On July 1, 1914, at Felice's parents' home, her engagement to Kafka had become official. On July 12, under equally public circumstances, in a hotel—the Askanische Hof—the engagement was broken. Eleven days later, Kafka wrote in his diary the famous entry: "The tribunal in the hotel. Trip in the cab. F. 's face. She patted her hair with her hand, wiped her nose, yawned. Suddenly she gathered herself together and said very studied, hostile things she had been saving up" (Kafka 1972: 293).

By the end of the month, the general mobilization for the war overburdened the figure of the tribunal. Instead of expressing relief or sorrow for not being drafted immediately, Kafka observed, on July 31: "Now I receive the reward for living alone. But it is hardly a reward; living alone ends only with punishment" (p. 300).

Between the two entries—the subpoena to the family tribunal and the punishment for having been spared by the Austrian military administration—Kafka confided to his diary, on July 28, the paralysis that had overtaken him. Work alone could save him: "I am more and more unable even in the office. If I can't take refuge in some work, I am lost" (p. 295). In the following months, Kafka was to seek refuge in the composition of *The Trial*. As was often the case with him, the writing was checked by an impasse. Kafka put his novel aside and proceeded with his search for salvation by beginning "In the Penal Colony." He finished the story between the first and the second week of October 1914.[9]

Analyzing the relations between the two texts, Corngold stresses the importance of the explorer's presence in "The Penal Colony." As an external element, uninvolved with the values that underlie the nature of the process he

9. For a precise dating of the composition of *The Trial*, see Pasley and Wagenbach 1965: 55–83. On the nonlinear way in which work proceeded until the novel was abandoned, in January 1915, see Pasley's comments on the edition that adheres to the manuscript strictly (Pasley 1990: 359–65). On the composition of "In the Penal Colony" and possible influences, see Wagenbach's remarks in Wagenbach 1985, particularly pp. 15–22.

is witnessing, the foreigner can easily cast doubt on, and finally deny, the legitimacy of the sentence about to be carried out. Corngold still associates the function of the explorer's eye in the narrative with a therapeutic effect on the author himself: " 'In the Penal Colony' casts doubt on the fact of anyone's guilt and hence on the efficacy of punishment for redemption. It does so radically for Kafka the author: it breaks up a paralyzing belief in the machinery of exculpation, and to this extent the story is redemptive" (Corngold 1988: 235).

It was this therapeutic function, Corngold believes, that allowed Kafka to take up *The Trial* once again: " 'In the Penal Colony' frees Kafka, too, for the worthy task of condemning Joseph K." (p. 237). But if we leave it at that, then the only merit of "In the Penal Colony" is to have given Kafka the strength to return to his novel. It is as if he had "used" the shorter work as he had "used" Felice before. So "In the Penal Colony" is seen as no more than an inferior text, the sole importance of which lies in its psychological effect on the author. This would be another, unexpected link with "The Judgment." In our reading of the earlier story, we failed to consider the figure of Georg's friend, frustrated and lost in the immensity of Russia. But now he has become important to our purposes.

Kate Flores seems to have been the first author to establish a nexus between Georg and an "outer" Kafka, a man with a profession and possibly a career, and between Georg's friend and an "inner" Kafka, a writer who places his trust in a rather problematic literature (Flores 1958, particularly p. 12). Greenberg accepts this association, but then adds: "Kafka intended to represent the conflict between marriage and writing as an integral part of the father-son opposition. . . . Here he failed. The friend in Russia is unable to come alive in the story with the meaning that Kafka wished him to have. He remains a ghostly ineffectual presence, a mystery whose explanation must be sought in Kafka's life" (Greenberg 1968: 61). A similar argument would have to be developed in connection with "In the Penal Colony"; if Corngold did not do so, it would seem that it was just because he did not dare take the necessary step. But is his interpretation correct? Is "In the Penal Colony" similar to "The Judgment" in presenting an inner deficiency or, on the contrary, does a comparison between the two bring out its superiority? To show that the second hypothesis is the right one, let us examine the story from the beginning.

What is the role of the explorer, to the extent that he is uncommitted to the administration of justice, if not that of providing the narrative with an axis on the basis of which the Law may be interpreted? Deleuze and Guattari observe that, in Kant, the Law is disconnected from the metaphysical tradition and from then on becomes independent of "a preexistent Good that might confer matter on it"; it turns into "pure form on which the good depends as such" (Deleuze and Guattari 1977: 65). Kafka, they add, moves in this direction. To him, the issue is "*to dismantle the mechanism* of a machine . . . which needs this image of the law only to put its gears in order and make them function together 'with perfect syncretism' " (p. 65).

In "The Penal Colony," the machine is the one of which the officer is in charge. As its dedicated servant, he not only explains its operation in detail to the visitor but also complains that the machine, which was invented by the previous Commandant, is disliked by the present Commandant and the wives of the other officers. Its three parts function in synchrony. Thus, "the Bed" moves sideways and vertically, so as to favor the work of "the Designer," which, with the teeth of "the Harrow," inscribes on the prisoner's body, deeper and deeper, the commandment (*Gebot*) he has disobeyed. The prisoner in question, for instance, is about to have written on his body the sentence "Honor thy superiors!"

Asked by the explorer whether the prisoner knows his sentence, the officer answers: "No. . . . There would be no point in telling him. He'll learn it on his body" (Kafka 1971: 145). To tell him the sentence would have been a waste of time, and as the sole judge, the officer follows to the letter his own principle (*Grundsatz*): "Guilt is never to be doubted" (p. 145). True—and this is one of the officer's complaints—much of the function of the execution has been lost with the adoption of new customs. It is no longer the spectacle it once was:

> How different an execution was in the old days! A whole day before the ceremony the valley was packed with people; they all came only to look on; early in the morning the Commandant appeared with his ladies; fanfares roused the whole camp; I reported that everything was in readiness; the assembled company—no high official dared to absent himself—arranged itself around the machine; this pile of cane chairs is a miserable survival from that epoch. . . . The Commandant in his wisdom ordained that children should have the preference. . . . How we all absorbed the look of transfiguration on the face of the sufferer, how we bathed our cheeks in the radiance of that justice, achieved at last and fading so quickly! (pp. 153–54)

Although he imagines the explorer is "conditioned by European ways of thought" and thus is opposed to capital punishment, the officer-judge tries to win him over. Because he fails, because he is unable to make his visitor accept justice-as-spectacle to any degree, the officer realizes his time has come; he frees the prisoner and decides to use the machine, which is no longer quite in order, for the last time: he will be its victim now. But after he dies the expression on his face denies the redemptive function he associated with the exercise of justice. The narrator speaks for the visitor:

> And here, almost against his will, he had to look at the face of the corpse. It was as it had been in life; no sign was visible of the promised redemption; what the others had found in the machine the officer had not found; the lips were firmly pressed together, the eyes were open, with the same expression as in life, the look was calm and convinced, through the forehead went the point of the great iron spike. (p. 166)

The combination of motives—writing as a kind of sentence and the carrying out of justice as a way of reaching redemption, the latter a frequent theme in Kafka's private reflections on his literary vocation—incorporates the author's personal obsession into the narrative. But what might be a help to interpreters proves, in this particular case, an obstacle. It seems possible that writing "In the Penal Colony" had a therapeutic effect on Kafka; but it would be an oversimplification to see it as no more than that. If parts of "The Judgment" did depend on a focus that had no autonomous existence outside Kafka's personal problems, the case of "In the Penal Colony" is different.

It little matters whether or not Kafka's intent was to denounce the machine at the service of the Law; what is decisive is the demonstration of the insubstantiality of the Law, which is easier to perceive by dint of its difference from and discordance with the European viewpoint—the colony is placed on a tropical island, so that the "backward" nature of its system of administration of justice is made verisimilar. Seen by an explorer, the colony provides Kafka with an opportunity to demythify the question of the Law and, not without irony, to force first-world readers to think about it. (We single out first-world readers because third-world readers are hardly likely to have mythified the Law; rather, they have probably simply accepted it because such things are "incontestable." Thus, their effort will be both slighter—not for them the problem of the desubstantialization of the Law—and much bigger: they will have to imagine the social and intellectual context in which the Law can be called into question.)

According to the system of justice that is still in force in the colony, the injustice of the procedure and the inhumanity of the execution are, as the explorer says to himself, unquestionable; such forms of justice have been superseded in Europe. In order to understand this part of the explorer's monologue—which is indispensable for an understanding of the effective link between this story and *The Trial*—we must ask: what is this other, supposedly more advanced, form of justice? The very formulation of the question allows Kafka to take a decisive step: more than just liberating him psychologically to take up his novel again, "In the Penal Colony" creates a fictional homologue of the history of the administration of the Law. Having discarded the mythology that justified expiation—the transfiguration of the victim—and questioned the principle underlying the judgment—guilt is not to be doubted, Kafka now denies the desideratum: the example and comfort received by those who, witnessing the execution, see the Law being carried out and confirmed. What is left of it all? Only two elements: the suffering of pain and the power that causes it. The Law is what mediates between the two and justifies them. The object of the exercise of power, the Law is the form that legitimates the suffering imposed. The spectacle of pain is historically—and not just as a fictional experiment—prior to the technical, rational administration oriented by a hygienic and impersonal "Panopticon."[10]

If we are right and Corngold is wrong, what remains to be said about the statement we inferred from his analysis? According to the statement, the therapeutic importance of "In the Penal Colony" is related to its interpretive undecidability. To be more explicit, we can say that its sole univocal value is extraliterary; except for this value, the interpreter should acknowledge that no conclusion about textual production could be sufficient and unassailable.

Two stands may be taken. First, there is no undecidability in the story at all, for regardless of what the author's intentions may have been it is clear that his intuition is built on a historical and political soil. Thus, what Christine Lubkoll says about *The Trial* may be equally applied to "In the Penal Colony": "Clearly the novel treats the problem of incorporation into social 'processes' . . . first and foremost as a historical experience" (Lubkoll 1990: 289). Second, it is not denied that the poles "suffering" and "power" are the real terms derived from the dismantling of the machine and the demythification of the Law. But it should be added that despite the univocity of these terms there is a multiplicity of semantic networks between them, piling up on one another, overlapping, so that it is impossible to unravel them completely. It is on the basis of this disharmonic multiplicity that the religious, existential, psychoanalytical, and other readings of Kafka can be erected. And because each is opposed to all the others, none of them being able to prove that any other is unfounded, the interpretation of the text is undecidable. Does the second point imply that the base is univocal but the structure built on it is undecidable?

10. The reference to the "Panopticon" brings to mind Foucault's historical and philosophical study of the exercise of power in modernity, *Surveiller et punir* (Discipline and punish) (1975). On the other hand, the archaeological links we have established between the two texts help to visualize the analysis of modern capitalism proposed by Robert Kurz: in it, "fetishism has become self-reflexive, and so abstract work has turned into a self-justifying machine" (Kurz 1991: 18). Fetishism is the common element joining the different historical times of the two narratives.

I repeat, stressing that this conclusion is mine alone, that if the poles "suffering" and "power" are univocal, undecidability a posteriori attacks these poles, and in so doing fits them to each interpretation. If we were to ask interpreters to omit the two poles (but how could we justify such a request?), one would automatically have to conclude that such interpretations are no more than ornamental, and thus discardable, fabrications.

It is not yet the time to choose between the two alternatives. Not least because of the links between "In the Penal Colony" and *The Trial*, our analysis will benefit from the preliminary examination of the shorter narrative and will be in a better position to focus on the issue of undecidability.

The Trial

The earliest reference to *The Trial* (*Der Prozeß*—or, as Kafka himself wrote, *Der Proceß*) is in a diary entry of July 29, 1914:

> Joseph K., the son of a rich merchant, one evening after a violent quarrel with his father—his father had reproached him for his dissipated life and demanded that he put an immediate stop to it—went, with no definite purpose but only because he was tired and completely at a loss, to the house of the corporation of merchants which stood all by itself near the harbour. The doorkeeper made a deep bow, Joseph looked casually at him without a word of greeting. "These silent underlings do everything one supposes them to be doing," he thought. "If I imagine that he is looking at me insolently, then he really is." And he once more turned to the doorkeeper, again without a word of greeting; the latter turned towards the street and looked up at the overcast sky. (Kafka 1974: 297)

As can be seen, of this early sketch hardly anything was to find its way into the novel. Off and on, Kafka was to work on it throughout the latter half of 1914; in January 1915 he abandoned the manuscript. The unfinished novel was given to Max Brod, who was ordered to burn it. His friend not only failed to keep his word but also meddled with the text, to the dismay of interpreters ever since.[11]

Published in 1925, one year after the author's death, the novel at first received a religious interpretation, started by Brod. This reading was to change immediately after World War II, gradually acquiring existentialist overtones; and this new version remains, with due changes, the standard reading of Kafka.[12]

11. Brod's changes have been identified and can now be corrected, particularly thanks to the work of Malcolm Pasley (cf. postscript to Kafka 1990: 350).

12. For an examination of the British, French, and North American receptions of Kafka, see Beicken 1974: 33–51.

Since it is not my intention to review the ever-growing body of Kafka interpretation, I shall limit my observations to two paradigmatic analyses. The first of these, by Erich Heller, will be the object of a more cursory examination, since our interest in this case is more generic: to relate Kafka to the meaning assigned to the world in Western thought.

To Heller, Kafka is less a religious writer than someone obsessed with the demise of the spiritual interpretation of the cosmos. This interpretation, "the sacramental model of reality," had been subverted during the Reformation. The sacramental model integrated faith and knowledge, represented the unifying principle of all human experience, and thus gave a meaning to life and death, to the destiny of the soul and the moral law (Heller 1975: 211). Beginning with the Reformation and encouraged by "the sudden efflorescence of physical science in the seventeenth century," this principle of integration went astray and the material world began to be seen as the only reality, "the sole provider of relevant truth, order and lawfulness" (pp. 212–13). The contraposition between the sacramental and the physical-realist models was to be expressed by the antagonism between symbol and allegory highlighted by Goethe, in which it is the task of the former and not of the latter to manifest "the final and irreducible truth of reality" (p. 214). The collapse of the integrating model was then inevitable. The most dramatic moment of this collapse took place in Kafka's lifetime. "Kafka writes at the point where the world, having become too heavy with spiritual emptiness, begins to sink into the unsuspected demon-ridden depths of unbelief. In this cataclysm . . . Kafka's heroes struggle in vain for spiritual survival" (pp. 214–15). Thus, Kafka is the spokesman for "negative transcendence."

It would not be adequate, then, to read Kafka as a religious writer. However, though Heller rejects this sort of interpretation, his own reading is only a variant of religious exegesis. It will become clearer later that Heller does not interpret Kafka's fiction in the light of any established religious doctrine but instead sees it as the expression of a stage in human existence characterized by the absence of a church or an *ecclesia*, in the literal sense of "assembly of the people." I do not say this reading is false; rather, I observe that it heads in the direction opposite to the one we followed in our analysis of "The Judgment." The clash between the two hypotheses requires that we attempt to understand what the source of the disagreement is.

It has to do with Kant's reflections on the limits of the understanding in connection with reason's totalizing designs. Implicitly, Heller adopts Kant's solution: the identification of knowledge as what can be experienced, set out in the first *Critique*, together with the corollaries of the impossibility of knowledge of God, the soul, and freedom, the displacement of morality to the sphere of the practical, and the impossibility of providing ontological justification for moral precepts, which are all consequences and mere reflections of the heritage of the Reformation. Thus, the struggles of Kafka's characters for "spiritual survival" could be visualized as a historical consequence of "the use of reason as a mere instrument," in which Theo Elm sees Kafka's criticism of the Enlightenment, in *The Trial* (Elm 1979: 436).

The above summary makes it easier to understand the tradition to which Heller's interpretation belongs. We call it existential, considering both its rejection of the scientific view of the world and its commitment to the defense of everyday existence, which due to its "disenchantment" is increasingly marked by anomie and desperation. Now, it would be absurd to deny that these parameters apply to Kafka's work. His raw materials are indeed despair, isolation, and confusion. But if we take seriously the hypothesis we began to formulate in connection with "In the Penal Colony" and agree to see the situations described in the story as related to a desubstantialization of the Law—that is, to the lack of a unified, imperative worldview that determines what is likely to take place—our investigation will necessarily proceed at a different pace; whereas the existential reading tends to be nostalgic, this alternative interpretation is combative. Is this sense of commitment and combativeness present in Kafka's work? If yes, then should the analyst not be in a condition to deal with it as well?

Since we are only beginning our examination of *The Trial*, it seems reasonable to consider the efforts of previous interpreters. Let us then go on to say that, according to Heller's reading, Kafka is a conformist—in which reading Heller is by no means alone: Lukács founded his criticism on the very same argument (see Lukács 1960). Our reading, on the contrary, holds that in a significant part of Kafka's texts, including *The Trial* and *The Castle*, there are clear political overtones, involving an epistemological questioning of the Law that legitimizes modernity. However, even if we accept that the existence of these political overtones can be demonstrated, one would still have to prove that Kafka was not a conformist. If we failed to do that, the logical conclusion would be the coexistence of these two opposing interpretations. Either as a result of incompetence or as a strategy, we would be forced to acknowledge that interpretation is undecidable.

This, then, is the situation at which the present analysis finds itself at the moment: it is dissatisfied with the existential reading of Kafka, but can do no more than state two opposite images. Further, the problem of undecidability is again relevant. Since the conclusions of our first discussion of the issue are not sufficient, it would be pointless to return to it for the moment. A better idea is to consider an evaluation of Heller's interpretation by another analyst working along the same lines.

Beda Alleman's analysis is a close textual comment. A more careful examination, then, is necessary to bring out its major points.

Alleman begins with an observation as simple as it is brilliant: *The Trial* begins with an unusual sentence—the statement that somebody must have accused Joseph K. of something, which led to his arrest. What is unusual, even paradoxical about the sentence is that the arrest in question does not imply legal restraint on K.'s person by the police. "Thus it is equally unlikely that the cause of the arrest was an accusation" (Alleman 1963: 234). And he adds: "The apparent [logical] necessity of the accusation disappears . . . as soon as it becomes clear that the arrest is different from what one might suppose it to be" (p. 237). The paradox, then, underlies the basic narrative process of *The Trial*. It is grounded on the "particular insistence" on the "purely hypothetical condition" of justice, to such an extent that, "at the end of the novel," the nature of the trial itself is more uncertain than ever. This applies not only subjectively to Joseph K. but also to the reader, "insofar as he has failed to reach his own meaning, either in a psychological, metaphysical, theological, or sociocritical way" (p. 237).

The hypothetical and yet permanent nature of justice, the shadow that is always visible, although it is impossible to identify the nature of the object projecting it, is associated by Alleman with the fundamental "narrative principle" of the novel, from which proceeds the decisive role played in it by deception or illusion: "The necessity of deception is a fundamental law [*Grundgesetz*] of the world of *The Trial*" (p. 244), a law that is never converted into its opposite—that is, the affirmation of a truth.

The fundamental law of the novel imposes on the analyst the condition that only the letter is to be trusted. The structure of the novel, then, seems to present two consecutive justifications for the nature of the trial to which the protagonist is submitted. The first is of a legal nature: Joseph K. tries to justify himself on the basis of the principle that attack is the best defense. And he does so by arguing that the tribunal is incompetent. Alleman comments: "However, it becomes apparent that the tribunal is not refutable, at least not through legal argument. Thus Joseph K., in his legal quest, comes face to face with the void" (p. 255). If, then, the first way of responding to the threat proves futile, both character and interpreter must attempt a second path.

Joseph K.'s second justification presupposes the failure of his first attempt—that is, the acknowledgment that he was wrong about the nature of the tribunal. Instead of implying the recognition of a level in the legal process that has the power to create shadows and obstacles, this second justification has to do with existence itself. To support his thesis, Alleman quotes a reflection by Kafka dated February 25, 1918: "It seems as though he were underpinning his existence with retrospective justifications, but that is only psychological mirror-writing [*Spiegelschrift*]; in actual fact he is erecting his life on his justifications" (Kafka 1991: 52). This seems to mean that the latter was just as deceptive as the former. That is: when it comes to justifications presented before the tribunal of life, all arguments are useless and flawed. Observes Alleman: "This is carried so far in *The Trial* that Joseph K. seems not to realize or to admit that his entire existence is at stake. He believes that a couple of simple, 'supplementary' measures could put everything to rights again" (p. 257). He is then responsible for the reduplication of the error. The one-year period during which the trial took place was the necessary time for him to understand " 'naked existence' " (p. 257). The price he pays is to be killed like a dog.

In our review of the literature on Kafka, we found few interpreters as respectful of their object and as penetrating as Beda Alleman. Nevertheless, his exegesis perhaps falls short of his goal. To show this, all we need do is check a slightly earlier passage by Kafka, written on February 24, 1918: "*Can you know anything other than deception? If ever the deception is annihilated, you must not look in that direction or you will turn into a pillar of salt*" (Kafka 1991: 51). If the tribunal, in the legal or in the existential sense, is the institution that demands justifications from the defendant, any justification is necessarily an illusion, for there is no possible access to the substance of the Law, or—what is virtually equivalent—because the Law has no substance.

Now we begin to realize—and Alleman indeed deserves credit for providing a basis for this perception—that the inevitability of delusion is the basic principle in *The Trial* because Kafka projects the effects of Kant's desubstantialization of the Law. To put it in the terms of Theo Elm, the analyst who comes closest to the hypothesis we are proposing, Kant is present in Kafka not only on the ethical plane, as the thinker who did the most for the Enlightenment pragmatization of reason, but also on the epistemological plane, to the extent that Kafka demonstrates the radical consequence of desubstantialization of the Law. This desubstantialization—the term itself does not appear in Elm—is inscribed in the letter of the text, which moves between "the orientation provided by the schematism of pure reason and, at the same time, by the impossibility of apprehending a truth with definitive validity" (Elm 1979: 429).

An earlier passage of the diaries (December 9, 1917) reinforces this point:

"The observer of the soul cannot penetrate into the soul, but there doubtless is a margin where he comes into contact with it. Recognition of this contact is the fact that even the soul does not know of itself. Hence it must remain unknown. That would be sad only if there were anything apart from the soul, but there is nothing else" (Kafka 1991: 30). We have already underscored the objectifying tone of Kafka's introspection. If this is associated with Joseph K.'s dilemma, its impersonal character becomes clear. His dilemma is everyman's. Hannah Arendt observed that "Kafka's heroes are not really people," for they "are only models, and remain anonymous" (Arendt 1976: 107). The model objectivity of the protagonists is a consequence of the fact that each requires from himself supplementary justifications that always prove to be illusions. If this result is inevitable, it can only be because they stand before the tribunal without knowing the Law that accuses them—that is, their own Law as well. In Kafka, the desubstantialization of the Law is all the more drastic because it affects both the sphere of the cosmos and that of the mind.

How, then, can we fail to take into account the similarity between the passage we have quoted and interpreted and the issue raised by Kant? Alleman, like Heller, does not see this nexus, and for this reason he gives partial emphasis to the pathos of Joseph K. (as real as it is ironical). To Alleman and the existential interpreters, Joseph K. is a pathetic figure, one that is unable to laugh. The existential approach does not touch on humor, lest laughter might sully the sublime melancholia of despair. But Kafka's creatures are less forlorn than light, volatile, unsubstantial.

However, we still must face the most serious objection: how can we draw a parallel between Kafka's fiction and Kant's epistemology if Kafka always claimed to be uninterested in philosophical abstractions and never mentioned Kant or his *Critiques*? Nonetheless, between Kafka and Kant there stands the figure of Heinrich von Kleist. The despair Kant's system made him feel was mentioned in Chapter 2. Although there is no evidence that Kafka felt the same, it is clear that he was seriously affected by the lack of a center of gravity that might guide individual action; and this effect was sharpened by his sensation of social, linguistic, and cultural rootlessness, Kafka being the member of an assimilated Jewish family, speaking and writing a language that did not belong to the nation where he had been born and where he lived all his life. The revelation of the nonexistence of the Law that rules mankind, or of the impossibility of knowing its substance, had an even stronger impact on his delicate and sensitive mind. But the effect on Kafka of the realization that the soul—in the religious or the psychological sense—cannot be known was not only pathos, but also a tendency opposite to the intimist expressivism that had its roots in Romanticism.

It is precisely this point that the existential interpretation misses and, as it simplifies matters, distorts. It is true that there is in Kafka a profound despair over—but not nostalgia for—the absence of a ballast in the world. I am not saying that his work is rooted only in a sharp critical perception of his time. But the two views are true as parts of a more complex insight. Because the desubstantialization of the Law does not affect contemporary reality alone—because it creates a "black hole," as it were, which draws into itself the world as such—a fiction that dramatizes it, such as Kafka's, may practice a sort of asceticism of historical material without necessarily being ahistorical in nature. As Adorno observed in a different context, to bring Kafka's work down to the level of the "universally human" is to falsify it in a conformist way (Adorno 1969: 261). By associating Kafka's work with the Kantian question of the Law, we make sure that it is not seen as oblivious to History, deaf or indifferent to contemporary reality. On the contrary, its asceticism only underscores its character as a response to what is taking place here and now. Thus, it is not enough to point out, as Theo Elm does, an ethical and an epistemological front, in which Kant appears as Kafka's unnamed interlocutor; it is also necessary to show that these two fronts are connected to a third, which is political.

It seems that our analysis has now reached a more comfortable situation. Indeed, we have been able to go beyond the dance of opposing images; we have taken a few steps that are at least apparently promising and show how Kant's epistemological question is present in Kafka's work. But what about undecidability? Is it not affected by our conclusion about how contemporary reality is present in Kafka's fiction? The answer is clearly yes: we have now begun to historicize our statement concerning Kafka's undecidability. Let us do so in an explicit way.

In my comment on Erich Heller's analysis, I observed that it was representative of a kind of approach I called existential, which dealt with its object in a way quite different from, and even opposed to, an approach that took into account the relation between Kafka and the Kantian problem of the Law. Discussing Beda Alleman's essay, I saw that the examination of his analytical proposal—the hypothetical nature of justice in *The Trial*—made it possible to look at Kafka's work in connection with the Kantian issue. As a consequence of this analytical transformation, instead of emphasizing the pathetic tone of our object I showed that this was no more than one of its sides, others being objectification and critical humor.

Now, the fact that a line of interpretation may be transformed into another does not imply that there is no opposition between them. If, then, we suppose that the second—the one I am elaborating now—may be developed to the point of becoming reasonably consistent, the two alternative readings will then make up an undecidable pair. Thus, undecidability results from consideration of the work under two opposing paradigms, both generated by the same originating experience of modernity. These paradigms oppose each other because they visualize in contrary ways this originating experience: to the existential interpreters, the failure of what Heller calls the sacramental model; to us, the desubstantialization of the Law. What makes the interpretation of Kafka's work undecidable from the outset is uncertainty about which paradigm should be related to it. Undecidability is, then, not a consequence of the kind of textual organization of the object, but of a precise historico-cultural environment in which its consideration takes place. Thus, the question is posed in a precise moment in time.

The examination can and should go further. For this, however, we need to determine whether undecidability is present only in the confrontation between opposing paradigms or also within each. Could it be that in each paradigm there is a limit to what can be decided? No extended consideration is necessary to show that, owing to the irreducibly hypothetical character of Kafka's Law, illusion and deception (to use Alleman's concepts) make up the guiding principle of the novel. It is because it is grounded on illusion and deception that the novel encourages religious or psychological interpretations. That is, although neither Heller nor Alleman explicitly endorses either reading, each is led to them by the very procedure he adopts. Since neither of their interpretations postulates the undecidability of Kafka's text, but on the contrary affirms that it has such and such a character, they pose the limits of existential undecidability. That is: on the basis of undecidability, each interpretation privileges and affirms a specific orientation of meaning.

Something of the kind occurs with the interpretation I favor. When we speak of pain and power as *real terms*, are we not acknowledging the univocity of these elements? Thus, the interpretive dilemma posed by the Kant-Kafka relationship founded on the problem of the Law on the one hand historicizes the question of undecidability, and on the other helps to show that, within each position, something is taken to be decidable. One need only add that, in the second interpretation, the production of meaning—pain and power as univocal terms—requires treatment in reality, on the plane of society, rather than on that of existence in the abstract.

We must then see what we are to make of this discovery.

THE "NATURE" OF THE TRIAL

Whoever feels the need to do more than examine a few of Kafka's stories is liable to get the impression that the more one reads, the less one feels secure about being able to understand them—a strange effect for a text written in standard syntax. And the reader's feeling of insecurity will not be dispelled if he or she resorts to interpretations of Kafka. One interpreter, the representative of an extreme version of undecidability, writes: "Kafka's aesthetic compulsion . . . in *The Trial* as elsewhere is to write so as to create a necessity, yet also as to make interpretation impossible rather than merely difficult" (Bloom 1989: 192). This is the "profitable" way of resolving a tension that is present at the very act of writing. As Theo Elm has observed: "Given the hypothetical character of the narrative (B. Alleman) and the paradoxes that destabilize narration (G. Neumann) . . . the self-evidence of univocal adjudications of meaning is discredited and the reader's rational potency is attacked, although at the same time no doubt is cast on the operational validity of the meaning of the novel, the logic of its form as expression of a rational thought" (Elm 1979: 424). Now, this impasse is caused not by any pedantic strain in Kafka, nor by any "avant-garde" intention of shocking the reader's expectations of meaning, but by the "inexorable contradiction between Enlightenment logic and the paradox that destabilizes freedom of meaning" (p. 424) that is the stuff of *The Trial*.

What Bloom's observation points to is not a singularity of Kafka's prose. Flaubert's *Madame Bovary*, Kleist's "Marionettentheater" (Puppet theater), Beckett's plays and novels are all modern works in a similar vein. They are characterized by extreme semantic instability. In this, they point to a direction opposite to that followed by the classical novel: "The development of the classical novel corresponded to the slow retrogression of the *citoyen* [citizen], who, in the French Revolution and in Kantian philosophy, had tried for the first time to rule the world by man-made laws. . . . All these novelists, whether they described the world realistically or imagined other worlds fantastically, were in a constant competition with reality" (Arendt 1976: 104–5). From the interpretive viewpoint, to compete with reality meant to extend to fictional situations the evaluative standards that were applicable to it. The bourgeoisie had been able to legitimate literature as the basic vehicle of nonspecialized culture to the extent that the poet and the novelist had preserved at least the minimal evaluative standard that was defended by the bourgeoisie in the real world.

Thus, it is extremely pertinent to examine the accusation that the prosecutor Ernest Pinard raised against Flaubert in court:

What is the title of the novel? *Madame Bovary*. That is a title that says nothing in itself. There is a second title, in parenthesis: *Moeurs de province*. That is also a title that does not explain the author's position, but hints at it. The author did not intend to follow this or that true or false philosophical system, but to present some genre paintings, and you ought to see *what* paintings these are!!! (Pinard 1964, 2: 725)

The indifference towards minimal canonical values—the defense of marriage and the condemnation of adultery—is carried to such extremes in the novel that no voice is raised against the heroine: "Who, in this book, could blame this woman? No one" (p. 731). And this is extremely serious, the prosecutor implies, for some reader—particularly a female one—might attempt to act as freely as the protagonist of the novel. This was not due to any revolutionary intent of the author's; on the contrary, his conservatism was beyond challenge.

With *Madame Bovary*—as with *Les Fleurs du mal* (Flowers of evil), a book published around the same time—literature gave up competing with reality, even to criticize it from an enlightened viewpoint, and began to assume a position increasingly unnerving for the standardized habits of "literary" reading. Kafka is the apex of this process. Naive mimesis—the work seen as an expression of the author's intention, the plot and the fate of the characters seen as obeying minimally homogeneous values—is threatened.

The question is then raised in the context of interpretive discussions: how can Kafka be read? Reading, formerly a pleasant form of entertainment, becomes a shock, even a nightmare. (Not surprisingly, seekers of fiction as entertainment tend to prefer other media these days.) And here the non-specialized character of Kafka's language works against it. His interpreters, not being from the outset motivated to question the values that guide reading, but rather taking it as a "natural" opportunity for the "attribution of meaning," often perceive such works as if they did not imply a break with literary tradition. This way of thinking—or of not thinking—only multiplies the mistakes. In order to avoid them, two approaches may be adopted: either to face the question in strictly theoretical terms, or to concentrate on one particular work, going into theoretical discussions only when this becomes inevitable. Given the procedure we have been adopting in the present chapter, our choosing the first option would be out of place. So we must rely on the second: let us focus our analysis on *The Trial* and then do the same with *The Castle*. And we shall adopt those lines of reading that, after their examination, have amounted to more than an allegation in favor of undecidability. The first has to do with the "nature" of the trial. (The quotation marks underscore that what we are seeking is not its substance, but its textual form.)

On the morning of Joseph K.'s thirtieth birthday, two men come to his rented room to tell him he is under arrest.

The story of *The Trial* begins in media res. We are not told what it was that K. did, or who denounced him. The two men are formal and rude. They laugh when K. asks them to tell him their names and the authority they serve. Nor do they answer K. when he asks them what he has been accused of; they have not been instructed to give him this information. Their job is merely to seek out or keep an eye on those who are singled out by the Court. But they do not waste time. While Joseph K. dresses, they hint at bribes and unceremoniously have breakfast. The accused man does not know how he ought to react. For, after all, he was living in a constitutional state (*Rechtstaat*), and the laws were in force. How could procedures have been started against him if he had not been told what he had been accused of? No, it could only be a joke perpetrated by his colleagues in the Bank.

Joseph K., a high-ranking official who has achieved success early, solely on the basis of his own merits, addresses in a somewhat superior tone those he sees as his social inferiors—and among these he certainly includes the boorish policemen. Thus, when they tell him to come into the next room to be interrogated by the Inspector, K. believes all will soon be resolved. Surely the Inspector could only be a person of more quality. But he is mistaken: the Inspector is every bit as formal and as rude as his subordinates. And he knows no more than they why K. is being arrested. His logic is the same as theirs: he hints at threats, pretends to give advice, preserves the rigid police hierarchy— no, it is not usual for accused persons to take a seat. Two different logics clash here. K., a citizen who is aware of his rights and duties, asks in vain for information that is denied him by those who have the power. But they all do have one point in common: neither the Bank official nor the authorities the inspector represents intend to disturb the proper functioning of society.

Kafka's irony here is unmistakable. Beda Alleman was perceptive enough to point out that in the opening passage of the novel, arrest does not keep the person arrested from moving about freely. This, however paradoxical it may seem from a logical viewpoint, is not paradoxical from the viewpoint of social functionality: the arrested person is allowed to go on doing his duty. Now one begins to perceive that the strict logic of the Enlightenment seems strange here, because something has happened in society that has moved it outside of the scope of this logic.

In addition, the analysis should not be restricted to the textual immanence, but should also consider the relation between the text and the material on which it feeds. Paradox and ambiguity, then, are to be seen as a function of this interrelation. Thus, the Inspector explains, rather ambiguously, why three of K.'s colleagues from the Bank were called as witnesses: they are there, he says, so that K.'s arrival at the Bank will be as unobtrusive as possible, whereas the reader sees this as evidence of the omnipresence of the repressive apparatus. But it is not the accused man, puzzled by a situation that does not fit the logic he has internalized, who comes to this conclusion. To him, these figures are so devoid of importance in the institution where they all work that he cannot even see them as his colleagues.

Thus ends the first chapter. Joseph K. believes the incident will not affect his everyday activities. It is only one of those intriguing, inexplicable situations, the impact of which gradually dies down until they dwindle into a mere topic for idle conversation. But at the Bank he is notified by telephone that the first interrogation in his trial has been scheduled for the following Sunday. Kafkan irony reappears: the authorities clearly do not wish to disturb K.'s service to society. After all, are not police authorities and banking institutions seen euphemistically as serving society? Joseph K., in any case, feels that, given the rights and privileges assured to people of his social status, he will be able to put an end to the trial at the very first interrogation and will need no help; all he need do is complain of the careless way the address of the Court was given to him. How could his convictions as a citizen disturb the possibility of interference of another kind of logic? Through K.'s security, it is the logic of the citizen that makes him confident of the existence of the rule of law. How could he—or his reader, even today—logically admit the existence of a different state of affairs? Such a supposition seems so absurd that the gallows humor of the text goes unacknowledged; instead, it is subsumed under a general pathetic tone.

In the courtroom, Joseph K. remains assured of his social distinction. And indeed he seems to be right. The poor neighborhood he is forced to pass through, the sorry state of the building where the Court meets, the very solicitude with which his requests for information are met, the dress and the aspect of the people he finds in the courtroom—everything seems to confirm his superiority. He answers the judge in a firm tone, and he is inwardly pleased when the audience applauds him. Certain that some of the people support him, he becomes more daring and accuses the Court of being part of a powerful, corrupt, and arbitrary organization. But then he realizes his mistake as to the meaning of the applause: everyone in the audience wears the same badge as the judge. They are all officials. Secure about his own position in society, conscious of his rights as a citizen (and why do Kafka's interpreters hardly ever observe the paradox formed by these two convictions, which imply that only "first-class citizens" can be secure of their rights?), Joseph K. had been led on to act in an exciting theatrical performance. The applause that had pleased him indicated not agreement, but instead surprise and amusement. The logic of the citizen had had an effect of *estrangement*. Unwittingly, the defendant is seen as an exotic character. The clash between different logics—which comes unexpectedly to K. and tends to go unnoticed by the reader—changes the accused man's self-defense into, of all things, an aesthetic experience. But K. still fails to realize the risk he is running. His reply to the Examining Magistrate shows that his sense of his own superiority remains intact: " 'You scoundrels, I'll give you an interrogation yet' " (Kafka 1974: 57).

His conviction remains unshaken when, the following Sunday, K. realizes that the books the judge kept consulting were in fact not legal tomes, but pornographic material. Nor is his self-confidence affected when he finds that the other accused men are terrified and subservient. In fact, the details described by the narrator seem to be autonomous, unconnected to the protagonist's consciousness, as if there were a locked door between K. and the action he is involved in.

Nevertheless, independently of what might be going on in his consciousness, the power that accuses him and that at first seemed flimsy, primitive, and toothless turns out to be an octopus with a thousand tentacles. K.'s tour of the Court reveals that there is no clear separation between its rooms and the humblest dwellings of its minor employees, and that its long punishing arm extends even to the lumber-room in the Bank. Invisible, seemingly decrepit and mean, "justice" is omnipresent. One of the warders being punished observes in passing, with no intent to terrify K., that the proposal he had made at the time of K.'s arrest—he had asked to be allowed to keep K.'s underwear—would imply an insignificant loss, "for what importance can such things have for a man who is unlucky enough to be arrested?" (p. 95). The punishment of the warders in the Bank underscores the close interconnection between society's repressive apparatus and its financial institutions, just as the judge's books introduce the third element present in the image of power: "Manifestly, sex, in its links to the legal and economic orders, exerts its effect, as the third central field, on the principles of power" (Lubkoll 1990: 282).

The ramifications of the system of justice, the realizations that the trial is serious and that the plot extends much further than the accused man can see are hinted at by everyone around him. In the end, all seem to know what only he himself ignores. His uncle tries to alarm him; the Advocate, as it were, was already expecting his visit; Leni had heard comments about his behavior. His amusing performance in the courtroom had reflected badly on him. The play he had improvised had not taken place on a stage. At least in this the logic of the citizen agreed with the Court's: a courtroom is not the proper place for aesthetic estrangement.

But Joseph K. remains oblivious of everything. The visit to the Cathedral, which he supposes to be dictated by his professional interest, turns out to have been planned by the priest who summoned him. Nonetheless, Joseph K. remains confident that the logic of the police is adopted only by the court officials, whereas elsewhere in society the logic of the citizen still holds. The accused man's resistance derives from his unwillingness to acknowledge the absolute interpenetration between the sphere of the police and the justice system and the civil sphere. The liberal logic of the citizen ignores the threat of the omnipresent law, which not only supervises but also penetrates every nook and cranny of society. K. and his reader respectively have learned and believe that under the rule of law legislation cannot oppose the rights of society.

However, contrary to what the constitutional state affirms, the procedures apparently followed by the trial are not public but secret, and the Court is invisible. Beginning with Gerhard Kaiser, a whole lineage of interpreters, of which Beda Alleman is the most outstanding, conclude from this that in Kafka the trial is juridically irrelevant! "His trial has nothing in common with the usual meaning of legal process; with its invisible judges, a hidden accusation, and an execution without an adequate final sentence, it is in fact a simulation of regular legal procedure" (Kaiser 1958: 25). These analysts fail to see that the Court's invisibility is correlated with the fact that civil society not only does not oppose it, but also has been infiltrated with agents, informers, and stool pigeons, in accordance with the Court's ruling logic. The trial drags on, as K.'s advocate observes, unpredictable and remote. As the painter-informer explains, the accused men's allegations of innocence are null because the Court is never convinced of it. If the interpreter fails to take this clue into consideration, he or she holds on to the security provided by the feeling of superiority that characterizes Joseph K. most of the time. It is as if the novel's protagonist and its interpreters said to one another: we know that this sort of thing could not possibly happen here in our society, to "decent" people.

These interpreters prove to be misguided when they fail to realize that K.'s reaction gradually changes. The incident in which he faints in the stifling air of the Court suggests his weakness. His earlier arrogance, motivated by the security he felt because he had a position in the Bank, changes into resignation, helplessness, and finally defeat. The "nature" of the trial is then a consequence of the connection between the invisibility of the Court and the hidden nature of a Law that is nonetheless inexorable. If we are to take the Advocate's word for it, the conclusion ought to be the opposite: "For the Defence was not actually countenanced by the Law, but only tolerated, and there were differences of opinion even on that point, whether the Law could be interpreted to admit such tolerance at all" (Kafka 1974: 128).

The Law itself rules the randomness of the procedures. Hidden, it commands the invisible chambers that enforce it. Its logic is inaccessible to the eye of society. But it would be a fatal mistake to conclude from this that it does not exist. The logic of the Law is none the less logical because those who control it are not publicly identifiable. From this viewpoint, *The Castle*, which presents the lives of the town's rulers, is a sequel to and goes further than *The Trial*. But for the moment we will not resort to Kafka's last novel. The ensuing abstraction is not so excessive that we cannot see ramified power as the true keeper of the Law.

Power is not someone, but something that is disseminated and concretized by its agents—and this is not affected by the fact that only lower-echelon officials appear in the novel. The invisibility of the Court makes the invisibility of the higher judges even more necessary. To see it as evidence of the religious or existential character of *The Trial* is just as reductionistic as to read it as a critique of bureaucratic capitalism, Austrian style (Lukács 1960: 82). This local flavor of Kafka's work, which was made even more vivid by W. M. Johnston's research (see Johnston 1972, particularly chapter 3, pp. 45–50), might have contributed to an understanding of Kafka had Johnston been able to discover the question of power that his work poses. Since he failed to do this, the Marxist-sociological interpretation of Kafka became as reductive as the existential one. These interpretations abolish the possibility of inner connection. The legal and the spiritual planes are seen as necessarily hierarchized, and the priority given to the one favored by the interpreter relegates the other to a condition of near futility.

Against the reductionistic approach, it is instructive to compare the different accounts of the Law given by the Advocate, the priest, and the painter (in *The Castle*, the same function may be attributed to the superintendent's viewpoint). A representative of civil society apparently ruled by a constitutional state, the Advocate should not be complacent about the actual practice of the courts. The secrecy—"the proceedings were not only kept secret from the general public, but from the accused as well" (p. 129)—the difficulties raised for the defense and for the very legitimation of the Advocate are described by him as routine things, which have been accepted for a long time. Hence, we see the importance of advocates' personal relationships with judges and officials, both to obtain information on cases and to oil the necessary palms; Dr. Huld boasts of the private knowledge he has acquired by such means. His words even show that he is secretly satisfied with the current practices. It matters not at all to him that theoretically they are the very negation of proper legal procedure. Although he is not an official of the judicial system, the Advocate is perfectly integrated into it.

The priest at the Cathedral, who calls Joseph K. by his name, identifies himself plainly as the prison chaplain. It is as such that he knows about K.'s case and now proceeds to advise him. Thus, when K. protests that he is innocent, the priest argues that "that's how all guilty men talk" (p. 232). This dialogue is all the stranger for the fact that when K. introduces a religious (or existential-religious) argument in his protest—" 'But I am not guilty,' said K.; 'it's a misunderstanding. And if it comes to that, how can any man be guilty?' "—the priest answers him with a strictly police-type argument: " 'That is true,' said the priest, 'but that's how all guilty men talk' " (p. 232). The priest's words reinforce the "advice" he had heard from the Inspector: "Don't make such an outcry about your feeling innocence" (p. 19). The subtle priest—the reader will surely feel as much admiration as K. for the extreme skill with which he deals with the various interpretations of the parable of the doorkeeper—thus feels the same about the accused man's attempts to defend himself as does the rude Inspector. Priest and policeman—the Advocate being the middle term between them—are officials of the same Law. All, then, are agents of a praxis which is the opposite of the vaunted constitutional state.

Is it the case, then, that of this Law we can know nothing aside from the extension of its use? Is the impossibility of knowing it all we can know of it? Another person associated with the Court has something relevant to say about this. Titorelli, the artist who paints portraits of the judges, tells K. about his experience in the courts. Once one is accused, one must opt for one of the possible forms of postponing the trial. K. is surprised to hear this, and Titorelli explains that this is so because acquittal seems impossible. "Never in any case can the Court be dislodged from that conviction" (p. 166). Perhaps that is why he insistently asks the accused man whether he considers himself innocent. By reiterating this claim unhesitatingly, K. makes his case more attractive to the painter. In other words, Titorelli reinforces the opinion of the officer-judge in "The Penal Colony": guilt is inexorable. Thus, the more the accused man proclaims his own innocence, the more the intermediary stands to profit from the case.

But the comparison with "In the Penal Colony" can be misleading. Strictly speaking, it is not the same justice that is involved in the two cases. As we have seen, the machine operated by the officer belonged to a time that, from the prevailing European viewpoint, was marked by objectionable legal practices. In his research on the novella, Wagenbach observes that Kafka knew about the penal colonies of European powers (New Caledonia, Devil's Island, Port Blair; see Wagenbach 1985: 67–68). If the machine was still in operation, it was only because it was on a tropical island, far from the enlightened metropolis.

The sort of justice practiced there was the opposite of the secret system that Joseph K. must face. In the colony, death was a public spectacle for the edification of participants. It concretely wrote its sentence in the condemned man's body; furthermore, it was incisive and particularizing. If, then, we take the Panopticon as the symbol of the disciplinary society that, between the late eighteenth and the early nineteenth centuries, eliminated physical torture, and in which "punishment tended . . . to become the most hidden part of the penal process" (Foucault 1975: 15), we may see Kafka's penal colony as a remnant of an earlier form of justice, with its public nature and its rhetoric of torture. Surely *The Trial* is not a fictional homologue of the same historical period. Is there, then, a period of which it *is* the homologue? The question may seem ludicrous. It is well known that Kafka refused to place his stories in specific historical contexts. Are we then using Foucault in order to find historical and cultural "references" for Kafka's stories? Let us look into the matter more carefully.

When I discussed "In the Penal Colony," I observed that the writing of the novella may have helped the author to return to the composition of *The Trial* to the extent that it created a "diachronic" context for mechanisms of punishment. We know how adverse Kafka was to confessional texts. We have also seen that he despaired of the possibility of literature ever ceasing entirely to rely on metaphor. The "diachrony" implied—fictional, not referential— was the material substance on which he was to build his "objective correlative."[13] What might seem to be an unjustifiable method was in fact quite sensible.

If our hypothesis is reasonable, what then is the actual reality to which the system of justice described in *The Trial* corresponds? There is an interval of time separating the justice of the penal colony—particularized, emotional, physical—from this other justice, impersonal, hidden from the public eye, meant for large numbers (the accused men seen by Joseph K. in chapter 3 sat "along a row of wooden benches fixed to either side of the passage" [p. 73]), and aiming at social rationality (K.'s arrest does not interfere with his

---

13. "Objective correlative" is perhaps the expression that has had the most equivocal fate in contemporary criticism. T. S. Eliot used it in a 1919 essay and never employed it again; when he mentioned it later it was with manifest regret. In spite of its creator's rejection, I believe it is a most useful concept, less for its implications of depersonalization of the literary text than for the idea of objectification it implies. Although I agree that this shift in emphasis would require a reexamination of the concept's definition, the fact remains that it was originally presented as follows: "The only way of expressing emotion in the form of art is by finding an 'objective correlative'; in other words, a set of objects, a situation, a chain of events which shall be the formula of that *particular* emotion" (Eliot 1975: 48).

professional activities). The historical phenomenon that defines this dia-chronic development is the so-called rule of law, or constitutional state. It was by this that the accused man felt protected. (Ironically, it is precisely because they take the rule of law for granted that some interpreters are puzzled by the—to them unquestionable—difference between the trial described in the novel and "civilized" legal proceedings.)

Thus, it seems justified to speak of the legal system in force in the penal colony as pre-Panopticon. Consequently, the justice system of *The Trial* may be said to be post-Enlightenment. It was the philosophy of the Enlighten-ment that provided the basis for the constitutional state, which assigned to all citizens the same rights and duties. Early in chapter 1 Joseph K. is shown as a man who is not used to learning from experience. It makes sense, then, that he should face police logic with his own citizen's logic. Nevertheless, inde-pendently of the worldliness of his interlocutors, what K. says in his conversa-tions about the trial shows him to be the representative of a species on the verge of extinction. The impersonal and cold narrator never makes this point explicitly. But the careful reader will observe that K.'s old landlady is not surprised by the arrival of the warders. Nor does K.'s neighbor, a girl prepar-ing to work in a law firm, find anything amiss in what has been going on. The uncle and the client who try to help him do not question the existence of the punishing institution. The same applies to the advocate to whom his uncle introduces him, and to Leni, who is so knowledgeable about the inner work-ings of the courts. In short, nobody sees anything odd in what is going on. Joseph K. seems to have slept for too long, so that, upon waking, he finds himself in a world in which his assumptions about the constitutional state no longer hold.

It is curious that a work such as Kafka's, which contains no explicit references to time or place, and thus seems to abstract any historical back-ground, should implicitly brand as fiction the staunchest convictions of its protagonist. But perhaps this fact seems curious only because our perspective is too narrow. For it was Kafka himself who wrote about the coming of the Messiah: "The Messiah will come as soon as the most unbridled individual-ism is possible in faith—as soon as nobody destroys this possibility and nobody tolerates that destruction, that is, when the graves open" (Nov. 30, 1917; Kafka 1991: 27). Shortly before, he had written: "It is only our conception of time that makes us call the Last Judgment by this name. It is, in fact, a kind of martial law" (p. 27).

Could it be that the abolition of the opposition between the Enlighten-ment logic of the citizen and the logic of the police state—the infiltration of society by the state—is precisely what Kafka means by the time of "the most unbridled individualism," and thus the moment of the "martial law"? If so, then Joseph K. may well be accused of believing in a "fiction": the idea that legal procedure is founded on the substance of legal texts, whereas in fact juridical norms are based only on the form of their regulations, a form that is not an expression of justice, but rather a manifestation of power. The "nature" of the trial then has to do with the desubstantialization of the Law, which—reduced to mere form—ultimately consists of no more than the power that uses it and is legitimated by it. And Heinz Politzer's characterization of Kafka is then a transparent paradox: "Kafka was a realist of unreality" (Politzer 1978: 275).

In more prosaic terms, *The Trial* is made up of nearly dreamlike material. The nightmare that provides its substance has to do both with the disintegration—on the plane of reality—of the practices of the constitutional state and with the author's most idiosyncratic obsessions, whether they had a religious origin or were merely individual. The point, then, is, contrary to usual interpretive practice, not to hierarchize the planes on which the process took place and affirm the secondary role of the juridical plane in order to emphasize the existential plane, but instead to see the intimate connection between the two. The shift between the different planes is dreamlike; it is, however, governed by a principle that provides the basis for Kafka's fiction: the principle of objectification. In short, the point is not to consider the literary work as if it were a dream, but to see dream-logic operating in a literary construction.

The above formulation will allow us to return to the question of undecidability. The successive returns to this question point to the importance I attribute to it.

Accused of believing in something that had turned into fiction, since it no longer had any links to the real world, Joseph K. has no alternative other than painful resignation. It corrodes all his power to resist. When he submits to his executioners, K. surrenders to the reality principle. Here, then, we again find the two poles on which *The Trial*, like "In the Penal Colony," is based: personal pain, ending with death, and the power to which the living are subject. These univocal poles are counterposed to the affirmation of undecidability and allow the postulation of a reading of Kafka that is active and political rather than quietist: according to such a reading, Kafka's work would then be the denunciation of the permanence of the constitutional state as a fable, a fiction.

What has just been said would be no more than a tentative hypothesis were it not for chapter 9 of *The Trial*. The ordering given by Max Brod to Kafka's manuscript, which is reproduced in M. Pasley's critical edition, gives that statement strategic importance. Since the priest introduces himself as an official of the courts, the parable of the doorkeeper that he tells, and particularly the various interpretations he discusses, do not seem to support the interpretation we have proposed. One should think that the priest's statement—"The right perception of any matter and a misunderstanding of the same matter do not wholly exclude each other" (Kafka 1974: 238–39)—applies to the novel itself, making it extremely undecidable. Rather than jump at such a conclusion, let us consider the parable of the doorkeeper.

Politzer underscores the double sense of the phrase "man from the country" (the man who approaches the doorkeeper) in Hebrew. *Am-ha'arez*, a word appearing in the November 26, 1911, entry of the diaries as "Amhorez," is commonly used in the sense of "one who is ignorant in doctrine and in life, an obtuse man" who "before the law is a primitive who understands only what he can touch with his hands and understand with his senses" (Politzer 1978: 279). In biblical times, however, the phrase referred to humble people—fishermen, shepherds, craftsmen, men of the plain—as opposed to the population of Jerusalem, "who lived in the shadows of the sacred" (p. 280), that is, the poor and ignorant, unable to understand the prescriptions of the law (p. 281). Joseph K., Politzer adds, "is an Am-ha'arez, who concentrates on concrete everyday activities and is horrified at the thought of busying himself with the incomprehensible abstractions of the law" (p. 281).

Given the counterposition between the priest and the protagonist, however, Kafka himself does not choose a single alternative. If, on the one hand, in the "Letter to His Father" Kafka blames his father for his unbelief and his lack of knowledge about Jewish tradition, which would place him on the side of the priest, on the other hand, he found in himself contradictory links with both his mother and his father. "I [am] a Löwy with a certain basis of Kafka, which, however, is not set in motion by the Kafka will to life, business, and conquest, but by a Löwyish spur that impels more secretly, more diffidently, and in another direction, and which often fails to work entirely" (Kafka 1976: 11). And Politzer concludes: "Within the parable form that Kafka gave to his novel, this guilt becomes utterly impenetrable" (p. 283). It is, then, as if Kafka had made his personal impasse between his mother's family, the intellectualized and somber Löwys, and his father's, the active, ignorant Kafkas, the inescapable umbilicus of his narrative.

If we compare the conclusion we arrived at on the basis of the decisive passage from chapter 9 with what we have just said above, we find that the two statements contradict each other, and there is no possible interpretation into which the two might be subsumed. The conflicting exegeses of the parable of the doorkeeper do not allow us to conclude whether the doorkeeper merely did his duty or whether he abused his power; whether he deceived the man who sought the Law or whether, in fact, he himself was deceived. However, our reading of *The Castle*, which contains a sequence that has no counterpart in *The Trial* (see the section "The Corridors of the Law" in the discussion of *The Castle*, below), will allow us to go beyond this limit. Only when we do so will we be able to reach a conclusion about the question of undecidability.

As long as we remain within the bounds of *The Trial*, however, we must conclude that the demythifying view of the Law—being devoid of substance, the Law is a mere form by means of which power manifests and legitimates itself—clashes with the undecidability reading. Neither is able to go beyond or absorb the other. Therefore, this conclusion means that although it may be quite reasonable to assume the radical undecidability postulated by Bloom, it is no less necessary to assume a moderate undecidability. Whereas the radical version implies that interpretation is impossible, the moderate one assumes that the text is structured in such a way that it is constituted of a basic semantic instability. Our earlier reflections have already made it clear that what we mean by "moderate undecidability" is explicitly defined as the undecidability resulting from the desubstantialization of the world in Kafka. This is what makes his text uniquely volatile; and this conflicts with the reader's expectations, which are in turn a consequence of his or her background. Like Kafka's narrator, his reader has an Enlightenment view of meaning. The text's volatility destabilizes it—that is, it shows the reader's assumptions to be incompatible with the social experience described in the text.

In order to demonstrate this incompatibility, one must take into account the question of power in *The Trial*: "Power is shown in the novel not as a localized instance of a dominion, nor as a hierarchically apprehensible structure, but as an extensive, decentralized system with component functions [*Teilfunktionen*]. This structure may be described by the image of a system with multiple ramifications" (Lubkoll 1990: 280). This is consistent with what Janouch claims to have heard from Kafka himself: "Capitalism is a system of dependencies that range from the internal to the external, from the external to the internal, from the higher to the lower, and from the lower to the higher. Everything is dependent, everything is linked. Capitalism is a condition of the world and of the soul" (Janouch 1951: 90).

Before we can say that the analysis is complete, we must examine some specific aspects that reinforce or enrich the results at which we have arrived.

WHO IS JOSEPH K.?

The scene of Joseph K.'s arrest shows us the clash between the citizen's expectations and the logic of the police. But the dialogue between the accused man and the warders highlights an even more palpable difference. The ironical allusions, the veiled threats, the hints of small bribes, the passing comment on life in prison are all indicators of the policemen's mind-set; but a small gesture of the second warder betrays his class background: as he tries to convince the accused man to give him his underwear, his belly "kept butting against him in an almost friendly way" (Kafka 1974: 10). This intimate physical contact both reiterates the invasiveness of the warder's attitude and points to the fact that he belongs to a class that has no respect for personal territoriality. The bodily contact reaffirms the violence expressed or suggested by the warders' words and indicates their social background.

In contrast, Joseph K.'s sense of superiority is expressed by his avoidance of physical contact. The citizen's territoriality is formulated in words and does not rely on the body. His superior education, the fact that a police inspector is among his acquaintances, his senior position at the Bank, where he is called to private meetings with the vice-director and the director, all make him presume that soon the misunderstanding will be cleared up. But the only gesture permitted by bourgeois territoriality—a handshake among gentlemen—is ignored by the policemen. What in any other situation would be no more than rudeness here is something far more serious: the man who refuses the handshake deliberately asserts his contempt for the social hierarchy in which the accused man believes. But K.'s self-confidence is still unaffected; when he speaks to the Inspector, he complains of the neighbors' curiosity. Other people's indiscretion affronts his gentleman's sense of propriety.

Later, K.'s consciousness of his status is apparent in the irritation he feels because he has not been properly notified of the precise time and place he is to appear before the Court—as well as in the fact that he makes a point of not being strictly punctual, which would have been humiliating. His "class consciousness" goads him into the mistake of assuming that the crestfallen, submissive crowd he finds before the Examining Magistrate will be "easy to win over" (p. 47). Similarly, early in chapter 8, the mere sight of an old client of the Advocate's in his shirtsleeves reinforces his sense of security: "The mere possession of a thick greatcoat gave him a feeling of superiority over the meagre little fellow" (p. 185). With his heightened awareness of his good position in society, Joseph K. not only fails to give any importance to the trial but also, encouraged by what he believes to be the successful impact of his first words before the audience, begins to speak as a defender of the insulted and injured:

> "What has happened to me," K. went on, rather more quietly than before, trying at the same time to read the faces in the first row, which gave his speech a somewhat distracted effect, "what has happened to me is only a single instance

and as such of no great importance, especially as I do not take it very seriously, but it is representative of a misguided policy which is being directed against many other people as well. It is for these that I take up my stand here, not for myself." (pp. 50–51)

According to Max Brod, when Kafka read his writings he displayed such impressive histrionic skills that his listeners doubled up in laughter. Perhaps the passage just quoted is one that provoked such a reaction from those who heard him. Joseph K.'s arrogance remains comical even when one returns to the text for the tenth time. K.'s self-importance eggs him on to assume quixotic attitudes. And it remains intact even after he penetrates the labyrinths of the Court.

His conversation with the Law-Court Attendant is particularly significant. This man, having confessed his inability to defend his wife against the ridiculous student who constantly importunes her, says that he believes K. can help him, apparently betraying the humility of the socially inferior. How could this be possible, if he himself had just said that in the Court most cases were "*aussichtslosen Prozesse*" (foregone conclusions)? Thus, the husband's protests seem to be part of the same predictable game. His experience as a court employee has given him some insight into the psychology of accused men: at first they are always determined to protest the corruption of the machinery of justice. Joseph K.'s situation as a neophyte is so obvious that the Attendant's wife has already concluded that he intended "to improve things" (p. 60). Without saying so explicitly, the husband who claims to be affronted expects to take advantage of his own situation: "Then he gave K. a confidential look, such as he had not yet ventured in spite of all his friendliness, and added: 'A man can't help being rebellious'" (p. 72).

K.'s quixotism, founded on the belief in the privileges that the constitutional state supposedly ensured him, remains unshaken because he is oblivious to all evidence to the contrary. Certainly he would not be able to preserve his smug sense of security if he were really listening to the commercial traveler's description of the behavior of other accused men: "Common action is out of the question. An individual here and there may score a point in secret, but no one hears about it until afterwards, no one knows how it has been done. So there's no real community" (pp. 193–94). The Court encourages defendants to assume an extremely individualistic position. Again, how could K. remain quixotical if he had related this statement to what he had heard from the girl at the Law-Court Offices: "Perhaps none of us are hard-hearted, we should be glad to help everybody, yet as Law-Court officials we easily take on the appearance of being hard-hearted and of not wishing to help" (p. 82). The girl, then, believes there is no personal guilt involved. Rather, it is their professional position that requires officials to be indifferent. At the same time, accused men are forced to act individualistically. The machine imposes a kind of behavior that seems unthinkable to K., who does not realize he has already been singled out.

In the Advocate's house, the lessons K. has heard from Block, the "commercial traveler," are reinforced by the conversation between Block and Dr. Huld, which he is allowed to hear. The conversation between the Advocate and his old client displays the careful manipulation of the forms by means of which power is exerted. Huld is a master performer. The client is his humble servant. The ritual of obedience imposed on him is a kind of litany: " 'Who is your Advocate?' 'You are,' said Block. 'And besides me?' asked the Advocate. 'No one besides you,' said Block. 'Then pay no heed to anyone else,' said the Advocate" (p. 211).

The bright young priest and the old Advocate, an invalid who can no longer go out, are equally authoritarian and effective. To Joseph K., the scene with the commercial traveler simply demonstrates that Block is unable to see that the other man is using him to affirm his own power: "The client ceased to be a client and became the Advocate's dog" (p. 214). But in fact K. underestimates the old commercial traveler's cunning. To Joseph K.'s Enlightenment convictions, fear, humiliation, and shame are not possible forms for ensuring a man's survival. Thus, his beliefs are contrary to all that everyone is telling him all the time. K.'s principles make it impossible for him to understand.

And, in addition to what is going on with people, K. fails to realize that the Court is invisible. But its power resonates even in the majestic shadows of the Cathedral and gives strength even to an old bed-ridden invalid. Internally, K.'s quixotic stance is slowly corroded, though his outward behavior is unaffected. To others, his attitude still seems clumsy and haughty. The contrast between his behavior and Block's is evidence of this. However, the continuation of the passage quoted above shows that his consciousness contrasts with his conduct: "K. listened to everything with critical detachment, as if he had been commissioned to observe the proceedings closely, to report them to a higher authority, and to put down a record of them in writing" (p. 214). The allusion to "a higher authority" is ambiguous, ultimately undecipherable. We may understand it in a quixotic sense: an authority that would correct the revolting goings-on that K. was witnessing. Or it might be taken in a "realistic" sense: an even more powerful authority that could humble the Advocate himself. But K. is well aware of the fact that no such authority exists, no such resource is available. He must either remain as unshakable as Don Quixote or else "cure" himself.

For Alonso Quijano, the cure is to die in his own bed, surrounded by his loved ones and giving signs of repentance and contrition. For K., the cure is simply to resign himself to the fate of dying like a dog. If, however, we look at it from the viewpoint of the linear narrative, this resignation never actually takes place. The accused man remains quixotic when he is again sought by two men. He realizes that he is doomed; even so, he tries to make things more difficult for his executioners. But by the time he sees a policeman in the street, K. is already aware that it would be useless to call for his protection—or, perhaps, he is simply tired of resisting. He will no longer attempt to run away, as he did earlier; he will not try to disappear in a crowd. Meekly he rests his head on the boulder and lets the men open his shirt. But he has a last flare of quixotism just before he dies:

> His glance fell on the top floor of the house adjoining the quarry. With a flicker as of a light going up, the casements of a window there suddenly flew open; a human figure, faint and insubstantial at that distance and that height, leaned abruptly far forward and stretched both arms still farther. Who was it? A friend? A good man? Someone who still sympathized? Someone who wanted to help? Was it one person only? Or were they all there? Was help at hand? Were there some arguments in his favour that had been overlooked? . . . Where was the High Court, to which he had never penetrated? (pp. 250–51)

In a remarkable observation, Adorno associates this passage with the tradition of expressionist painting: "Many decisive parts in Kafka read as if they had been written in imitation of Expressionist paintings" (Adorno 1969: 264). The undecipherable gesture makes concrete what could not be expressed verbally. Because resignation had never been complete in him, Joseph K., even just before the execution, can only accept death as a shameful thing. If, as Alleman wrote, justification of the Dasein is as necessary as it is inaccessible, in the case of *The Trial* this is so not on account of any existential explanation, but because the will to dismantle the machine of the Law clashed with its omnipresence and impersonality—no official is responsible for it, and one can never be sure who is or is not an official—and its nonfunctionality. Thus, the will to dismantle the machine fails because it is restricted to a single Don Quixote, who assumes a logic the universality of which turns out to be deceptive.

But what is peculiar about Joseph K.'s quixotism? To the other characters in Cervantes' novel, the Knight of La Mancha was mad because he took seriously norms that had fallen into disuse long before. The reader of the work is happy to identify with those who laugh at or fight with the crazy hero. It was only to "the Knight of the Rueful Countenance" that the world was mad; and so his exploits amused all, nobles and plebeians. K. is a peculiar kind of Quixote because the values he affirms are theoretically in force. They at least appear to be shared by the reader, who is assumed to be as convinced as K. that he or she lives under the rule of law. If the immediate effect of Don Quixote's actions is comic, it is because the reader immediately recognizes them as insane. The response is tragic and sublime because, in his madness, the hero lives in a bygone world of chivalry, to which he devotes his impeccable character and spotless behavior.

In contrast, the immediate effect of K.'s actions is tragic, and the reader falls under the spell of the pathos of the labyrinth. Identifying with the protagonist, the reader finds solace in the idea that the trial in the story has nothing to do with the actual administration of justice. The reader, like most interpreters, tends to preserve the identification with the defendant, even if this obscures the economy of the text. This may happen in two ways: first, through a technical way—the reader fails to realize that the difference between *Don Quixote* and Kafka's work has to do with the different relation between narrator and protagonist; and second, through a thematic way—the denial of the trial's juridical relevance and the emphasis on the existential plane, associated with the simultaneous need for and impossibility of human Dasein. Let us examine the two obstacles.

As to the first, in Cervantes' novel the narrator is a priori much more distanced from the hero than in Kafka's work. The narrator, who introduces himself as the translator of an Arabian manuscript, presents scenes in a pure state. By adhering to the values in force in the real world, the fiction of *Don Quixote* denounces the fictitious nature of chivalric romances. The reader, pleased to share this viewpoint, has the right not only to laugh at the follies of innocent madness but also to be moved by them sometimes. In a word: the narrator's "impartiality" and the hero's obsolete values ensure the reader's security.

The situation in *The Trial* is quite different. The reader, identifying from the outset with K. as he suffers arbitrary persecution, seeing it as similar to what might happen to anyone in actual existence, tends to lose sight of the peculiar nature of the narrator. For this reason, the reader will fail to realize that Joseph K.'s sense of superiority—which he or she will tend to feel as well—and K.'s quixotic stance derive from his inability to acknowledge the lack of a match between his own expectations, founded on the rule of law, and actual reality. The reader sees his or her own reflection in K. and therefore does not question the narrator's position. The reader cannot perceive that the narrator is unreliable and that K. is not a hero, not even someone with whom he or she can identify. In other words, Cervantes' novel called for a simple response: here is a lovable madman, whose only mistake was to be born at the wrong time. But Kafka's novel presents something more complex: here is an ordinary man who believes in all that we believe in, persecuted by a fate that can only be understood as motivated by the intricacy of existence. What is peculiar about Kafka's Quixote is only in the uncertainty about the age to which the protagonist's values belong, and consequently how to explain his predicament in relation to the values in force. The existential solution does not even conceive of this peculiarity, since it takes for granted that Joseph K.'s predicament is timeless. This has the additional effect of obscuring what the two Quixotes, after all, do have in common: both are conceived as characters of fictional works that focus on the fictionality of values.

Let us turn to the second obstacle. Even if the professional critic is aware of the critical detachment and the irony that characterize the narrator's presentation of K., he or she will give little attention to these elements, either because the problem in question is ontologized or because he or she considers it absolutely undecidable. To underscore the deceptions and red herrings that Kafka supposedly placed in his text, as Corngold and Bloom do, is far from sufficient. The affirmation of radical undecidability does no more than defend an insufficiently critical analysis. Such a reading misses the opportunity to understand Kafka's inversion of Cervantes' text: *The Trial* is a fiction that, by presenting the machinery of justice as omnipresent, denounces the fictitious nature that the constitutional state has acquired. Like the Knight of the Rueful Countenance, K. is a figure of the past. But the reader cannot brand him as mad without running the risk of being labeled mad as well, or of becoming so cynical that he or she no longer cares if the norms of the civilized world are seen as fictions.

Perhaps it is only now, decades later, that we can read *The Trial* from a third perspective: as a fiction that, whatever the author's intention may have been, demonstrates the fictitious nature of the constitutional state. Without the benefit of hindsight, one of the first critics to recognize Kafka's importance could write that the court that Kafka submits to his jurisdiction "takes us to a time before the law of the twelve tables, a primitive world, against which the institution of written law was one of the earliest victories" (Benjamin 1974b, 2, 2: 412). Benjamin, following Haas, still saw the time of Kafka's narratives as the night of primeval eras. But, even more emphatically than Haas, he added a rectification: "It is very significant that the world of the officials and the world of the fathers are one and the same to Kafka. This similarity does not honor them" (p. 411). It should not be thought, however, that the mere passage of time has the magical effect of unveiling what had remained obscure even to the most perceptive interpreters. Rather than proceed to draw the consequences of the fictitious nature of the constitutional state, let us conclude the observations of the present subsection.

By questioning the identity of Joseph K., we have attempted to relate the situation of the constitutional state in the post-Enlightenment period to the quixotic nature of the hero of *The Trial*. We found that Joseph K. is a member of a species on the verge of extinction: the individual whose legal expectations are the actualization of the logic of the citizen. Assuming that the reader subscribes to this logic as well, we may say that the reader identifies with K. to the extent that his or her understanding of the novel is impaired. But lest one misunderstanding be replaced by another, let us examine some other procedures used in the novel, procedures that—among other functions—have the effect of encouraging misguided interpretations.

THE UNRELIABLE NARRATOR

It was Ernest Pinard—not a literary critic but a public prosecutor—who was the first to point out the unique position assumed by the narrator in *Madame Bovary*. As we have seen, Pinard observed that the narrator never reproaches the heroine for her conduct.

Flaubert criticism in the earlier half of the twentieth century appropriated Pinard's insight, discarding its condemnatory tone. Thus, Auerbach writes: "His opinion of his characters and events remains unspoken; and when the characters express themselves it is never in such a manner that the writer identifies himself with their opinion, or seeks to make the reader identify himself with it. We hear the writer speak; but he expresses no opinion and makes no comment" (Auerbach 1974: 486). Today this does not seem to do justice to the complexity of the object it purports to describe. According to Auerbach, the narrator's detachment from the fate of the characters resulted from Flaubert's choice of a narrative mode—free indirect speech—which contrasts with the two more ordinary modes, direct and indirect speech. In it the role of the narrator, Auerbach explains, is limited to selecting events and converting them into language, under the conviction that language is able to speak for itself. "Every event, if one is able to express it purely and completely, interprets itself and the persons involved in it far better and more completely than any opinion or judgment appended to it could do" (p. 486).

Almost twenty years later, this simplifying tendency can be seen in Beda Alleman, who writes of Kafka's narrative that "the art of free indirect speech [*erlebte Rede*] consists in remaining in between objective reporting and the personal perspective of the character that the narrative concerns" (Alleman 1963: 239).

Both authors fail to observe that this narrative mode affects the reader's expectation of what the work has to offer him or her—information concerning the world that, however metaphorical in nature, should conform to what is counted as rational; that is, in conformity with the functioning of Enlightenment reason. By disconnecting the narrator from the universe of the characters and taking the narrator's comments independently of the characters' actions, Flaubert made his readers insecure as to what was the proper way of receiving the plot as a whole. To the extent that the narrator no longer controlled the expected understanding, the text no longer contained the *representative of society*, the character in charge of formulating the adequate interpretation from the viewpoint of the legitimated values. The old markers of direct speech, what the characters say, and of indirect speech, what the narrator comments, helped divide responsibilities and, ever since the consecration of subjectivity, confirmed the primacy of the self.

How could it be possible now to determine with any precision the opinions of the authorial self? Flaubert, Pinard reasoned, does not condemn adultery; therefore he is guilty of not reinforcing an established value. Auerbach, affirming that the novelist trusted language's ability to make things clear by itself, places himself in a position symmetrically opposite to that of the prosecutor. Both, however, rely on the same assumption: language is commanded by the speaker's intention. Nor does Alleman seem to perceive the threat to the prerogative of intentionality: there is an intermediary value between direct speech and indirect speech, and it is able to reconcile objective and subjective exposition.

The allusion to *Madame Bovary* will suffice to show that the two interpreters rushed to the conclusion that their analytical instruments were enough to do the job. Who, for instance, is Emma's husband? A fool, an almost idiotic man with provincial pretensions, or an angel lost among devils? What is the difference between the mayor's "agricultural" speech and Rudolph's suave words in Emma's ears, if both have the intention to seduce? What is the difference between the pharmacist Homais and Father Bournisien if both, after all, are serving the same interests? What is the clear meaning of the language of free indirect speech if not that the narrator refuses to play the part of stage director because the "portrait" of society he presents is a portrait of chaos, of utter mismatch between personal motivation and stated principles?

If we assume that the interpretation holds for Flaubert himself, then this must also be recognized as authorial intention. However, it no longer takes the form of a program for society. Kant had supposed that the lack of a substance to be converted into a moral precept was not detrimental to the latter's status as law, for it resulted from the transformation—effected on the individual level—of freedom into duty. The importance of free indirect speech underscores the failure of this transformation. Once it is desubstantialized, the law, on the moral and social planes, is no more than a prescription, a machine that imposes itself on individuals and forms with them a multiplicity of heterogeneous circuits that cannot possibly be reduced to the will of any agent; thus, power cannot be confused with the determination of a certain place. We then have not individual subjects, invested with what we have been calling the logic of the citizen, but rather an anonymous power, infiltrated throughout society, making no difference between its lay and its religious branches—Dr. Homais and Dr. Huld, Bournisien and the prison chaplain.

Kafka, an admirer of Flaubert, made his narrator just as impassive as the narrator in *Madame Bovary*. Alleman acutely observes that *The Trial* concerns the arguments and reactions of Joseph K., "but never speaks *about* Joseph K." (Alleman 1963: 238). The narrator reports the protagonist's opinions and reactions but neither presents him from within nor explains him with an illuminating comment. To say that the narrator is unreliable is, in a way, to judge it on terms other than its own. A reliable narrator was one that assumed the existence of a pact with the reader, through which it made sure that social values circulated within the work. Thus, trust in the narrator was the effect of a wider trust: ultimately, in the Law that ruled society. Expressed in the form of the novel that flourished in the eighteenth and early nineteenth centuries, this trust corresponded to the period during which, even though God had been dethroned, not everything was possible—that is, in the period during which the loss of belief in the absolute substantiality of the Law that ruled the world had not yet been replaced by the experience of vertigo of which Kleist and Kafka were to be masters.

To say that in Kafka the narrator is unreliable is to say that the functions of the reader and of the interpreter have become much more complex. The former no longer has a guide he or she can rely on; and the task of the latter can no longer be defined as discovering an intention. The reader and the interpreter no longer see themselves as belonging to a single community of values. Since the bases of their stability—the idea of expression of nationality and that of authorial intention—have been shaken, the question "What is literature?" again becomes crucial, as it had been in the late eighteenth century (see Chapter 2). And the return of this question makes it necessary to understand better the status of fiction. Up to the time of such "reliable" novelists as Fielding or Thackeray, Balzac or Stendhal, it was possible, in a more or less crude fashion, to explain fictional products in terms of the author's will or some theory of social conditioning of which the work was the proof. But by Kafka's time the significance of the unreliable narrator was such that it became necessary to understand the very discursive form that favored semantic indeterminacy.

To mention this problem is tantamount to pointing out the difference between the semantic instability of fictional works and undecidability as to which interpretation is correct. The former comes to be seen as the defining property of the fictional. (Unmistakable since Flaubert or—in English-language fiction—Henry James, its presence is, however, already quite clear in Balzac.)[14] Undecidability, by contrast, is an attribute of only a few works—this seems to be the case of Kleist's writings. Of these works it is then said that no approach can excel another; the competition between different interpretations is a struggle without a winner. Undecidability is the limit case in fictional discourse, a discourse that rests on no solid semantic soil and thus cannot receive a definitive interpretation.

Although I realize that this discussion deserves a much more extensive treatment, I shall do no more than repeat that the narrator's indifference concerning the characters' fates questions the habits of the passive reader—the reader who is used to being guided by the narrator's comments, and the prenotion of interpretation as the way to arrive at the "truth" of the text. Let us see how this passivity and this prenotion are disturbed by another characteristic of Kafka's work.

THE FALSENESS OF REPRESENTATIONS

Two passages in *The Trial* deal with the fraud and deception that permeate society. K. is taken by his uncle to the Advocate's house, and instead of listening to the two men's conversation, he goes looking for Leni. A large portrait of a judge catches his eye. K. says that the judge might be the one in charge of his trial. Leni replies that she knows the man in question, and that he looks quite different from the portrait. " 'That's all invention,' said Leni, with her face bent over his hand. 'Actually he sits on a kitchen chair, with an old horse-rug doubled under him' " (Kafka 1974: 120–21). But why should the reader trust this information? Leni is being seductive. Does she really have the knowledge she claims to have, and can she really help K. with her connections? The narrator is not just "indifferent" to the hero; he is unconnected from the entire world in which the characters live, so that the reader is left on his or her own.

The situation is much the same when the defendant talks to Titorelli, the painter, who is working on a portrait of another judge. K. is curious about a figure in the middle of the chair or throne from which the judge seems to be

14. In this connection, see Michel Butor's essay on the "*mobile romanesque*" (novel as mobile) of the *Comédie humaine* (see Butor 1960: 79–93).

about to rise. He asks what it is intended to represent; the painter tells him it is Justice. " 'Now I can recognize it,' said K. 'There's the bandage over the eyes, and here are the scales. But there are wings on the figure's heels, and isn't it flying?' " (p. 162). Titorelli argues that he did as he had been told to do and adds that he never really saw the judge or his throne; like a patient teacher, he explains that "it's all invention," for the portraits are not supposed to be faithful likenesses but are painted according to preestablished conventions.

Since Titorelli's words confirm Leni's, it might seem that they are to be believed. But, again, is Titorelli any more to be trusted than Leni? For the painter, like Leni, is also trying to win over K., to extract money from him with the argument that since he has access to the authorities, he might be able to help him. To both Titorelli and Leni, K. seems to be an easy prey. This does not mean that Kafka's Quixote is a naif, easily fooled by those who are well schooled in the world of the Court. The attraction he feels for Leni will be explained when we discuss K.'s relationship with Frieda in *The Castle*. As to Titorelli, Joseph K. is less a victim of his own innocence than a man who wants to learn the rules of the game he has to play. The painter has been recommended to him by an important client, who is presumably knowledge-able about the underground justice that is persecuting K. And Titorelli's game is quite venal and brazen: for the right amount of money, he will pull all the strings in favor of the accused man.

Whence, then, does the strength of Leni and Titorelli proceed, apart from the assumption that they have close access to power? K.'s quixotism lies not in estrangement from reality, but in his conviction that he is protected by his social status. When he examines the rooms of the building where the Examining Magistrate hears the accused men, his thoughts concentrate on two points: first, "That was not an arrangement likely to inspire much re-spect, and for an accused man it was reassuring to reckon how little money this Court could have at its disposal"; and second, "The possibility was not to be excluded that the money was abundant enough, but that the officials pocketed it before it could be used for the purposes of justice" (p. 69). His sense of class makes him aware of the advantages that the poverty of the Court might imply. The precariousness of the building is reassuring, because it seems to suggest the possibility of intimidating or bribing the officials. And the hypothesis that the sorry condition of the court building is a consequence of corruption is even more heartening.

Thus, the chivalric ideal of Cervantes' Quixote is here replaced by some-thing the basis for which is a comfortable social situation. As an upper execu-tive who may rise even higher in his profession, a man who has enough money to nurture the ambition to buy a house for himself, who is already able to frequent the cafés and pick and choose a lover, Joseph K. believes that he has an unquestionable right to privacy and to his privileges. It is as a man of his time that the defendant is a man of his class; his quixotism is founded on the logic of the citizen. Rather than oppose the constitutional state as the place of freedom to the arbitrary totalitarian state, *The Trial* shows quite clearly that the constitutional state takes social inequality for granted, so that the modern Quixote could not possibly be a bankrupt aristocrat.

What separates the Enlightenment aspiration for the rule of law from the post-Enlightenment state in which Joseph K. lives is not a sudden, inexplicable, tragic catastrophe. Kafka's genius was to exacerbate the situation of inequality that underlay the logic of the citizen to the point at which, one fine morning, a citizen wakes up to find himself outside reality.

It is in his sleep that Gregor Samsa is transformed into an unclassifiable insect [*Ungeziefer*]. It is as he wakes up that Joseph K. finds himself transformed into a unique sort of Quixote. Just as the past days of chivalry were seen as a golden age only by the Knight of the Rueful Countenance, the time before Joseph K.'s awakening seems a time of justice only for those who identify with the logic of the citizen—who do so to such an extent that they fail to see exactly how Kafka depicts this time.

I do not mean that this is the interpretation that the author himself would agree with. One may even suppose that he left the narrative unfinished because its development ran into an obstacle he was unable to overcome. My proposal, then, does not rely on the notion of authorial intention, but it does take into account a quite conspicuous aspect of Kafka: his extreme sensitivity to power. Canetti, to whom we are indebted for this sharp insight, sees it even outside Kafka's work, in the very physical presence of the man: "Confronted as he was with power on all sides, his obduracy sometimes offered him a reprieve. But if it was insufficient, or if it failed him, he trained himself to disappear; here the helpful aspect of his physical thinness is revealed . . . By means of physical diminution, he withdrew power *from himself*, and thus had less part in it; this asceticism, too, was directed against power" (Kafka 1978: 71).

This extreme sensitivity to signs of power materializes in his work both in the features he attributes to his protagonist and in his subtle apprehension of the multiple forms of social hierarchy. Let us mention only one of these: the episode in which one of the warders is beaten because of K.'s complaint. The warder complains of the logic of the citizen because, were it not for K.'s action, he and his comrade might soon be promoted and become whippers like the one who is punishing them (Kafka 1974: 95–96).

In short, we have been trying to demonstrate that the narrator's unreliability is paralleled by the falsity or, at any rate, the doubts concerning representations. This is sometimes an effect of the vanity of those who exert power—the judges and their portraits—or of the will to power of those who are close to the powerful, Leni and Titorelli. This has the consequence of affecting the privilege traditionally granted to the interpreter of being seen as the one who *evaluates* the true meaning of a textual object. Rather than corroborate this certainty, the analysis of some of the proceedings used in *The Trial* shows semantic instability—the impossibility of nailing down the text to a single meaning—as a constitutive element of the work. This does not imply that it is semantically undecidable. For *The Trial*—the story of a character to whom, one fine morning, it becomes clear how mistaken he has always been about the juridical practices of his country—is the analysis of the legal machinery of a society that operates on the basis of a Law that does not correspond to any substance. The norm which K. intends to follow is not unknown to others; the difference is that they are aware that, at some point, it became a dead letter.

In the case of "In the Penal Colony," the island's distance from the mother country explains the officer's indignant reaction to the change of the norm. *The Trial* relies on a similar strategy; but whereas in the novella the change is recognized as the correlate of what has indeed taken place in the recent history of Western nations, in the novel the strategy is based on projection. While K. slept, liberalism died out. As a surviving member of an extinct species, K. behaves in a way that allows the narrator—who in this sense corresponds to the explorer in "The Penal Colony"—to observe the attitudes of a type of man no longer existent. These attitudes—both K.'s claims to his rights and the extreme awareness of his own social privileges—are the only signs indicative of the changes that took place while he slept at night.

On the macroscopic plane, *The Trial* cannot be considered a text the interpretation of which is undecidable because its subject is the power that operates a juggernaut. Power, made impersonal, is not to be identified with and is not limited to the invisible higher judges but depends on the collaboration of the various sectors of society. That is: the logic of the citizen disappears together with the individual subject, which—like Joseph K. himself—is often seen in a corridor or *Gang*, a German word that also means "gear" or "cogwheel."

But, though it is absent on the macroscopic plane of the work, the devil of undecidability is in the details. From the outset, the very existence of the higher judges is no more than a hypothesis. (Could undecidability then be the ironical product of an "excess" of reason, which is, according to Kant, responsible for explanations of the nature of freedom, the soul, and God?)

We do not deny, then, that there is a certain margin of undecidability in

The Trial. But we insist that this undecidability is subordinated to the overarching scheme the poles of which are pain and power. Being unsubstantial, the Law is a phantasmagoria, a ghost that justifies power. But irradiated throughout society, with no stronghold housing and identifying its officials, power cannot be captured in a flow chart. In Kafka, it is the very representation of the unlimited spatial expansion of power in a society that is drastically changed.

Let us now turn to *The Castle* in order to refine our conclusion.

The Castle: *A Religious Novel?*

The Castle (*Das Schloß*), probably written in 1922 (see Politzer 1978: 341–42; Pasley and Wagenbach 1965: 71–72), belongs to the last phase of Kafka's life. His correspondence seldom touches on the novel. From Planá he wrote to Max Brod, on September 11, 1922, that his week-long stay there had not been happy, "for I will evidently have to drop the Castle story forever" (Kafka 1977: 357).

The novel was published in 1926, and the interpretation of it that became standard followed the lines established by Kafka's literary executor and biographer, Brod: the work's religious character was seen as self-evident. Thus, in his preface to the U.S. edition (which was published in German only in 1949), Thomas Mann declared: "Kafka as a writer is perhaps best characterized as a religious humorist" (Mann 1949: 67). Later he defines the central theme of the novel as follows: "The grotesque disconnection between the human being and the transcendental; the incommensurability of the divine, the strange, sinister, demoniac illogicality, the inexpressibility, the tyranny—yes, the immorality, according to any human standards, of *The Castle*" (p. 69). Similarly, in his introduction to *The Castle*, Edwin Muir, a fine translator but an unoriginal interpreter, wrote that the novel should be read as a modern *Pilgrim's Progress*: "*The Castle* is, like *The Pilgrim's Progress*, a religious allegory" (Kafka 1948: iii). In the years immediately following World War II, this interpretation was gradually replaced by the existential reading (see the discussion of *The Trial*). Since we have examined that reading already, it seems relevant to consider here the factors that probably favored the religious interpretation.

Two possible factors may be suggested. First, the Western intelligentsia that had been brought up early in the century was much more open to religious values than the generation that began to distinguish itself in the mid-1940's. In addition, the religious explanation proposed by Brod—unlike the one formulated by Willi Haas—gave an a priori meaning to Kafka's writings, so that the reader would be spared any bewilderment. In our present time, those who advocate this kind of interpretation have an even more concrete goal: that of preserving a positive view of liberal society, reaffirming the stabilizing role of religion (see Schirrmacher 1987 and particularly Esch-weiler 1990). Second, for early-twentieth-century intellectuals, the horrors of World War I had not had the effect of destroying the ideals of the liberal society in which they had been brought up. Consequently, they still had a potentially organic conception of society, on which a functional view was to be erected, one that was adverse to the idea of the managed society that "negative dialectic" would show to be characteristic of the contemporary developed world.

These two factors may be seen as interacting rather than operating in isolation. If society is seen as potentially organic, structurally made up of functional institutions, the horrifying view of it we find in Kafka could only be explained by the emphasis on a certain dysfunctionality. And this could only affect religion, the legitimacy of which had been questioned since the Enlightenment and the importance of which for the everyday existence of social groups was clearly decreasing. These interpreters of Kafka were not necessarily religious persons themselves. Nor was it necessary that they see the author as one obsessed by the emptiness of religious unbelief. But for them Kafka's vision of society could be conceived only as vertigo or night-mare, an *Alptraum*, the product of the author's own morbid tendencies (which provided a point of departure for Oedipal interpretations). One may even minimize the influence of Brod's view of his friend as a spiritually tormented man, for Brod's "testimony" was a much less important motivating factor than the preservation of belief in the values of liberal society. This was what led its champions to identify Kafka's spiritual misery as religious emptiness.

Therefore, except for a narrow psychoanalytical interpretation, the only way to explain the terrible dream of *The Trial*, *The Castle*, and the shorter stories was to see them as referring to the inscrutability of divine justice. Such was the credibility of the constitutional state that it was inconceivable that the root of Kafka's fiction might be a questioning of its existence. More exactly, it was inconceivable that Kafka's fiction might be rooted in the issue of the desubstantialization of the Law. This is not to deny the presence of religious unease in Kafka. But I do claim that the proponents of Brod's reading are unable to understand Kafka's work in any other way than reducing it to the spiritual-religious dimension—and, as I have mentioned, this is applicable even to the most recent defenders of this approach.

What we find in the analysis put forth by one of Kafka's earliest admirers is something quite different from reductionism. In his tribute to Kafka upon the tenth anniversary of his death, Walter Benjamin wrote:

[Kafka's parables] are constructed in such a way that they may be quoted from and narrated for didactic purposes. But do we know the doctrine that is contained in Kafka's parables and taught by K.'s gestures and the motions of his animals? No; all we can say is that here and there it is alluded to. Kafka would perhaps have said: These passages convey it as its residues; but we may just as well say: They pave the way for it as its harbingers. In any case, what is in question here is the organization of life and work in the human community. (Benjamin 1974b, 2, 2: 420)

In his elliptical style, in so many ways reminiscent of Kafka's, Benjamin stresses the peculiarity of Kafka's parables: the doctrines underlying them do not exist, but passages from these parables are residues or harbingers of them. Since there is no doctrine corresponding to them, Kafka's parables do not point to a religious credo. But they indicate an unmistakable ambiguity—the passages are residues of an unknown doctrine or harbingers paving the way for it. The religious element appears not as a center around which the parables dispose themselves, but as a remainder or forerunning sign.

But how can we be justified in seeing this sign as pointing to a religious doctrine? The ending of the passage from Benjamin reinforces the suspicion that such a reading would be arbitrary, for it stresses the fact that in Kafka the concern with life and work in the human community replaces the religious concern with fate. Acceptance of this conclusion would be comforting, for it would simplify our task: we could then affirm that the religious interpretation of Kafka is no more than an unwarranted projection made by anxious liberal interpreters.

But Benjamin himself, developing Haas's insight, forces us to choose a more difficult path. In a letter to Gershom Scholem dated July 20, 1934, replying to a letter from Scholem accompanying a copy of *The Trial* to which he had added a poem, Benjamin not only acknowledged the theological character of the interpretation proposed in the poem but also added: "I hold that my own work also has an ample theological side, although it is covert" (Benjamin 1978, 2: 613). In the same letter we find the following, more explicit, passage: "I tried to show how Kafka attempted to project [*erstatten*] on the reverse of this 'nothingness,' on its lining. This assumes that every way of overcoming this nothingness, as it is conceived by the theological commentators who follow Brod, would have been abhorrent to him" (p. 614). What distinguishes Benjamin's essay, then, is not that it denies the presence of the theological issue in Kafka, but that it links redemption with the reverse of nothingness, and—if we associate the passage just quoted with the passage from the essay quoted earlier—that it identifies the reverse of nothingness with the organization of the human community.

One may surely question Benjamin's interpretation by arguing that it is difficult to find, in Kafka's novels, just where the possibility of redemption is emphasized. Though this is indeed difficult, depending as it does on a most unlikely chance, as we shall see when we analyze K.'s interview with the Secretary Bürgel, there is nothing arbitrary about it. For, despite the similarities to *The Trial*, *The Castle* is distinguished from the earlier novel both by the impossibility of penetrating the motivation of characters' actions and by the unlikeliness of reducing the theological question to the social plane. Although this argument requires further elaboration, it should be stated from the outset that the passage from Benjamin's essay is most important because it forces us to see that the emphasis on the religious dimension of *The Castle* cannot be reduced to a mere projection of liberal values. As we have said, the mind-set of liberal expectations predisposed interpreters to acknowledge that dimension. But its flaw, we added, is that the religious was emphasized to the detriment of what was not consistent with the defense of the liberal view of society. It was Benjamin's unique brand of Marxism that allowed him to put his finger on the blind spot of the religious reading and at the same time avoid the blind spot of Marxism: its inability to take into account the question of theological redemption.

But could it be that our praise of Benjamin, with its emphasis on his sensibility to Kafka's subtleties, is no more than a naive acceptance of what amounts to a contradiction in Benjamin's text? Only Kafka himself can provide us with the decisive evidence. Particular attention should be given to the diary entry of January 16, 1922. Kafka speaks of the anguish he experiences because of the lack of synchronization between the inner and the outer clocks—"The clocks are not in unison" (Kafka 1972: 398–99). While the outer one follows a mechanical rhythm, the inner one "runs crazily on a devilish or demoniac or in any case inhuman pace," as it pursues its trains of thought unbridled.

> This pursuit . . . carries one in a direction away from [men] [nimmt die Richtung aus der Menschheit]. . . . 'Pursuit,' indeed, is only a metaphor. I can also say, 'assault on the last earthly frontier,' an assault, moreover, launched from below [Ansturm von unten], from mankind, and since this too is a metaphor, I can replace it by the metaphor of an assault from above, aimed at me from above. (p. 399)

And the final paragraph in the entry begins with the statement: "All such writing is an assault on the frontiers; if Zionism had not intervened, it might easily have developed into a new secret doctrine, a Kabbalah" (p. 399).

The passage would be even more extraordinary if we could associate it with the writing of *The Castle*. But this cannot be done with any certainty. It is not quite clear when Kafka wrote the novel, though Brod remembers that, on March 15, 1922, Kafka read to him the first chapter (see Brod 1977: 163). Thus, it is only probable that the diary entry was written while Kafka was working on *The Castle*.

Just how, then, does the long passage from Kafka quoted above confirm Benjamin's interpretation? Pursuit away from men, assault on the last earthly frontier—these are images that point to the search for a beyond. More important than these images is the final statement: such an assault could easily lead to a new esotericism, if it were not for Zionism. Kafka's integrating effort to reestablish the link with the roots of his people does not take place in consistency with a religious propensity; on the contrary, it counterbalances such a propensity and—at least from the viewpoint of its extreme form—neutralizes it. If we take into account that, in its technical sense, the word "Kabbalah" means "tradition," we can understand better the ambiguity that Benjamin intuited: not being at the service of a codified doctrine, the new Kabbalah— that is, the one that Kafka's work propounds—contains residues of the older one and announces a new one, yet to take shape. Thus, we find that, at least with regard to *The Castle*, there is a clear theological concern involved.

However, even if we acknowledged that the definitive proof depended on a detailed study of the novel itself, it would be premature for us to take this early conclusion as in any way decisive. For we must consider the opposite movement contained in the same passage: whereas the assault points to a new Kabbalah, Zionism neutralizes it. Like Benjamin, whose interest in the Jewish people and in the possibility of moving to Jerusalem never became definitive, Kafka cannot be said to have joined the Jewish movement. True, his concern with and interest in Zionism increased noticeably beginning in late 1918; he supported Felice's participation in community projects sponsored by a Jewish organization; he encouraged Brod to join the movement body and soul; but he himself did very little in this way. The impasse finally immobilized him.

This inability to overcome a devastating contradiction reflects on his own work. In a letter to Scholem dated September 15, 1934, Benjamin stressed the importance, for an interpretation of Kafka, of considering "the historical aspect of his failure" (Benjamin 1978, 2: 619–20). He returns to the same subject toward the end of a letter to Scholem on June 12, 1938: "To do justice to the figure of Kafka, in its purity and its specific beauty, one should never lose sight of the fact that it is the beauty of failure" (p. 764). It may be argued, though, that Benjamin does not state with any clarity where exactly Kafka failed; nor does he do so in his 1934 essay. Let us then turn to Adorno, whose admiration for Kafka was as intense as Benjamin's. Without detracting from his admiration, Adorno admitted that there were flaws in Kafka's work: "Among the defects, which become obvious in the great novels, monotony is the most striking. The presentation of the ambiguous, uncertain, inaccessible, is repeated endlessly, often at the expense of the vividness that is always sought" (Adorno 1969: 254).

These last observations may strike the reader as unnecessary details. If so, the reader is asked to consider no more than the basis of the argument: Benjamin's interpretation not only confirms the existence of a theological argument in *The Castle* but also shows that the novel contains an unresolved tension with the earthly territory of the human community.

But here the most serious objection of all can be raised: Is this acknowledgement not inconsistent with the argument of our essay? Our criticism of other interpreters and our analysis of "The Judgment," "In the Penal Colony," and *The Trial* refused any exegesis that saw as essential in Kafka the pressing and frustrating search for a justification for existence. We proposed, as an alternative, a positive, political approach that highlighted the question of the exercise of power in a context where the Law has lost its substance. In short, we attempted to show that the root of Kafka's problem was to be found in Kant's restriction of the Law to what can be experienced. The noumenon, in the positive sense, is not for us, since "the doctrine of sensibility is likewise the doctrine of the noumenon in the negative sense" (*CPR*, B 308). If, then, we admit that *The Castle*, one of Kafka's great texts, presents an unmistakable theological content, is this not a flagrant contradiction?

The apparent contradiction, however, only reinforces our viewpoint all the more. Kant's assertion that the humanly conceivable Law lacks substance—that is, that it concerns not noumena but only phenomena—should not, to be sure, be construed as a positivistic questioning, which sees the scientific as all that is worth knowing. I assume that the reader is aware of the fact that, to Kant, the Ideas lost none of their dignity for being incompatible with the work of concepts. The philosopher criticized theology not because it investigated the divine, but because it claimed to be knowledge of the divine. Kant's problem is even more conspicuous in Kafka because the latter was unable to solve his dilemma: on the one hand he was attracted by what was beyond the human, and on the other he remained obsessed with the organization of the human community. For—except for the alternative of giving up, of submitting to what was incomprehensible or beyond reason—the dilemma could be definitively solved only if Kafka postulated a *nature* for the Law that had in it a place for the human.

This was what the romantics had attempted. As we saw in Chapter 2, by concentrating on the self or on the products of the self, even when—as the young Schlegel did—they tended to treat poetical procedures as autonomous, the romantics never gave up the search for the restoration of unity, a unity that somehow reestablished what had been destroyed by critical philosophy. Closer in time to Kant, the romantics were, however, more distant from his problem than Kafka was. The romantics' question—which was simultaneously a reproach—was: In a world where one has no access to noumena, how is one to live if not in a state of active distraction?

The above considerations not only emphasize the connections between the present chapter and the one preceding it but also state its basic line of argument more clearly and show explicitly under what conditions we find it acceptable to speak of a theological and an existential plane in Kafka's work. There is nothing wrong with such a reading as long as these planes are seen as aspects to be integrated and not as a unifying view. It should also be noted that we are not naively supposing that religious angst has anything to do with the Kantian problem of the Law. As a religious feeling, angst may well be a despairing of the divine. But this is not necessarily the same as Kafka's angst, which requires the permanence of ambiguity and uncertainty. One may even speculate that Kafka's psychological inability to overcome his impasse provides the condition for this result. It should also be added, however, that this can be valid only if we are careful to note that this particular psychological state led to this particular textual result because it operated in tandem with Kafka's equally characteristic need for objectification.

I hope it is not unduly optimistic to say that the above discussion will make things much easier for our analysis of *The Castle*.

K., THE LAND SURVEYOR

Like *The Trial*, *The Castle* begins in media res. All we know about the protagonist is that he comes from another village and that he is responding to a job offer. The scenery of the opening passage is so stark that it seems an unlikely beginning of a story: "It was late in the evening when K. arrived. The village was deep in snow. The Castle hill was hidden, veiled in mist and darkness, nor was there even a glimmer of light to show that a castle was there" (Kafka 1966: 9).

K. is a land surveyor. But even his professional qualification and the job offer he mentions are immediately questioned. The inn where he lodges is called the *Herrenhof* (Lords' Inn), a name that seems a good omen for one who intended no more than to be hired and, through work, to become integrated into the life of the community. But his qualification is called into question by an authority who, though decidedly minor, is nonetheless quite arrogant. This seems to be an unimportant obstacle. The Castle administration is called by phone and confirms K.'s allegation. K., as naive as the protagonist of *The Trial*, thinks that he is as good as hired already. He has arrived in the territory of a certain Count West-west—a redundancy interpreted by Greenberg as indicating the farthest reaches of the Western world (see Greenberg 1968: 162–63 n.)—whom he is willing to serve. Things seem simple enough to him, and in a conversation with the landlord K. says he is not sure whether he will want to live in the Castle, which is usual for employees, because he fears he may not like the place. His argument will soon come to be seen in an ironical light: "I like to be my own master" (Kafka 1966: 13). And since he had not been able to see the Castle, now he goes out in order to take a look at it.

The sight is somewhat disappointing, and mentally he compares the Castle tower with that of the church in his home town. Whereas the church tower pointed up, there seemed to be a childish touch of insecurity and carelessness in the tower he saw before him: "It was if a melancholy-mad tenant who ought to have been kept locked in the topmost chamber of his house had burst through the roof and lifted himself up to the gaze of the world" (p. 16). There was something insane (*etwas irrsinniges*) about the tower. If the narrator in Kafka were reliable, no discussion would arise as to whether or not the novel contained a religious allegory, for the narrator's comment would somehow "correct" the character's reflection. But the passage just quoted is in free indirect speech. As such, it expresses more than K.'s disillusionment; it also represents the thought: was it to become a part of that shapeless monster that he had made his journey? As the narrative proceeds, the reader realizes that K. has already made a number of small mistakes. Since they are all mistakes of interpretation—believing that the Castle's reply amounted to a confirmation of the job offer, believing that he would certainly be invited to live "up there"—why should the comparison between the two towers not also prove to be a mistake of the same kind? The narrator incorporates its voice with the character's precisely because it does not intervene, making it impossible for the receiver to distinguish whose opinion is being expressed.

Still under the effect of the optimism inspired by his success in his first "test," the Land Surveyor no longer doubts that he has been accepted and is disappointed with the sight of the place he already considers his future residence. Shortly before, in his conversation with the landlord, he said he had not yet seen the Count. The landlord, out of malice or cruelty, is not surprised to hear this. But soon the Land Surveyor, or at least the reader, will realize that this was an important point. K. meets the village schoolmaster, who in passing makes two revelations: first, there is no real difference between the peasants and the Castle; second, when K. asks him if he knows the Count, the teacher answers: "Why should I?" For safety's sake, he switches to French to add: "Please remember that there are innocent children present" (p. 16). K.'s question is then a gross obscenity. Although the reason for this may not seem clear at first, one may conclude that it is a consequence of the fact that the teacher's mentality is the same as the villagers'. What links the peasants to the inhabitants of the Castle is the extreme reverence and terror the latter inspire in the former. And this terror is the cause of their unfriendliness towards strangers, which has been mentioned by the teacher and affirmed by the old man whom K. meets in his first walk.

The reader, then, begins to realize that K.'s optimism is unjustified. But is the peasants' hostility to all strangers really the general rule? More specifically, could it not be that since there is no difference between them and the people in the Castle, the villagers are not as certain about K.'s acceptance as K. himself is? The Land Surveyor is in the predicament of having made a journey in search of a job and being received with mistrust and hostility by the villagers. This is the axis around which the entire novel will turn: the relationship sought by someone who has been called with the "thing" that called him.

This relationship seems more secure to K. when he receives his first letter from the Castle. Still assuming that it is up to him whether to accept or to refuse the offer, K. reflects on the letter's contents:

> There was of course a danger, and that was sufficiently emphasized in the letter, even elaborated with a certain satisfaction, as if it were unavoidable. This was sinking to the workman's level. . . . If K. were willing to become a workman he could do so, but he would have to do it in grim earnest, without any other prospect. K. knew that he had no real compulsory discipline to fear, he was not afraid of that, and in this case least of all, but the pressure of a discouraging environment, the pressure of the imperceptible influences of every moment, these things he did fear, but that was a danger he would have to guard against. (Kafka 1966: 30)

Naive, optimistic, confident of his own powers, K. is fundamentally mistaken. His position in society does not allow him to assume the quixotic position of Joseph K. Although he is struggling in the name of a right of which there seems to be not a sign—that what has been promised in writing must be carried out—he does not seek anything more than to accomplish his intention of being integrated into the village. The common trait he has with the hero of *The Trial*—the will to struggle—is not sufficient to say that the two are one and the same. K.'s humble social status does not ensure him anything more than the condition of a workman (*Arbeitsein*); not for him the arrogance that is the prerogative of the logic of the citizen. To him it would be unthinkable, for instance, to bribe the officials—as it would be to Amalia's father, in his attempts to rehabilitate his daughter.

The similarities and differences between K. and Joseph K. come out clearly in K.'s conversation with Barnabas, the messenger. Like Joseph K., the

Land Surveyor is naive; this is manifested in his belief in his own superiority in relation to the villagers. If they are hostile to him or avoid him, K. remains unaffected, because he feels he has already been accepted by the Castle. Joseph K.'s naiveté led to his quixotism; K.'s naiveté is expressed in his eagerness to establish communication with the Castle.

Another similarity is clear, in spite of their different trajectories and social positions: the Law, in its tortuous, enigmatic way, always operates against the intruder. From this perspective, the peculiar Quixote (Joseph K.) and the Stranger (K.) are one and the same. It is because of this effect of the Law that we can think of *The Castle* as a variant of *The Trial*. Thus, we may use elements of one in order to illuminate the other. But before we attempt this, we must carry our preliminary investigation somewhat further.

The second similarity we have referred to—the constitution of the figure of the Intruder by the minions of the Law—engenders a third: the Intruder, whether in his own town or in the farthest reaches of the West, is exiled because of the segregation that victimizes him. The evident alliance between masters and slaves—judges and informers, castellans and peasants—which, however, in *The Castle*, being based on the terror of the villagers, only makes all the more flagrant the exclusion of the Intruder, in *The Trial* was still disguised by the apparent solidarity that Joseph K. met with.

Out of the set of features we have examined, then, only social status and the desire for integration distinguish K. This means that the novel is a reflection on power and its relation to the Law, but from a perspective different from that of *The Trial*: the workman is not the citizen; the logic of one is different from the other's; both, however, are marked by the same excessive behavior. This change in perspective of the power-Law relation is brought out more vividly by an examination of K.'s relationship with Frieda.

Although Frieda's status in the Herrenhof is lowly and her features are plain, K. becomes obsessed with her, falls in love with her, when he learns that she is the lover of Herr Klamm, the chief. K.'s seduction of Frieda is manifestly the search for a way of gaining entry to the Castle. K., though an anti-Quixote, is as daring as Joseph K. in his attempts to get close to power, and his boldness is increased by the feeling of exclusion aroused in him by the unmistakable antipathy with which the villagers treat him. Anxious to find legitimation, something Frieda can give him only in a provisional way, facing general hostility, K. embraces Frieda in a love scene that involves lust and dirt, in addition to the consciousness that, in the adjoining room, sits the chief and K.'s rival, Klamm.

In a few lines Kafka condenses the Land Surveyor's ambition and his humble Dasein:

> There, hours went past, hours in which they breathed as one, in which their hearts beat as one, hours in which K. was haunted by the feeling that he was losing himself or wandering into a strange country, farther than ever man had wandered before, a country so strange that not even the air had anything in common with his native air, where one might die of strangeness, and yet whose enchantment was such that one could only go on and lose oneself further. (Kafka 1966: 46)

The vertigo that K. experiences, the overpowering strangeness of the air in comparison with that of his native town (*Heimatluft*), could not be mistaken for the madness of passion. What intoxicates him is not the smell of beer coming from the floor where he rolls with Frieda, but the duplicity between eros and power. Frieda is more than a mere pragmatic tool, but she is surely a door that may take him into the corridor he is eager to reach.

Finding himself in the inn where the masters stay, K. believes his goal is just around the corner: he will speak with Klamm, be received by him, with no mediators. At first, all K. wanted to achieve by this was to secure his job. After his conquest of Frieda, something more personal is added: he wants to speak to Klamm as one man to another, compensating for his apparent inferiority with what he thinks he has already secured—his right to keep Frieda. Once he reaches the door that will give him access to his rival, he will always be able to get in, even if Frieda leaves him. Thus, when he later learns from her substitute at the Herrenhof that Klamm is in the adjoining room and about to leave, K. dares to go where only authorities are allowed, reaches the yard where the coachman awaits his master, goes into the sledge, has a drink, enjoys the warmth reserved for officials, forces Klamm to postpone his journey, is admonished, and finally leaves the battlefield.

Has K. scored a victory? The mismatch of forces is so great that he himself is aware of it. Before, when he was completely naive and certain of his acceptance, he said he wanted to be his own master. The idea of freedom, which again comes back into his mind—he "had won a freedom such as hardly anybody else had ever succeeded in winning" (p. 105)—on the one hand reinforces his old way of being, but on the other signals the end of his naive hopes:

> It seemed to K. as if at last those people had broken off all relations with him, and as if now in reality he were freer than he had ever been, and at liberty to wait here in this place usually forbidden to him as long as he desired, and had won a freedom such as hardly anybody else had ever succeeded in winning, and as if nobody could dare to touch him or drive him away, or even speak to him; but— this conviction was at least equally strong—as if at the same time there was nothing more senseless, nothing more hopeless, than this freedom, this waiting, this inviolability. (p. 105)

But the disappointment is not so strong as to make him give up his goal. The reflections that had been inspired by the loss of the opportunity to speak with Klamm had been no more than a flash, a brief delusion. That way lay defeat and nothing else. So K. blocks it out of his consciousness, and his old naiveté reappears as stubbornness. Obstinately, as if he has learned nothing from his recent experience, K. affirms to himself his inexorable goal:

> He, who with all his powers strove to get a glimpse of Klamm, valued very little, for instance, the post of a Momus who was permitted to live in Klamm's eye; for it was not Klamm's environment in itself that seemed to him worth striving for, but rather that he, K., he only and no one else, should attain to Klamm, and should attain to him not to rest with him, but to go on beyond him, farther yet, into the Castle. (p. 109)

One will not be able fully to understand K.'s desire for integration unless one considers that it also involves an obsessive purpose of ascent. This is important because it helps us, with hindsight, to desublimate Joseph K.'s struggle. We have been seeing him as a quixotic figure. But we failed to see a further irony. Joseph K.'s quixotism was that of a man who defended the rights reserved to those whose posts were now sought by the Land Surveyor. This also affects our reading of "In the Penal Colony." There the stranger, a traveler whose social status is secure, is another observer and analyst. In *The Castle*, the stranger becomes the Intruder because he insists on penetrating a social order that rejects him. Joseph K. and the officer–judge belong to an order that is no longer in force, even though this order corresponds diachronically to different times: the pre-Panopticon era and the age of the Panopticon. The priest, the painter, the Advocate and his lover, and the countless officials in *The Trial*, like the new commandant and the wives of the other officers in the colony, belong to the new, invisible order. As he focuses different objects under a constant Law, Kafka creates in each case, for his text, a different space, so that his permanent question is seen in various perspectives.

This mobility, together with the cold analysis it allows, highlights the fact that there is no particular empathy for any of the characters. None stands for the author, for in each the examination begins anew that aims at the very least to understand his impasse, since to escape it seems impossible. Curiously enough, the most aggressive attitudes belong to the character whose one goal is to achieve integration. Although frustrated, K. is a sort of self-made man reduced to his minimal expression; or, to use an image more congenial to Kafka, a man of the country trying to break into the fortress of the Law.

The similarities between the *Am-ha'arez*, the man of the country, and the Land Surveyor have already been pointed out (see Politzer 1978: 345–51), but in a different sense. In *The Trial*, the man of the people was stopped by the first doorman, and his story was dissected by the subtle and erudite prison chaplain. In *The Castle*, the Land Surveyor is similarly stopped by lower-echelon officials. The excessiveness we saw as a characteristic of his conduct is a quality that signals the adoption of the viewpoint of the social order into which he desires to be integrated. Is the Law that justifies this order a religious one? Is, then, the meaning of the story theological? Although we do not deny that religious overtones are present and that K. may be a character in the "new Kabbalah" that Kafka felt attracted to, it is no less clear that this religious way takes place by a strictly secular path: that of the questioning of power, even more explicitly in *The Castle* than in the earlier novel. The villagers support the power established in the Castle, whether by fear or by terror, and thus confirm it. It is this pact between masters and slaves that makes the Land Surveyor an Intruder. The villagers are hostile to him because they are aware that his acts deviate from the routine they follow and cherish. This much is said by the least aggressive of the characters.

The landlord cannot understand why K. is leaving the Herrenhof when he is expected to be received by Klamm's secretary. K. explains that he has not allowed himself to be examined, which would have meant giving in to an official whim. But K. feels that the landlord accepts his explanation only out of politeness and asks him whether the examination was important. " 'Well, yes,' replied the landlord. 'I shouldn't have refused," said K. 'No,' replied the landlord, 'you shouldn't have done that' " (Kafka 1966: 114). The landlord's politeness is really a form of indifference to the Land Surveyor's strangeness.

The landlord's wife, however, does not conceal her indignation. She sees the stranger not as a naif, but as an ambitious man, who used Frieda as a stepping-stone. Frieda tells him:

> The landlady doesn't claim to know what you want from Klamm, she merely maintains that before you knew me you strove as eagerly to reach Klamm as you have done since. The only difference was this, that before you knew me you were without any hope, but that now you imagine that in me you have a reliable means of reaching Klamm certainly and quickly and even with advantage to yourself. (p. 148)

The landlady's opinion is probably the same as the one the reader has arrived at. The unreliability of the narrator in Kafka does not make it impossible to understand the protagonist's goal. Rather, this goal is presented in the starkest fashion, both in the hero's monologues and in the comments of those who observe him. But the counterpart of this stark clarity, as we shall see shortly, is the fact that not all of the Land Surveyor's motives are shown. The persistence of his naiveté is manifested in his inability to learn from his mistakes.

Kafka's protagonists are one-way streets. It is precisely the lack of substance of the humanly conceivable Law that makes it impossible for them to grasp its order. Thus, even if we admit the existence of a theological plane in Kafka's work, it is not arbitrary to observe its similarities to the religious-negative version. But clearly this is not—even in *The Castle*—the most salient plane in the texts; what is most conspicuous is the detailed, punctual presentation of the machinery of the Law, the impossibility of having access to it by rationally conceived tactics of defense (Joseph K.) or attack (the Land Surveyor). This is not to say that in Kafka power is fate; this would be, once again, to treat his themes as if they were timeless and to fail to see their unmistakable concreteness. Nor is it to say that in Kafka power has no logic of its own: what is meant is that this is a logic of administration. As such, power acknowledges only those who command and those who obey; the obedient are rewarded with a certain amount of commanding power.

Those who are excluded from the circuit of power are nonetheless necessary as well. They are the Intruders. No romanticizing will reward them. They are excluded not because they are better, or because their human substance is less corruptible, but because without them the machinery would not run against any friction. It is the excluded who make it possible to conceive of transcending the machinery of the Law. But since this transcendence can only be negative—that is, it can never be substantialized—to describe the excluded is to highlight the conveyor belts and the temporal corridors of the Law. The task of the excluded is not condemned, identified with a hubris that cannot understand the order of the gods: since there is no substance, there are no gods. And they are not replaced by the absurd, as was often said in the days when French Existentialism was popular. To speak of the absurd is still to presume some kind of substance.

THE CORRIDORS OF THE LAW

It is Kafka's work in its entirety, and not just the texts we are concerned with here, that shows his obsession with the issue of power and its operation. The fact that he deals with it in a context from which History seems to have been excluded, in contrast with what a writer such as André Malraux does in *Man's Hope* and *Man's Fate*; the semantic instability of the narrative; the religious anxiety; and the frequent adoption of the form of the fable and the parable, usually associated with biblical literature—all of these made it difficult for criticism to recognize the nature of Kafka's work. And matters were made even worse by the narrowness of Czech Marxist critics, who were best positioned to understand it. Their observations—"We have spoken of the archaic character of Kafka's work that results from the fact that he sees the individual social strata as closed worlds. . . . In his attitude toward the working class,

Kafka is intellectually on the level of the utopian socialists" (Goldstücker 1981: 73), or "Joseph K.'s guilt cannot be defined with any law of petty bourgeois society. He is guilty 'only' through the complete superfluity and senselessness of his life, which is based only on apparent values" (Hájek 1981: 114)—are discouragingly mediocre.

If, however, we manage to break through the obstacles, we find that Kafka's obsession with the issue of power explains the monothematic, one-way nature of his protagonists. Given a certain problem, Joseph K. and the Land Surveyor will fight to the end. For the former, there is but a single alternative to quixotism: giving up any attempt at self-defense. Since *The Castle* was left in a less complete form than the earlier novel, we cannot tell how K. would have reacted when his situation reached its nadir. As it is, when K. takes refuge in the squalid room that Pepi shares with her roommates we see that his desire for integration is at its lowest point.

Once we identify the features of power in Kafka's monothematic works, it becomes more difficult to accept the existence of a real theological and religious dimension in his novels. As the seriousness of the Law-power theme comes to the fore, one tends to de-emphasize the religious aspect, though, as we have seen, not to deny that it is present, duly subordinated to the main axis.

Could it be that the two difficulties that challenge critics are conse-quences of Kafka's mistrust of metaphor? We have seen that he believed the language of analogies was fraudulent because it implied anthropomorphiza-tion. Thus, he was left with the alternative of dealing with the nonhuman by means of allusive language, which does not eschew metaphor but cannot be seen as being founded on it. Now, how could it be possible to reconnect the human and the divine in a nonanthropomorphized way if not by unfolding what can be experienced—that is, what is materialized as an event, fact, or accident experienced or witnessed by someone? And how can one rely on experience, with a view to a relationship that cannot be experienced, if not by alluding, by means of a radical projection, to what can be inferred from the plane of interhuman relations? On this plane, the Law-power pair becomes the privileged axis, since the Law has form only—that is, it does not translate and hence does not rely on any properties belonging to things themselves. Power operates on the same level as the Law because, analogously with the relation between the human and the divine, it assumes the link between unequals, the principle of subordination. Last, it should be considered that Kafka, unable to treat the divine analogically, could present his work only as allegory—that is, as a form the parts of which are not organically connected, where instead there is a constitutive gap.

If, then, we are right, with regard to Kafka the alternative between a religious or a "sociological" interpretation is simply not relevant. If we admit that the issue of power can be framed in sociological terms (no quotation marks here, meaning that a sociological interpretation is not necessarily seen as reflexology), we can say that the religious plane is integrated into it. Apprehended by an *allusive projection*, the divine is not named by analogy, but by contiguity.

The village ruled by the Castle is a much less complex society than the city in which Joseph K. lived. Thus, it comes as no surprise that the signs of hierarchy are much less differentiated. They are based on the primary distinction between those who live in the Castle and those who live in the village. Within the first category there is further differentiation between the higher officials, their secretaries, the messengers, and provisional employees, such as Barnabas. Within the second, there are those who serve the Castle—the Superintendent, the teacher, the people who work for the inn patronized by the lords of the Castle—and those who are afraid, the extreme case of this category being Amalia, directly responsible for her family's disgrace. Interpersonal relationships are regulated by the degree of proximity to or distance from power. Thus, there are effective relationships—such as those between higher officials and the Castle's representative in the village, the Superintendent, or that between the Superintendent and the teacher; relationships that are theoretically possible but actually unviable—between the Land Surveyor and his would-be superior; and inconceivable relationships—exemplified by K.'s question whether the teacher personally knew the Count.

Although it does not involve an inconceivable relationship, the Land Surveyor's obstinate attempts to secure an interview with Klamm are impossible in themselves: "Just listen to me, sir. Herr Klamm is a gentleman from the Castle, and that in itself, without considering Klamm's position there at all, means that he is of very high rank. But what are you, for whose marriage we are humbly considering here ways and means of getting permission? You are not from the Castle, you are not from the village, you aren't anything" (Kafka 1966: 52). True, nobody confirms the landlady's opinion, and Frieda's previous contention that it would be impossible to satisfy the Land Surveyor's wish might be taken as an effect of the landlady's influence on her. And it could also be that the villagers, in their contacts with their masters, developed habits that made access even more difficult. But the fact is that there is a marked separation between those who are above and those who, at the opposite end, are nothing.

Thus, the stranger's attitude can only be interpreted as arrogance and presumption. The village is indeed as primitive as it seemed to him upon his arrival. This is expressed by the acceptance of the manifest chasm between those who exercise power and those who are subject to it. K. is animated by his will to ascend; the self-made man in him identifies these lands in the "farthest reaches of the West" as integrated into the archaeological time in which *The Trial* is set. Our previous knowledge of what the earlier novel says about a *later* time indicates that integration in this different order will not have any major impact on the fate of the Intruder. In other words, whereas at the time corresponding to the rural setting of *The Castle*, under the sway of Count West-west, social mobility seems inconceivable, in Joseph K.'s big city it is perfectly possible, but the Law remains equally invisible in both places (see note 15 to this chapter).

The archaeology we mentioned in connection with a less complex society permits a simpler view of the operation of power. Although its representatives and mediators can be seen down below, from the outset its location is clear: the seat of power is up there, in the Castle, whereas in the "later" context of *The Trial* the system of justice is ramified throughout the whole of society. Again, in *The Castle* the authorities still have names. Count West-west is too remote for his existence to be at all certain, but Klamm, though his standing in the hierarchy is never made clear, is too concrete to be seen as an impersonal entity. Instead, he is the very embodiment of the inscrutability of power.

The Castle, however, does more than simply repeat what *The Trial* affirms. The inscrutability of power does not mean that complainants are absolutely unable to find the way to the Law. The episode of the Land Surveyor's conversation with Bürgel is one the counterpart of which is missing in *The Trial*. An analysis of this episode will retrospectively illuminate our reading of the earlier novel.

The Land Surveyor is sleepy and no longer expects that anything of any use will ever come from a conversation with a secretary not directly involved with his case; but Bürgel explains to him what the officials of the Law think about the possible chances of applicants and their pleas. Secretaries resort to a number of evasive measures in order to prevent applicants from gaining access to the official who is competent to hear them. Theoretically, however, it is not impossible that chance might favor the applicant; if Bürgel himself has never heard of such a thing actually happening, this does not necessarily mean that the possibility does not exist. "That everything should be lost is yet more improbable than the most improbable thing itself" (p. 252). But the Land Surveyor does not profit from this conversation: "K. was asleep, impervious to all that was happening" (p. 254).

Could it be that this is precisely the moment when the Land Surveyor loses his chance of solving his problem? The narrator's impartiality does not allow us to add a single word. Irony mingles with hope—it cannot even be said to stifle it. Before the Law, the pure form that is the instrument of power, not everything is lost from the outset. But the occurrence of a redeeming lucky chance only reaffirms arbitrariness.

The archaeology employed is useful for yet another purpose: to decode K.'s behavior. We have seen that the landlady's interpretation of it does not necessarily negate the motivation for K.'s interest in Frieda described in the passages in free indirect speech; both the landlady and these passages indicate that the Land Surveyor saw the girl as a tool by which to approach Klamm. This greater clarity about the character's motivation, in turn, makes it possible for Kafka to present a more complex view of the Land Surveyor. Let us analyze K.'s answers concerning his feelings for Frieda.

The most important element in the Land Surveyor's counterattack is not his accusation that, with the pretext of telling him the landlady's opinion, Frieda is also giving her own, but rather his contention that, though he acknowledges the fairness of contrary opinions, these criticisms fail to take into account the whole problem. For, he argues, if he had sought Frieda only because of the reasons she and the landlady mentioned, she would be no more than a pawn (*Pfand*) in his hands; but this would be true only if Frieda did not love him in return. In other words, the accusation would be true only if there had been no mutual love "interest"; in that case, K., in his calculated attempt to use Frieda as a tool to approach Klamm and even as a bargaining chip, would be like a crafty predator dragging his helpless prey. But if there was mutual love involved, then K.'s use of Frieda was in the interest of both (see Kafka 1966, chapter 13, especially the passage beginning on p. 147).

On the basis of this summary, then, it would seem that the Land Surveyor distinguishes between "pure" and "honest" reason. The former is pure because it is entirely ruled by mental material—calculation (with which ethical criticism returns to Kant). It is as if K. were saying: "My purpose is to get to Klamm, not in order to stop there, but as a stage in my ascent to the Castle. It is in his interest to see me because I have stolen his lover; it is in mine because I need his permit in order to marry." This implicitly contains the possibility of striking a bargain: "I am willing to make certain sacrifices, perhaps even to sacrifice my relationship with Frieda, if Klamm will open the door to me." Now, the Land Surveyor denies that such "purity" is the case, because his interest in Frieda is caused not only by his acknowledged will to ascend but also by the attraction he feels for her. Thus, reason becomes "honest" when something cloudy, emotional, passionate interferes. K. does not argue that false motives are being attributed to him, but that he is being misunderstood in that half of his motivation is not being taken into account.

Thus, power may be said to be more perfectly carried out the "purer" the reason that guides it, and, conversely, accused men and applicants stand most to lose when they are guided by "honest" reason. In this way, *The Castle* might be said not only to introduce an element that is absent in *The Trial*—the fact that, despite the insubstantiality of the Law, chance may intervene against the minions of the Law—but also to insert a Nietzschean strain in the Kantian theme.

But we shall not explore this new possibility. Instead, in order not to lose sight of our object, let us simply ask: How reliable is K.'s counterargument? Is it more than just a self-serving defense? The Land Surveyor's discussion with Olga bears him out. Although Olga's criticism of Frieda makes sense, K. not only defends her, perhaps even unreasonably, but also sees her as responsible for what he thinks he has already achieved in the village:

> True, I was engaged to come here as a Land Surveyor, yet that was only a pre-text, they were playing with me, I was driven out of everybody's house. They're playing with me still to-day; but how much more complicated the game is now that I have, so to speak, a larger circumference—which means something, it may not be much—yet I already have a home, a position and real work to do, I have a promised wife who takes her share of my professional duties when I have other business, I'm going to marry her and become a member of the community, and besides my official connexion I have also a personal connection with Klamm, although as yet I haven't been able to make use of it. (p. 187)

My purpose is not to justify the Land Surveyor or, on a more general plane, to determine which characters are reliable. (That is why we will not present an in-depth analysis of Frieda, a much more difficult character to understand than K.) What I want to do is to underscore the defining charac-teristic of *The Castle*, on the basis of the archaeological position the novel occupies in relation to the time of *The Trial*. We may then say that in *The Castle*, because it corresponds to a time previous to that of the constitutional state[15] and because it deals with a community in which social relationships are more elementary, the operation of the pair Law-power is more palpable. In this context, the explanation of K.'s conduct could be made more explicit by the introduction of an argument—the difference between "pure" and "hon-

15. This anteriority may be construed either in a diachronic or in a synchronic sense. The first possibility is more remote or less useful: the fact that the Castle officials use a telephone indicates that the time here could not possibly be much removed in the past. It seems more reasonable to think of the Count West-west's village as a contemporary of Joseph K.'s city, the difference between the forms of the Law involved being explained simply by the spatial distance. We may further hypothesize that the village is also contem-porary with the penal colony in the earlier story, both of them being spatially remote from the metropolis, with its more "advanced" system of legislation.

est" reason—which would be more difficult to make in the more complex urban environment.

Thus the two novels deal with two different instances of positive application of the Law. (Unlike "In the Penal Colony," what is involved here is not two different moments in time but rather two synchronic instances; see note 15, above.) Here, it would be interesting to consider the difference between the drawn-out trial to which Joseph K. is subjected and the summary ostracism that isolates Amalia's family. At the stage represented by the village in *The Castle*, relationships remain fundamentally personal, and an offense against an official implies the immediate punishment of the guilty person's family, without the intervention of courts of justice.

These differences, however, are more important for the way they characterize the Law-power pair. Power is asymmetrical; the Law that justifies it is so desubstantialized that those who clash against it can be successful only if they are favored by a most unlikely chance. The corridors of the Law—made up of dozens of cubicles around a courtyard, where busy minor officials deliver, claim, or negotiate exchanges of petitions, where everyone is bad-tempered, haughty, and in a hurry—are gears of a machine that is ever active, ever alert, ever feared. In *The Castle* the machinery of the Law, not disguised as the constitutional state, shows itself to the naked eye: it creates applicants only to evade their petitions. Servants exist so that, in cahoots with their masters, they will operate the machinery of power. Desubstantialized, the Law is a fiction all the more effective for being perceived as an unquestionable truth, a fiction the efficacy of which depends on its denying that it is a fiction.

The mechanism of the Law is all the more powerful for the fact that both rulers and subjects are equally convinced that the form of the Law is the form of reality. Consequently, we can also understand that the unreliability of the narrator in Kafka is less a technical procedure, the possibilities of which had been explored earlier, than a consequence of the fact that his characters are unreliable. They are unreliable not because they are necessarily unscrupulous, but because they are forbidden to be transparent to themselves. Honest reason is an impure reason because, when the purity of reason is confused with the pure calculation on which it might focus, the honesty of reason consists in its ability to see itself as moved by nonrational interests. We may even reiterate our statement in a more sophisticated form: "pure" reason is best defined not as that which is guided by a pure use of the mind, pure calculation, but as that which appears to be so because it is unable to acknowledge its nonrational motivation or because it conceals such motivation from itself.

Now we can understand better why it is that, in the novels we have analyzed, undecidability is present side by side with the painstaking and inexorable analysis of the operation of power. And, finally, we can see why both assume a lack of substance, which must be concealed so that the Law hides the absence that is constitutive of it. Thus, we can understand better why the active political aspect of Kafka's work is not incompatible with its quietist tendency.

On the basis of our analysis of *The Castle* as the rural stage of the process presented in *The Trial*, we must now turn to a final point. This has to do with the status of fictional discourse.

The Desubstantialization of the Law and the Status of the Fictional

Clearly, no serious analysis of Kafka can sidestep the subtle problems raised by his work. But the present book is not addressed only to specialists. In this section, concerned as it is with a topic of general interest, a broader approach is convenient.

What do we mean when we say a text is literary? If, given the various kinds of appreciation of literature, we ask this question, we find that three criteria are extant. First, as a part of so-called belles lettres, literature implies beautiful writing. Second, a text is said to be literary when it has a fictional or documentary plot and presents the image (potentially, the portrait) of a state of society, or represents an image of life. Third, a literary text is one that actualizes in words a discursive mode: fictional discourse.

These criteria could not but be discordant, even inconsistent, since they belong to different times, though the effort is seldom made to place them in history and spell them out clearly. The first is derived from Renaissance poetics: literature is seen not as an autonomous territory, but as a part of rhetoric. As such, its study benefited from the examination of the rhetorical treatises of classical antiquity and concentrated on questions of proper diction and discrimination of figures of speech. The discomfort we feel before its characterization of literature as beautiful writing is a consequence of the fact that today it is no more than the residue of a classification no longer in force. For in relation to what other kind of text is literature said to be beautiful? When is an author not expected to write a beautiful text, or when is one *not* expected to trouble oneself with beauty? In the Renaissance, a play and a historical narrative were supposed to be equally beautiful. Written in ornate language, avoiding the commonplace and the trivial, plays, lyrical poems, letters, and historical essays were all addressed to the attention of a sophisticated public. Attention is perhaps not the best term here: it might be better to say instead "the ears of a sophisticated public." For this writing was meant more for the ear than for the eye. All language considered vulgar or obscene, arousing belly laughter or redolent of the street or marketplace, the sort of popular and frank language that Rabelais inherited from the medieval genres, was not in conformity with the decorum that was expected of belles lettres, seen as a sign of distinction, a mark of social differentiation.

When, in the present times, whether or not aware of this historical background, we apply the first criterion, not only do we fail to say anything of any use about literary objects but we confuse the common reader. Freud, for instance, was awarded a literary prize for works that distinguished themselves for their sophisticated use of language. More recently, the same prize was given to a contemporary philosopher. Does this mean that the panel considered these two writers fine novelists? Quite probably both of them would be offended by such praise. Such reactions would be unthinkable until the late eighteenth century, for the criterion of belles lettres did not assume either the existence of the novel or that of the humanities, let alone the differentiation between philosophy and each of them that arose only when these different modalities were recognized as such. That is, the criterion of belles lettres implied the existence of discursive alternatives quite different from those that came to be known in the modern age. These alternatives disappeared, together with the criterion of distinction—the man educated for the court, the perfection of the courtier—they presupposed. Instead, another basis was founded: the acknowledgment of the self, of individual subjectivity as a theme for exploration.

The second criterion is much more recent. Though already legitimated in Montaigne's *Essays*, it became more widespread in the early decades of the nineteenth century. As an expression of the creator's individuality, literature was seen as the means through which a time, an era, a social and human situation were represented. With the "normalization" of Romanticism, literature became a potentially differentiated discourse—that is, freed of norms and requirements proper to other modes of writing. Its immediate object was neither to edify nor to delight the reader, but to express the author. The very term "author" had suffered a significant shift: whereas the Latin root of "author," *auctor*, earlier connoted authority, with the full legitimation of individual subjectivity the author became responsible for what he or she wrote, and a literary author came to mean one who expresses what takes place in his or her subjective world. It would be interesting to examine how, in this way, recognition of literary expression involved the problem of the relations between the rights of the individual and society. Here we shall do no more than note that the assertion of the individual was decisive for the idea of a discourse potentially freed from collective requirements, and equally decisive for the concept "literary work," as long as individual aspirations and collective values did not clash. Now, this clash is quite visible in the trials of Flaubert and Baudelaire, both accused precisely of attacking moral values, and it is an important element of Poe's prestige in Europe; thus, by the mid-nineteenth century the defining criterion of literature as expression of individuality was problematic. This criterion became increasingly vague and inadequate.

Let us add that the conception of "literary work" as the expression of authorial individuality assumed that the author and the society he or she lived in had compatible values. We are not saying that this was actually the case, but that it was assumed by the criterion. Thus, the affirmation of the literary character of a work was subject to the previous evaluation of the values it propagated as acceptable or unacceptable to those who represented power. It is often said that in the nineteenth century literature came to be seen as an indispensable ingredient in the education of a refined person. But it is not always added that such literature was not to offend one's good feelings or to lead one astray from the ideals of the "good society." The formation of the literary canon—that is, the list of works considered obligatory for higher culture and the kind of interpretation they were submitted to—presupposed both society's acknowledgment of the individual subject and the latter's acceptance of the basic values thus legitimated. Let us also add that it is not by accident, incompetence, or negligence that this definition of literature fails to delimit the field of literature properly. One may well ask, for instance: Why should a different kind of text, whether or not it contained a socially legitimated justification, be seen as a minor expression of a state of society?

This question, if indeed it was ever asked, had no historical consequence. The reason for this is simple: it is only apparently that the characterization on which the criterion is based—language as an expression of a state of society— is descriptive. It is, in fact, a normative criterion: the works we recognize as literary are those that allow an interpretation showing the state of society acceptable to the legitimated point of view. The criterion does not apply to texts meant for a specialized public. It would be otiose to ask whether these do not also express the state of society that gave rise to them. The question would be useless because the criterion presiding over their circulation would not be the same. In any case, since throughout the nineteenth century the literary text was the form of socialization par excellence, it had to respect, endorse, and propagate the hierarchy of values and modes of conduct. Thus, the criterion singularized the literary text explicitly and gave it prestige even as it imposed a social function on it.

Now, as the examples of Flaubert and Baudelaire make clear, this requirement of homogeneity came to be questioned in actual practice. The guiding focus of adequate reception, the narrator or lyrical voice, became either unreliable (Flaubert) or provoked a shock experienced by the reader as an aggression (Baudelaire). It will be worthwhile to quote Sainte-Beuve on Baudelaire here. Excusing himself for not having written about his friend's book, the famous critic imagines he would have told him: "You are too suspicious of passion, natural passion. . . . Let yourself go, do not be so afraid of feeling as others do, never fear being too ordinary" (Sainte-Beuve 1933: 44). The passage is a masterpiece of euphemism. Under the pretext of giving the poet advice, the critic accuses him of laying too much emphasis on "natural passion" and being hamstrung by the fear of "feeling as others feel!" The problem, then, is not that Baudelaire felt differently from everyone—a serious crime against social homogeneity—but only that his style was negatively affected by a fear that was in fact unfounded.

What Sainte-Beuve could not possibly have predicted was that the task of official critics would become increasingly embarrassing, that the styles of authors were to become more and more offensive. From then on, the criterion emphasizing the homogeneity of values would rely either on excluding rebels from the pantheon of canonical writers or on avoiding the propagation of their lesson. Since the first alternative, though it was tried, ultimately failed, and since the example of rebel writers was propagated in their own countries and abroad, the criterion could satisfy only the smug or the lazy.

In other words, it was the literary object itself that called for criteria taking into account their discursive specificity. As we saw in the previous chapter, this requirement did not appear first in the mid-nineteenth century; it was already clear to the early German romantics. But, as was shown, this criterion was short lived and was soon replaced by historiographical description in the work of the man who had been its major champion. In other words, historiographical description, as well as the criteria that attempted to explain the character and quality of the literary work as a function of social mechanisms, were the means through which the subsystem of literary power attempted to reconcile the basis of the criterion—literature as the expression of individuality—with the norms that could be legitimated in post-Napoleonic society.

As literary studies acquired legitimacy, together with the rise of History as a branch of knowledge and the appearance of the "human sciences," it came to be necessary that the study of literature also become "scientific." Thus, to take literary works as expressions of an environment—geographical, sociohistorical, ethnic, and so on—was the way to bring to light the homogeneity manifested by the work. To treat it otherwise would be to fall back on the dangerous individualism of the romantics, to return to the otiose conflict between the rights of the individual and the obligations imposed by society.

The idea of science intervened in favor of the homogeneity that must be assured. It had the additional advantage of not forcing the critic to endorse values already official. This interpretation may emphasize another form of homogeneity: for instance, to elect an author for his or her rebelliousness, as long as it is added that this rebelliousness points to a different social order. Another solution also presented itself: the aestheticization of literature, art, and life itself (see the final section of Chapter 2).

The third criterion, then, reflects the need to return to the critical path opened by the early German romantics. If what characterizes a discourse is the fact that it establishes a *territoriality*, its identification by the receptor will depend on the presence of specific marks—that is, traits that the reader expects to find in a work belonging to the discursive mode in question. The contemporary reader, for instance, expects both an autobiography and a historiographical essay to be truthful accounts of the past. But the two expectations do not have identical parameters; otherwise, autobiography and historiographical essay would be one and the same thing. In addition to reporting true facts, autobiography is assumed to be restricted to the viewpoint and individuality of the one who presents the facts. This is why autobiography is often seen as a literary genre: for are we not told that literature is the expression of individuality?

This observation will serve at least to provide a quick insight into the difference introduced by the criterion of fictionality and the attempt to use it to characterize the literary work. What, then, is the specificity of fictional discourse? That is: Why would it be arbitrary to say that if there is no substance to which the term refers, all discourse is fictional?

Fictional discourse is characterized first by its peculiar position in relation to the question of truth. All other discursive forms, from the various forms of actualization of pragmatic everyday speech to religious, scientific, and philosophical discourse, have in common the assumption of truth. Hence, there are penalties and sanctions for those who are caught in a lie or falsification, and excommunications for those who dare to interpret the affirmed truths their own way. The assumption of truth holds from the humblest rites of everyday life all the way to the allegation that such and such an experiment validates a given scientific hypothesis. What is different about these various discursive modalities is the apparatus of truth. Validation of hypotheses works in science but not in religion; the role played by inner belief or conviction in religion has no place in philosophy, whose truth apparatus rests on the effectiveness of the problematization offered, and so on.

Fictional discourse is in a class all its own because it suspends the question of truth. It does not say that this question ought to be abolished as irrelevant to its purposes; rather, it places the issue at a sufficient remove to allow it to be seen in perspective. If the reader is unfamiliar with this reasoning, let him or her picture the situation of a spectator in a theater. The scene is recognizable to the spectator. However, aware of the fact that the scene in question is not connected with the pragmatics of everyday life—that is, that the actors and actresses are performing—the spectator is in the privileged position of being able to see from a distance the workings of values, customs, habits, and automatic attitudes that may be his or hers. That is, the depragmatization of familiar or conceivable situations allows the spectator to see them from a critical remove. Thus, fiction operates by means of disconnection from ordinary pragmatics—whether that of everyday existence or that of another discourse—in order to actualize its own pragmatics: that of placing in perspective, or in question, or allowing the critical viewing of, norms, values, and behaviors that the receiver recognizes or even shares.

Whether our knowledge of this characterization of the literary object is more or less refined will not make a fundamental difference, for from a general point of view what matters first of all is that it provides the means for evaluating the contemporary receiver. But from this it should not be concluded that the acknowledgment of the fictionality of the work of art today is no more than a routine mark, one that requires no further reflection. We shall simply say that it is a part of the expectations of a reasonably well-informed person.

Only now can we see what these considerations point to. If it is true that the idea of fictionality is a part of the contemporary expectations of the common reader of literary works, one can understand the disturbance brought about by Kafka's works. But for this to become perfectly clear one further point must be elaborated. We have said that the pragmatics of the fictional are related to the possibility of questioning "truths" that are recognized or shared by the receiver. For this to take place, this questioning must not involve the norms and values in force in their entirety. Perspectivization itself rests on the soil that remains stable. For instance, if one is to be moved to tears, one must be sure that one is at the theater. If the theater is to question the world, the very existence of the theater must remain unquestioned. If every questioning has a destabilizing effect, the questioning made possible by the fictional assumes that something remains stable. For, however unique fictional discourse may be, it, like any other discourse, rests on a social pact. And it is this pact that bars unlimited questioning.

Once the notion of a pact is introduced, it must be said that it is not through the pact itself that criticity is actualized by the literary work. To say this would be tantamount to saying that, since the late eighteenth century,

Western society has been so liberal as to legitimate a discourse the purpose of which is to criticize Western institutions![16] Criticity imposed itself in spite of the pact. The direct intervention of the pact takes place only through the acceptance of a discourse that provides intellectual pleasure. That is, fictional discourse, as it is socially legitimated, contains a double and not always consistent motivation: it is the discourse that gives the receiver intellectual pleasure and, at the same time, the discourse that makes it possible to question in part, or at least in nonabsolute terms, the truths in force. The effectiveness of the fictional depends on the interaction of these two properties: the pleasure it provides and the relative questioning it provokes. If, on the one hand, it is fundamentally questioning and critical, it is identified as philosophy; if, on the other, it is fundamentally a source of pleasure, it is seen as entertainment. In either case it loses its identity and finds itself in a position of disadvantage in which to be compared with other modes of expression.

We are then in a position to explain why Kafka's work affects socialized expectations about fictional discourse. What he does, particularly in the novel closest to his readers' actual experience, *The Trial*, is precisely to destabilize the entire theater. We have been shown the stages through which the Law was converted into a positive norm, up to the advent of the state in which Western readers believe they live. In *The Trial*, full recognition of the constitutional state is accompanied by the corrosion of its reality. The narrator's remove from the protagonist creates for the reader a gap that he or she cannot fill by means of identification with any other character. Hence, we can see the attractiveness of religious and existential explanations: to endorse one or the other amounts to asserting that something remains unquestioned in the novel (religious search or the need to justify existence). But if these dimensions are subordinated to or compromised by the protean ramifications of the machinery of the Law, where can the reader find a ground on which to base his or her customary reception of fiction? Where can he or she find something to hold on to?

Thus, either this invading Law is the harbinger of the postliberal era or

16. Contrast the naiveness of such a hypothesis with the bluntness of a defender of the pact, indignant about the opportunists who take advantage of it: "Only the societies of the modern Western world have been wealthy, confident, and tolerant enough to support institutions like literature whose *raison d'être* has been to criticize the established social order and its central values. In more traditional societies, all institutions function strictly as legitimators of the existing order, and even in modern Western society other institutions, like religion, the media, and the law, that to some degree criticize the establishment, always end as the stoutest defenders of the *status quo*, revealing weaknesses only to preserve strength. . . . Only the arts, and particularly literature, continue at every opportunity to bite the hand that feeds them" (Kernan 1990: 24–25).

else this development is the consequence of something inherent to the insubstantiality of the Law as a human creation. The identification of Kafka's world with Nazi terror or Stalinist totalitarianism was an actualization of the first hypothesis. But this would imply that Kafka had a prophetic capacity that Benjamin, even before this reading was popularized, had already questioned, in a letter to Gershom Scholem dated June 12, 1938: "Kafka lives in a *complementary* world. (In this he is quite close to Klee, whose work is as essentially *isolated* in the sphere of painting as is Kafka's in that of literature.) Kafka discerned the complement without discerning what surrounded it . . . ; no comprehensive view, also no 'prophetic gift.' Kafka listened to the tradition attentively, and he who strains to hear does not see" (Benjamin 1978, 2: 762). The complementary world that Kafka perceived had nothing to do with prophecy because it was an aspect of the present. The complement has to do with what was already contemporary to the constitutional state in which Joseph K. still believes he lives.

Having discarded the prophecy hypothesis, let us see what the second one has to offer us. What does it mean to say that the unlimited arbitrariness of the Law is the consequence of a growth that is inherent to it? It means that Kafka, like Kleist, is overwhelmed by the terror resulting from the fact that the ambition of reason is not commensurate with the results of the understanding. If man can know only the objects of experience, then he can know only the appearance (*Schein*), the phenomenon. This is the only possible object of science, which reaches its goal when it formulates the law of phenomena. Thus, phenomena are not valid for the field of morals.

How, then, can the philosopher speak of moral law? Although the word used is the same, "law," its meaning is quite different. The universality claimed by moral law assumes an operation radically different from that claimed by scientific law. The latter homogenizes a result because the intuitions of sensibility and the categories with which the understanding operates find the proof of their objectivity in experience, whereas through practical reason man represents only what ought to exist (see Kant 1965: 526). It may then be said that moral law amounts to a *necessary fiction*. The fact that moral law is the product of the internalization of freedom as duty had seemed to Kant sufficient to protect it against the instability brought about by fictions. What obsesses Kafka, in contrast, is the instability, the lack of a basis in something demonstrable that might translate into a precept of moral law. We need not, then, invest him with a prophetic gift in order to understand his nightmare: instability was complementary to his world.

Why do we say *his* world rather than the human world? To understand this restriction, it is necessary to explain more fully the social context on the basis of which Kafka's peculiar sensibility developed. "His world" refers not only to what is proper to the world he knew, but to what is complementary to it—that is, every world capable of being perceived as a complement of what his world was.

Given the available documentation, no one would dare affirm that Kafka was obsessed by the question of the Law from his reading of Kant. It was his *Umwelt*, his particular circumstance, and within it the influence of the Jewish tradition emphasized by Haas and Benjamin, that was responsible for his perception of the "complement." It was because of this sensibility to the complementary aspect of the world he lived in that Kafka's fiction ventured outside the bounds of the fictional experience legitimated in modernity. Let us repeat: this experience assumes that values may be questioned as long as some value remains stable; that is, a limit is set to fictional questioning. If, instead, everything is questioned, the questioning source itself becomes socially intolerable because everything is destabilized. But this is precisely what Kafka does. In his works, the fictional object never allows one to say, in relief: "Well, after all, the world is not like that—or, in any case, there's more to it than that"; or, in concrete terms, "Outside the world of *The Trial*, laws are still respected and the police can't knock on my door whenever they want to." In *The Trial*, the basic fiction *is* the rule of law in a constitutional state. Kafka's, then, is a fictional work that, without claiming to be the truth, for it asserts none, questions "truths" as fictions.

Let us make one final clarification: It would be a misunderstanding to conclude that what is said in the present section concerning Kafka's position vis-à-vis the status of fiction in modernity applies to literary works in general. If the concept of fictionality is applied outside the temporal scope of modernity, the mistake is inevitable. For instance, René Wellek attacked Auerbach's *Mimesis* for allegedly failing to respect boundaries and for containing "a conception of criticism and scholarship" he considered "an extremely dangerous one" (Wellek 1954: 305); one might then conclude that I am implicitly on Wellek's side. Nothing could be further from the truth.

No historical criterion, precisely because it is historical, can account for what we call a literary object. Since there is no match between a criterion taken from the praxis of a historical period—as fiction in the case of modernity—and the presence of literary works, we must either develop a meta-historical criterion, like Auerbach's realism, or—what is less risky—develop a historico-cultural analysis of the functions carried out by the discourses in force during the period in question. It should be stressed, then, that this criterion of the fictional is no Procrustean bed that excludes from literature everything that does not fit into it. It is a tool in the hands of the historico-textual intelligence of a mode of discourse, not a resource to be put to use in any taxonomy.

Kafka's Context

I have been presenting a certain line of interpretation of Kafka's work. This could now be extended and applied to a larger corpus, but I believe it will be more effective instead to discuss Kafka's background. Such a discussion might be out of place if my purpose were to write a study of Kafka's work and not, as is the case, to use an analysis of it to draw conclusions about a number of interrelated issues.

Kafka's family belonged to the Jewish community of southern Bohemia, the legal emancipation of which had been one of the measures taken as part of the celebrations of the coronation of the emperor Franz Joseph in 1849.

The writer's father, Hermann Kafka, the son of a Jewish butcher, was born in 1852, in the town of Osek. After a childhood marked by a poverty his own children would never experience, Hermann moved to Prague, where, thanks to his economical habits and his marriage to Julie Löwy, he eventually became the prosperous owner of a medium-sized business. Hermann and Julie had quite different backgrounds. The Löwys, a family of rabbis, represented a tradition of spirituality, of contact with the living forces that ensured the survival of the Jewish community in spite of the Diaspora. In contrast, Hermann, who had been forced to work hard to escape extreme poverty, stood for rough edges, strength of will, and a rigid work ethic. Having received a traditional upbringing, Julie never objected to Hermann's harsh way of treating his children; on the contrary, she backed up her enterprising husband at all times. Thus, the fact that their mother belonged to a rabbinical family had no impact on the children's education, only nominally Jewish.

Franz, the eldest child, was born in Prague, in the old part of the town, close to the ghetto, which by the time of his birth had already been destroyed. Although the ghetto itself no longer existed and the Jewish population had been integrated in order to join the labor force, out of its ashes had grown the symbolic ghetto that Kafka was to know as a young man: "the German 'ghetto,' as the phrase went" (Hermsdorf, in Kafka 1983: 8). Living in the capital of the Czech renaissance, the Germans were "merchants, professors, upper-echelon officials, employees of the state administration," but "there was hardly a German proletariat to speak of" (p. 9). Thus, integrated into the machinery of empire and the professions but disconnected from the mass of common workers, the Germans were a separate group; in his introduction to

Kafka's stories, Klaus Hermsdorf emphasizes that they had few relations with the Czech population outside of business. For this reason they were viewed with mistrust by the Czech majority, who accused them—and not without reason—of defending the Austro-Hungarian status quo.

The first conflict, then, is this: Jewish emancipation meant, in actual practice, the absorption of Jews into another non-Czech group, whose language they appropriated, whose schools their children were sent to, even as their link with the Jewish tradition, centering on the synagogue, was reduced to the bare minimum. However, this absorption did not ensure the Jews freedom from the ghetto. Identified as Germans, they remained an unassimilated body within the nation but were not accepted by the minority with which they tried to identify. Although to the Czechs the Jews, as a minority that defended a regime from which the Czechs wanted to free themselves, were not differentiated from the Germans, to the German population the Jews were just as undesirable. Thus, they were caught between two masses, belonging to neither and facing the hostility of both.

This was the situation in Prague just before the Great War. According to Hermsdorf, "nowhere else in Europe was the sense of the unreality of reality as palpable . . . as it was in German Prague before World War I" (pp. 10–11). Another biographer observes that Prague offered Kafka the knowledge "of the various ways of modern alienation" (Wagenbach 1964: 135). Whereas Hermsdorf highlights the view of the city from the standpoint of the finished work, Wagenbach does it from that of its own heterogeneity. Both, however, see Prague as the opposite end of the umbilical cord of Kafka's work. Further, the numerous references to the city in his letters and diaries are negative. Yet, though he often planned to move away, he did so only toward the end of his life, for a period shortened by the catastrophic situation of postwar Berlin and by his own delicate health. Like opposite poles, Prague and Kafka attracted each other. Although only those who have been there will be able to see the city in his works, any reader can sense it in the abstract as the "unreal city," the center of modern alienation (*Entfremdung*).

Whether because he needed to depend on his family or because he feared the discomforts of migration, the fact is that Kafka remained as a witness to the particular babel of his city. Thus, we must examine the conflicts between the three peoples who lived in it. What was behind these conflicts?

The legal emancipation of the Bohemian Jews had the effect of making them seek integration into the German community. In this a politico-economic factor must have been decisive: since German was the official language of the Habsburg empire, integration into German culture was an easier way to overcome the economic and social obstacles implied by the marginalization of the Jews. In contrast, identification with the Czechs promised no more than the prospect of entering a war of nationalities and adopting a language without a country and without prestige. The generation of Kafka's parents had worked hard at acculturation. Although Hermann's everyday language must have been Czech, and his German was only barely adequate—Wagenbach observes that a letter of his to Julie, then his fiancée, closely follows a model in a letter-writing manual—it must have seemed to him that the only way to gain socioeconomic status was to be assimilated into the German-speaking community, which was quite small: "In 1900, only 34,000 of the 450,000 inhabitants of Prague spoke German" (Wagenbach 1964: 16). This conviction was probably shared by most of the recently emancipated Jewish population. Otherwise it would be hard to explain why the Jewish elementary school should be German-oriented, a fact that champions of Czech autonomy saw as responsible for the preservation of German influence in Bohemia (see Riff 1976: 10).

The pro-Germanism of Jews encouraged anti-Semitism, particularly among the lower classes. In this way anti-Semitism became a political instrument in the conflicts that sharpened increasingly from the 1890's on. Riff mentions a number of events that were certainly known to Kafka and all his contemporaries.

In 1892, a member of the *Reichsrat* (Council of the Empire), E. Schneider, in a visit to Prague, recommended that the alliance of Czechs be founded on "the anti-Semitic question." In the absence of a cause, a cause was duly fabricated: Jews were accused of the "ritual murder" of Christians. The climate of mass hysteria culminated in 1899 with the trial of Leopold Hilsner, accused of killing Agnes Hruza, in Polná (northeastern Bohemia). The episode started a wave of anti-Semitic riots that reached Prague and did not involve Czechs only: "The antisemitic Austrian priest, Father Josef Deckert, published one of the first pamphlets alleging that Agnes Hruza was the victim of a ritual murder. In Vienna, the anti-Jewish newspaper, *Deutsches Volksblatt*, echoed him, but both publications were seized and appeals to higher courts against confiscation were rejected" (Riff 1976: 12).

However, the intervention of the imperial courts did not put an end to the issue. Antagonized by the German communities, the Jews were seen by Czech patriots as an antinationalistic minority. In late 1897, in Prague, there were attacks against cafés patronized or owned by Jews, the synagogues, and the new German theater. Martial law was imposed on the city, but it served only to contain the most conspicuous forms of violence. Anti-Semitism smoldered on, and Hilsner was twice found guilty (in 1899 and 1900). It was only in 1918 that his innocence was proved and his freedom ensured.

Our purpose here is less to emphasize the significance of the Hilsner trial, which would not have ballooned to such proportions if not for the animosity directed at Jews—and if one thinks of the Dreyfus affairs, also taking place at the time, one realizes that such feelings were by no means restricted to the uneducated classes of a subject nation—than to underscore the failure of the Czech Jews' attempt at assimilation. The generation that had opted for assimilation had tried to join a group that now rejected it. In the process, the Jews had reduced their contacts with their own roots to a minimum; their religious practices were no more than a half-forgotten, automatized routine; and their children were encouraged to speak German as their native language, to see German culture as their heritage. The same process was going on in other countries as well: in Germany, it began with the generation of the parents of Auerbach, Benjamin, Scholem, Löwenthal, and Adorno, the generation of Cassirer.

But in Czechoslovakia the catastrophe, though less bloody, took place earlier. The only heritage that assimilated parents bequeathed to their children was their own deracination. Even more than in "Letter to His Father" ("Brief an den Vater"), it was in a letter to Milena, dated May 30, 1920, that Kafka emphasized the effects of failed acculturation:

> The insecure position of Jews, insecure within themselves, insecure among people, would make it above all comprehensible that they consider themselves to be allowed to own only what they hold in their hands or between their teeth, that furthermore only palpable possessions give them the right to live, and that they will never again acquire what they once have lost but that instead it calmly swims away from them forever. From the most improbable sides Jews are threatened with danger, or let us, to be more exact, leave the dangers aside and say that they are threatened with threats. (Kafka 1954a: 50–51)

This reflection is applicable not only to his parents' generation but also to his own. In this way Kafka justifies his father's attachment to material things; he and others like him can feel safe only about what they can grab because they have rid themselves of all symbolic links. Less objectively, in the letter he was never to send to his father, Kafka accused Hermann of indiscriminately abusing Jews, Germans, and Czechs, and of seeing himself as a unique point of firmness, decisiveness, and worth. The passage from the letter to Milena explains this aspect of his father's behavior: whatever has autonomous existence and freedom of movement threatens his sense of security. With respect to Kafka's own generation, the reality is just as grim or even worse: the parents still trusted their own teeth and hands; the children feel endangered to such a degree that threats themselves threaten them.

Twenty years later, the world would see that Kafka's evaluation of the situation was by no means paranoid. In this marginal country, which was to achieve autonomy only with the collapse of the Austro-Hungarian Empire, and that in our own times has opted for partition into two states, the assimilation of the Jews had not only ended in failure but also led to complete deracination. Therefore, as Riff observes, Zionism, Socialist activism, and mysticism were responses to an otherwise unbearable situation.[17] Kafka was drawn particularly by the first and the third of these responses, though he cannot be said to have been indifferent to the second. But to him the only really meaningful option was literature. It was in his writing that he drew, to the utmost and most painful extent, the consequences of his situation as a pariah. Thus, the case of Kafka fits Stölzel's description of the attitude that came to characterize Jews: "To oppose the inevitable accusation of double loyalty, the Jews had no alternative other than to torment themselves with the same accusation that was directed at them by the majority" (Stölzel 1988: 109). That is why Kafka adopted "from Zionism . . . the political masochism" (p. 134). In his case, however, the psychological reaction is not the whole answer.

It is true that access to his work is made easier by an acquaintance with his environment, a nightmare setting that made even the act of writing problematic. But this is not enough to give us the key to his achievement. We would be falling back on a causal interpretation if we concluded that the conditioning factors of the author's background are enough to determine the work. The purpose of this section is a more modest one: to provide the frame of reference for Kafka's textual strategies. Between this frame of reference and the textual strategies there are mediations that are actualized only in the text itself.

The most elementary of these mediations is the principle of inexorable objectification, magnified by Kafka's hostility to introspection. We have already mentioned the passage from Benjamin: "It is very significant that the world of the officials and the world of the fathers are one and the same to Kafka. This similarity does not honor them" (Benjamin 1974b, 2, 2: 411). Rather than project into his text the complaints he directed at his father, he objectifies them by projecting them on the outer world, fusing this world with that of the authorities, taking it as a condensation of the threats that threaten him. This example is enough to show why we refuse to posit a causal chain joining context to text, in which the former would condition the latter. Objectification is the product of a verbal chemistry in which living experience is transformed into text. It is impossible to reconstruct such a process. All we have is the raw material and the finished product.

17. For an excellent analysis of the Jewish question in Europe in the early twentieth century, particularly of the Jewish intelligentsia, see Löwy 1989, especially chapter 3.

The failure of the older generation's attempt to assimilate left Prague's Germanized Jewish intelligentsia without a country. Let us see how Kafka positioned himself in relation to each term: the Czechs, German culture, and the Jewish community. With respect to the first, we need no more than a few elementary observations. Much more than his friends Max Brod and Franz Werfel, Kafka was interested in contemporary Czech literature and spoke the language fluently, though with mistakes (see his diary entry of November 28, 1911—Kafka 1972: 127) that were particularly conspicuous in the written language. Thus, in a letter to Ottla sent from Berlin, thanking her for translating into Czech a letter sent in his name to the insurance company he worked for, Kafka wrote: "What am I to do now, since I have already launched into the world the lie about my splendid Czech, a lie that probably no one believes" (Kafka 1982: 89). Further, since to him German was no more than an instrument of culture, Kafka could not be suspected of any Pan-Germanic sentiments. It should also be added that his disapproval of his father's conduct toward his employees made him sympathize with all the disinherited, whether they were Czechs or Oriental Jews. His position was, then, one of clear respect for those whom his father mistreated in his firm; but we can find out little else about it before we consider his relations with the Jewish community.

To Jews, assimilation implied forgetting their group of origin and thus led to the disintegration of the outcast. The failure of assimilation led to a clash, sometimes openly hostile, between assimilated parents and deracinated children. The somewhat frequent allusions to the Jewish question in Kafka's letters and diaries testify to his anxious desire to find a place for himself. But what could such a place be when it no longer existed by the time he was born? In these passages what we see is not the attempt to regain what has been lost, but rather that of healing the wound of deracination.

Since what concerns him is not the reconstruction of the abandoned community, Kafka shows no sign of wanting to restructure religious life centering on the synagogue. Religion is not the means by which this lonely man attempts to find the comfort of communion. This is certainly curious, given the mystical tendencies he manifests in dozens of fragments and aphorisms. Instead of the wide road of religion, Kafka seeks an entrance by means of the contact with a humble company of Jewish actors who, in the cafés of Prague, enact a modest repertoire of Yiddish plays.

The long diary entry of October 5, 1911, tells of Kafka's first meeting with this group. The dryness of the text betrays his emotion, born of the identification with what is familiar and, simultaneously, a gesture of exclusion: "Some songs, the expression 'yiddische kinderlach' [Jewish children], some of this woman's acting (who, on the stage, because she is a Jew, draws us listeners to her because we are Jews, without any longing for or curiosity about Christians) made my cheeks tremble" (Kafka 1972: 65). The Yiddish phrase elicits complicity from the spectator, who excludes Christians from his communal pleasure. What is included in this momentary community? Not the Western Jew, educated, polished, and well-off, sometimes fearful of betraying his roots, but the Oriental Jew, poor and despised even among Jews. It is about the lives of these people, their customs and their literature, that Kafka wants to learn from the actor Jizchak Löwy.

However, though he keeps a correspondence with Löwy (see Wagenbach 1964: 71), and though in the benefit of his group he organizes an artistic evening in which he is to present an introductory lecture, Kafka soon realizes that he has aimed too high:

When I saw the first plays it was possible for me to think that I had come upon a Judaism on which the beginnings of my own rested, a Judaism that was developing in my direction and so would enlighten and carry me farther along in my own clumsy Judaism, instead, it moves farther away from me the more I hear of it. The people remain, of course, and I hold fast to them. (January 6, 1912; Kafka 1972: 167)

Although the experience did not keep him from writing and giving the lecture on Yiddish, from reflecting on the situation of minor literatures and concerning himself with Jewish history and literature (see Kafka 1972: 172–76, entries of January 24 and 26, 1912), in any case his knowledge of this "minor" theater did not make him overcome his hesitations concerning Judaism. Throughout his life, Kafka was to hesitate before taking the next step, to remain distant even when just an inch away from his goal. This ambiguous, existentially shattering position was nevertheless the condition for maintaining his critical measure. Thus, even in his phase of closest involvement with Judaism, he is able to write:

Today, eagerly and happily began to read the *History of the Jews* by Graetz. Because my desire for it had far outrun the reading, it was at first stranger to me than I thought, and I had to stop here and there in order by resting to allow my Jewishness to collect itself. Towards the end, however, I was already gripped by the imperfection of the first settlements in the newly conquered Canaan and the faithful handing down of the imperfections of the popular heroes [*Volksmänner*] (Joshua, the Judges, Elijah). (Kafka 1972: 98–99)

Nine years later, the same distancing from what nevertheless remains near can be observed in a letter to Max Brod, dated August 7, 1920. Kafka compares the religious prescriptions of the Greek and Jewish cultures and concludes that he cannot subscribe to either. The Greek law, he writes, "was less profound than the Law of the Jews, but perhaps more democratic (scarcely any leaders or founders of religion among the Greeks)" (Kafka 1977: 242). Opposed to the figure of the man of action and tending, because of his indecision, to paralysis, in his moments of lucidity Kafka ponders the reasons for his unintegrated state: he criticizes the Greek heritage for its shallowness and the Jewish for its reliance on leaders and heroes.

But intellectual restrictions do not weaken his thirst for integration; the all-embracing warmth of the community is stronger than any qualms he may have. So, as he reflects on the life of the Jewish community, he mentions as its distinctive trait the fact that its members "come together at every possible opportunity, whether to pray or to study or to discuss divine matters or to eat holiday meals whose basis is usually a religious one and at which alcohol is drunk only very moderately. They flee to one another, so to speak" (December 25, 1911; Kafka 1972: 152). This characteristic, incidentally, does not impress him solely when he finds it among those by whom he had the possibility of being accepted: "The tremendous advantage of Christians who always have and enjoy such feelings of closeness in general intercourse, for instance a Christian Czech among Christian Czechs . . ." (July 1, 1913; Kafka 1972: 222).

If we compare this emphasis on the closeness he finds outside his immediately surrounding world with what his biographers tell us about the situation in Prague, particularly the isolation of Czech Jews, Benjamin's observation and question are all the more relevant: "[Kafka] was no clairvoyant, nor was he the founder of a religion. How could he stand this atmosphere?" (Benjamin 1974b, 2, 2: 424–25). Such a question could find no answer; Kafka lived all his life in the throes of this unanswered question. During his only relatively long sojourn abroad, he wrote to Robert Klopstock, on December 19, 1923: "To me the Academy for Jewish Studies is a refuge of peace in wild and woolly Berlin and in the wild and woolly regions of the mind" (Kafka 1977: 402).

The Promised Land has vanished with the time of the fathers; the New Canaan proves to have imperfections that echo those that were handed down by the ancient leaders; in Prague, when hostilities do not erupt, they simmer just below the surface; Berlin, which has attracted him for so long, welcomes him when life had already become impossible. As long as he can stand this atmosphere, Kafka formulates it in his writings. This is his everyday world, his motivation. But it would be foolish to think of it as an explaining cause. For Kafka's aversion to introspection—which we have mentioned as his first step towards the kind of text he was to produce—and his objectifying effort meant not the attempt to depict an environment, but to produce the record of what underlay it, of what could not be seen.

However illuminating an analysis of Kafka's relations with Judaism may be, such an analysis can be misleading unless it is accompanied by a similar study of Kafka's feelings towards German culture.

The strangeness of Kafka's situation in relation to his mother language, the language in which he always wrote, may already be detected in one of his earliest letters to Milena: "I have never lived among German people, German is my mother-tongue and therefore natural to me, but Czech feels to me far more intimate [*ist mir viel herzlicher*]" (Kafka 1954a: 30). His affection was then associated with a language he could not write without relying on external assistance, whereas the language he employed he had never used in the living community of its speakers. Thus, what we have come to recognize as "Kafkaesque" is already present in Kafka's relationship with the language he wrote in. The appropriateness of this relationship, in both its tragic and its combative aspects, comes out clearly in his diary entry of October 24, 1911:

> The Jewish mother is no "Mutter," to call her "Mutter" makes her a little comic (not to herself, because we are in Germany), we give a Jewish woman the name of a German mother, but forget the contradiction that sinks into the emotions so much the more heavily, "Mutter" is peculiarly German for the Jew, it unconsciously contains, together with the Christian splendor Christian coldness also, the Jewish woman who is called "Mutter" therefore becomes not only comic but strange. (Kafka 1972: 88)

How could German be his *Muttersprache* (mother tongue) if "die jüdische Mutter ist keine Mutter" (the Jewish mother is no "Mutter")? Nevertheless, German *is* his mother tongue.

If we forget that this dilemma was actually experienced by a human being, the juxtaposition of the two texts may seem to pose a puzzle. The dilemma is all the more inescapable because it exists before the intervention of the writer. Kafka's original language was a borrowed tongue. On the basis of his testimony, to Czech Jews German never came as naturally as it did to German Jews. (Or, for that matter, to Elias Canetti, to whom German was, in the veritable babel of his childhood, literally his mother tongue, the one closest to his affections.) The antagonism that came between Czechs and the German and Jewish minorities and caused the Jewish minority to be rejected by the German one, together with the German minority's identification with Austrian power, gave the German spoken in Prague its peculiar stamp. "Under the pressure of isolation, Prague German increasingly turned into a holiday language [*Feiertagsidiom*], a language supported by the state" (Wagenbach

1964: 56). In order to escape this artificial situation, he would have to convert either to Zionism or to Czech nationalism. But Kafka could not even break away from Prague.

There was, then, no alternative to relying on a language that, though used in his everyday life, remained to him a foreign tongue. Thus, "Kafka's characteristic purism, his sobriety of construction, his phrases, his starkness of vocabulary would be unthinkable without Prague German in the background" (p. 56). This particular German, "dry, a paper language, was incapable of close familiarity; the language itself always contained a remnant of strangeness" (p. 56).

It would be simplistic to imagine that Kafka saw himself as the victim of some malignant demon and for this reason pestered his friends with expressions of suffering. It would be even more mistaken to see him as a stoic. Kafka simply experienced in extreme form the situation of a writer who does not belong to a metropolitan culture, who is forced to work, in one way or another, always or occasionally, with borrowed instruments.

One of the documents that best describes the impression caused by his German is an ironical and humorous passage in a letter to Max Brod and Felix Weltsch, dated April 10, 1920. Kafka was then in a sanatorium in Merano. Here are Kafka's impressions of his fellow inmates:

> Today, when I went into the dining room the colonel (the general was not there yet) invited me so cordially to the common table that I had to give in. So now the thing took its course. After the first few words it came out that I was from Prague. Both of them—the general, who sat opposite me, and the colonel— were acquainted with Prague. Was I Czech? No. So now explain to those true German military eyes what you really are. Someone else suggested "German-Bohemian," someone else "Little Quarter." Then the subject was dropped and people went on eating, but the general, with his sharp ears linguistically schooled in the Austrian army, was not satisfied. After we had eaten, he once more began to wonder about the sound of my German, perhaps more bothered by what he saw than by what he heard. At this point I tried to explain that by my being Jewish. At this his scientific curiosity, to be sure, was satisfied, but not his human feelings. (Kafka 1977: 233)

What was it about Kafka's German that sounded odd to the Austrian officer? This man was acquainted with the Prague accent, as his reference to the "Little Quarter" (*Kleinseite*), the part of the city where most Germans lived, indicates. Besides, in a letter to his sister Ottla, dated April 6, 1920, also sent from Merano, Kafka said that his landlady identified his accent the moment he walked in (see Kafka 1982: 43). But his answer fails to satisfy his exacting interlocutor. The only answer that comes close to doing so is his explanation that he is Jewish. Ultimately one arrives at the inevitable conclusion: here is a man who speaks his mother tongue as if it were a foreign language. The general would probably have been even more surprised if he had been told that the strange creature in question was a writer.

Kafka's case is not comparable to that of Joseph Conrad, who even though he came to master English was never able to speak the language without a foreign accent, and in whose text specialists detect telltale remnants of his native tongue. Even less is his case similar to that of Samuel Beckett, who came to have complete mastery of French to the point of becoming perfectly bilingual. Kafka has the uncomfortable distinction of being a writer who uses a borrowed language. This alone is sufficient to explain why he saw himself as alone in his diaspora, watching the world go by from the window in his room—or, to take an image from an early entry in his diary, why he felt deracinated: "All those things, that is to say, those things which occur to me, occur to me not from the root up but rather only from somewhere about their middle" (Kafka 1972: 12).

Thus, an examination of Kafka's contacts with the Czech, Jewish, and German communities suggests the image of interruption, of something that never takes root. To the Czechs, Kafka was a German speaker; to the German community, he was a Jew. And what was he to the Jews? Being neither assimilated nor a Zionist, what could he be? However, it was precisely this man without a country, stigmatized by his lack of a place, who formulated, in two short texts, the fundamental reflection on marginal literatures.

With his "Rede übere die jiddische Sprache" (Speech on the Yiddish language), Kafka intended to open the fund-raising evening for the benefit of Jizchak Löwy's troupe. The speech, read at Jewish Town Hall on February 18, 1912, left "his audience somewhat astonished, even scandalized" (Robert 1988: 49). The very theme—an analysis of a despised language, made in a tone that indicated disdain for his speakers—could only sound offensive to his audience of assimilated Jews: "For all that, I believe I have convinced most of you, ladies and gentlemen, that you will understand not a single word of the jargon" (Kafka 1953: 306). Rather than sport professorial condescension, or adopt the humble posture of one who seeks help, Kafka seems to amuse himself with his audience of respectable citizens. Thus, after seeming to comfort them—"Fortunately, everyone who knows the German language will be able to understand the jargon"—he again sounds an unpleasant note when he adds that it is impossible to translate Yiddish into German: "One cannot translate the jargon into German. The connections between them are so tenuous and significant that they are destroyed as soon as Yiddish is retranslated into German, that is, it can only be rendered into something unsubstantial" (p. 308).

From the viewpoint of the material purpose of the evening, the lecturer's attitude was unjustifiable, for it hardly encouraged the Jewish community to come to the support of the poor Jewish troupe. But what concerns us is less Kafka's tactlessness than his position in relation to Yiddish. He makes no attempt to praise or ennoble the language. Instead, he emphasizes its character as a language made up of borrowings—"it is wholly made up of foreign words"—a language so fluid and dynamic that it really has no grammar to speak of. But Yiddish is not just movement, ad hoc appropriation of words to describe what is going on at the moment; it also has an opposite aspect: the preservation of archaisms. "Whatever comes once into the ghetto does not easily leave the ghetto" (p. 307). Thus, the only dignity of this language made up of multiple borrowings lies in the fact that its rags point both to the contemporary marketplace and to the depth of history.

Kafka then introduces to his assimilated audience a repertoire of plays the excellence of which he intends to emphasize, plays spoken in a language that the audience just might be able to follow. Is Kafka trying, like an avant-garde artist, to offend his own public? Though the aggressive intent is surely present, it is no more than a means to make a point: "You will come quite close to the jargon if you understand that, apart from knowledge, there are in you active forces and a chain of forces that allow you to understand it with your feelings [*Jargon fühlend zu verstehen*]" (pp. 308–9).

Kafka's idea is to get Prague Jews to activate their feelings in order to reterritorialize their deterritorialized language. If, as a pro-Zionist initiative, the effect of Kafka's speech was negligible, the text is nonetheless an extraordinary document for what it says about his social and linguistic consciousness. This is seen more clearly when we relate the speech to a passage from a letter to Brod in which Kafka reflects on the situation of Jewish writers whose native language is German:

> They existed among three impossibilities. . . . These are: The impossibility of not writing, the impossibility of writing German, the impossibility of writing differently. One might also add a fourth impossibility, the impossibility of writing (since the despair could not be assuaged by writing, was hostile to both life and writing; writing is only an expedient, as for someone who is writing his will shortly before he hangs himself—an expedient that may well last a whole life). Thus what resulted was a literature impossible in all respects, a gypsy literature which had stolen the German child out of its cradle and in great haste put it through some kind of training, for someone has to dance on the tightrope. (Kafka 1977: 289)

There is a clear connection between this text and the speech on Yiddish. German words, once they were appropriated by Yiddish, externally turned into rags, and internally entered a different circuit, so different that their return to the original circuit made them insubstantial. Used by Jews, who were foreigners, the German word was, as it were, stolen.

The passage might be taken as an example of what Stölzel refers to as Kafka's "political masochism." But the laceration it speaks of is much more terrible than that. The instrument of a triple or quadruple impossibility, each of which contradicts the following one, and the multiple shock of which conditions this very particular breakthrough that materializes in Kafka's text, the "stolen" word is living proof of a deterritorialization: the use by gypsies of a prestigious language. The passage from the letter to Brod directs us to Kafka's observations concerning minor literatures.

On December 25, 1911, under the impact of his "discovery" of the actor Löwy, Kafka commits to paper what he sees as the characteristics of the literatures of small nations.[18] This is the longest sentence Kafka ever wrote. On the basis of this text, Deleuze and Guattari offer two characterizations of a minor literature. The first is: "A minor literature is not the literature of a minor language, but one made by a minority with a major language" (Deleuze and Guattari 1977: 25). And the second is: "The three characteristics of a minor literature are the deterritorialization of language, the ramification of the individual into the immediately political, the collective administration

---

18. "What I understand of contemporary Jewish literature in Warsaw through Löwy, and of contemporary Czech literature partly through my own insight, points to the fact that many of the benefits of literature—the stirring of minds, the coherence of national consciousness, often unrealized in public life and always tending to disintegrate, the pride which a nation gains from a literature of its own and the support it is afforded in the face of a hostile surrounding world, this keeping of a diary by a nation which is something entirely different from historiography results in a more rapid (and yet always closely scrutinized) development, the spiritualization of the broad area of public life, the assimilation of dissatisfied elements that are immediately put to use precisely in this sphere where only stagnation can do harm, the constant integration of a people with respect to its whole that the incessant bustle of the magazines creates, the narrowing down of the attention of a nation upon itself and the accepting of what is foreign only in reflection, the birth of a respect for those active in literature, the transitory awakening in the younger generation of higher aspirations, which nevertheless leaves its permanent mark, the acknowledgment of literary events as objects of political solicitude, the dignification of the antithesis between fathers and sons and the possibility of discussing this, the presentation of national faults in a manner that is very painful, to be sure, but also liberating and deserving of forgiveness, the beginning of a lively and therefore self-respecting book-trade and the eagerness for books—all these effects can be produced even by a literature whose development is not in actual fact unusually broad in scope, but seems to be, because it lacks outstanding talents. The liveliness of such a literature exceeds even that of one rich in talent, for, as it has no writer whose great gifts could silence at least the majority of cavillers, literary competition on the greatest scale has a real justification" (Kafka 1972: 148–49).

of enunciation. It should be stressed that 'minor' no longer qualifies certain literatures, but rather the revolutionary conditions of every literature contained within what we call a great (or established) literature" (p. 28). Both formulations are faithful to Kafka's text, but the second abstracts what was contingent in his situation—a Czech Jew writing in a major language—and thus stresses its operative potential.

The deterritorialization of language is not a consequence of someone's using a language in relation to which he or she is a foreigner, but of a writer's making the language in which he or she writes "foreign." Put more simply, it consists in going against the grain of the conventional use of a language. In this sense, literary Brazilian Portuguese is deterritorialized by Guimarães Rosa (*The Devil to Pay in the Backlands*), with his combination of archaisms and neologisms, his Faustian pact with questions for which no doctrine has an answer; by Graciliano Ramos (*Barren Lives*), with his bone-dry syntax; by João Cabral de Melo Neto (*A Knife All Blade: Or Usefulness of Fixed Ideas*), with his knife-and-vinegar antilyricism. These examples also show the simultaneous presence of the three characteristics mentioned above, even though in Rosa the political element is too dated (restricted to the level of the plot) for it to have the significance it has in Ramos and Cabral. But it is not our intention to give the impression that the justification of a long essay is an observation concerning Brazilian literature in the end. The examples of Brazilian writers have the sole purpose of illustrating modes of deterritorialization known to Brazilian readers—which leads, in turn, to another observation concerning the possible fruitfulness of the concept of minor literature.

In discussions of the culture and literature of peripheral nation-states, it is common to treat their relations with metropolitan cultures by adopting a colonized viewpoint—whatever is thought in the periphery is inevitably a dilution of what has already been thought, more cogently, abroad; or by defending a chauvinistic position—let us exalt our roots and protect them from corrupting foreign influences; or yet by opting for a dialogic alternative— there must be interchange with dominant cultures.

The category "minor literature" suggests a different attitude: the practitioners of a minor literature—not in spite of, but precisely because of their condition as such—are able to detect movements that go unnoticed in the metropolis because from the standpoint of stable metropolitan institutions, they seem remote. No cause-and-effect explanation is meant here; we are not saying that because Kafka was such and such a man, the member of a conformist, middle-class Jewish family in a dependent European nation, then . . . This would be to indulge in a crude a posteriori logic, incongruously combining Platonic fervor and materialistic endeavor. Once this qualification is made, it should be said that the decisive part of the interpretation we have presented may be linked with what has been said about minor literatures.

We have agreed with Benjamin's statement that Kafka was no prophet foreseeing the state of society in the future, but rather a man who, as an individual, formulated what was complementary to him. Our subsequent observations concerning the situation of Prague's Jewish community made this idea of complementarity more palpable. Put simply, Kafka's literature is the counterpart of the threats that result from threats. But it is also true that, when he objectifies his answer, Kafka shifts planes: what had been complementary to the individual only—that is, the effect of a specific idiosyncrasy of his—is made the correlate of a social threat, the threat that the (social, moral) Law will reveal its own insubstantiality, the fact that its stability no longer holds.

Then we saw that the modern status of fiction depended on this very stability. That is, the supreme political achievement of the Enlightenment, the establishment of the rule of law, expressed by a constitution applying to each and every member of the society, was the indispensable precondition for the legitimation of a discursive form—fiction—founded on the possibility of questioning the values of society without exposing writers to legal sanctions. Its critical capacity assumed a division into territories. If the territory of the fictional was to be able to place in perspective the socially accepted truth and the practices and values associated with it without exposing authors to the risk of legal persecution or plunging readers into uncertainty, outside the territory of fiction this truth must remain pragmatically in force. Once these parameters were respected, it was (and is) possible to define both an honest practice of fiction and somewhat reproachable practices, such as the supposedly critical review of past values through facile, marketable, uncommitted, and pleasurable "historical" fiction, or the equally facile criticism of present situations in order to present an alternative in didactic "fiction."

Fiction—with no quotation marks or qualifications—presupposed, and still presupposes, a peculiar pragmatics: its statements, in themselves nonpragmatic (since they are neither true nor false), deal with values that the receiver identifies with, or at least can identify as values. Now, particularly in *The Trial*, it is precisely this stability of the rule of law that is seen as an illusion. Trials and judges are invisible; the minions of justice are everywhere; the process is infinite, or at least it is impossible to know when it will end.

The character of this process was distorted when it was seen as a prophetic anticipation of totalitarian regimes, for what is singular about it is not an exclusive or even a characteristic property of these regimes: the existence of a society in which differences of territoriality have been abolished. In *The*

Trial, the absence of checks on the apparatus of justice is, therefore, parallel to the dissolution of a territory properly belonging to the fictional. To say this is to superimpose the plane of the narrative, where justice has no bounds, upon the plane of the experience of reading the narrative, where the reader feels the lack of a ground from which he or she could see in perspective the values being questioned.

The absence in Kafka of stable territorialities makes what previously seemed fixed part of a chaotic game, the rules of which either do not exist or else are unknown. It is as if—to use a category that had not yet been formulated in Kafka's time—the language games mentioned by Wittgenstein in his *Philosophical Investigations* had all of a sudden gone wild and, one fine morning, began following paths hitherto prohibited. But let us not forget that this sudden disruption of language games is perceived only by the quixotic Joseph K. No one else thinks there is anything the matter. It is only to him that the world has become a fiction. Although we are not told why, to everyone else this fiction has already been accepted as reality. To them, the insubstantiality of the Law makes no sense; they have never thought of such things, and the very question is above their understanding.

Could it be that this insubstantiality of the Law, from which derives its conformity to those who manipulate it, this subversion of the stability of the status of the fictional, has become a worldwide phenomenon now that we live increasingly in a world of images? I mean to do no more than make this question comprehensible.[19] It has been said that billboards today are part of our unconscious. But we cannot fully apprehend the impact of the world of images if we consider no more than the amount of time we spend exposed to its influence. Nor does the world of images have the relevance it seems to have now because the socialization of children takes place more through the electronic media than through reading. The point is that the socialization and legitimation of the forms of power necessarily take place through the medium of images.

Ever since Plato, Western thought has tried to establish the criteria and hierarchies by means of which images—*eidola*—could be submitted to fixed, immobile, superlunary truth, the expression of a timeless substance. It might seem as if the everyday dominance of images in the present world could be interpreted as the salutary corrosion of the metaphysics of truth. Did not the attempt of modern thought to arrive at an emancipating reason take a definitive step when, with Kant, it gave up the identification of the real with the rational?

To be sure, Kant is the originator of the problem of the Law that we have

19. For an examination of this possibility, see Godzich 1991: 747–59.

been taking as the basis for an understanding of Kafka. But in Kant the fact that the moral law is not constitutive does not imply that it is capricious, manipulative, or arbitrary. It is rather a "necessary fiction," something man imposes on himself *as if* it were indeed inscribed in the order of things. The denial of the substantialist basis of classical metaphysics in Kant was accompanied by the appearance of the categorical imperative. In the particular case of images, they had their territory well defined in the place where imagination, instead of serving the understanding, was its equal. This entire construction assumed that truth—the truth of the phenomenon or of the circulation of regulating Ideas—had a territory of its own and occupied a central place. Today, when a real war can be watched as if it were a video game, when certain governments attempt to solve their financial difficulties by suddenly changing the "laws" of the market, the necessary "fictions" seem to lose their quality of necessity and tend to be seen as no more than fantasies that are manipulated by those who have the power to do so. The "victory" of the market economy over "real socialism" only postpones awareness of the real meaning of the empire of electronic images.

But this omnipresence of unqualified fiction does not mean that the fictional is no longer controlled. It was the hypothesis of the control of the imaginary, exerted on its own product par excellence—the fictional work—that initially suggested a study of Kafka. In the course of our study we perceived its connection with the Kantian problem. When we analyzed it, we realized not only that it would be possible to historicize Kafka's problem, relating it to that of the early German romantics but also, in a consideration of Kant's third *Critique*, to examine an ambiguity we had not perceived before—the one between aestheticization and criticity. The aestheticization we noted and its development served as the basis for the contemporary cult of the image. Thus, in an even more surprising way, Kant and Kafka meet: whereas the philosopher paved the way for aestheticization, through which the cult of the image was legitimated, the writer inaugurated the possibility of reaffirming the criticity exalted by Kant, which, in the case of literature, was soon stifled.

It was thanks to this criticity—or else to this illusion of criticity—that we were able to understand the subversive impact of Kafka's work on the established status of the fictional. This does not mean that the control of the imaginary has been abolished. The acknowledgment of a mode of discourse as fictional, a step that has by no means been taken by most students of literature, was in fact a compromise with control. That is, those who admitted it, rather than take the work as the expression of a truth present elsewhere, could afford not to meddle with the truth claims of their colleagues in other areas, since at least in their own field it was recognized that their objects treated truth differently. The situation now has different parameters. The subversion of an area as proper to the exercise of a pleasurable and questioning discourse no longer implies that Truth is in force elsewhere. Kafka's work belongs to a time when the control of the imaginary dispenses with the idea of truth, its philosophical or religious elaboration, and makes of this control the principle on which the action of the multiple agencies of power is based. In other words, truth is no longer affirmed on the basis and as the function of a certain rationality; rather, it is identified with the brute fact that a certain power wants, asserts, and imposes this or that.

The now direct connection between truth and power, as it expands through the multiple incidence of images, at the same time annuls the basic criterion of fictional discourse: its questioning force. Not that the fictional is now directly censored—this would be the truly totalitarian variant. It seems hardly accidental that Western democracy today should see totalitarian regimes as affronts to good taste: the power founded on images, which imposes itself by means of insistent images, generates an adhesion that makes overt violence unnecessary. The truth transmitted and constituted by images, power as truth, dispenses with unpleasant repression because the receiver, accustomed to the chaotic multiplicity of electronic images, sinks into an attitude of indifference. "What does it matter whether it is or isn't art, as long as it allows me to relax for a while?" Or, "Why carry on this boring discussion over ready-mades when museums have already bought them?"

However, we are too much persons of our time, and therefore too incompetent, to realize that the world of images actually assumes the predominance of contented indifference, an attitude of bored indifference in relation to criticity, the merely residual survival of fictionality. Most likely we cannot even see the metamorphosis that the idea of fictionality is experiencing. How many other metamorphoses may be taking place?

It may even be, then, that Kafka's great achievement signals not as much an end as another beginning. We can see what it is the end of. One of the best interpreters of Kafka today writes that "the structure of the Kafkan paradox" consists in the fact that it contains, on the one hand, the "history of the disappearance of the hero, brought about by the game of life," and, on the other, "the desperate search for the very rules of this game, the disappearance of which is being asserted" (Neumann 1990: 19). The question is then whether this game still has any rules. But as long as human society exists, how could these rules be missing? Thus, the devastating critique of the tyranny of electronic images may fail to see a positive possibility: that the image, precisely as it corrodes the old metaphysical belief in Truth, may open the way for a less imperial, less imposing idea of truth, one that is historically and culturally mutable, and that is powerless to control "nontrue" discourses.

In a certain sense, Kafka places us in a situation reminiscent of Montaigne's. It took two centuries for Montaigne's practice to be legitimated in gnosiological terms by Kant. We cannot even be sure if the comparison is valid. All we know is that the consecration of the individual lost its grounding a long time ago. This, to be sure, is not enough to allow us to discern what Kafka is the beginning of.

Reference Matter

References

Adorno, T. W. 1958. *Noten zur Literatur*, vol. 1. Frankfurt: Suhrkamp Verlag.

———. 1969. *Prisms.* Trans. Samuel and Shierry Weber. Cambridge, Mass.: MIT Press.

Alleman, B. 1963. "Kafka: *Der Prozess.*" In B. von Wiese, ed., *Der deutsche Roman*, vol. 2. Düsseldorf: Bagel.

Arendt, H. 1976 [1948]. "Der Mensch mit dem guten Willen." In *Die verborgene Tradition: Acht Essays.* Frankfurt: Suhrkamp Verlag.

Aristotle. 1952. *On Poetics.* In *Aristotle*, vol. 2. Trans. I. Bywater. Chicago: Encyclopaedia Britannica.

Auerbach, E. 1974 [1946]. *Mimesis: The Representation of Reality in Western Literature.* Trans. W. R. Trask. Princeton, N.J.: Princeton University Press.

Ayrault, R. 1961. *La Genèse du romantisme allemand*, 4 vols. Paris: Aubier.

Bakhtin, M. 1981 [1975]. "Forms of Time and the Chronotope in the Novel." In *The Dialogic Imagination.* Trans. C. Emerson and M. Holquist. Austin: University of Texas Press.

Beaujour, M. 1980. *Miroirs d'encre: Rhétorique de l'autoportrait.* Paris: Seuil.

———. 1983. " 'Consideration sur Ciceron' (I, XL), l'alongeai comme marque générique: La lettre et l'essai." In M. Tetel, ed., *Actes du colloque international Montaigne (1580–1980).* Paris: Nizet.

Beicken, P. U. 1974. *Franz Kafka: Eine kritische Einführung in die Forschung.* Frankfurt: Athenaion.

Benjamin, W. 1974a [1919]. *Der Begriff der Kunstkritik in der deutschen Romantik.* In R. Tiedemann and H. Schweppenhäuser, eds., *Geammelte Schriften.* Vol. 1, bk. 1. Frankfurt: Suhrkamp Verlag.

———. 1974b [1934]. "Franz Kafka: Zur zehnten Wiederkehr seines Todestages." In R. Tiedemann and H. Schweppenhäuser, eds., *Gessammelte Schriften.* Vol. 2, bk. 2. Frankfurt: Suhrkamp Verlag.

———. 1978. *Briefe.* 2 vols. Ed. G. Scholem and T. W. Adorno. Frankfurt: Suhrkamp Verlag.

Blanchard, M. E. 1990. *Trois portraits de Montaigne: Essai sur la représentation à la Renaissance*. Paris: Nizet.

Blanchot, M. 1949. "Kafka et la littérature." In *La Part du feu*. Paris: Gallimard. (*The Work of Fire*. Trans. Charlotte Mandell. Stanford, Calif.: Stanford University Press, 1995)

Bloch, H. 1991. *Medieval Misogyny and the Invention of Western Romantic Love*. Chicago: University of Chicago Press.

Bloom, H. 1989. "Freud and Beyond." In *Ruin the Sacred Truths: Poetry and Belief from the Bible to the Present*. Cambridge, Mass.: Harvard University Press.

Böhm, G. 1985. *Bildnis und Individuum: Über den Ursprung der Porträtmalerei in der italienischen Renaissance*. Munich: Prestel.

Bohrer, K. H. 1989. *Die Kritik der Romantik: Der Verdacht der Philosophie gegen die literarische Moderne*. Frankfurt: Suhrkamp Verlag.

Born, J., ed. 1979. *Franz Kafka: Kritik und Rezeption zu seinen Lebzeiten (1912–1924)*. Frankfurt: S. Fischer Verlag.

———. 1983. *Franz Kafka: Kritik und Rezeption (1924–1938)*. Frankfurt: S. Fischer Verlag.

Brod, M. 1977 [1954]. *Über Franz Kafka*. Hamburg: Fischer Taschenbuch Verlag.

Brody, J. 1982. *Lectures de Montaigne*. Lexington, Ky.: French Forum Publishers.

Brown, M. 1979. *The Shape of German Romanticism*. Ithaca, N.Y.: Cornell University Press.

Brown, P. 1969 [1967]. *Augustine of Hippo*. Berkeley: University of California Press.

Butor, M. 1960 [1959]. "Balzac et la réalité." In *Répertoire*. Paris: Minuit.

———. 1968. *Essais sur les Essais*. Paris: Gallimard.

Canetti, E. 1978. "Kafka's Other Trial." In F. Kafka, *Letters to Felice*. Trans. James Stern and Elizabeth Duckworth. Harmondsworth, Eng.: Penguin.

———. 1989. *Voices of Marrakesh*. Lewes, Eng.: Guild Quality.

Cassirer, E. 1963 [1927]. *Individuum und Cosmos in der Philosophie der Renaissance*. Darmstadt: Wissenschaftliche Buchgesellschaft.

Cave, T. 1979. *The Cornucopian Text: Problems of Writing in the French Renaissance*. Oxford: Clarendon Press.

Chédin, O. 1982. *Sur l'esthetique de Kant et la théorie critique de la répresentation*. Paris: J. Vrin.

Chytry, J. 1989. *The Aesthetic State: A Quest in Modern German Thought*. Berkeley: University of California Press.

Corngold, S. 1988. *Franz Kafka: The Necessity of Form*. Ithaca, N.Y.: Cornell University Press.

Costa-Lima, L. 1980. *Mimesis e modernidade: Formas das sombras*. Rio de Janeiro: Graal.

———. 1989. *A aguarrás do tempo: Estudos sobre a narrativa*. Rio de Janeiro: Rocco.

———. 1991. *Pensando nos trópicos*. Rio de Janeiro: Rocco.

———. 1992. *The Dark Side of Reason: Fictionality and Power*. Trans. Paulo H. Britto. Stanford, Calif.: Stanford University Press.

Davis, N. Z. 1986. "Boundaries and the Sense of Self in Sixteenth-Century France." In T. C. Heller, M. Sosna, and D. E. Wellbery, eds., *Reconstructing Individualism*. Stanford, Calif.: Stanford University Press.

Deleuze, G. 1983 [1963]. *La Philosophie critique de Kant*. Paris: Presses Universitaires de France.

Deleuze, G., and F. Guattari. 1977 [1975]. *Kafka: Por uma literatura menor.* Trans. J. Castañon Guimarães. Rio de Janeiro: Imago. (*Kafka: Toward a Minor Literature.* Trans. Dana Polan. Minneapolis: University of Minnesota Press, 1986)

Diderot, D. 1965 [1762]. "Éloge à Richardson." *Oeuvres esthétiques.* Ed. P. Vernière. Paris: Garnier.

Dietz, L. 1965. "Drucke Franz Kafkas bis 1924." In J. Born et al., *Kafka-Symposium.* Berlin: Verlag Klaus Wagenbach.

Eichner, H. 1955. "The Supposed Influence of Schiller's *Über naive und sentimentalische Dichtung* on F. Schlegel's *Über das Studium der griechischen Poesie.*" *Germanic Review* 30, 1.

Eliot, T. S. 1975 [1919]. "Hamlet." In *Selected Prose of T. S. Eliot.* Ed. Frank Kermode. New York: Farrar, Straus & Giroux.

Elm, T. 1979. "*Der Prozeß.*" In H. Binder, ed., *Kafka-Handbuch.* Vol. 2, *Das Werk und seine Wirkung.* Stuttgart: A. Kröner Verlag.

Eschweiler, C. 1990. *Der verborgene Hintergrund in Kafkas "Der Prozeß."* Berlin: Bouvier Verlag.

Fichte, J. G. 1988 [1794]. *A doutrina-da-ciência de 1794 e outros escritos.* Trans. Rubens Torres Filho. São Paulo: Nova Cultural.

Flores, K. 1958. "The Judgment." In A. Flores and H. Swandler, eds., *Franz Kafka Today.* Madison: University of Wisconsin Press.

Fontenelle, B. 1742. "De l'origine des fables." In *Oeuvres de Monsieur de Fontenelle*, vol. 3. New enlarged ed. Paris.

Fontius, M. 1983 [1977]. "Literatura e história—desenvolvimento das forças produtivas e autonomia da arte." Trans. P. Naumann et al. In L. Costa-Lima, ed., *Teoria da literatura em suas fontes.* Rio de Janeiro: Francisco Alves.

Foucault, M. 1975. *Surveiller et punir: Naissance de la prison.* Paris: Gallimard.

———. 1984. *Histoire de la sexualité: Le souci de soi.* Paris: Gallimard.

Freccero, J. 1986. "Autobiography and Narrative." In T. C. Heller, M. Sosna, and D. E. Wellbery, eds., *Reconstructing Individualism.* Stanford, Calif.: Stanford University Press.

Freedberg, D. 1989. *The Power of Images: Studies in the History and Theory of Response.* Chicago: University of Chicago Press.

Friedrich, H. 1949. *Montaigne.* Bern: A. Francke AG Verlag.

Fumaroli, M. 1978. "Genèse de l'épistolographie classique: Rhétorique humaniste de la lettre, de Pétrarque à Juste Lipse." *Revue d'histoire littéraire de la France* 78.

———. 1980. *L'Age de l'éloquence: Rhétorique et "res literaria" de la Renaissance au seuil de l'époque classique.* Geneva: Librairie Droz.

Ginsburg, C. 1987 [1976]. *O queijo e os vermes.* Trans. Maria Betânia Amoroso. São Paulo: Companhia das Letras.

Godzich, W. 1991. Vom Paradox der Sprache zur Dissonanz des Bildes." In H. U. Gumbrecht and K. L. Pfeiffer, eds., *Paradoxien, Dissonanzen, Zusammenbrüche.* Frankfurt: Suhrkamp Verlag.

Goldstücker, E. 1981 [1965]. "Franz Kafka in the Prague Perspective: 1963." In K. Hughes, ed., *Franz Kafka: An Anthology of Marxist Criticism.* Hanover, N.H.: University Press of New England.

Gracián, B. 1986 [1646]. *El Discreto. El Criticón. El Héroe.* Mexico City: Porrúa.

Greenberg, M. 1968. *Kafka: The Terror of Art.* New York: Horizon Press.

Greenblatt, S. 1986. "Fiction and Friction." In T. C. Heller, M. Sosna, and D. E. Wellberry, eds. *Reconstructing Individualism*. Stanford, Calif.: Stanford University Press.

Greene, T. 1968. "The Flexibility of the Self in Renaissance Literature." In P. Demetz, T. Greene, and L. Nelson, Jr., *The Disciplines of Criticism: Essays in Literary Theory, Interpretation and History*. New Haven: Yale University Press.

Haas, W. 1929a. "Über Franz Kafka." *Die literarische Welt* 35 (Aug. 30): 3–4.

——. 1929b. "Über Franz Kafka." *Die literarische Welt* 36 (Sept. 6): 5–6.

——. 1929c. "Über Franz Kafka." *Die literarische Welt* 37 (Sept. 13): 7.

Habermas, J. 1987. *The Philosophical Discourse of Modernity: Twelve Lectures*. Trans. F. Lawrence. Cambridge, Mass.: MIT Press.

Hájek, J. 1981. "Kafka and the Socialist World." In K. Hughes, ed., *Franz Kafka: An Anthology of Marxist Criticism*. Hanover, N.H.: University Press of New England.

Hartman, G. H. 1980. *Criticism in the Wilderness: The Study of Literature Today*. New Haven: Yale University Press.

Heidegger, M. 1972 [1938]. "Die Zeit des Weltbildes." In *Holzwege*. Frankfurt: V. Klostermann.

Heller, E. 1975 [1952]. "The World of Franz Kafka." In *The Disinherited Mind: Essays in Modern German Literature and Thought*. New York: Harcourt Brace.

Hirsch, E. D., Jr. 1976. *The Aims of Interpretation*. Chicago: University of Chicago Press.

Horkheimer, M. 1988 [1938]. "Montaigne und die Funktion der Skepsis." In *Gesammelte Schriften: Schriften 1936–1941*. Vol. 4. Frankfurt: S. Fischer Verlag.

Huppert, G. 1973 [1970]. *The Idea of Perfect History*. Trans. F. and P. Braudel. Paris: Flammarion.

Iser, W. 1983. "Os atos de fingir ou o que é fictício no texto ficcional." In L. Costa-Lima, ed., *Teoria da literatura em suas fontes*, vol. 2. Rio de Janeiro: Francisco Alves.

Janouch, G. 1951. *Gespräche mit Kafka: Aufzeichnungen und Erinnerungen*. Hamburg: Fischer Taschenbuch Verlag.

Jauss, H. R. 1970 [1967]. "Schlegels und Schillers Replik auf die 'Querelle des anciens et des modernes.'" In *Literaturgeschichte als Provokation*. Frankfurt: Suhrkamp Verlag.

Johnston, W. M. 1972. *The Austrian Mind: An Intellectual and Social History*. Berkeley: University of California Press.

Juhl, P. D. 1980. *Interpretation: An Essay in the Philosophy of Literary Criticism*. Princeton, N.J.: Princeton University Press.

Kafka, F. 1948 [1927]. *The Castle*. Trans. Willa and Edwin Muir. New York: Knopf.

——. 1953. *Hochzeitsvorbereitungen aus dem Lande und andere Prosa aus dem Nachlaß*. Ed. Max Brod. Frankfurt: Fischer Taschenbuch Verlag.

——. 1954a [1952]. *Letters to Milena*. Ed. Willy Haas. Trans. Tania and James Stern. New York: Schocken.

——. 1954b [1953]. *Dearest Father*. Trans. Ernst Kaiser and Eithne Wilkins. New York: Schocken.

——. 1966 [1927]. *The Castle*. Trans. Willa and Edwin Muir. Harmondsworth, Eng.: Penguin.

——. 1971 [1946]. *The Complete Stories*. Various translators. New York: Schocken.

——. 1972 [1949]. *The Diaries of Franz Kafka*. Ed. Max Brod. Trans. Joseph Kresh and Martin Greenberg. Harmondsworth, Eng.: Penguin.

———. 1974 [1926]. *The Trial*. Trans. Willa and Edwin Muir. Harmondsworth, Eng.: Penguin.

———. 1976 [1953]. *Letter to His Father/Brief an den Vater*. Trans. Ernst Kaiser and Eithne Wilkins. New York: Schocken.

———. 1977. *Letters to Friends, Family, and Editors*. Trans. Richard and Clara Winston. New York: Schocken.

———. 1978 [1973]. *Letters to Felice*. Trans. James Stern and Elizabeth Duckworth. Harmondsworth, Eng.: Penguin.

———. 1982. *Letters to Ottla and the Family*. Trans. Richard and Clara Winston. New York: Schocken.

———. 1983. *Das erzählerische Werk*, vol. 1. Berlin: Rütten & Loening.

———. 1984. *Oeuvres complètes*, vol. 3. Trans. C. David. Paris: Pléiade.

———. 1989. *Gesammelte Werke*, 8 vols. Ed. Max Brod. Frankfurt: Fischer Taschenbuch Verlag.

———. 1990 [1926]. *Der Proceß*. Frankfurt: Appartband, S. Fischer.

———. 1991. *The Blue Octavo Notebooks*. Cambridge, Mass.: Exact Change.

———. 1992. *Nachgelassene Schriften und Fragmente*, vol. 2. Ed. J. Schillemeit. Frankfurt: S. Fischer.

Kaiser, G. 1958. "Franz Kafkas *Prozeß*. Versuch einer Interpretation." *Euphorion, Zeitschrift für Litteraturgeschichte* 52.

Kant, I. 1922 [1799]. "Erklärung in Beziehung auf Fichtes Wissenschaftlehre." In vol. 3 of *Kant's Briefwechsel (1795–1803)*, *Kant's gesammelte Schriften*, vol. 12. Ed. Königlich Preußischen Akademie der Wissenschaften, Berlin and Leipzig: Walter de Gruyter.

———. 1965 [1781]. *Critique of Pure Reason*. Trans. Norman Kemp Smith. New York: St. Martin's Press; Toronto: Macmillan.

———. 1971 [1788]. *La Critique de la raison pratique*. 6th ed. Trans. with an introduction by F. Alquié. Paris: PUF.

———. 1974a [1781, 1787]. *Kritik der reinen Vernunft. Werkausgabe* (1st and 2nd eds.). Vols. 4–5. Ed. W. Weischedel. Frankfurt: Suhrkamp Verlag.

———. 1974b [1789]. *Kritik der Urteilskraft*. In *Werkausgabe*. Vol. 10. Ed. W. Weischedel. Frankfurt: Suhrkamp Verlag.

———. 1974c [1791]. "Erste Fassung der Einleitung in die *Kritik der Urteilskraft*. In *Werkausgabe*. Vol. 10. Ed. W. Weischedel. Frankfurt: Suhrkamp Verlag.

———. 1982a [1789]. "Critique of Aesthetic Judgement." In *The Critique of Judgement*. Trans. James Creed Meredith. Oxford: Clarendon Press.

———. 1982b [1789]. "Critique of Teleological Judgement." In *The Critique of Judgement*. Trans. James Creed Meredith. Oxford: Clarendon Press.

Kernan, A. 1990. *The Death of Literature*. New Haven: Yale University Press.

Kleist, H. Von. N.d. [1801]. *Sämtliche Werke*. Ed. P. Stapf. Munich: Emil Vollmer Verlag.

———. 1982. *An Abyss Deep Enough: Letters of Heinrich von Kleist*. Trans. Philip B. Miller. New York: E. P. Dutton.

Köhler, E. 1974 [1956]. *L'Aventure chevarelesque*. Trans. E. Kaufholz. Paris: Gallimard.

Koselleck, R. 1976 [1959]. *Kritik und Krise*. Frankfurt: Suhrkamp Verlag.

Kristeller, O. 1965. *Renaissance Thought*. Vol. 2: *Papers on Humanism and the Arts*. New York: Harper and Row.

Kurz, R. 1991. *Der Kollaps der Modernisierung: Vom Zusammenbruch des Kasernensozialismus zur Krise der Weltökonomie.* Frankfurt: Eichborn Verlag.

Lacoue-Labarthe, P., and J.-L. Nancy. 1978. *L'Absolu littéraire: Théorie de la littérature du romantisme allemand.* Paris: Seuil.

Lebrun, G. 1970. *Kant et la mort de la métaphysique.* Paris: A. Colin.

Lévi-Strauss, C. 1991. "En relisant Montaigne." In *Histoire de lynx.* Paris: Plon.

Lloyd, D. 1985–86. "Arnold, Ferguson, Schiller: Aesthetic Culture and the Politics of Aesthetics." *Cultural Critique* 2: 137–69.

Löwy, M. 1989 [1988]. *Redenção e utopia: O judaísmo libertário na Europa central.* Trans. P. Neves. São Paulo: Companhia das Letras.

Lubkoll, C. 1990. "Man muß nicht alles für wahr halten, man muß es nur für notwendig halten." In W. Kittler and G. Neumann, eds., *Franz Kafka Schriftverkehr.* Freiburg: Rombach Verlag.

Lukács, G. 1960 [1958]. *La Signification présente du réalisme critique.* Trans. M. Gandillac. Paris: Gallimard.

———. 1974 [1911]. *Soul and Form.* Trans. Anna Bostok. London: Merlin Press.

Mann, T. 1949 [1948]. "Dem Dichter zu Ehren: Franz Kafka und *Das Schloß.*" *Der Monat* 819: 66–70.

———. 1960 [1918]. "Zum Tode Eduard Keyserlings." In *Gesammelte Werke, Reden und Aufsätze,* vol. 10. Oldenberg: Fischer Verlag.

Marquard, O. 1962. "Kant und due Wende zur Äesthetik." *Zeitschrift für philosophische Forschung* 16: 231–43 and 363–74.

Merleau-Ponty, M. 1960. "Lecture de Montaigne." In *Signes.* Paris: Gallimard.

Montaigne, M. de. 1933 [1580, 1588, 1590]. *Essais.* Ed. A. Thibaudet. Paris: Pléiade.

———. 1952 [1580, 1588, 1590]. *The Essays.* Trans. Charles Cotton, ed. W. C. Hazlitt. Chicago: Encyclopaedia Britannica.

———. 1983 [1580–81]. *Journal de voyage.* Ed. F. Garavini. Paris: Gallimard.

Moser, W. 1989. *Romantisme et crises de la modernité: Poésie et encyclopédie dans le 'Brouillon' de Novalis.* Quebec: Ed. du Préambule.

Muschg, W. 1968 [1929]. "Über Franz Kafka." In *Pamphlet und Bekenntnis.* Olten, Switzerland: Walter-Verlag.

Neumann, G. 1990. "Der Name, die Sprache und die Ordnung der Dinge." In W. Kittler and G. Neumann, eds., *Franz Kafka Schriftverkehr.* Freiburg: Rombach Verlag.

Neuschäffer, H.-J. 1969. *Boccaccio und der Beginn der novelle: Strukturen der Kurzerzählung auf der Schwelle zwischen Mittelalter und Neuzeit.* Munich: W. Fink Verlag.

Novalis. 1978a [1795–96]. "Philosophische Studien (Fichte Studien)." In *Werke, Tagebücher und Briefe,* 2 vols. Ed. H.-J. Mähl. Munich: Carl Hanser Verlag.

———. 1978b [1797]. "Philosophische Studien (Hemsterhuis- u. Kant Studien)." In *Werke, Tagebücher und Briefe,* 2 vols. Ed. H.-J. Mähl. Munich: Carl Hanser Verlag.

———. 1978c [1798]. "Logologische Fragmente." In *Werke, Tagebücher und Briefe,* 2 vols. Ed. H.-J. Mähl. Munich: Carl Hanser Verlag.

———. 1978d [1798–99]. "Das allgemeine Brouillon." In *Werke, Tagebücher und Briefe,* 2 vols. Ed. H.-J. Mähl. Munich: Carl Hanser Verlag.

———. 1978e [1799]. "Die Christenheit oder Europa." In *Werke, Tagebücher und Briefe,* 2 vols. Ed. H.-J. Mähl. Munich: Carl Hanser Verlag.

Pascal, B. 1957a [1655]. "Entretien avec M. de Saci." In *Oeuvres complètes*. Ed. J. Chevalier. Paris: Pléiade.

———. 1957b [1669]. *Pensées*. In *Oeuvres complètes*. Ed. J. Chevalier. Paris: Pléiade.

Pasley, M. 1990. "Zu dieser Ausgabe." In *Der Proceß in der Fassung der Handschrift*. Frankfurt: S. Fischer.

Pasley, M., and K. Wagenbach. 1965. "Datierung sämlicher Texte Franz Kafkas." In J. Born et al., *Kafka-Symposium*. Berlin: Verlag Klaus Weinbach.

Perrault, C. 1964 [1688–97]. *Paralèlle des anciens et des modernes*. Introduction by H. R. Jauss and comments on art history by M. Imdahl. Facsimile of original Paris ed. Munich: Eidos Verlag.

Pessoa, Fernando. 1965. *Obra poética*. Rio de Janeiro: Aguilar.

Peter, K. 1978. *Friedrich Schlegel*. Stuttgart: J. B. Metzlersche Verlagsbuchhandlung.

Pinard, E. 1964 [1857]. "Le Procès de *Madam Bovary*." In G. Flaubert, *Oeuvres complètes*, vol. 2. Intr. and notes by B. Masson. Paris: Masson.

Politzer, H., ed. 1973. *Franz Kafka*. Darmstadt: Wissenschaftlicher Buchgesellschaft.

———. 1978. *Franz Kafka: Der Künstler*. Frankfurt: Suhrkamp Verlag.

Preisendanz, W. 1967. "Zur Poetik der deutschen Romantik I: De Abkehr vom Grundsatz der Naturnachahmung." In H. Steffen, ed., *Die Deutsche Romantik: Poetik, Formen und Motive*. Göttingen: Vandenhoeck & Ruprecht.

Proust, F. 1991. *Kant: Le ton de l'histoire*. Paris: Payot.

Regosin, R. L. 1992. "Critical Discussions." *Philosophy and Literature* 16, 1 (Apr.).

Reiss, T. 1992. *The Meaning of Literature*. Ithaca, N.Y.: Cornell University Press.

Riff, M. A. 1976. "Czech Antisemitism and the Jewish Response Before 1914." *Wiener Library Bulletin* 39, New Series: 8–20.

Robert, M. 1988 [1979]. *Seul, comme Franz Kafka*. Paris: Calmann-Lévy, Agora.

Rousseau, J.-J. 1953 [1782]. *The Confessions*. Trans. J. M. Cohen. Harmondsworth, Eng.: Penguin.

Sainte-Beuve, C.-A. 1933 [1860]. "La Morale en l'art." In W. T. Bandy, *Baudelaire Judged by his Contemporaries (1845–1867)*. New York: Columbia University Press.

Schiller, F. 1967 [1795]. *Letters (On the Aesthetic Education of Man)*. Ed. E. M. Wilkinson. Oxford: Clarendon.

———. 1978 [1795]. *Über naive und sentimentalische Dichtung*. Postscript by J. Beer. Stuttgart: Reclam.

———. 1989 [1995]. *Über die ästhetische Erziehung des Menschen*. Postscript by K. Hamburger. Stuttgart: Reclam.

Schirrmacher, F., ed. 1987. *Verteidigung der Schrift Kafkas "Prozeß."* Frankfurt: Suhrkamp Verlag.

Schlegel, F. 1958 [Undated]. "Nachlaß." In *Kritische Friedrich Schlegel Ausgabe*, vol. 11. Ed. E. Behler. Munich-Paderborn-Vienna: Verlag F. Schöningh.

———. 1961 [1815]. *Geschichte der alten und neun Literatur*. *Kritische Friedrich Schlegel Ausgabe*, vol. 7. Ed. E. Behler. Munich-Paderborn-Vienna: Verlag F. Schöningh.

———. 1967a [1796]. Review of G. E. Lessing's *Humanitätsbriefe*. In *Kritische Friedrich Schlegel Ausgabe*, vol. 2. Ed. H. Eichner. Munich-Paderborn-Vienna: Verlag F. Schöningh.

——— 1967b [1797]. "Kritische Fragmente." In *Kritische Friedrich Schlegel Ausgabe*, vol. 2. Ed. H. Eichner. Munich-Paderborn-Vienna: Verlag F. Schöningh.

——. 1967c [1798]. "Athenäum Fragmente." In *Kritische Friedrich Schlegel Ausgabe*, vol. 2. Ed. H. Eichner. Munich-Paderborn-Vienna: Verlag F. Schöningh.

——. 1971a [1796]. "Jacobis *Woldemar*." In *Kritische Schriften*. Ed. W. Rasch. Munich: Carl Hanser Verlag.

——. 1971b [1797]. "Über das Studium der griechischen Poesie." In *Kritische Schriften*. Ed. W. Rasch. Munich: Carl Hanser Verlag.

——. 1971c [1797]. "Von Wesen der Kritik." In *Kritische Schriften*. Ed. W. Rasch. Munich: Carl Hanser Verlag.

——. 1975 [1798]. Letter to Novalis, December 2, 1798. In *Novalis: Schriften*. Vol. 4: *Tagebücher, Briefwechsel, Zeitgenössische Zeugnisse*. Ed. R. Samuel, H.-J. Mähl, and G. Schulz. Stuttgart: Verlag W. Kohlhammer.

——. 1980a [1797]. "Über Lessing." In *Werke in zwei Bände*, 2 vols. Berlin-Weimar: Aufbau-Verlag.

——. 1980b [1800]. "Gespräch über die Poesie." In *Werke in zwei Bände*, 2 vols. Berlin-Weimar: Aufbau-Verlag.

Schmitt, C. 1986 [1919]. *Political Romanticism*. Trans. Guy Oakes. Cambridge, Mass.: MIT Press.

Schopenhauer, A. 1970 [1851]. *Essays and Aphorisms*. London: Penguin.

Schulte-Sasse, J. 1988. "The Concept of Literary Criticism in German Romanticism." In P. U. Hohendahl, ed., *A History of German Literary Criticism*. Lincoln: University of Nebraska Press.

Seneca. 1987. *De la brevedad de la vida y otros escritos*. Trans. L. Riber. Madrid: Aguilar.

Sennett, R. 1978. *The Fall of Public Man: On the Social Psychology of Capitalism*. New York: Vintage.

Starobinski, J. 1982. *Montaigne en mouvement*. Paris: Gallimard.

Stierle, K. 1973. "Geschichte als Exemplum—Exemplum als Geschichte. Zur Pragmatik und Poetik narrativer Texte." In V. R. Koselleck and W.-D. Stempel, eds., *Poetik und Hermeneutik*. Munich: W. Fink Verlag.

——. 1987. "Montaigne und die Erfahrung der Vielheit." In W.-D. Stempel and K. Stierle, eds., *Die Pluralität der Welten: Aspekte der Renaissance in der Romania*. Munich: W. Fink Verlag.

Stölzel, C. 1988 [1975]. *Kafkas bösen Böhmen: Zur Sozialgeschichte eines Prager Juden*. Berlin: Ullstein Bücher.

Strohschneider-Kohrs, I. 1977. *Die romantische Ironie in Theorie und Gestaltung*. Tübingen: Max Niemeyer Verlag.

Suzuki, M. 1991. Introduction to *On Naive and Sentimental Poetry*, by F. Schiller. Trans. M. Suzuki. São Paulo: Illuminuras.

Szondi, P. 1978 [1968, 1973]. "Frederic Schlegels Theorie der Dichtarten" and "Das Naive ist das Sentimentalische: Zur Begrifsdialektik in Schillers Abhandlung." In *Schriften*, vol. 2. Frankfurt: Suhrkamp Verlag.

Taylor, C. 1989. *Sources of the Self: The Making of the Modern Identity*. Cambridge, Mass.: Harvard University Press.

Thibaudet, A. 1963. *Montaigne*. Ed. Floyd Gray. Paris: Gallimard.

Torres Filho, R. 1975. *O espírito e a letra: A crítica da imaginação pura em Fichte*. São Paulo: Ática.

Ullman, W. 1966. *The Individual and Society in the Middle Ages*. Baltimore: Johns Hopkins University Press.

Vance, E. 1973. "Le Moi comme langage: Saint Augustin et l'autobiographie." *Poétique* 14.

———. 1989 [1986]. "Augustine's *Confessions* and the Poetics of Law." In *Marvelous Signals: Poetics and Sign Theory in the Middle Ages*. Lincoln: University of Nebraska Press.

Wagenbach, K. 1964. *Kafka*. Hamburg: Rowohlt.

———. 1985 [1975]. *Franz Kafka: In der Strafkolonie: Eine Geschichte aus dem Jahr 1914*. Berlin: Verlag Klaus Wagenbach.

Walzel, O. 1973 [1916]. "Logik im Wunderbaren." In H. Politzer, ed., *Franz Kafka*. Darmstadt: Wissenschaftlicher Buchgesellschaft.

Weber, H.-D. 1973. *Friedrich Schlegels "Transzendentalpoesie."* Munich: Fink Verlag.

Wellek, R. 1954. "Auerbach's Special Realism." *Kenyon Review* 16.

———. 1982. "The Attack on Literature." In *The Attack on Literature and Other Essays*. Chapel Hill: University of North Carolina Press.

White, H. 1982. "The Politics of Historical Interpretation: Discipline and Desublimation." In *The Content of Form: Narrative Discourse and Historical Representation*. Baltimore: Johns Hopkins University Press.

Witte, B. 1990. "La Naissance de l'histoire littéraire dans l'esprit de la révolution." In M. Espagne and M. Werner, eds., *Philologiques I. Contribution à l'histoire des disciplines littéraires en France et en Allemagne au XIXe siècle*. Paris: Edition de la Maison des Sciences de L'Homme.

Zeitlin, J. 1928. "The Development of Bacon's *Essays*—with Special Reference to the Question of Montaigne's Influence upon Them." *Journal of English and Germanic Philology* 27, 4 (Oct.): 496–519.

Index

In this index "f" after a number indicates a separate reference on the next page, and "ff" indicates separate references on the next two pages. A continuous discussion over two or more pages is indicated by a span of numbers. *Passim* is used for a cluster of references in close but not consecutive sequence.

Absence, 26–30 *passim*, 49f, 53f, 56, 59f, 63–68 *passim*, 116; and portrait, 49f, 53

Adorno, T. W., 62f, 144, 187, 218, 226, 246, 264, 278–79, 306

Aestheticization, 11f, 68, 102, 111f, 121f, 127–31 *passim*, 135f, 140–45 *passim*, 161, 163, 171, 180ff, 298, 319; private, 141f, 149, 176; public, 114, 141f

Aesthetics: autonomy of, 3, 62, 84, 93f, 97; and education, 119–20, 126f, 139, 144, 164; and experience, 12, 63, 90–101 *passim*, 114, 119–23 *passim*, 127–30 *passim*, 135f, 146, 154, 162f, 181, 218, 226, 252; and judgment, 80–97 *passim*, 129, 163, 166, 181, 188; normative, 163; objective, 154, 163, 173; systematic, 151, 163, 166. *See also* Ethics and aesthetics

Allegory, 125, 161, 232, 241, 288

Alleman, B., 243–47 *passim*, 250, 253, 264, 267ff

Arabesque, 49ff, 161ff, 185, 218

Archaeological hypothesis, 292

Archaeological position, 292

Arendt, H., 245, 248

Aristotle, 6, 82, 168

Arnim, L. von, 184

Arnold, M., 181

Art, religion of, 176

Art critic (*Kunstkritiker*), 106, 146f

Art judge (*Kunstrichter*), 146f, 154, 156

Artaud, A., 189

Auerbach, E., 30, 53, 267

Augustine, 35–36, 197

Autobiography, 33–37 *passim*, 50–51, 56, 59–60, 106

Ayrault, R., 152

Bakhtin, M., 6

Balzac, H. de, 234, 269f

Baudelaire, C., 218, 296f

Bauer, C., 192, 194

Bauer, F., 189–95 *passim*, 199–203 *passim*, 223, 226, 230, 235f, 278

Bayle, P., 43

Beaujour, M., 56, 64

Beautiful, the: and interest, 90–91; and the sublime, 83, 90–93 *passim*, 97, 181–82, 218

Beckett, S., 248, 313

Beicken, P. U., 186, 240

Benjamin, W., 103–7 *passim*, 146–52 *passim*, 167, 186, 266, 275–79 *passim*, 301f, 306f, 310, 317

Benns, G., 48–49

Blanchard, M. E., 48–49, 66
Blanchot, M., 200, 215
Bloch, G., 195
Bloch, H., 50
Bloom, H., 193, 248, 260, 266
Boccaccio, 4f, 44, 160
Boétie, E. de la, 13, 49f, 56, 65
Bohrer, K. H., 111ff
Boileau, N., 146
Born, J., 184f
Brod, M., 186, 195, 204f, 223f, 240, 258, 262, 275–78 *passim*, 308, 312
Brody, J., 9
Brown, M., 162
Brown, P., 35f
Butor, M., 54, 64ff, 270

Calderón de la Barca, P., 179
Canetti, E., 102, 200, 203, 272, 311
Cassirer, E., 9, 306
Castiglione, B., 158
Cave, T., 66
Cellini, B., 106
Cervantes, M. de, 4, 145, 178, 265f
Chamfort, S.-R. N., 152
Chamisso, A. V., 184
Chédin, O., 81, 97–101 *passim*
Chytry, J., 130
Cicero, 8
Coleridge, S. T., 103, 146
Confession, confessional, 35f, 64, 152, 161, 197, 208–9, 232, 256
Conrad, J., 313
Corngold, S., 187, 213f, 233, 235–36, 239, 266
Criticism, ix, 64, 107, 128, 145–57 *passim*, 166, 171–76 *passim*, 180f; modern, 148
Criticity, ix, 63, 102–7 *passim*, 118–21 *passim*, 129ff, 135f, 142–50 *passim*, 161–76 *passim*, 180f, 299–300, 319; and ethics, 130
Crotesque, 49f
Custom: role of, 47f; in Montaigne, 18, 32–33

Dante Alighieri, 179
Davis, N. Z., 21
Deckert, J., 305
Deleuze, G., 97, 197, 236–37, 315
Democracy, bourgeois, 111
Descartes, R., 18, 24–25, 26, 215f

Desubstantialization, 132, 260. *See also* Law: desubstantialization and insubstantiality of
Diderot, D., 4, 10, 127, 146, 156
Dietz, L., 183
Diomedes, 123
Discourse and territoriality, 317
Disenchantment (*Entzauberung*), 96, 242
Dogmatism, 105, 129
Dreyfus, A., 306
Dymant, D., 195

Ecriture, 54–55, 56, 65
Eichner, H., 151
Eisner, M., 204f
Eliot, T. S., 256
Elm, T., 242, 244, 248
Epigram, 152
Epistemological skepticism, 28, 38ff, 215
Erasmus, D., 37, 64
Eschweiler, C., 275
Essay, 15, 18, 51f, 58, 64, 152f, 157, 166
Essays (Montaigne), 3, 9, 13–69 *passim*, 295
Ethics and aesthetics, 130, 210, 226
Event, 198
Exemplum and exemplarity, 23f, 28, 30
Expressionism, 188, 222, 264

Fact: and history, 42, 52; and individual subject, 41
Ferguson, S., 181
Fichte, J. G., 104–9 *passim*, 133–39 *passim*, 143, 145, 152, 155, 173
Fiction, fictional, fictitious, 11f, 44, 56, 62f, 102, 128, 130, 156, 170, 176, 187, 201, 214–19 *passim*, 227, 269f, 299, 302, 320
Fictional: discourse and truth, 298ff, 317; ban on the, 128
Fielding, H., 234, 269
Finality, regulating character of, 88
Flaubert, G., 218, 232, 234, 248, 267–70 *passim*, 296f
Flores, K., 236
Fontenelle, M. de, 115–16
Fontius, M., 143
Foucault, M., 6–7, 45, 112, 239, 256
Fragment, 59, 64, 152–60 *passim*, 166. *See also* Essay
Freccero, J., 36, 58
Free indirect speech, 232–34, 267, 268–69, 281, 291

Freud, S., 192, 195, 204, 231, 233, 295
Friedrich, H., 24f, 49, 54
Fumaroli, M., 8, 31

Galileo, 95
Gervinus, 180–81
Geulincx, 109
Glaucus, 123
Gnosticism, 192–93, 219
Goethe, J. W. von, 108, 125, 241
Goldstücker, E., 288
Gracián, B., 158
Greenberg, M., 231, 233, 236, 281
Greenblatt, S., 32
Greene, T., 3, 31
Gregory, 6ff
Guattari, F., 197, 236–37, 315

Haas, W., 186, 192f, 266, 274, 276, 302
Habermas, J., 127
Hájek, J., 288
Hegel, G. W. F., 63, 111f, 115, 121, 126, 149
Heidegger, M., 108, 113
Heller, E., 192f, 241–47 *passim*
Herder, J. G. von, 172
Hermeneutics, 165
Hermsdorf, K., 304
Hieroglyph, 161–62, 163, 179–80
Hilsner, L., 305f
Hirsch, E. D., Jr., 216f
History, as discipline, 121, 181, 297
Hobbes, T., 17
Hoffmann, E. T. W., 184
Hölderlin, F., 130
Homer, 123, 179
Horkheimer, M., 17f
Hruza, A., 305
Humboldt, W. von, 125
Huppert, G., 41–42

Image, contemporary cult of, 129, 319
Imaginary, control of the, 11, 44, 50, 56, 66f, 128, 187, 319f
Imagination, 11f, 22, 38–48 *passim*, 52–56 *passim*, 67, 75, 83f, 88–93 *passim*, 97–100 *passim*, 116, 121, 127f, 159, 319; and the imaginary, 56
Individualism, types of, 26, 29–30, 44, 68
Individuality, 19, 45, 91, 123, 142f, 152f, 199,

205, 226, 234, 296f; and the individual, 6; in antiquity, 5, 9
Individual subject, *see* Self
Infrasensible, 92, 98
Ingarden, R., 216
Intentionality, *see* Subject, intentionality of
Interest, 90f, 98. *See also* Beautiful, the: and interest
Interpretation, question of, 215–27 *passim*
Interpretive stability, 222, 224
Iser, W., 62, 170, 227

Jacobi, F. H., 150
James, H., 155, 270
Janouch, G., 211, 260
Jauss, H. R., 115f
Jesenská, M., 191, 195, 200
Johnston, W. M., 254
Joseph K. and Don Quixote, 263–66 *passim*, 271, 282–85 *passim*
Josephus, F., 36
Judgment: faculty of, 80f, 85–87, 88, 92, 96; question of, 79–80
Juhl, P. D., 217
Jünger, E., 108

Kabbalah, new, 278, 286
Kafka, F., 39, 62–63, 68, 104, 155, 183–227, 230–63, 267–94 *passim*, 299–321; critical humor of, 246; and the complementary world, 301f, 317; as experimental writer, 231; and the logic of the citizen, 252f, 257, 269, 272f, 282; "objective" vision and objectivity of, 246, 258, 310f
Kafka, H., 187, 193, 303, 305f
Kaiser, G., 253
Kant, I., 1, 3, 11f, 18, 26, 63, 67, 71–107 *passim*, 135–39 *passim*, 143–46 *passim*, 162f, 180f, 188, 279f, 301f, 319, 321; Kantian morality, 77, 90
Kernan, A., 217, 300
Kierkegaard, S., 112, 148, 186
Klee, P., 301
Kleist, H. von, 132, 184, 218, 245, 248, 269f, 301
Klopstock, R., 191
Köhler, E., 8
Koselleck, R., 17
Kristeller, O., 8
Kurz, R., 114, 182, 239

Lacoue-Labarthe, P., 152, 167
Language: allusive use of, 213, 221–22, 288;
  analogical use of, 213, 288; games, 134,
  318; staging by means of, 198f
La Rochefoucauld, F.-A.-F., 158
Law, 1, 2, 26, 33, 67f, 75–78 *passim*, 97, 107,
  112, 128, 135, 144, 187, 225f, 236, 254f,
  260, 274, 279, 285–94 *passim*, 300–301;
  ancient, 18, 41, 48; desubstantialization
  and insubstantiality of, 238, 244ff, 292f,
  317f
Lebrun, O., 81–82, 84, 206
Lessing, G. E., 146, 151
Lévi-Strauss, C., 27, 87–88
Literature: and fictional discourse, 59–60, 63;
  minor, 104, 315ff; modern conception of,
  3, 53f; Renaissance conception of, 3, 8,
  294
Lloyd, D., 181
Löwenthal, L., 306
Löwy, Jizchak, 202f, 220, 309, 313, 315
Löwy, Julie, 303, 305
Löwy, M., 307
Lubkoll, C., 239, 260
Lukács, G., 60–64 *passim*, 112, 148, 242, 254

Machado de Assis, J. M., 1
Machiavelli, N., 3
Malebranche, N., 16, 43, 109
Malherbe, F. de, 9
Mallarmé, S., 10, 218
Malraux, A., 287
Mandeville, J., 72
Mann, T., 10f, 274
Marquard, O., 95f, 121
Marx, K., 130
Maximes, 152
Melo Neto, J. C., 155, 162, 316
Mendelssohn, M., 177
Merleau-Ponty, M., 58
Metaphor, 213f, 222, 231f, 256, 288
Method, 63; order of, 5, 63
Metternich, K. F. von, 177
Mimesis, 112, 198, 208f, 220; order of, 4–5,
  6, 8, 169
Mirandola, P. della, 3, 31
Modernity, 74f, 96, 107–16 *passim*, 126, 129f,
  148, 150, 173, 215f, 226, 242, 247
Montaigne, M. de, 1–72 *passim*, 131, 215,
  295, 321; essays of, 3, 9, 13–69 *passim*, 295;

and ideal self, 45, 52; relativism in, 27, 48;
  role of custom in, 18, 32–33
Moser, W., 159
Muir, E., 274
Muschg, W., 185

Naive genius, and poetry, 122, 124f
Nancy, J. L., 152, 167
Napoleon, 95, 133, 172, 177
Narrator, unreliability of, 269–70, 272–73,
  286, 293
Neumann, G., 248
Neuschäffer, H., 4
Newton, I., 41, 95
Novalis, 1, 10, 104, 109f, 130–45 *passim*, 159,
  175ff
Novel, 5, 10, 106, 159–62 *passim*, 166, 248

Objective correlative, 211, 223, 256
Occasionalism, 109, 112; modern and Ro-
  mantic, 110
Ornament and ornamentality, 162f

Paré, A., 32
Pascal, B., 9–10, 43, 57, 59, 186
Pasley, M., 183, 235, 240, 258, 274
Pasquier, E., 42
Paul, 6
Perrault, J. B., 115
Pessoa, F., 208
Petrarch, 3
Pinard, E., 248–49, 267f
Plato, 6
Play impulse, 119–20
Plutarch, 47
Poetry: progressive, 115, 118, 123, 165–66,
  173; sentimental, 115, 122–26 *passim*, 141;
  transcendental, 166f
Politzer, H., 258f, 274, 285
Portrait and absence, 14, 16, 48
Power, 150, 203, 239, 254, 260, 272, 274,
  279, 284–94 *passim*, 320
Power-Law relation, 283, 288, 292f
Preisendanz, W., 163
Proust, F., 78, 158, 212
Public and private, 16–17, 21, 47

Rabelais, F., 12, 44, 295
Ramos, G., 316
Ranke, I., 181–82

Reason, modern, 25f, 97, 121
Referent, 112
Regulating principle, 173–74
Reiss, T., 4
Relativism, 27; in Montaigne, 27, 48
Religious intentionality, 167
Representation, 112f, 127, 168, 201, 205–12 *passim*, 216, 218
Representational scene, 211
Riff, M. A., 305, 307
Rigosin, L., 53
Rimbaud, A., 170
Robert, M., 313
Romantics, early German (*Frühromantiker*), 60, 68, 103–13 *passim*, 132, 134, 144–54 *passim*, 159, 176, 184, 199, 205, 297f
Rosa, J. G., 316
Rousseau, J.-J., 9, 26, 57ff, 67, 106, 161, 197f

Sainte-Beuve, C.-A., 297
Schematism, 97
Schiller, F., 1, 68, 107, 115–30 *passim*, 135, 139ff, 147–50 *passim*, 160, 166, 181, 197
Schirrmacher, F., 275
Schlegel, F., 1, 103–8 *passim*, 115, 130, 132, 136, 143–82 *passim*, 279; and Schlegel brothers, 108, 145
Schleiermacher, F., 159, 165
Schmitt, C., 21, 107–14 *passim*, 121f, 127, 129, 134, 144
Schneider, E., 305
Scholem, G., 276, 278, 301, 306
Schopenhauer, A., 10
Schulte-Sasse, J., 146f
Science, mystical conception of, 133, 135f
Secundus, J., 44
Self: acknowledgment of, 39f, 295f; autonomy of, 5, 18–19, 139; consecration of, 3, 9, 11, 18–19, 26, 39, 43, 56, 67, 128, 321; ideal, 45, 52; infinity of, 10; primacy of, 9, 11, 18, 44, 48, 53, 67, 150, 268; univocity of, 220
Semantic instability, 223, 227, 248, 260, 270, 273, 287
Semantic stability, 217ff, 222f
Seneca, 31, 45
Sennett, R., 114
Shakespeare, W., 159
Silent communication, universality of, 91, 100, 119, 154

Similitude, 6
Skepticism, 18, 26, 30, 38, 41, 48, 105, 129, 150
Speaker, intention of, *see* Subject: intentionality of
Starobinski, J., 54ff
Stendhal, 234, 269
Stierle, K., 5, 19, 29, 48, 65
Stölzel, C., 307, 315
Subject: intentionality of, 40, 67; modern, 3
Subjectivity: 24f, 72f, 76, 80, 90f, 94, 98, 106–11 *passim*, 118, 123, 131, 152–57 *passim*, 187, 215, 222, 268, 295; primacy of, 2, 26; Romantic, 111f. *See also* Self; Subject: modern
Sublime, experience of the, 84, 92f, 98, 162
Substantialist conception, 5, 18, 168f
Supersensible, 80f, 84, 92f, 98, 218
Suzuki, M., 125
Syntax, semantics, and aesthetic experience, 101f
Szondi, P., 106f, 115, 122, 126

Taste, judgment of, 91, 100, 127
Taylor, C., 25f, 28
Teleological conception, 115
Teleological judgment, 81, 87–90 *passim*
Telesio, B., 8
Thackeray, W. M., 269
Thibaudet, A., 14, 38
Tieck, L., 145
Torres Filho, R., 105
Travel writing, 68–69, 72f
Troyes, C. de, 7
Tucholsky, K., 184f

Ullmann, W., 7
Undecidability, 224–25, 239f, 242, 246f, 258, 260, 266, 270, 273f, 293–94
Understanding, archaeology of faculty of, 93
Uyttersprot, H., 187

Valéry, P., 146
Vance, R., 33–36 *passim*
Veit, D., 177
Vicente, G., 12
Vico, G. B., 74, 84, 215f
Voice and aesthetic experience, 101

Wagenbach, K., 183, 235, 255, 274, 304f, 311
Walzel, O., 183–84

Weber, H. D., 173
Weber, M., 79
Wellek, R., 302
Weltsch, F., 312
Werfel, F., 210, 308
White, H., 181–82
Wilkinson, E. M., 125
Willoughby, L. A., 125

Wit, 152, 157ff, 164, 205; and event, 212
Witte, B., 181
Wittgenstein, L., 318
Wohryzek, J., 195
Wolff, K., 212, 220

Zeitlin, J., 64
Zenge, W. von, 132

Library of Congress Cataloging-in-Publication Data

Lima, Luiz Costa
[Limites da voz. English]
The limits of voice / Luiz Costa-Lima ; translated by Paulo
Henriques Britto.
p.   cm.
Includes bibliographical references and index.
ISBN 0-8047-2540-3 (alk. paper)
1. Literature—Philosophy.   2. Criticism.   3. Literature—
Aesthetics.   I. Title.
PN45.L47513   1996
801—dc20   95-36712   CIP

⊗ This book is printed on acid-free, recycled paper.

Original printing 1996
Last figure below indicates year of this printing:
05 04 03 02 01 00 99 98 97 96